DATE DUE

IMAGINING
THE MIDDLE EAST

IMAGINING
THE MIDDLE EAST

The Building of an American Foreign Policy, 1918–1967

MATTHEW F. JACOBS

The University of North Carolina Press   Chapel Hill

Designed by Courtney Leigh Baker and set in Quadraat and Univers by Tseng Information Systems, Inc. Manufactured in the United States of America. The paper in this book
meets the guidelines for permanence and durability of the Committee on Production
Guidelines for Book Longevity of the Council on Library Resources. The University of
North Carolina Press has been a member of the Green Press Initiative since 2003.

Library of Congress Cataloging-in-Publication Data
Jacobs, Matthew F.
Imagining the Middle East : the building of an American foreign policy, 1918–1967 /
Matthew F. Jacobs.
p. cm.
Includes bibliographical references and index.
ISBN 978-0-8078-3488-6 (cloth : alk. paper)
1. Middle East—Foreign relations—United States. 2. United States—Foreign
relations—Middle East. 3. Middle East—Foreign relations—20th century. 4. United
States—Foreign relations—20th century. 5. Middle East—Politics and government—
20th century. 6. Islam and politics—Middle East. 7. Arab-Israeli conflict. I. Title.
DS63.2.U5J34 2011
327.7305609′041—dc22
2011006662

A portion of this book was published, in somewhat different form, as "The Perils and
Promise of Islam: The United States and the Muslim Middle East in the Early Cold War,"
Diplomatic History 30, no. 4 (September 2006): 705–39. Used with permission.

15 14 13 12 11   5 4 3 2 1

To Jessica, Ally, and Jeremy

CONTENTS

ACKNOWLEDGMENTS

Far more people contributed to this book than I can possibly thank in the lines that follow. Nonetheless, the place to begin is with those who provide the resources—both financial and archival—that make our work as scholars possible. Over the years, I have benefitted from the generous support of the Eisenhower World Affairs Institute, the Lyndon Baines Johnson Foundation, the Graduate School of the University of North Carolina at Chapel Hill, and the Humanities Scholarship Enhancement Fund from the College of Liberal Arts and Sciences at the University of Florida. I would not have been able to complete the project without their support, for which I am truly grateful. I also have been fortunate to work with outstanding archivists at the Truman, Eisenhower, Kennedy, and Johnson Presidential Libraries, as well as the National Archives in College Park, Maryland, the Middle East Institute in Washington, D.C., the Council on Foreign Relations in New York City, and the Seeley G. Mudd Library at Princeton University. I benefitted profoundly from these archivists' deep knowledge of their respective collections and their ability to suggest materials that I had no idea existed.

I wish to reserve special thanks for those at the University of North Carolina Press who ushered me and my book through the publication process. Chuck Grench—ably supported by Katy O'Brien, Beth Lassiter, and Sydney Dupre—has been an outstanding editor ever since his initial expression of interest in my work in summer 2008. His faith in me and his careful interventions at crucial moments proved indispensible to the project's successful completion. Paul Betz provided invaluable guidance and oversight as project editor, and I am truly grateful for Jeff Canaday's thorough copyediting. Working with each of them has been a real pleasure.

Several individuals have offered insightful advice over the years, either by reading drafts of chapters, commenting on my work at conferences, or participating in conversations about my work. These include Mark Bradley, Nathan Citino, Frank Costigliola, Peter Hahn, Walter Hixson, Paul Kramer,

Sheryl Kroen, Douglas Little, Ussama Makdisi, Melani McAlister, Robert McMahon, Joseph Spillane, Michael Tsin, and Salim Yaqub. Of these, I would like to single out Peter Hahn, Doug Little, Melani McAlister, and Salim Yaqub for their more sustained engagement with my work and the many suggestions they have made over several years. I would also like to thank the two reviewers for the University of North Carolina Press, who evaluated the full manuscript on two occasions. Their careful readings made the finished product immeasurably better. Of course, any errors or problems that remain are entirely my responsibility.

As an undergraduate at Cornell University, I had the tremendous good fortune to take multiple classes with Tim Borstelmann and Walter LaFeber. Both are exceptional teachers, though in very different ways, and proved crucial to my decision to pursue a career researching, writing, and teaching about the history of U.S. foreign relations. Walt's lectures, seminars, and research acumen still inspire me and set a standard that I continually strive to meet. Tim helped me undertake my first large research project while also proving that it is possible to pursue it all—a career, a family, and other passions.

At the University of North Carolina at Chapel Hill, I was part of cohort of Ph.D. students working with Michael Hunt that included Chris Endy and Alan McPherson. Both Alan and Chris are excellent scholars and good friends, and each readily gave assistance and support whenever I asked for it. Sharing the graduate school experience with them was truly a pleasure.

Yet, among all the individuals I have mentioned thus far, none is more responsible for my becoming the historian I am today than Michael Hunt. He taught me how to ask questions and how to look for answers. He taught me that thinking historically is not just a discipline, but a way of life. I am also fairly certain he spent far more time than he wanted to teaching me to write. Michael was an excellent mentor, constantly pushing me to look deeper, to think harder, and to own my work, despite its flaws. He and Paula became my lifelong friends, whom I look forward to reconnecting with every time I return to Chapel Hill.

The history department at the University of Florida has proven to be an exciting and intellectually stimulating place to work. Bill Link has been an exemplary mentor, in both formal and informal ways. He knows the ins and outs of the academic world better than anyone I know, and has provided wise counsel on occasions too numerous to count. Joe Spillane has been both an excellent department chair and friend, reading through some early drafts of material, talking through the project, and protecting my time. Michelle

Campos, Nina Caputo, Elizabeth Dale, Mitch Hart, Sheryl Kroen, Jon Sensbach, and Ben Wise are among the many great colleagues and trusted friends with whom I have the pleasure to work, and all allowed me to bend their ears at opportune moments. Former colleagues Fitz Brundage, Fred Corney, Bob McMahon, Michael Tsin, Brian Ward and Bob Zieger all helped me settle into the department—professionally, intellectually, and socially—during my early years in Gainesville. Of course, no history department is complete without an excellent administrative staff. In our department, Linda Opper, Erin Smith, and Rutecleia Zarin are among those who make everybody else's work much easier.

Teaching is the most enjoyable aspect of my job, and I have been very fortunate to have a large number of highly engaged students who challenge me. Four in particular stand out. Evan Hentschel took my course on U.S.–Middle East relations the first time I offered it many years ago, and his probing questions during class and office hours forced me to rethink not only how I presented some of the material, but also some of the arguments that would ultimately take shape in this book. Roommates Alexia Ash and Anna Prusa must have made whatever apartment complex they called home the smartest in Gainesville, and over the course of several classes, independent studies, and Anna's honors thesis, they revealed intellectual interests and senses of humor that were uncannily complementary, and that made teaching them as much of an educational experience for me as it was for them. Finally, and more directly relevant to the subject of this book, Kris Malham was one of many students in my classes who served in Afghanistan or Iraq, or both. Our many conversations in class and office hours, and particularly the three hours we spent going through photographs from his first tour in Iraq, remind me why I believe a book like this one is necessary.

Gainesville is a fine environment in which to live and work, and has made completing this book a much more bearable endeavor. The many long hours spent on roads and trails—first as a runner and now as cyclist—in and around Gainesville over the years offered exercise, solitude, and time, and served as crucial breaks from the manuscript or moments of epiphany. These were hours when I did some of my best thinking.

I would like to express my gratitude to Alex Rudnick, Helen Rudnick, and Lindsey Knauff. All were exceptional babysitters and over five years became extensions of our family. In addition, Alex, a budding historian in her own right, provided critical assistance with the bibliography.

Last but far from least is my family. My in-laws have each made their own sacrifices and contributions. Ed and Beverly Harland have made many trips to Gainesville to watch their grandchildren so I could keep working on the book. They have always done so with generous spirit and good cheer. Julie, Dave, Doug, and Bradley Rouse have also offered their endless support, often in the form of short vacations, golf games, and good humor. Julie deserves special mention, though, as she never shied away from asking me the tough questions about the status of the book. Though I see Randy, Dana, Jory, and Marc Harland less frequently, not least because getting back and forth to Paris on a regular basis is a bit more difficult than is the trip to and from North Carolina, our time together is no less enjoyable or valuable, and serves as a useful reminder of the enduring importance of family.

Growing up the youngest of fourteen children on a dairy farm in northern New York taught me perseverance, which has served me well during this long journey. Even more important was developing a thick skin and a sense of humor. I owe a special debt, in this regard, to Pete, Brian, and Steve Lister. Pete has the most common sense of any individual I have ever met, and he and his wife Kathy and their kids Jennifer, Kristin, Melissa, Jessica, Nicole, and Justin offer their own form of inspiration to me. Brian's artwork hanging in our house inspires my own creativity as a historian. Steve's crazy antics and relentless commentary prove, if nothing else, that at least the rest of us are sane. I am also grateful to my sister Caryn Woodfin, upon whom I have always been able to rely.

My son Jeremy has an amazing and seemingly endless desire to watch any sporting event, from the NBA championships to the World Cup to the Super Bowl to the Tour de France, and then to attempt somehow to re-create it in our house, yard, or neighborhood. I relish the moments when I get to participate in those endeavors, even if doing so detracts from my work. And though he cannot yet fully comprehend what this book is about, I have been touched by his frequent expressions of interest in it, especially his request that I show him where the Middle East is on a map. I also appreciate his willingness to do whatever he could to help me finish, whether that meant forcing me to take a break to play with him, going over to a friend's house, or putting up with yet another babysitter so that I could work. My daughter Ally has been a real trooper. She was born as my wife was finishing her dissertation, was old enough to ask for daily updates as I completed my own, watched as my wife then shifted to writing her book, and graciously celebrated when the final version of mine went in the mail on her eleventh birthday. Clearly, her patience for such things far exceeds my own. Looking back over that time,

I am amazed at the changes she has undergone. Her intellectual curiosity, athletic ability, and kind spirit consistently impress me and challenge me to do better as a father and search for more time to spend with her. I hope that at some point down the road both she and Jeremy will find some value in the book and thus understand in some way the sacrifices they made (knowingly and unknowingly) as I completed it.

Finally, my wife Jessica is a stellar historian and colleague in her own right, and she put her considerable skills to good use in reading multiple drafts of the manuscript. She was particularly effective—and persistent—at getting me to talk through challenging points, but she also seemed to know when to tell me to shut up, write, and "J. P. P." (Just Push Print) already! It would not be the book it is without her invaluable contributions. Yet, somehow, it was everything she did outside the context of the book—cooking dinners, running the kids around town, encouraging me to spend time on the bike, and all the other things big and small—that matter most. Simply put, her presence makes my life infinitely better in every respect, and I hope she realizes how much I love and appreciate her. It is to her, Ally, and Jeremy that I dedicate this book, and I thank them for the life we are making together.

IMAGINING
THE MIDDLE EAST

INTRODUCTION

Imagining the Middle East

When President George W. Bush addressed the nation in the aftermath of the terrorist attacks of 11 September 2001, he framed the event in an apparently self-evident five-word question: "Why do they hate us?" His answer to that question appeared equally obvious: "They hate our freedoms — our freedom of religion, our freedom of speech, our freedom to vote and assemble and disagree with each other." Leaving aside the fact that both the question and the answer left who "they" were largely undefined, it is important to note that the exercise met a rhetorical need at a particular moment in time as people tried to make sense of such terrible acts. It was reasonable to ask, albeit in a more sophisticated manner, what ideas these terrorists held about the United States that inspired them to take such actions. Of course, framing the issue as President Bush did suggested another equally important and ill-defined question: What do "we" think of "them"?[1]

It is that very big question that I address in *Imagining the Middle East*. My foremost premise is that the exercise of U.S. power — cultural, economic, military, and political — in the Middle East has been enabled, justified, and sustained through the ways Americans have thought about and interpreted the region, the people who inhabit it, and the forces at play there. Thus, I examine the ways in which, to borrow a phrase from David Engerman's work on nineteenth- and twentieth-century Russian and Soviet experts in the United States, academics, business persons, government officials, and journalists who were "paid to interpret" the Middle East "for American audiences" understood the region in the twentieth century, from roughly the end of World War I through the late 1960s. I argue that, over time, these analysts, commentators, experts, observers, and specialists interpreted the Middle East in two primary ways. First, they imagined the region possessed certain characteristics, and their beliefs about the region were revealed in a series of discourses about its people, religions, political movements, social structures, polarizing conflicts, and defining moments. Second, they imagined the Middle East as they hoped it might become as a consequence of outside involvement in the region. These individuals believed the Middle East would change as other countries—especially the United States—became more deeply involved in regional affairs. The ways in which they imagined the Middle East of the past and present came in part to justify or explain policies designed to create an imagined Middle East of the future.[2]

These arguments require that the book take shape around specific themes and issues, rather than along a more traditional chronological narrative. I have reduced the emphasis on the Cold War that generally dominates scholarship on the history of U.S.–Middle East relations. While the Cold War remains, in this analysis, crucial, it is just one of several factors at work, as is demonstrated by the exploration of persistent, though shifting, perceptions of the region that predated, existed alongside, and outlasted that conflict. Chapter 1 examines the evolution of expertise and the production of knowledge regarding the Middle East as they were increasingly driven by expanding U.S. economic and national security interests in the region. Chapter 2 turns to the issue of religion, the most obvious marker of difference between the United States and much of the Middle East, and analyzes the different understandings of Islam, its impact on the Middle East itself, and its implications for U.S. involvement and interests there. The third chapter investigates interpretations of and responses to nationalist movements across the region, while the fourth chapter tackles directly a secular, modernizing impulse that I argue has long animated U.S. involvement in the Middle East. Finally, chapter 5 addresses the primary issue, the Arab-Israeli-Palestinian conflict, that caused the greatest consternation among, and revealed deep tensions between, those involved in the very complex process of imagining the Middle East.

As a consequence of this thematic organization, the book is neither an all-inclusive overview of the history of U.S. relations with the Middle East, several fine examples of which already exist, nor is it a deeply detailed case study of U.S. relations with a specific country in the region. Instead, it is an effort to grapple with how professional observers of, commentators on, and makers of policy toward the Middle East understood the region in its entirety. To be sure, these individuals did address specific countries in their commentaries or policies, but they often did so through a larger conception of the region as a whole. Two examples demonstrate the point. First, an April 1951 National Intelligence Estimate noted, "From the point of view of US security

interests, the Near East must be considered as an entity. Defense of Western strategic interests in the region (oil installations, communications, and
strategic air facilities) would require the use of military bases and the free
movement of defending forces throughout much of the area." Hence, policy
toward a single country could not be divorced from the larger regional context. Second, and as chapter 2 demonstrates, specialists characterized Islam
as a "totalitarian" religion that dictated how all of its adherents thought and
acted. Obviously such an assessment was highly problematic and there is no
intent to perpetuate it here, but it does reveal the extent to which American
and other observers of the time viewed the Middle East as an entity. It is therefore important to understand how such a reading came into being and its
implications for U.S. relations with both specific countries and the broader
region.[3]

The book's thematic organization makes it possible to read each chapter
independently, but several threads tie the chapters together into a cohesive
examination of how professional Middle East watchers imagined the region.
First is my broad methodological interest in combining approaches that
focus on national security concerns, diplomacy, and economics with interpretations that emphasize the cultural, ideological, or intellectual contexts,
as well as the nonstate actors who influenced the course of U.S. foreign relations. Too often, scholars view these approaches as mutually exclusive, rather
than mutually supportive. A more useful formulation might recognize that
the protection or pursuit of national security concerns or economic interests often motivated policymakers, but that cultural, ideological, or intellectual contexts impacted how those interests were defined, articulated, and
pursued.[4]

There can be little doubt that scholars must combine the two approaches
when wrestling with the history of U.S.–Middle East relations. U.S. policymakers clearly focused on economic interests, especially oil since the 1920s,
and national security concerns, particularly during and after the Cold War
with the Soviet Union. But culture and ideas were central to how policymakers and average Americans understood both economic and security
issues. Oil quickly became the most critical feature of increasingly mechanized and technologically advanced militaries, as well as of a new consumer
culture that first expanded rapidly across the United States, then Europe,
and eventually other parts of the world in the twentieth century. Access to
Middle Eastern oil for the United States and its allies therefore became crucial, in both economic and military terms, to preserving what policymakers

and scholars have referred to as "the American way of life." Americans understood the Cold War conflict with the Soviet Union in similar ways, as a contest for the survival of the U.S. cultural, economic, and political system at home as well as a concomitant universalist vision of the world as a whole. Hence, as U.S. policymakers, and the academics, journalists, and businesspersons who supported them, worked to define and protect those national security interests in the Middle East, they were forced to try to understand the region itself. That effort, in turn, brought them face to face with their own ideas about the people, religions, social structures, political movements, and other aspects of the Middle East. It was virtually impossible to design policies without taking such ideas into consideration.[5]

The second thread running through these chapters, closely connected to the first, is a focus on the changing nature of expertise and authority in the United States with respect to the Middle East specifically and to foreign relations more broadly. Through much of the nineteenth century, missionaries, tourists, and travel writers constituted the majority of "experts" on the Middle East. By the late nineteenth century, that group expanded to include academics interested in ancient Near Eastern and biblical studies. It grew again in the early twentieth century to include businessmen involved in trade with the Middle East and the nascent regional oil industry, an emergent group of policy and strategy intellectuals, as well as some European academics and political commentators. Even so, at the time of World War II, there were few people in the United States who could be characterized as authorities on the modern Middle East. That state of affairs began to change during the war, which brought people from other specialties to focus on contemporary U.S.–Middle East relations. The rise of the Cold War in the late 1940s then provided the policy justifications necessary to win significant funding for the creation of modern Middle East studies as a specific discipline. From that point forward, the number of people claiming expertise in Middle Eastern affairs continued to grow.

I contend that these individuals came to constitute an informal network defined by certain basic features. Most fundamentally, all members of this network shared a professional and policy-oriented interest in the Middle East and sought to convey a sense of the region's role in a broader conception of international politics. They shared the common goal of contributing to policy and public discussions about the Middle East and its relationship to the United States. They self-identified in some way as—and were paid to be—professional analysts, commentators, experts, observers, or specialists with respect to the Middle East. There also existed a certain level of intertextuality within this informal network, which is to say that many of its members were familiar with the work of their peers and communicated with each other, either directly or indirectly, at professional meetings, through letters, or by reading, citing, and responding to each other's work. There were even institutional expressions of this informal network's existence through meetings convened by organizations such as the Council on Foreign Relations or the Middle East Institute. Finally, while most participants were from the United States and received much of their training at U.S. academic, government, or business institutions, the network was also transnational in scope. It relied particularly on European experts—people like Valentine Chirol in the years surrounding World War I, Hamilton A. R. Gibb from the 1930s through the 1950s, and Bernard Lewis from the 1960s to the present, among many others—both to serve as voices of authority but also to train Americans. But this informal transnational network also drew on individuals from the Middle East itself, especially those from Lebanon, either as educators of future experts or as interlocutors who might lend credibility to various assertions about the region and its peoples.

The network examined here shares some features with, but also departs in significant ways from, other acknowledged networks. In her work on the Freemasons, historian Jessica Harland-Jacobs defines a network as "an interconnected system; more specifically, it is an interrelated group of people who share interests and concerns and interact for mutual assistance. While some networks operate only on a local scale, others . . . function concurrently on a variety of levels: local, national, regional, and even global." The Freemasons constitute a more formal and wide-ranging network than did the Middle East specialists I discuss, but the notion that specialists were interconnected, that they shared interests and concerns, and that they interacted to pursue a mutually agreed upon goal (even if not to provide mutual assistance) is applicable. That said, the network of Middle East specialists I discuss was not nearly as tight-knit as "the Vulcans" described by journalist James Mann in his recent study of Republican Party foreign policy operatives who had come of age politically in the 1970s and 1980s, and who returned to power with the administration of George W. Bush. Self-named after "the Roman god of fire, the forge and metalwork," the Vulcans were an exceptionally tight group of similarly minded officials who worked assiduously to dominate U.S. foreign policy, especially in the aftermath of the Clinton administration. A more useful comparison can be made with the "Sovietologists" David Engerman has investigated. Engerman examines a politically and intellectually diverse group of "professor-consultants" drawn together by their shared interest in contributing to U.S. Cold War policies as they participated in the creation and repeated reshaping of an entire field of academic study. Much as the specialists in my own study did with respect to the Middle East, for decades Engerman's subjects helped to define the boundaries of debate and discussion with respect to the Soviet Union.[6]

While I contend that an informal transnational network of analysts, commentators, experts, observers, and specialists emerged, I am keenly aware of the limits of that network and my arguments regarding it. There were no clear guidelines for determining membership in the network, the individuals about whom I write never explicitly spoke of themselves as members of a network, and so there remain certain individuals in the pages that follow who resist easy classification and labeling. Nonetheless, I do find the idea of an informal transnational network of professional specialists a useful concept through which to examine how Americans have imagined the Middle East. I also must be clear that by employing the concept of an informal transnational network I am in no way suggesting that all individuals agreed on all of the major issues of the day or that they exercised inordinate power when it came to specific policy decisions. In fact, many issues engendered significant debate among members of the informal network, and even basic agreement on a particular issue did not always lead to a single policy prescription. It is more useful to consider the expertise these individuals claimed and the interpretations they put forth as helping to establish the boundaries or parameters for debate and discussion regarding regional affairs and the U.S. role in them. Finally, for ease of writing and reading, I deploy terms such as "analysts," "commentators," "experts," "observers," or "specialists" when generically referring to participants in this informal transnational network, but I use discipline-specific identifiers such as "academic," "government Middle East specialist," or "journalist" when describing particular individuals or segments of the network. I avoid using the term "Arabist" altogether, as it suggests language skills that few professional observers of the Middle East possessed prior to the mid-1950s and because it has become a contentious and even derogatory term, with significant political implications since the early 1970s.

Examining this informal transnational network of Middle East specialists concerned with interpreting the region for American audiences allows us to build upon David Engerman's notion of "knowledge *for*, *of*, and *as* global power." In the first of these categories, knowledge for global power, academics and other specialists worked on issues regarding the Middle East with the explicit purpose of assisting policymakers. At the same time, many individuals, particularly in academia or the media, saw themselves playing a crucial role in educating the broader public about the region, its place in the international political arena, and the U.S. role there. In this way they promoted the acquisition of knowledge of global power as a fundamental responsibility of all Americans. Finally, many specialists relied heavily on new and allegedly neutral or objective ways of identifying, labeling, and quantifying certain characteristics of the region. Measuring literacy rates, poverty rates, food production, and economic output, among other things, provided a means of categorizing countries, regimes, social systems, or even people, and could be used to place them within a perceived broader international hierarchy of states and peoples.[7]

That point leads to a third thread running through this book: the consistent efforts of the members of this informal transnational network of academics, businesspersons, journalists, and policymakers to imagine a transformed or modernized Middle East. This impulse to transform was a product of the intersection of two broader, universalizing visions of the United States and its project in the world. Anders Stephanson has referred to this project as "a peculiar fusion of providential and republican ideology that took place after the Revolution, a most dynamic combination of sacred and secular concepts." The sacred concept was the belief that the United States was a special place "providentially selected for divine purposes." The secular concept, meanwhile, drew from the notion that the United States was an experiment in republican virtue, liberty, and orderly progress that served as an "exhibition of a new world order" that might benefit "humankind as a whole." From the early nineteenth century onward, this sense of sacred and secular mission has suggested that Americans have a unique role to the play in the Middle East. Nineteenth-century missionaries saw the educational and philanthropic institutions they founded across the region as not only potentially leading Muslims and indigenous Christians to convert, but as fulfilling a broader biblical prophecy of a new Jerusalem emerging to redeem the old Jerusalem. Through the first half of the twentieth century, the emerging network of specialists understood the potential for political transformation in rising secular nationalist forces in part as an outgrowth of this U.S. missionary experience but also as a response to both European colonialism and what Americans perceived to be Islamic despotism. At the same time, a parallel narrative of socioeconomic transformation grew from the participation of U.S. companies in the development of Middle Eastern oil resources and the intervention of the U.S. government in the region more broadly. Institutions like the Arabian American Oil Company (ARAMCO) worked assiduously to promote themselves as bringers of progress and development to the peoples of the area, even when facts on the ground suggested the story was much more complicated. These dual narratives combined with new forms of social scientific knowledge by the late 1950s and early 1960s to support U.S. government policies explicitly intended to modernize the Middle East. When the flawed assumptions underlying those policies led to their failure, specialists relied upon entrenched ways of imagining the Middle East to explain the region's inability to transform itself.[8]

Envisioning a unique transforming mission for the United States in the Middle East relied on closely connected and equally powerful sacred and secular imaginings of the region. Since at least the early nineteenth century, Americans have imagined the Middle East either as "the cradle of civilization," as the "birthplace of three great religions," or, more simply, as "the Holy Land." When U.S. interest and involvement in the region increased in the twentieth century, sacred concerns about the role of Islam as a "totalitarian" force influenced American efforts to support the rise of secular nationalist movements across the region. But when those movements failed to conform to U.S. wishes, policymakers and members of the network promoted secular models of socioeconomic transformation, or modernization, the failure of which also came to be read through closely connected sacred and secular lenses. And the most vexing problem of all, the Arab-Israeli-Palestinian conflict, appeared to observers as a product of the intersection of sacred religious and secular nationalist concerns among both Jews and Arabs.

Examining these imaginings of a sacred and secular mission to create a modern Middle East requires one to investigate what "modern" meant in the minds of specialists. From World War I forward, it increasingly came to mean a reliably secular and national state that pursued policies to formalize legal and constitutional systems protecting individual rights, promoting consumer-oriented economic growth, and providing social services, especially in education and health care, that would improve the daily lives of the citizens of the state. For many observers, the model modern nation was Turkey under the rule of Mustafa Kemal (known more familiarly as Atatürk), who hoped to weaken Islam and the connection between the masses and their Ottoman past by declaring an independent Turkish republic, eliminating the caliphate, and changing the alphabet, among other things. Particularly in the late 1940s and early 1950s, members of the informal network of specialists held him up as the type of leader they hoped to see rise to power in states across the region.

Yet the pursuit of modernity in the Middle East occasionally took a back seat to building reliable military and political alliances that would help protect U.S. national security interests. The tensions between these two visions of the Middle East were nowhere more apparent than in the evolving relationships between the United States and Egypt on the one hand, and the United States and Saudi Arabia on the other. In the 1950s and 1960s, the United States forsook a relationship with Egypt, a state that could reasonably be characterized as one pursuing many aspects of the modern agenda described above, but also as one not willing to subordinate itself to U.S. political and military wishes. Instead, the United States solidified its economic, political, and military relationship with a decidedly antimodern Saudi Arabia (as it is defined above), a reliable regional ally in possession of enormous petroleum reserves, all while Americans involved in ARAMCO continued to promote the company as the modernizer of the desert kingdom.

The focus on transformative visions of the Middle East and their implicit opposites — concerns about "backwardness" or "tradition" in the region — serves to highlight the fourth thread running through these chapters: my effort to contribute to what Melani McAlister has called a "post-orientalist" understanding of the multifaceted relationship between the United States and the Middle East. McAlister refers to Edward Said's highly influential *Orientalism*, which argued that first Western Europeans and then Americans utilized a series of essentializing discourses to exercise both intellectual and material dominance over the "Orient." The Orientalist discourse Said identified was citational, as the primary authorities built a mutually reinforcing web of references to each other. The discourse worked to feminize the Middle East in Western European and American thinking by characterizing the people of the region as weak, emotional, or irrational, and it established an intellectual relationship between the Middle East and the West that was based on binaries — strong and weak, feminine and masculine, backward or traditional and modern. Historians of U.S. foreign relations have hesitated to accept Said's argument and approach for several reasons. In general, they have been uncomfortable with how he removed his sources from their distinct historical contexts and presented his own essentializing claims about the nature of Western European and U.S. relations with the Middle East. Moreover, many scholars of U.S. foreign relations have struggled to embrace approaches and arguments that could not demonstrate a distinct causal link between specific cultural representations, popular perceptions, and actual policies.[9]

One way to arrive at a post-Orientalist interpretation is to focus on individuals and groups who thought on nearly a daily basis about the Middle East and how it figured in the international orientation of the United States. Unearthing their assumptions, guiding interpretive frameworks, and narratives about the Middle East and its place in the world does not always lead us to specific policies, but it does help us restore sources to their proper historical context while also acknowledging their explicit political motivations. Moreover, it allows us to understand the intellectual environment within which debates about the nature and direction of U.S.–Middle East relations took place.

Examining the ideas of those who thought about the Middle East on a daily basis thus permits us to challenge and push forward some of Said's arguments. My focus on an informal network of professional Middle East watchers suggests that there was indeed a citational aspect to American imaginings of the region. While members of this network did not always agree on specific issues, they did develop mutually reinforcing ways of understanding the region that helped to establish the boundaries of debate. But those imaginings utilized much more than just a feminizing discourse. The following pages reveal a tendency to personify certain understandings of the Middle East, to encapsulate in specific people the hopes, dreams, fears, anger, and other emotions and ideas of Americans regarding broader movements and trends in the region. Feminizing individuals such as Iran's Mohammad Mossadegh was one among several negative discursive paths along which this process played out, but it could also follow the opposite avenue, as was the case when analysts held up Turkey's Kemal as the model of a secular, modernizing leader they hoped others might emulate. In either case, such characterizations of key individuals were part of a larger effort to confer either legitimacy or illegitimacy on regimes in the region. The focus on people also extended beyond specific individuals to entire populations. There were numerous efforts to educate American audiences about the allegedly inherent character traits of "the Arab," "Moslems," "Muslims," or "Mohammedans." Finally, while binary characterizations (strong/weak, feminine/masculine, etc.) were important features of how specialists imagined the Middle East, the process as a whole was much more complicated. For example, focusing on binaries alone overlooks the possibility and dynamic of transformation, a fundamental part of how network members imagined U.S. involvement in the Middle East.

In combination, the interpretive threads detailed above reveal at least the outlines of what Timothy Mitchell calls in his work on the British colonization of Egypt an evolving "framework of meaning"—an intellectual structure designed to render complex and disparate things orderly and understandable within a specific context. That framework provided a way for academic, business, government, and media specialists to make the Middle East more comprehensible and, by extension, locate the region and the various forces at play there within a broader international context in which the United States was emerging as the world's most powerful country with significant interests in the region. To be sure, the different components of that framework at once complemented and conflicted with each other. The ways in which many Americans conceived of their country's Cold War and oil-based national security interests in the Middle East sometimes contradicted those same individuals' conceptions of the Arab-Israeli-Palestinian conflict, of the role of religion, or of the broader sense of the sacred and secular mission that animated U.S. involvement in the region. Likewise, attempts to understand and respond to nationalist movements often ran counter to similar efforts to define the role of religion. These tensions are not the only ones inherent in the larger framework of meaning I discuss in the following pages, but they do demonstrate just how complex that framework was.[10]

By laying out this framework of meaning, I have no intention of propagating or perpetuating a variety of deeply flawed perceptions of and stereotypes about the Middle East and its peoples. These misapprehensions range widely, from overlooking religious diversity, both across different faith traditions and between different sects within individual religions, to what were at times explicitly racist and derogatory characterizations of the people of the region. Rather, my objective is, first, to try to recreate the Middle East that an informal network of policy-oriented specialists from a variety of professions imagined they knew and, second, to understand how those imaginings factored into discussions of the United States' role in the region and the wider world. Thus, much of what follows, including quotations that refer to "Moslems," "Mohammedans," or a variety of other insensitive terms, is more about the people doing the imagining than it is about the subject of their imagination. For it is only by first understanding the origins of such a framework of meaning that we can hope to move beyond it.

I do not use Arabic-language sources, as I do not believe the questions this book seeks to answer require them for the most part. There are many keys to understanding the history of U.S.–Middle East relations, one of which we can locate by examining how an informal network of policy-oriented specialists in the United States and their affiliates from Europe and the Middle East understood the region and conveyed those understandings to American audiences. Other keys emerge through studies that draw widely or exclusively on Arabic-language sources. Indeed, such a project would be the exact opposite of what I have undertaken here, and would rely largely on Arabic-language sources to explore how people in the Middle East have imagined the United States. The history of U.S.–Middle East relations is incredibly complex, and understanding that history demands a variety of studies and approaches. Even so, I do rely at certain moments on current scholarship based on Arabic-language sources to correct views expressed in some of the English-language sources I have utilized. Finally, for both consistency and ease of reading and recognition, I have utilized current common spellings of Middle Eastern names, places, and terms.

While I draw on a wide range of scholarship to develop the arguments of this book, several key works have offered both models and points of departure. Two path-breaking books—Douglas Little's *American Orientalism* and Melanie McAlister's *Epic Encounters*—focus specifically on the Middle East. Little's first chapter analyzes nineteenth-century travel writing and twentieth-century cultural products, such as *National Geographic* and the movie *Aladdin*, to argue that American ideas about the Middle East have mattered in the formulation of policy. He then undertakes an excellent policy history organized around specific themes (oil, national security, the Arab-Israeli conflict, etc.) but unfortunately focuses less on ideas than his opening chapter suggests he should. McAlister, on the other hand, analyzes movies, comedy skits, political cartoons, and literature, among other media, to examine how the Middle East and U.S. relations with the region have factored into or been reflected in American culture. Again, the book is outstanding, but it says very little about actual relations between the United States and the Middle East. My own research aims for a spot somewhere between the two, where ideas and culture matter in a policy-oriented way. In this sense, readers familiar with the two works might view them as the interpretive bookends to the present project. Finally, David Engerman's two award-winning works on Russian and Soviet specialists in the United States—*Modernization from the Other Shore* and *Know Your Enemy*—serve as revealing case studies of the intersection of expertise, knowledge production, and international politics. He brings to bear a keen understanding of both the Russian/Soviet and U.S. contexts, while also making important contributions regarding the professionalization of expertise in the United States, and thus offers useful guidance for my own work.[11]

Captives, Missionaries, Tourists, and Orientalists

Before investigating how twentieth-century specialists imagined the Middle East, we must first see how their eighteenth- and nineteenth-century forebears encountered and thought about the region and examine the perceptions and assumptions that were handed down to successive generations. From the founding of the United States through the mid-nineteenth century, one's authority regarding what was then known as part of a much larger "Orient" or, more specifically, as the "Near East," rested largely on whether or not one had experienced it firsthand. Most Americans' encounters with the Orient took place through the commentary provided by a variety of captives, missionaries, tourists, and travel writers. By the last quarter of the nineteenth century, the new field of ancient Near Eastern studies, or biblical studies, lent academic credibility to American understandings of the region. Academics and firsthand commentators brought their own approaches to imagining the Middle East and claimed some special authority or expertise, but the knowledge they produced was layered on top of that which came before, and often reflected the same basic themes.

The Orient, as early Americans imagined it, appeared as an obstacle to both the sacred and secular missions that Anders Stephanson argues were at the heart of the new nation's conception of its place in the world. Islam and indigenous forms of Christianity came to represent challenges to the extension of the sacred Christian vision, while Islam, monarchy, and despotism seemed to thwart the spread of the secular republican model. Read through these lenses, much of what passed for authentic U.S. knowledge of the Orient in the nineteenth century drew from sensationalized and highly impressionistic reporting of particular events and was based on fundamentally religious narratives that elevated a particular group of American Protestant Christians over indigenous Christians and Muslims.

The most widely read early U.S. commentaries about the Orient were the few biographies of "Mahomet," the occasional travel book, and the narratives of sailors who had been held as captives of the North African powers in the late eighteenth and early nineteenth centuries. Historian Robert Allison's analysis of this body of colonial and early American literature reveals it was fundamental to defining the future of the United States. Allison claims that experiences with and readings about the Muslim world caused early Americans to see "an example of the kind of political society they did not want to create." Depicting an antirepublican society characterized by religious despotism, weak political leadership, sexual licentiousness, and a history of capturing and enslaving enemies in warfare, the texts presented an image of the kind of government and society that Americans hoped to avoid replicating. Such perceptions, regardless of their accuracy, became so embedded in the political discourse of the day that Americans of any political persuasion in the early republic could find in these popular and familiar stories justifications for the widely divergent positions they advocated with respect to their new country. The Orient thus served as a metaphor through which the "Founding Fathers" in the United States criticized and delegitimized one another. John Quincy Adams, for example, defended his father's concerns that too much liberty might lead the young country down the road to anarchy, and perhaps tyrannical rule, by denigrating Thomas Jefferson for his support of Thomas Paine's *Vindication of the Rights of Man*. Adams labeled Jefferson an "Arabian prophet" for the "Islam of democracy." In Allison's words, the Muslim world portrayed by these early authorities offered "a lesson for Americans in what not to do, in how not to construct a state, encourage commerce, or form families. Power had to be controlled, liberty had to be secured, for men and women to prosper and for societies to progress."[12]

The conflicts with the North African powers were resolved by 1815 and it was not long before Christian missionaries departed for the Mediterranean and gave voice to the sacred and secular American vision. The first missionaries from the United States arrived in the Ottoman Empire in 1820, and their successors came to constitute the largest U.S. concern in the region by mid-century. Missionaries soon realized that, despite their hard work, converting Muslims was unlikely. Learning Arabic, however, allowed them to extend their reach beyond religious issues into other areas, most notably education. By 1900, American missionaries, along with philanthropists and independent educators, had opened over eight hundred elementary and secondary schools serving nearly forty thousand students across the region, as well as several institutions of higher learning, including Robert College in Turkey and Syrian Protestant College (renamed the American University of Beirut in 1920). In these schools, Arabs were taught a secular curriculum based on European and American experiences: the Enlightenment, the rise of nationalism, and the development of democracy following the American and French revolutions.[13]

What motivated missionaries to pursue this agenda in the Middle East, especially given the fact that conversions to Christianity were so rare? They fervently believed that the United States and the Holy Land (holy for both Christians and Jews) were providentially intertwined. Indeed, missionaries to the Orient embodied the sacred and secular American vision perhaps more than any other group of nineteenth-century Americans. Driven by a spiritual connection to the Holy Land and a complex reading of both the Bible and history more generally, American Protestants saw the creation of the United States as the fulfillment of the biblical prophecy of a new Jerusalem. It was up to missionaries, as well as educators and philanthropists, from this new Jerusalem to redeem the old Jerusalem, which they believed had been defiled over the centuries. These desires to transform the Orient in both sacred and secular terms remained powerful motivating forces for Americans involved in the region from the middle of the nineteenth century through the beginning of the twenty-first.[14]

Missionaries pursuing this redemptive project wrote letters home and reports to their congregations in which they described the many obstacles they encountered, including threats to their health and personal safety. As in most of the rest of the world in the nineteenth century, disease was rampant and many areas lacked law enforcement and were beyond government control. In his overview of U.S. involvement in the region from 1776 to the present, historian Michael Oren liberally quotes missionary descriptions of Muslim violence and perfidy, almost continuous illness, and the rigors of travel in an effort to present the region as a uniquely inhospitable place and to suggest that it was against enormous odds that the missionary community came to thrive. Fuad Sha'ban deploys similar evidence to make a different point. Citing statements such as the missionary Eli Smith's declaration that "the nearer you approach to Jerusalem, the less will be your desire to visit it; from the expectation of more pain from views of present wickedness, than of pleasure from reflections upon its ancient glory," Sha'ban argues that missionary writings played a crucial role in propagating negative American imaginings of Islam and the Orient.[15]

Yet, as historian Ussama Makdisi has demonstrated, this missionary way of imagining the Orient was not limited to the region's Muslims; it was also applied to indigenous Christians. The missionaries denigrated Muslims, to be sure, but they also had to present themselves as the bearers of the true Christian faith by showing, according to Makdisi, "that Oriental Christianity was not only corrupt but selfish, bigoted, and out of touch with the common man." Thus, "in the minds of the missionaries, Oriental Christianity and Islam were coupled as the two pillars of temporal and spiritual corruption that had to be struck down." Makdisi's findings challenge Edward Said's emphasis on Islam to the exclusion of local Christian sects as the focal point of Western European and U.S. discursive efforts to "other" the Orient, a point with which I generally agree though, as I will argue, Islam was one of several critical lenses through which Americans viewed the Middle East.[16]

Reactions to the deaths of Reverend J. G. Coffing and Reverend Merriam, both of whom were murdered in separate incidents in the early 1860s, offer telling examples of how Americans understood the Orient during this period. The two attacks appeared to have been carried out by thieves preying on small groups of travelers. Edward Joy Morris, head of the U.S. legation in Constantinople, worked strenuously to ensure the alleged killers were caught and punished—in this case with death sentences—and in conveying the results back to Washington. In doing so, he commented freely on the characteristics of the Middle East. The decapitation of one of Coffing's accused murderers was "conducted with unusual solemnity, in order to make a lasting impression on the public mind," which Morris believed responded favorably to such displays. This swift application of "justice" was all "the more striking because of the impunity which criminals have too often enjoyed who have murdered the subjects of other Christian powers." Speaking more generally of the conditions he encountered in the area, Morris characterized the Ottoman government as "hydra-headed" in its reliance on provincial governors who were appointed due to their success as courtiers rather than as administrators. He proclaimed his constant vigilance against "the prejudices of race and religion, more obstinate and violent in this empire than in any other part of the world, and the fear which always exists with the Porte of exciting civil war between neighboring districts of opposite faiths."[17]

As real as these events were, Morris's commentary on them, as well as the broader missionary narrative of experiences in the Near East, contributed to a distorted image of the place, its inhabitants, and its animating forces and issues. The central missionary narrative was one of decline and redemption, of the new Jerusalem cleansing the Holy Land of all its corrupting influences—be they Islamic, Oriental Christian, or otherwise—and reviving it for the present and the future. Through schools in particular, this narrative went, missionaries would teach and spread American and Western European ideas and values, hoping eventually to create educated, liberal, middle-class reformers who would realize this missionary vision. Receptive American congregations enthusiastically awaited this outcome, and were kept informed of both the obstacles to and progress toward this goal through the missionaries' letters to individuals and formal reports to the American Board of Commissioners for Foreign Missions, the body that oversaw missionary work. Indeed, some communications were published in what were effectively the earliest periodicals in the United States that dealt with the Near East: the *Missionary Herald*, the *American Theological Review*, and the *Moslem World: A Quarterly Review of Current Events, Literature, and Thought Among Mohammedans, and the Progress of Christian Missions in Moslem Lands*. Thus, through their activities and their communications with congregations back home, missionaries became the most recognized nineteenth- and early twentieth-century authorities on the Orient in the United States, and their interpretations proved instrumental in shaping how Americans came to imagine the region and their country's role there.

By the mid-nineteenth century a variety of adventurers, businessmen, engineers, soldiers, tourists, and other figures began traversing the area and presenting their own accounts of the Orient, which helped perpetuate these sacred and secular ways of imagining the region. The "Holy Land" became a primary destination of a new class of American tourists, many of whom traveled to the area hoping to experience firsthand the lands they had read so much about in the Bible. These voyages generated a large and widely read body of travel literature, and therefore served as an encounter not only for those who made the trip, but also for those who lacked the resources to do so. Mark Twain's *Innocents Abroad*, a product of his own Middle Eastern journey, was the best known of these works. Twain sought to convey a sense of the places that so many Americans had read about in their religious texts. The book opens with travelers bubbling with anticipation, fueled by their romanticized assumptions about the Holy Land. It ends with their dreams dashed by the unfamiliarity, poverty, and filth encountered abroad. Other authors and travel writers, including Herman Melville and a Louisiana slave named David F. Dorr, who traveled the world with his master before fleeing to Ohio, told similar tales. In the process, they strengthened the dominant image of the Orient and Islam as backward, dangerous, violent, and exotic.[18]

The discipline of ancient Near Eastern studies added yet another layer to these missionary and tourist imaginings of decline and redemption in the

Orient. In the United States, the academic study of the region originated in the early 1840s in two institutions, both of which were closely connected to the missionary enterprise in the Near East. The first was Yale University, which in 1841 appointed Edward Salisbury professor of Arabic and Sanskrit in response to the extensive interest in the Bible that existed across New England and that had at once produced and benefited from the missionary efforts in the Near East. Salisbury, who trained as an Orientalist in Europe, was the first professor in the United States to focus on the region. Over time he helped create at Yale a center of training in ancient languages that could compete with European, particularly German, universities. The second institution was the American Oriental Society, formed in 1842 to coordinate and report on the study of the Orient, including virtually anywhere east of Europe. The society was also closely connected to the missionary movement, as sixteen of its original sixty-eight participants were members of the American Board of Commissioners for Foreign Missions.[19]

Academic interest in the Near East continued to grow over the ensuing decades, and by the 1870s and 1880s several universities began to develop programs in ancient Near Eastern studies. Bruce Kuklick has shown that scholars working in Semitic studies, Assyriology, Egyptology, philology, and archaeology were initially motivated by a spiritual desire to confirm or better understand the contents of the Bible. Over time, however, their motivations became more secular in nature as they grew more interested in professional scholarship, detached observation, and understanding the human experience in both spatial and temporal terms. At the same time, the university presidents who supported these new specialists at Yale, the University of Pennsylvania, the Johns Hopkins University, the University of Chicago and others competed for supremacy in the field. They worked to present their schools and their specialists as the best authorities on the history of ancient civilizations, early Christianity, or, in some cases, early Islam. In the process, they hired top European specialists, often German, in the various fields, bringing a distinctly transnational character to ancient Near Eastern studies in the United States. These universities thereby established a precedent for the later study of the modern Middle East, when foreign specialists again provided much of the initial expertise required to train Americans, especially in languages and the study of Islam.[20]

Scholars of U.S. or European origin who studied ancient civilizations, early Christianity, or Islam in the late nineteenth or early twentieth centuries generally did so within an "Orientalist" framework. As Zachary Lockman has demonstrated, this way of understanding the Orient emerged in concert with the extension of European imperialism from the late eighteenth through the nineteenth centuries. British and French scholars were the first to engage in serious study of the region, though by the late nineteenth century German scholars and universities had also risen to prominence in the field. A central premise of the Orientalist framework held that the world of Islam was a distinct civilization that had stagnated for hundreds of years before entering a state of upheaval as it encountered a vastly superior European and U.S. civilization. Emphasizing Islam itself as an unchanging entity, scholars trained in the appropriate languages, philology, and foundational texts presumed to be able to explain all things Islamic, regardless of the era or place in which they existed. Orientalist scholars came to form an insular and self-replicating group, as they were placed in departments by area of focus, rather than by professional discipline, and often used essentially the same methodologies. Orientalism remained the dominant framework for training new academic specialists and for imagining the Middle East until World War II forced scholars to develop new ways of thinking about the region.[21]

These nineteenth-century academic, business, journalistic, missionary, and touristic imaginings of the Orient as an obstacle to the achievement of the sacred and secular American project had several deep and enduring legacies. On the most basic level, they left a community of people with a web of connections whose descendents utilized their presence to claim special knowledge and expertise in U.S. relations with the region for generations to come. In some instances, these connections literally assumed the form of a family affair over the course of the nineteenth and twentieth centuries, as the Dodge family history illustrates. Philanthropist William Earl Dodge (1805–1883) was a founder of the American mining firm Phelps, Dodge & Company. He had two sons, William Earle Dodge Jr. and David Stuart Dodge. William Jr. took over the mining interests, while David went to the Middle East and in the 1860s helped found Syrian Protestant College with money from the mining company. The younger William's son Cleveland Hoadley Dodge rose through the ranks of Phelps Dodge and helped fund Woodrow Wilson's presidential campaigns. Cleveland's twin sons, Cleveland Earl and Bayard, followed the family paths, as Cleveland stayed in mining and Bayard took up the family's interests in the Middle East, where he began as a faculty member at Syrian Protestant College in 1913 and then ran the university as its president from 1922 to 1948. The family's mining and missionary interests ultimately combined in Bayard's son David. David worked first for ARAMCO from 1949 to

1954, and then for the Trans-Arabian Pipeline (TAPLINE) from 1954 until his retirement in 1976. He came out of retirement to take over as president of American University of Beirut in 1981, only to become, as Robert Vitalis has noted, "America's first hostage in Lebanon" when Shi'ite militants kidnapped him in the midst of the Israeli attack on Beirut in 1982. The Dodges are perhaps the best example of a family with long-standing and multifaceted connections to the region, but there are others—the Eddys, the Hoskinses, and more—who became involved in the region as part of the nineteenth-century missionary and educational enterprises and remained critical players in the network of Middle East specialists decades later.[22]

In addition to creating a lineage of influential individuals who claimed expertise on the region, the missionaries, along with ancient Near East academic specialists, businesspersons, consultants, and travel writers, were critical in creating and sustaining in the United States a narrative of Middle Eastern backwardness. That narrative emphasized not only Muslims, but also Christians within the region. After all, if American Christian missionaries in the Middle East were going to redeem the region, they had to demonstrate that their version of Christianity was not only more valid than Islam but also the versions of Christianity that already existed there. The missionaries therefore characterized Christians just as they did Muslims. In glossing over religious and sectarian differences in the nineteenth century, missionaries, travel writers, and others established the precedent of placing virtually all inhabitants of the Middle East within a narrative of backwardness that would last well into the twentieth century.

These nineteenth-century authorities also imagined the Orient and U.S. involvement there in two fundamentally ahistorical ways, both of which relied heavily on the integrated sacred and secular project of the United States. The American missionaries, tourists, and authors and readers of travel literature who imagined a Holy Land awaiting redemption by the United States perceived the region either as it might have been two thousand years earlier in the time of Jesus or as it might exist in the future, after a sacred conversion to a particular form of Christianity and a secular conversion to the U.S. political and social model. Late nineteenth-century academic specialists in ancient Near Eastern studies perpetuated these ways of thinking about the area, denying its own distinct historical present by focusing almost exclusively on the ancient Near East and neglecting to study the region in contemporary terms. The second ahistorical imagining—equally powerful and just as problematic—concerned the United States and its agents in the Middle East. The

United States appeared in this rendering as a fundamentally different type of state and society than had heretofore existed. It was, in effect, a country that stood outside the historical problems and processes that other countries and places experienced. Moreover, through missionary and educational activities abroad, the United States and its citizens assumed responsibility for uplifting and transforming others by bringing the benefits of that allegedly exceptional U.S. model to the Middle East and the rest of the world. In combination, these two ahistorical imaginings suggested that the Orient was incapable of changing on its own, and that the United States was therefore the only legitimate source of change for the region. This way of imagining the United States in the Orient became deeply embedded in U.S.–Middle East relations over the coming decades, and its influence continues to the present.[23]

CHAPTER ONE

THE TASK . . . FALLS TO THE AREA SPECIALISTS

National Interests, Knowledge Production, and the
Emergence of an Informal Network

In 1947, the University of Pennsylvania's E. A. Speiser published a broad over-view of the Middle East and U.S. interests there. In *The United States and the Near East*, Speiser argued that U.S. "policy towards the Near East should be based on a thorough understanding of the present social and political conditions of the region." He sought to create space for a new group of participants in the policy process, claiming, "The task of furnishing the necessary informa-tion about the foreign scene falls to the area specialists. They contribute the basic intelligence—process it, to use the jargon of the recent war—and keep it up to date. In due time, this material is deposited within reach of those who frame foreign policy." Speiser went on to recognize that "many intermedi-ate stages" existed between the analysts and the policymakers, and policy might "not always reflect the best judgment of the specialists." Nonetheless, according to Speiser, "the end result depends largely on the ability and com-petence of the analysts all along the way."[1]

Speiser called for regional experts to begin playing a critical role in the development of policy because he found Americans woefully ignorant of the Middle East. He averred that the United States lacked the "trained and experi-enced men and women to handle our growing commitment in the region. . . . In recent years, while our stake in the Near East has been steadily growing, the system under which the necessary area work has to be carried on has not been subjected to anything like a corresponding expansion and modernization." Speiser was quick to absolve the State Department and any other specific organizations of blame for this state of affairs, claiming instead, "Fault lies with the system rather than with the individuals." To his mind, prewar U.S. interests in the region had not demanded a highly qualified group of specialists, and even if they had, hard-to-learn Middle Eastern languages and the quick transfers of staff into and out of areas worked against the development of such a group.[2]

In calling for a new approach to Middle Eastern studies in the United States, Speiser criticized a type of specialist and system of knowledge production that he himself exemplified. Born in 1902 in what is now Ukraine, Ephraim Avigdor Speiser came to the United States in 1920 to study ancient Hebrew. After attending the University of Pennsylvania for his master's degree and Dropsie College for his doctorate, Speiser joined the faculty at the University of Pennsylvania and remained there for the rest of his career as an archaeologist, philologist, and scholar of Semitics. His defining academic achievement was his participation in and reporting on a series of excavations in Iraq in the 1930s. During World War II, he brought his expertise in the ancient Near East to Washington, D.C., where he worked as head of the Near East section of the Office of Strategic Services' (OSS) research and analysis branch. There he supervised and worked closely with J. C. Hurewitz, who later became a towering figure in postwar Middle Eastern studies, on wartime intelligence and planning matters. It was Speiser's OSS work that led him to publish *The United States and the Near East*, one of the first postwar assessments of the new U.S. role in the region. In addition to calling for a new breed of area specialists, he urged the United States to accept its new global power and devote the necessary resources to developing a realistic yet regionally applicable policy independent of British or Soviet influence.[3]

This chapter provides the context necessary to evaluate Speiser's claims regarding the production and consumption of knowledge about the Middle East in the United States. It examines how the region came to be defined as an important interest for the United States and the consequences that designation had for knowledge production and the nature of expertise on the region from the early twentieth century through the mid-1960s. It begins by recounting the emergence of a more "professional," though still very limited, group of secular "experts" through the first four decades of the twentieth century. The established missionary and philanthropic community retained a powerful voice on Middle Eastern affairs, but academics, government officials, and journalists focused on international political and strategic concerns added their voices as well. The 1930s and 1940s in particular saw in-creased interest in the region, as the rising international oil industry and World War II drew more people and resources into the study of the Middle East. The heirs of the old missionary hands, ancient Near East specialists, and Orientalists from the United States and Europe originally attempted to meet this growing demand for knowledge about the contemporary Middle East. World War II and the early Cold War years then provided the context within which Speiser and others called for the "expansion and modernization" of the system of knowledge production about the Middle East. In response to those calls, there emerged an increasingly bureaucratized and institutional-ized, though still quite informal, transnational network of modern Middle East specialists. These new specialists relied heavily on U.S. national security concerns to pursue funding and to explain the fundamental interest of the United States in the region. This chapter concludes by reflecting on the field of Middle Eastern studies and the government use of scholarly research from the vantage point of the 1960s, when assessments of the efforts of this net-work first appeared.

Strategists, Orientalists, and the Problem of Knowledge Supply and Demand

The Americans who imagined or visited the Orient in the late nineteenth and early twentieth centuries did so in a rapidly changing international political context. A recently unified and rising Germany challenged British and French power in Europe, while the 1905 war between Russia and Japan revealed the former's weakness and the latter's growing strength. At the same time, the encroachment of European empires combined with a variety of internal prob-lems to weaken the Ottoman Empire. The economy of the empire grew con-siderably through the nineteenth century, but that growth was predicated on increasing integration into European affairs. Indeed, by the 1880s both the Ottoman Empire and Egypt were bankrupt and at the mercy of European creditors. Growing nationalist forces challenged Ottoman rule from within, culminating in the 1908 Young Turk Revolution that overthrew Sultan Abdul Hamid II. After World War I the Ottoman Empire ceased to exist and was replaced by a much smaller Turkey, with Britain and France acquiring con-trol over former Ottoman territory in Iraq, Transjordan, Palestine, Syria, and Lebanon under the aegis of the League of Nations. Meanwhile, the United States was ascendant. As the Ottoman Empire fractured and disintegrated, the United States first built a transcontinental, and then a trans-Pacific and Caribbean, empire of its own. When the Ottomans and Egyptians were bankrupt, the U.S. economy, though subject to substantial downturns, grew at an unprecedented rate and became the world's largest, surpassing Britain's and Germany's combined by the start of World War I. The war itself then demonstrated increasing U.S. economic power, as the country ended the war as the world's largest creditor nation.[4]

The missionaries, travel writers, and ancient Near East specialists who dominated late nineteenth-century U.S. discussions of the Orient never dealt explicitly with the implications of these developments. That task fell to a new class of secular strategists, foreign policy intellectuals, journalists, and government bureaucrats who emerged at the beginning of the twentieth century. World War I, its aftermath, and the pursuit of access to the region's bountiful petroleum reserves revealed, however, that the supply of specialists qualified to comment on contemporary Middle Eastern affairs was not large enough to meet the increasing demand for such individuals. The heirs of the old missionary and Orientalist hands, who imagined the region through the sacred interpretive frameworks within which they had been trained and lived, stepped in to fill the void. Thus, by the beginning of World War II, new forms of authority and knowledge characterizing the newly named "Middle East" as an area of growing U.S. interest and concern had been layered into the existing sacred and secular academic, adventurer, missionary, and Orientalist narratives of the region.

Naval theorist Alfred Thayer Mahan was one of the first Americans to connect these new global developments through systematic thinking and writing about the political and strategic relationship between the United States and the rest of the world. Mahan published numerous books and articles that emphasized the role of sea power in international affairs and was one of the primary intellectual forces driving U.S. overseas expansion in the late nineteenth and early twentieth centuries. He believed strongly in Anglo-Saxon superiority, claiming that over time and through both missionary zeal and government action the benefits of the sacred and secular American project might be spread abroad, particularly to Asia.[5]

Mahan's views regarding what he would soon term "the Middle East," which he visited in 1867 and 1894, were central to new perceptions of the region that focused on secular, as opposed to sacred, concerns. Writing in The Problem of Asia in 1900, Mahan identified a place between thirty and forty degrees north latitude and running from the Mediterranean basin in the west to

Korea in the east—an area he labeled "Middle Asia." "Within these bounds," Mahan contended, was "the debated and debatable ground," an area of international competition for the foreseeable future. Middle Asia was composed of two crucial pieces: a resource-rich eastern half and a western half that contained the lines of communication and travel—the Suez Canal, the Red Sea, and the Persian Gulf, as well as any potential overland railways—necessary to access the east. Mahan was not yet aware of the massive petroleum reserves that would make the western portion so important throughout the remainder of the twentieth century. He believed Russia and Britain were the primary contenders for control of the area, but also argued that the United States' new presence in the Philippines, its expanding economy, and its increasing international power gave it a growing stake in the region. Fortunately, in Mahan's view, the United States and Britain shared similar outlooks and interests, which for the time being Britain could defend. Nonetheless, Mahan cautioned that the United States needed to recognize its growing concern with which power controlled Middle Asia, particularly the access points and lines of communication contained in its western half, and prepare to defend that interest if necessary.[6]

Mahan refined his ideas regarding this large and ambiguous area of Middle Asia in his 1902 *National Review* article "The Persian Gulf in International Politics." In Mahan's assessment, the Persian Gulf emerged as "one terminus of a prospective interoceanic railroad" that would become "one link . . . in a chain of communication between East and West, alternative to the all-water route by the Suez Canal and the Red Sea." It was also here that Mahan renamed the region, referring to "the Middle East, if I may adopt a term which I have not seen." As in his earlier writing, Mahan identified the British and the Russians as the main contestants in the area, but noted that all commercially oriented countries had an interest in maintaining secure and stable access to it. Moreover, because Russia had direct access to Asia and the Pacific through its own Siberian railroad and because Britain held such crucial interests in India and Egypt, as well as in Asia more generally, Mahan deemed it necessary and appropriate for Britain to assert its control in the area. On the horizon, however, loomed a rising Germany, which was building its own Mesopotamian railroad and might have threatened British naval mastery. Britain, Mahan declared, "must maintain continuously supreme the navy upon which her all depends," and Americans should support British power deployed "in the general lines of our own advantage" in the Middle East. Thus, although Mahan did not assert a direct U.S. claim in the Middle East, he did tie U.S. fortunes there and in Asia more generally to the maintenance of British dominance in the region.[7]

Placed in the context of Mahan's other writings, "The Persian Gulf in International Politics" reinforced existing ways of imagining the Orient while also adding another layer to those imaginings. Combined with his previously stated and well-known beliefs regarding the superiority of Anglo-Saxon civilization, the essay buttressed the sacred missionary and Orientalist framework of decline and redemption by defining the region as a site for future American expansion. Yet renaming the region the Middle East and focusing on its political and economic value to the United States, rather than on the people and cultures in the area, also immediately conferred a geographical and political designation that fit within emerging U.S. views of the world as a whole. Moreover, Mahan advanced the process first begun by the academic ancient Near East specialists of claiming expertise and authority by presenting his material in a secular, scholarly manner that presumed detached observation and objectivity.

Shortly after Mahan wrote of the growing importance of the Middle East, an increasingly bureaucratic and professional State Department undertook its own reimagining of the region as a growing economic and strategic interest of the United States. Since the signing of a commercial treaty with the Ottomans in 1830 led to the creation of a U.S. legation in Constantinople, several other consular offices appeared across the empire, in Cairo and in Persia over the ensuing decades. But ill-prepared and underpaid Foreign Service officers expressed growing discontent over their inability to protect expanding U.S. interests across the world. As a consequence, the department implemented more professional training and compensation, as well as a more systematic organizational structure. It created a division of Near Eastern affairs in 1909, though the area for which the branch had responsibility remained quite large. According to historian Phillip Baram, it handled U.S. concerns in "the Ottoman, Russian, German and Austro-Hungarian empires, as well as Italy, Greece, the Balkans, Abyssinia, Persia, Egypt, and the Mediterranean colonies of Britain and France." Subsequent reorganizations over the next thirty-five years ultimately resulted by 1944 in the creation of an office of Near Eastern and African affairs broken into three divisions: Near Eastern affairs, Middle Eastern affairs, and African affairs. Near Eastern affairs dealt with Turkey, Iraq, Palestine, Transjordan, Syria, Lebanon, Egypt, Saudi Arabia, and the rest of the Arabian Peninsula plus Greece. Middle Eastern affairs handled Afghanistan, Burma, Ceylon, India, and Iran. And as the United

States became more deeply involved in World War II, it relied on Britain's Middle East Supply Center in Cairo to get men and material into North Africa, southern Europe, the Arabian Peninsula, and the rest of what previously had been known as the Near East. Thus, "Near East" and "Middle East" became essentially interchangeable terms in emerging specialist and popular imaginings of the region.[8]

Though the first State Department reorganization had taken place a few years earlier, it was really during and immediately after World War I that American "experts" undertook sustained analysis of the area that was becoming known as the Middle East. Questions regarding what to do with the territories of the former Ottoman Empire, the growing need for oil and its likely abundance in the Middle East, and tensions between Jews and Arabs in Palestine drew increasing attention. The problem, however, was that the United States lacked a group of specialists qualified to comment on contemporary affairs in the region. Thus, it was left to the ancient Near East specialists, the missionary hands, the Orientalists, and specialists from other areas to recast themselves as experts in the contemporary Middle East.

Their first opportunity to do so came with the creation of "the Inquiry," a clandestine group of academics, policymakers, and other individuals tasked with postwar planning. The Inquiry emerged out of several different proposals for planning for a postwar peace agreement that circulated within the government in 1917. President Wilson ordered his closest advisor, Colonel Edward House, to assemble experts to begin the planning process in September of that year, and House put his brother-in-law Sydney Mezes in charge. The choice of Mezes, who was a philosopher of religion and had no training in international politics, to lead the group indicated how the entire organization would be handled and made clear the limited supply of real specialists trained to work on international political issues in early twentieth-century America. House presumed Mezes would be able to manage the academic, departmental structure the Inquiry would assume because he had been a dean and president of the University of Texas. The other key administrative figure was Walter Lippmann, whom Wilson himself identified to be the secretary to run the day-to-day operations of the organization. The Inquiry pulled individuals from various academic institutions, particularly elite northeastern universities, as well as other research-oriented organizations such as the Carnegie Institution. It also relied heavily on various professional academic associations like the American Economic Association and the National Board for Historical Services, an affiliate of the American Historical Association created in April 1917 for historians offering their services to the government during the war. The Inquiry was initially housed at the New York Public Library, but eventually moved to the American Geographical Society when it became too large to continue meeting at the library.[9]

The Inquiry's staff was divided between various geographical and topical assignments, one of which was Western Asia. Though the numbers changed from time to time, there were roughly ten paid employees working on the area from the Mediterranean to Tibet and Mongolia. Of these individuals, a generous count suggests that no more than half had any previous exposure to the area they were studying, and most of these scholars worked on ancient, classical, or medieval history. One member of the group specialized in Latin American history, another in Native American anthropology, and a third possessed a general interest in the societal impact of geography. There were, of course, other scholars, such as the historian of colonialism and imperialism George Louis Beer, who were placed in other sections (Africa, in Beer's case) but worked on issues that led them to deal with the Middle East. Finally, there were numerous unpaid research assistants, some of whom were academics, while others came from missionary or ministerial backgrounds. Overall, only a very limited number of individuals who worked for the Inquiry could be classified as experts on contemporary international politics, and no more than a handful of them had dealt with the Middle East in any meaningful manner.[10]

The Inquiry's work thus reflected both the increasing importance of the Middle East in the minds of American policymakers and advisors, and the largely inadequate training those individuals possessed for the task they were undertaking. According to historian Lawrence Gelfand, approximately half of all reports on African, Asian, or Pacific issues focused on the Middle East. But few of these reports contained serious analysis useful in preparations for what would be some of history's most significant peace negotiations. Gelfand notes that "most frequently the sources were encyclopedias, missionary materials, handbooks, foreign trade statistics, and information derived through personal conversations and hearsay," and rarely did the authors of these reports take the time or effort to critique their sources.[11]

Given the background and training of members of the Western Asia group, it is not surprising that they adhered to the dominant narrative through which Americans had imagined the region throughout the nineteenth century. Negative comments about the people, the sociocultural practices, and structures of the region were common. According to one report, "Koords" were "passionate, resentful, revengeful, intriguing, and treacherous. They make good soldiers, but poor leaders. They are avaricious, utterly selfish, shameless beggars, and have a great propensity to steal." Another characterized Turks as "always inconsistent," subject to "inconsistent reasoning," and even implicitly criticized them while appearing to compliment them: "fully 20% of the Turkish boys were so instinctively good that their characters were developing for good at points even where that development had to run counter to national prejudices and tendencies." The title of another report made the point even more bluntly: "The Turkish Government—Analysis of Its Inherent Evils."[12]

The content of the Inquiry's work will be examined further as it is relevant to the topics of later chapters, but here it is important to recognize the overall role the organization played in American imaginings of the Middle East during World War I and shortly thereafter. The Inquiry was the first systematic and broad-based effort by American academics and policymakers to engage seriously with the question of what U.S. interests in the region were and how they might best be pursued. The individuals engaged in that endeavor brought to their efforts a distinctly nineteenth-century outlook characterized by visions of Middle Eastern backwardness and a keen sense of America's sacred and secular mission in the world as a whole, but particularly with respect to the Middle East.

The implementation of the postwar League of Nations mandates in the former Ottoman Empire also brought the Middle East greater attention in the United States in the period following the war. As part of that process, Woodrow Wilson appointed a U.S. delegation headed by Oberlin College president Henry C. King and businessman and philanthropist Charles R. Crane to crisscross the region and assess the problems posed by the dissolution of the Ottoman Empire. The commission's report highlighted many of the political, religious, and social forces and tensions in the region, but the question of what to do about Armenia, where U.S. missionaries had a large presence and witnessed the Turkish massacres of Armenians over the preceding three decades, was of most immediate concern. It generated significant debate over whether or not the United States should assume a new League of Nations mandate for Armenia. The King-Crane Commission also drew greater attention to the intensifying contest between Jews and Arabs in Palestine, a conflict that would ensnare the United States in the region for the remainder of the twentieth century and beyond. King and Crane found that the issue of Palestine could not be separated from the widespread opposition across the region to the possible extension of European colonialism through the implementation of the mandate system. The policy prescriptions of the report were ignored, but its existence demonstrated the need for awareness of Middle Eastern issues and thus signaled the transition to imagining the region through a more contemporary lens.[13]

The rapidly escalating international demand for petroleum was another equally important aspect of the years surrounding World War I, which revealed both the Middle East's increasing prominence in world affairs and the absence in the United States of individuals qualified to comment on such issues. Several oil-dependent technological advances changed the face of warfare on land and sea, as well as in the air. The last years of the war witnessed the transition from trench warfare to mechanized warfare, as horse-drawn artilleries slowly gave way to the tank and the use of trucks to transport troops and supplies. On the seas, the construction of ever-larger warships and the move from coal to oil transformed naval warfare, increasing ships' speed and range. Oil also proved crucial to diesel-powered German submarines that threatened British naval mastery and ultimately proved critical in drawing the United States into the war. Similarly, the advent of the airplane created the possibility of delivering munitions, troops, and materiel further inland and behind enemy lines. It also extended the horrors of modern warfare from battlefields into civilian population centers. All of these dynamics played out on a much larger scale in World War II, but World War I offered an early preview of what was to come and indicated that modern armies demanded a steady supply of oil.[14]

Just as oil transformed modern militaries, the rapid advance of a petroleum-based consumer culture in the United States and Europe—symbolized by the automobile—contributed to an entirely new level of demand for oil. According to one contemporary estimate, the number of registered automobiles in the United States in 1920 (9.2 million) was more than five times greater than it had been just six years earlier (1.8 million), even though a portion of the U.S. economy had been focused on the war effort. Moreover, if growth continued, more than 12 million cars and trucks would need fuel in 1923, a number that excluded "the enormous number of farm tractors, motor boats, aeroplanes, and gasoline power plants of which there are no official records." The greater demand for oil coincided with a 50 percent price increase from 1918 to 1920. By 1922, higher demand, concerns about a possible shortage, and growing international conflict over petroleum resources led one commentator to try to put the importance of oil into context: "Oil is without doubt one of civilization's most important natural resources. And yet we are just beginning to learn how dependent we are upon it. The wheels of machinery cannot turn, ships cannot move across the seas, our industrial age would come to a complete standstill—without oil." [15]

The new importance of the region led policy-oriented organizations and publications to deal with contemporary Middle Eastern issues on a more regular basis during the interwar period, though coverage reflected the limited supply of specialists qualified to meet the growing demand for knowledge on the topic. The Council on Foreign Relations, for example, was a New York City-based organization that emerged from the remnants of the Inquiry in the early 1920s. Focused on developing and promoting a broader understanding of contemporary international affairs, it ran its first Study Group on the Middle East, titled "Economic and Political Problems in the Near East," in 1927. The organization's journal, *Foreign Affairs*, published some articles on the region in the 1920s but did so much more regularly by the mid- to late 1930s and during World War II. The articles varied widely in topic, ranging from rising Arab nationalism to oil interests to the continuing problems in Palestine, and were largely descriptive rather than prescriptive of specific policies. Nonetheless, they reflected rising interest in the region.

Yet, even as expertise became more secularized and strategic in nature, European specialists—first relied upon during the emergence of ancient Near East studies in the United States—remained prominent, and Orientalist ways of thinking persisted. For example, non-Americans authored approximately half the articles dealing with Middle Eastern issues published in *Foreign Affairs* between 1922, when the journal was founded, and 1945. That fact highlights the absence of qualified experts on contemporary Middle Eastern affairs in the United States. In addition, many of these authors, such as Valentine Chirol, Hamilton A. R. Gibb, David G. Hogarth, and H. St. John B. Philby, were established Orientalists in academia or the media. It was quite common for a specialist on the ancient Near East (Halford Hoskins) to comment on the importance of "The Suez Canal in Time of War," or for one of the world's preeminent scholars of Islam (Gibb) to analyze contemporary movements "Toward Arab Unity." [16]

Edward Mead Earle, a historian of military affairs and diplomacy, recognized this tension between existing sacred, missionary, Orientalist ways of imagining the Middle East and emerging secular interests in contemporary affairs. Born in 1894, by 1920 Earle had earned his bachelor's degree, fought in World War I, earned his doctorate, and become a lecturer in history at Columbia. He traveled widely, particularly in the Middle East, following World War I and drew on those experiences to become one of the first Americans to comment extensively on contemporary Middle Eastern affairs. In 1923, he published *Turkey, the Great Powers, and the Bagdad Railway: A Study in Imperialism*, much of which examined how a supposedly backward and previously stagnant Turkey struggled to come to terms with modern European imperialism, nationalism, and numerous internal obstacles. Yet Earle also began to stake a claim for both increased U.S. involvement in the region and for a new group of specialists to manage those interests. Earle remarked at the outset, "American religious interests in the Holy Land, American educational interests in Anatolia and Syria, and American humanitarian interests in Armenia, are now supplemented by substantial economic interests in the natural resources of Asia Minor." These expanding U.S. interests led Earle to urge his fellow Americans "to take stock of this Near Eastern situation" because economic connections necessarily had political implications. "The enormous expansion of American commercial and financial interests" in the Middle East, Earle argued, brought "the United States face to face with new, difficult, and complicated international problems" that required careful analysis and "statesmanship."[17]

Earle's interest in U.S. involvement in the contemporary Middle East led him in 1929 to issue a more explicit challenge to the missionary and Orientalist framework for imagining the region, though he did not reject altogether the sacred and secular American project there. Recalling a century of involvement, Earle acknowledged what he found to be very real contributions and struggles of U.S. missionaries in the Middle East. Earle believed the missionaries brought much good to the region, as "throughout the Near East by 1890 were to be found the American preacher, teacher and physician; the American printing press, disseminating the Bible in every important native tongue, and the American dollar, busily engaged in erecting buildings in which to house these diversified institutions." Similarly, missionaries displayed great "heroism" in their efforts to assist the victims of anti-Armenian violence in the late nineteenth and early twentieth centuries. At the same time, however, Earle thought these accomplishments had come at a cost for Americans and their understanding of the Middle East. "If American opinion has been uninformed, misinformed and prejudiced," Earle suggested, "the missionaries are largely to blame. Interpreting history in terms of the advance of Christianity, they have given an inadequate, distorted, and occasionally grotesque picture of Moslems and Islam. While consciously preaching good-will, they sometimes have unconsciously sowed the seeds of misunderstanding." Earle was especially critical of missionary reporting of the conditions in the Ottoman Empire: "Because the missionary left many of the characters and many of the facts out of his picture, the American people received an incomplete impression of who were sinners and who were sinned against." Earle presented himself much as Mahan had, as a new kind of specialist able to offer more detached economic and political analysis of the Middle East, though he did not discount the need for a revised missionary narrative. Instead, he contended, "the missionary must find a new approach not only to his constituents in the Near East but also to his friends and his supporters at home." Doing so would mean "much to the cause of good-will and peace," particularly, Earle implied, if that narrative were supplemented with new, more contemporary expertise.[18]

Between 1900 and 1940, and particularly from the end of World War I to the beginning of World War II, policymakers, journalists, and academics came to recognize some of the limitations entailed in imagining the Middle East through the late nineteenth-century lens provided by missionaries, travel writers, and academic ancient Near East specialists. To be sure, the older sacred and secular narrative of the United States and its missionaries—religious, business, and political—redeeming a debased Middle East remained powerful, but the older narrative was now supplemented by new layers of authority, expertise, and knowledge filtered through the lens of contemporary politics.

The World War II Watershed

In World War I, the Middle East had been important largely because the Ottoman Empire sided with Germany and because the region served as a gateway to European empires farther to the east. By World War II, however, the exploitation of regional oil resources, the increasing mechanization of warfare, the more global nature of the war itself, and the potential consequences of an Axis victory gave greater importance to the Middle East. While the limited supply of specialists to meet the growing demand for knowledge on the contemporary Middle East became evident in the 1920s and 1930s, World War II demonstrated both the intellectual and personnel constraints of existing expertise. In addition to service in the Middle East itself, there were a number of organizations and committees at home—the OSS and the various wartime and postwar planning committees, for example—that needed staffing with knowledgeable individuals. The demand for Americans possessing knowledge about the Middle East had increased dramatically. The war therefore served as an opportunity both for older Orientalist hands who sought to market themselves as authorities on the region and for those with a more contemporary focus hoping to train themselves or others in modern Middle East affairs.

The heirs of the old missionary and philanthropic hands were quick to respond to the growing demand for regional expertise by offering their contacts, experience, and knowledge for government use as World War II began. The professional lives of three individuals—Harold Hoskins, William Eddy, and John Badeau—exemplify the career paths of those whose claim to expertise rested on their long connections to the region, and whose wartime work gave them a level of influence that lasted well into the postwar period. Harold Hoskins was born in Beirut in 1895, grew up as part of the American missionary community there, became fluent in Arabic, and developed extensive ties throughout the region at an early age. He joined the Marines shortly after graduating from Princeton, survived a German gas attack during World War I, and eventually became an officer. After the war, he entered private industry and became an executive for a textile company. When World War II began, Hoskins reenlisted in the military and put his language skills and various Middle Eastern connections to use by serving as an economic advisor, roving liaison, and intelligence operative in the region. At the same time, he built ties to well-placed government officials, resulting in Undersecretary of State Sumner Welles's recommendation that Hoskins be assigned President Roosevelt's personal Middle East operative. In this capacity, Hoskins met with Saudi Arabian king Ibn Saud in 1943 in an unsuccessful attempt to convince the monarch to meet with Chaim Weizmann about the controversy in Palestine. In the postwar period, Hoskins served as a consultant to the State Department and to private businesses, before assuming the directorship of the State Department's Foreign Service Institute in the 1950s. He remained a respected commentator on Middle Eastern affairs until the late 1950s, when his adherence to the missionary narrative and Orientalist framework finally put him at odds with a newer breed of regional specialists.[19]

William Eddy shared a very similar background with his cousin Harold Hoskins and was ultimately an even more influential U.S. informant on Middle Eastern affairs. Eddy was born in Sidon, Lebanon, to missionary parents and, like Hoskins, joined the Marines and lived through a German gas attack during World War I. Eddy, however, chose academia over the business world between the wars, becoming chair of the English department of the American University in Cairo and then president of Hobart College in New York State. Eddy also rejoined the Marines during World War II, though in the intelligence field as an OSS officer in North Africa, and remained closely tied to the government thereafter. He served as the first U.S. minister in Saudi Arabia from 1944 to 1946 and in that context as the translator for President Roosevelt, who, while returning to the United States from Yalta in 1945, met with King Ibn Saud. Eddy departed Saudi Arabia in 1946 to succeed Harvard historian William Langer as head of the State Department's branch for research and intelligence, a key intelligence post between the end of the war and the creation of the CIA in 1947. In what initially seemed a bold display of dissent, Eddy resigned from government service in 1947 to protest President Truman's decision to support the partition of Palestine. In actuality, however, Eddy continued to consult with the CIA under the cover of working for ARAMCO in Saudi Arabia. He commented frequently on policy document drafts and maintained extensive correspondences with a variety of individuals regarding Middle Eastern affairs until his death in 1962.[20]

John Badeau also moved into government service from a missionary and philanthropic career in the Middle East, though he had more formal academic training than did either Harold Hoskins or William Eddy. Badeau was born in Pittsburgh in 1903 and earned a Bachelor's Degree in engineering at Union College, a divinity degree from Rutgers, and a master's degree from Union Theological Seminary, where he also studied Arabic and Muslim philosophy. Between his educational endeavors, Badeau spent seven years as a missionary in Iraq. He returned to the region in 1936 to teach at the American University in Cairo. Like both Eddy and Hoskins, Badeau worked for the government during World War II, in his case as a specialist in the Office of War Information. He returned to the American University in Cairo after the war to assume its presidency. In 1953, Badeau resigned his post to become president of the Near East Foundation, a philanthropic organization based in New York City that provided funding for schools, health care, and small-scale local development projects. Badeau remained in that position until 1961, when President Kennedy appointed him U.S. ambassador to Egypt. The Johnson administration tried to convince Badeau to remain in Cairo, largely because of his excellent rapport with Egyptian leader Gamal 'Abd al-Nasser, but he was ready to return to private life and resigned in 1964. Badeau also published frequently on Middle Eastern affairs, especially regarding Egypt, in the 1950s and 1960s.[21]

Though none of these three specialists had specific training in the contemporary Middle East or as political analysts before the war, others acknowledged each of them as experts in some form based simply on their knowledge of Arabic, their experience in the region, and the contacts they had developed. Their wartime endeavors gave them enhanced credibility as observers of regional affairs in the postwar period. Each of them, and others like them, then capitalized on that authority to achieve even greater recognition as noted Middle East experts in the early postwar decades.

World War II also brought greater attention to academic specialists trained in ancient Near Eastern studies. Committed to the war effort and cognizant of the increased demand for any form of expertise on the region, archaeologists, philologists, and religious studies scholars brought their language and research skills to the various intelligence arms of the government. Like Badeau, Eddy, and Harold Hoskins, they had no formal training in the contemporary Middle East, but others recognized them as experts because of their experience in the region, their language skills, and general knowledge of a place that for most Americans was terra incognita.

E. A. Speiser, with whom we began this chapter, was this type of World War II–era expert, though Halford L. Hoskins, a Middle East specialist at the Fletcher School for Law and Diplomacy and the Library of Congress, was more influential over the long term. Apparently unrelated to Harold Hoskins, Halford Hoskins had been trained by and worked for the Library of Congress as a specialist in the ancient Near East but noticed the growing demand for expertise and began focusing on contemporary Middle Eastern affairs during the 1930s—particularly economic and political issues involving oil and the Suez Canal. He served in the State Department's Division of Special Research for postwar planning during the war and then worked occasionally as a consultant for the State Department following the war. His most enduring contribution to the postwar study of the Middle East was his assumption of the directorship of the School of Advanced International Studies and its subsidiary, the Middle East Institute (created in 1946), both of which were affiliated with the Johns Hopkins University. In addition to continuing as the director of the Middle East Institute after the two organizations split in 1948, Hoskins published a number of monographs and contributed frequently to *Annals of the American Academy*, *Current History*, and the *Middle East Journal* (the organ of the Middle East Institute). Hoskins's most important and influential work in terms of laying out a particular interpretation of the Middle East was his 1954 monograph, *The Middle East: Problem Area in World Politics*. There

Hoskins reviewed a number of regional issues, such as the importance of oil, Arab nationalism, and the conflict over Palestine, and tried to explain the U.S. interest in each of them. He became one of Senator Lyndon Johnson's advisors on Middle Eastern affairs in 1959 and continued to write and comment on Middle Eastern affairs until his death in the late 1960s.[22]

While the limited supply of experts on the contemporary Middle East during World War II offered the opportunity for the heirs of the missionaries and philanthropists to return to prominence and created the need for specialists on the ancient Near East or early Islam to shift their focus to contemporary problems, it also presented a set of circumstances in which a new kind of Middle East specialist emerged. This new Middle East specialist was one who focused solely on contemporary international political issues and concerns. Moreover, the war also allowed for the implementation of at least rudimentary new programs in which the training of these new specialists might occur. The various intelligence, planning, and language-training institutions of the government, particularly those based inside the United States, served as some of the first organized programs within which one could learn about the modern Middle East. The OSS, the State Department, and the War Department, as well as other sections of the government, each possessed its own research or intelligence arm. Most of these groups functioned much like graduate seminars, with wide-ranging discussion of research papers and presentations. World War II therefore accelerated the transition to a generally more professional, secular, and scholarly type of political expertise that had first begun with Alfred Thayer Mahan at the start of the century and continued with Edward Mead Earle in the 1920s.

Though it happened more by accident than design, Jacob Coleman "J. C." Hurewitz capitalized on these new training opportunities to become quite possibly the first U.S. scholar trained as a specialist in the contemporary Middle East. Hurewitz was born in Connecticut to an ordained rabbi of Russian and Polish origins and a Lithuanian mother, and enrolled at Columbia University as a Ph.D. candidate in history in 1936. He was determined to research and write a dissertation on "Americans in Ottoman Palestine," and chose the modern Middle East as his focus even though there was no such formal program of study at Columbia or anywhere else in the country. He won a grant to support a three-year tour of Palestine without having completed Columbia's course requirements and without approval from an advisor or the department for his planned dissertation topic. Hurewitz's time in the Middle East was cut short by the eruption of World War II, and he returned to New York City in 1940 to resume his coursework at Columbia. Drafted into the army, Hurewitz ended up in Washington, D.C., as the Palestine specialist in the research and analysis branch of the oss, where he worked under the guidance of E. A. Speiser. Hurewitz later characterized his time in the oss and the State Department's postwar Office of Intelligence Research as a continuation of his graduate education, which he returned to Columbia to pursue in 1946. He defended a revised dissertation on "The Road to Partition" in 1949 and published it in 1950 as *The Struggle for Palestine*. He went on to enjoy a distinguished career in modern Middle Eastern studies and remained a critical player in what was by this point an emerging loose and informal transnational network of modern Middle East specialists, particularly as a mentor for a new generation of scholars who began to move beyond the missionary and Orientalist model that had played such an influential role in shaping how Americans imagined the Middle East since the nineteenth century.[23]

Just as Hurewitz and the intelligence community established a precedent for training a new kind of Middle East specialist in the United States during World War II, Princeton University's role in the Army Specialized Training Program set an example for close cooperation between academia and the government. Yale University had first taught Arabic in 1841, but few other schools had followed its lead. According to one assessment, Harvard was the second school to offer Arabic language training, beginning in 1880, and by 1939 there were only ten universities in the United States that offered training in Middle Eastern languages: Yale, Harvard, Michigan, Columbia, Chicago, Pennsylvania, UCLA, Catholic University, Johns Hopkins, and Princeton. Princeton had offered a course on ancient Oriental literature for some years, though it did not begin offering language classes until it hired Lebanese-born Philip Hitti as assistant professor of Semitic languages and literature in 1926. Hitti slowly expanded course offerings over several years, and in 1933 Princeton created a committee on Near Eastern studies that occasionally offered seminars on more contemporary issues. When the United States became heavily involved on the North African and Asian fronts in 1943 and the army required a targeted language program, Hitti stepped forward. According to Hitti, the military sent him one hundred fifty soldiers who were to achieve basic competency in Arabic, Turkish, or Persian within six months. Hitti designed most of the lessons himself and contracted students of Middle Eastern descent studying at schools primarily in the northeast who were unable to return home during the war to serve as teachers. The program was a success inasmuch as it trained soldiers to carry on basic conversations, though the first group of graduates had little opportunity to display their skills, because the army deployed them to India instead of the Middle East.[24]

Nonetheless, several individuals who went on to become recognized specialists on the Middle East came through Hitti's program either as teachers or students. Instructor Farhat Ziadeh became one of the preeminent instructors of Arabic in the United States and editor of the Arabic desk at the Voice of America. Student Morroe Berger became one of the most respected sociologists working on Middle Eastern issues and a professor at Princeton. Student Roger Davies served on the Arabic desk at the Voice of America before becoming deputy secretary of state for Near Eastern and South Asian affairs, and ultimately U.S. ambassador to Cyprus. More importantly, the wartime program established the precedent for close cooperation between academics—particularly those at Princeton—and the government when it came to studying the Middle East and training people to work there. That relationship would be expanded dramatically in the decades following World War II.

From the early twentieth century through 1945, expanding U.S. interests and involvement around the world led an increasingly professional and secular group of specialists in the government, academia, the media, and the business world to pay increasing attention to the contemporary Middle East. New conceptions of U.S. interests and power, the rising international oil industry, and two world wars made Americans more aware of the region than ever before. In the process, specialists added new layers of knowledge and expertise on top of the sacred and secular missionary, Orientalist framework that had conditioned American imaginings of the region for nearly a century. Increasing professionalization meant that recognized expertise and authority on the Middle East no longer rested solely in the hands of missionaries, tourists, and travel writers as it had at the end of the nineteenth century. The cooperation between individuals from different groups—academia, the business world, government, and the heirs of the old missionary community—also served to plant the seeds and spread the roots of the emerging loose and informal transnational network. Yet, while a more professional and transnational network of observers and commentators did emerge to imagine and interpret the Middle East for U.S. audiences in the first few decades of the twentieth century, it and the expertise of the individuals who populated it had limits. World War II revealed that the growing demand for knowledge on the contemporary Middle East outran the supply of qualified specialists and the knowledge they could provide.

The Cold War and the Institutionalization of Middle East Expertise

It was against this backdrop that E. A. Speiser called in 1947 for the creation of a new class of specialists to produce policy-oriented knowledge on the contemporary Middle East. His was one of several efforts to draw attention and resources to this undertaking. There were ten universities teaching Middle Eastern languages in 1939, and by 1947 only three—Columbia, Michigan, and Princeton—offered broader coursework on the contemporary Middle East. The American Council of Learned Societies argued in 1949 that circumstances were even worse, claiming that no U.S. university could count an expert in the contemporary Middle East among its regular faculty. To remedy the situation, Speiser and others drew on their commitment to studying the emerging Cold War and the opportunity it provided for acquiring resources to create an increasingly institutionalized form of Middle East expertise. In the process, they strengthened the informal transnational network of Middle East experts and added another layer of knowledge about the region, its international role, and its importance to U.S. global power.[25]

Those academics, business-persons, government officials, journalists, and other groups and individuals who supported the postwar expansion of expertise on the contemporary Middle East relied heavily on the developing Cold War and U.S. national security concerns in the region to justify their cause. Just as William Eddy, Halford Hoskins, and E. A. Speiser had served their country during World War II, they returned to service during the Cold War. They and the individuals who succeeded them as Middle East experts were Cold Warriors who believed producing knowledge for government use was both necessary and honorable. They were products of their time and subject to the widespread anticommunist discourse that dominated U.S. politics from the late 1940s through the early 1960s. In that regard they were no different than experts involved in the broader expansion of area studies in universities and other professions after the war.[26]

We must also acknowledge, however, that these specialists not only capitalized on but depended on the opportunities the Cold War presented for raising funds for studying the contemporary Middle East and for expanding the influence of the new specialists that undertaking created. In the United States, the study of the modern Middle East lagged well behind that of other areas such as Asia and the Soviet Union, so contributing to the Cold War cause became almost a necessity for those who wished to expand Middle Eastern studies in the postwar period. Philip Hitti, who ran the Army Specialized Training Program during the war and chaired Princeton University's Department of Oriental Languages and Literatures after the war, clearly saw the benefits his university could reap when he offered its services to Assistant Secretary of State for Near Eastern, South Asian, and African Affairs George C. McGhee in December 1950. Hitti began a letter to McGhee by pledging his department's willingness to stand "ready in this national emergency to cooperate to the utmost limits of its resources with any agencies in Washington, civilian and military, in providing basic training in the languages and areas of the Arab Moslem world." The training that Princeton could provide might serve as a "kind of foundation on which" skills such as "cryptography, interpretation, censorship, intelligence and the like could be based." Hitti begged McGhee "to bear the service we can render in mind as you discuss problems relating to the Near East with any government agencies concerned." Harvard University utilized similar logic when it started its own Center for Middle Eastern Studies in the early 1950s: "Our international commitment to counter the Soviet threat in the Middle East, the fundamental importance of Middle-eastern oil to our economy, and the continuing crisis in the area make it imperative that American universities turn their attention to this vitally important but hitherto relatively neglected region." The goal was to create a program "designed both to train selected men for service in private industry and in government and at the same time to encourage scholarly basic research on the modern Middle East in the fields of economics, political science, anthropology, history, and social relations, including social psychology."[27]

Such was the power of Cold War thinking in the United States that framing these new intellectual endeavors in this way was sure to work. Responding to Hitti, McGhee felt "confident" the "splendid offer to assist in the national emergency will be received enthusiastically by those who are now thinking and planning for future programs." Harvard's nascent center also found success as it drew resources from wealthy organizations, most notably the Ford and Rockefeller foundations, which were willing to fund social science research that would contribute to the Cold War cause. The oil companies jumped in as well, further demonstrating the significance of oil as a fundamental national security interest. ARAMCO funded the academic study of the Middle East, and even created an in-house intelligence branch that had close ties to the CIA. Overall, this influx of funds led to the creation of new centers for Middle Eastern studies that brought together scholars from multiple disciplines—economics, sociology, history, and political science, to name a few—that collectively sought to produce policy-relevant knowledge and experts willing to work closely with the government.[28]

The emergence of the Cold War made finding money to expand contemporary Middle Eastern studies relatively easy, but it offered little help in addressing the equally important problem of identifying people to carry out that agenda. There were few people in the United States trained as specialists in the modern Middle East. Thus, as it had during the war, the task of training a new class of contemporary Middle East specialists fell to scholars of different areas, eras, or specialties. Institutions engaged in this process also relied on the precedent, first established during the late nineteenth century with the creation of the field of ancient Near Eastern studies, of drawing on established European scholars to lend credibility and authority to such efforts. Reviewing the case of Harvard University's Center for Middle Eastern Studies demonstrates this process and reveals much about the evolving nature of academic expertise on the Middle East in the United States.

Harvard's Center for Middle Eastern Studies took shape in the early 1950s under the guidance of several highly influential and internationally inclined academics. Among these were noted historian of imperialism and international politics, former head of the State Department's research and intelligence branch, and future president of the American Historical Association, William Langer; economist, head of Harvard's School of Public Administration and president of the American Economic Association, Edward Mason; and dean of the Faculty of Arts and Sciences and future national security advisor McGeorge Bundy. That the center began operating in 1954 under Langer's direction further indicated the limits of expertise on the Middle East in the United States, as he was also the director of Harvard's Russian Research Center and chair of the University's Committee on Regional Studies. Initially, Langer was one of just four scholars involved with the center, which lacked instructors for more than a fifth of the classes it proposed to offer at its inception. Richard N. Frye, a young professor of Semitic languages and history who focused on Turkey and Iran, worked closely with Langer to run the center. The other two specialists were Charles Ferguson, who brought to Harvard his experience running the State Department's postwar Arabic language training program in Beirut, and anthropologist Derwood Lockhard, who had been a government intelligence specialist.[29]

Harvard and other universities establishing similar centers in the 1950s and 1960s overcame this shortage of available specialists by recruiting internationally, drawing in established scholars from Europe, Canada, and even the Middle East itself. Harvard recruited Oxford professor, and England's most respected scholar of Islam, Sir Hamilton A. R. Gibb and his former student, the Canadian scholar of Islam Wilfred Cantwell Smith. Gibb, trained as an Orientalist, had already begun during World War II to question that intellectual and educational framework, and thus welcomed the opportunity to play a critical role in redefining the nature of expertise on the Middle East. Harvard was not unique in bringing foreign experts to the United States, as UCLA recruited Gustave von Grunebaum from Europe and other universities looked abroad. Universities also hired academics from the Middle East who had been educated either outside the region, most often in Britain, or at institutions such as the American University in Beirut. Columbia, Johns Hopkins, and Princeton, among others, filled out their Middle East offerings by hiring talented scholars from the region itself. And while the focus here has been on academia, one must recognize that a U.S. government increasingly concerned with regional expertise followed similar practices, employing individuals from the region who had been educated in Europe or the United States — generally in fields connected to agricultural production, economics, or resource management — who then brought their particular technical expertise to bear on U.S.–Middle East relations.[30]

Returning to Harvard, one of the first scholars to train within its emerging center was William R. Polk. Polk grew up in a prestigious family and included among his ancestors President James K. Polk and numerous influential businessmen and military leaders. His brother, journalist George Polk, was killed in Greece in 1948 as one of the Cold War's first casualties. William possessed a voracious appetite for education and earned two undergraduate and two graduate degrees, one of each from Harvard (B.A. and Ph.D.) and Oxford (B.A. and M.A.). He joined the Harvard faculty as an assistant professor of Semitic languages and history and as a member of the nascent Middle Eastern Studies Center. In 1952, just one year removed from earning his first undergraduate degree, Polk published an influential pamphlet titled, "What the Arabs Think," an essay that both reflected some traditional Orientalist views of the Middle East while beginning to move beyond them. Polk also edited and contributed to "Perspective of the Arab World," a 1956 supplement to the *Atlantic Monthly* in which some of the most respected Western scholars of the Middle East and authors from the region itself conveyed their sense of what the region was like at midcentury.[31]

Polk became one of the most influential Middle East specialists in the

United States in the 1960s. He served on the State Department's policy planning staff from 1961 to 1965. In 1965, Harvard published the first of several editions of his *The United States and the Arab World* for the American Foreign Policy Library. Former under secretary of state Sumner Welles and Harvard history professor Donald Mckay founded the series in 1945 to publish literature to guide the public and policymakers as they confronted a new postwar international political environment. One of the organization's first publications had been E. A. Speiser's *The United States and the Near East*, which Polk's work was intended to update. Polk's book became required reading for Americans interested in U.S.–Middle East relations in the postwar period, and thus remains one of the best pieces for "conventional wisdom" about the Middle East at the time. Also in 1965, Polk resigned from government service to help establish the University of Chicago's Center for Middle Eastern Studies. He further helped institutionalize Middle Eastern studies nationally by serving as a founding director of the Middle East Studies Association in 1967. He remained an active scholar and public commentator on current affairs forty years later, publishing two works on the U.S. war in Iraq.[32]

Academics were not the only members of the informal network who developed their own version of contemporary or modern Middle Eastern studies, as the Foreign Service Institute implemented a program of Arabic language and Middle East studies in 1946. The impetus for creating and building the program came, just as it did for academic centers, out of concerns that the State Department lacked people with skills and expertise commensurate with America's expanding postwar role in the region. Teresa Thomas has demonstrated how the program evolved over time so that successful completion required two years of intensive study, much of it at a training center in Beirut, that emphasized the development of a professional, multidisciplinary approach, as well as linguistic skills. Over the three decades of the program's existence (1946–75), dozens of graduates formed a close-knit group of career-minded Middle East experts. As a group, according to Thomas, most of the graduates of the program considered themselves "regionalists," as opposed to "globalists," which meant that while they were committed Cold Warriors they believed the United States had to deal with the Middle East and its issues in their own right, rather than read them through a global Cold War lens. In general, graduates also adhered to what Thomas refers to as "the Beirut Axioms." These axioms suggested that the Arab-Israeli-Palestinian conflict presented a real danger to U.S. interests in the region — Israel, oil access, military bases, trade — and that the defense of those interests required both the resolution of the conflict and that the United States not be tied too closely to either side in the conflict. While their position on Israel would lead some graduates of the program into conflict with high-level policymakers and some other members of the network, their assessments of other issues discussed in the pages that follow were more commonly held across the network.[33]

As more individuals from a variety of intellectual, personal, and professional backgrounds claimed expertise on the contemporary Middle East in the postwar period, they communicated with each other and functioned in ways that institutionalized the field and helped further the emergence of an informal transnational network of individuals and organizations concerned with analyzing the region as it fit within the international political perspective of the United States. How they did so comes into focus only by looking at the growth of specific nodes of that informal network, the places where its participants—academics, businesspersons, journalists, government officials, and others—came together to share ideas. A number of publications provided additional means of communication between the different constituencies. Examining these nodes reveals how this informal network functioned and how sacred and secular knowledge about the Middle East and the U.S. role there circulated.

Gatherings organized by the Council on Foreign Relations offer one set of examples of network nodes. In many ways, the Council on Foreign Relations was itself a network of well-placed and well-connected government officials, academics, journalists, and private businessmen interested in U.S. foreign relations. Gaining membership to this elite group, particularly from the end of World War II through the 1980s, was almost a necessary rite of passage for any would-be high-level policymaker. The council generally promoted an activist and internationalist U.S. foreign policy and helped solidify the bipartisan Cold War consensus that dominated U.S. political discourse from the late 1940s through the mid-1960s. The council was also deeply involved in the intellectual development of U.S. foreign relations, with material generated within the walls of Pratt House, where the Council was based after 1945, frequently providing the foundation of evolving policies.[34]

The Middle East factored into the council's discussions and publications before World War II—the first relevant study group was held in 1927—but it was identified as an area of special concern only in 1940. That year William Westermann released his conclusions from a study of the impact of nationalism on world affairs. Westermann was a Columbia University historian who had been trained as a specialist in the ancient Near East, served for a time on the Inquiry, and ultimately served as the head of the Middle East section of President Wilson's committee of inquiry for the Versailles negotiations. In 1940, he worked for a State Department planning committee. Westermann found the Middle East to be the region of the world most susceptible to the "disruptive force" of nationalism. In a series of War and Peace Studies from 1942 to 1945, the council again pinpointed the Middle East as an area ripe for problems and called for an expanded postwar U.S. presence there.[35]

The council used those assessments as starting points for its postwar analysis of the Middle East and from the late 1940s through the late 1960s organized ten "Study Groups" on the region. Typically, each study group had fifteen to twenty participants, a chairperson, a rapporteur whose task was to take and write up minutes of each meeting, a research secretary, and a different discussion leader for each of the monthly meetings, which occurred over a period of roughly six months. In most cases, the discussion leader for a given meeting submitted in advance a paper summarizing the issues for consideration. That responsibility might also fall to the research secretary who, along with the chairperson, generally wrote up the group's findings into an article or book manuscript once all meetings were concluded. The council then published the material in Foreign Affairs or as a separate monograph. Titles and topics of postwar Middle East study groups included "The Defense of the Middle East," "Islam and the Modern World," Arab nationalist foreign policy, and the Arab-Israeli-Palestinian conflict, among others. Frequent attendees included: Halford Hoskins, Harold Hoskins, William Eddy, Philip Hitti, John Badeau, J. C. Hurewitz, William Polk, Hamilton A. R. Gibb, journalist Hal Lehrman, Middle East specialists from the State Department, CIA Middle East specialists Charles Cremeans and Kermit Roosevelt, and ARAMCO executive James Terry Duce. Of these individuals, Badeau, Cremeans, Hurewitz, and Polk also published works under the auspices of the Council on Foreign Relations.[36]

The Middle East Institute was a second node of the informal transnational network of specialists. George Camp Keiser, an architect who spent time in the Middle East before World War II, founded the Institute in 1946 with the belief that Americans needed to know much more about the region than they did at the conclusion of the war. The organization was based in Washington, D.C., and was a subsidiary of the Johns Hopkins School of Advanced International Studies, established two years earlier. Ancient Near East specialist Halford Hoskins served as director for both institutions. Along with Keiser and Hoskins, other founding members included Massachusetts congressman and future secretary of state Christian Herter and a young Middle East specialist named Harvey Hall. The Middle East Institute became an independent organization in 1948. Over time, members of the Institute included John Badeau; State Department officials George McGhee, Parker Hart, and Raymond Hare; ARAMCO executive James Terry Duce; academics J. C. Hurewitz and William Polk; and CIA agent Kermit Roosevelt.[37]

The institute facilitated communication among specialists by sponsoring annual conferences that provided a forum for investigating timely issues and by publishing articles in its house periodical, the *Middle East Journal*. Conferences addressed topics such as "Islam in the Modern World" (1951), "Nationalism in the Middle East" (1952), "Evolution in the Middle East" (1953), "Tensions in the Near East" (1956), and "The Arab Nation" (1960). They were usually held over a weekend every spring when the institute brought in a number of distinguished academics and government officials, as well as people from the region itself. Conference participants over the years included Philip Hitti (1951), Wilfred Cantwell Smith (1951), J. C. Hurewitz (1952), James Terry Duce (1953), William Polk (1960), and John Badeau (1953 and 1960). The *Middle East Journal* first appeared under the editorship of Harvey Hall in 1947 and published articles addressing both contemporary and historical issues regarding the region itself and topics in U.S.–Middle East relations. Academics, businesspersons, journalists, and active or retired government officials published in the journal or served on its editorial board. The journal also included book reviews that were either authored by or were about works by many of the most influential experts of the time.[38]

The creation of the academic field of Middle East studies, the expansion of U.S. government interest in the region, and the emergence of organizations like the Council on Foreign Relations and the Middle East Institute as sites for communication between the new specialists effected the institutionalization of knowledge and expertise on the Middle East. The individuals and organizations discussed above, along with others, came to constitute an informal transnational network of specialists on the modern Middle East. Drawn from the United States, Western Europe, and even from the Middle East itself, these experts self-identified as professionals paid to imagine the region as it fit into the international orientation of the United States. Their task was to render comprehensible for both policymakers and wider America some of the animating forces in the region and critical issues in U.S.–Middle East relations. Many of these specialists moved between academia or the business world and government, and consulted with each other through meetings at places like the Council on Foreign Relations and the Middle East Institute.

Before examining the different lenses through which members of this informal network viewed the Middle East, it is important to note that the network's commentary in the late 1940s and early 1950s began with the same axiomatic assertions about the region's critical strategic significance during the Cold War that had been used to justify the expansion of Middle East studies. As the academic, wartime OSS officer, and later renowned CIA operative Kermit Roosevelt noted in 1949, the Middle East sat at the junction of Africa, Asia, and Europe. Deploying language not unlike that Alfred Thayer Mahan utilized half a century earlier, Roosevelt referred to the Middle East as "the hub of three continents." The young Middle East specialist William Polk added that the Middle East had "long been the pot of gold at the end of the foreign policy rainbows for the Western powers and for Russia. Circumstances have combined to make it a rich prize on the world market."[39]

For these new experts imagining the Middle East, the Suez Canal, running between the Mediterranean Sea and the Red Sea, constituted a very significant nugget in that pot of gold. The canal facilitated French access to colonial holdings in Asia, and the British labeled it their "lifeline to empire," especially to the "crown jewel" of India. The postwar decline of colonialism did not decrease the importance of the Suez Canal and other regional waterways such as the Persian Gulf. In fact, the opposite may have been the case. As the European grip on African, Asian, and Middle Eastern lands weakened, and as Cold War tensions with the Soviet Union heightened, it became all the more important to control the shipping routes through which resources, trade, and military equipment moved. Participation in a reformed, rebuilt, and revitalized postwar, international mass-consumer economy based on expanding worldwide trade demanded it. Failure to control the Suez Canal therefore would mean greater transport expenses for oil and other resources, which would have to be shipped around Africa, and would make it much more difficult to defend U.S. interests not only in the Middle East, but also in Asia.[40]

But it was access to and control over oil that was most important, as most commentators emphasized its critical role for maintaining both a strong military and a strong mass-consumer economy. Halford Hoskins, the former ancient Near East specialist at the Library of Congress, noted in 1950 that oil was "essential to the economic well-being of any modern state." As the fuel for all forms of modern transportation, Hoskins argued, "oil is power. It is power in time of peace to develop and maintain great industrial development, power in time of war to expand industry and to energize a nation in combat." The Middle East held the largest portion of the world's known reserves at the end of World War II, so it assumed immense international significance. All of these factors became more important and obvious in troubled postwar times, especially as U.S. oil reserves declined and the United States came closer to becoming a net importer of oil.[41]

Oil was also the crucial concern for intelligence analysts at the CIA who sought to quantify the importance of the Middle East to the U.S. and European economies. A 1951 national intelligence estimate on the importance of Iranian and Middle Eastern oil for Western Europe estimated that if access to all Middle Eastern oil supplies were lost, "a cutback of about 10 percent in the total oil consumption of the non-Soviet world would have to be imposed, even after a maximum practicable increase in production from other sources." Further highlighting the importance of the Middle East's primary resource, the report continued: "No way can be foreseen at present by which a satisfactory adjustment, over a longer period of time, could be made to the total loss of Middle East oil, unless new reserves are proved elsewhere, or new sources of energy developed. Western Europe therefore would not be able to compensate for the loss of Middle East oil save by profound changes in its currently planned economic structure." The loss of Middle Eastern oil, especially from Iran, would prove particularly acute for Britain, which controlled all petroleum development in Iran and, according to the CIA, received 70 percent of its oil from the Middle East.[42]

Post–World War II members of the informal network of specialists generally agreed with policymakers that oil and the Cold War conflict with the Soviet Union justified U.S. interest and involvement in the Middle East and demanded the production of more knowledge about the region. As E. A. Speiser had acknowledged in his 1947 call for more specialists, however, the producers and analyzers of information might not always recognize or agree with the policies that emerge at the other end of the line. In fact, later chapters will demonstrate that as the intellectual project to produce expertise on the Middle East proceeded, some of its participants came to see part of their mission as critiquing and working to redirect policies that they believed were wrongheaded. Yet from the vantage point of the late 1940s or early 1950s, such disputes were well off in the distance.

THROUGH THE MID-NINETEENTH century, U.S. knowledge about the Middle East had been based on adventurer, captivity, missionary, and tourist narratives that generally presented the region as a backward place in need of both sacred and secular redemption by the United States. The emergence in the latter half of that century of the academic discipline of ancient Near East studies only further emphasized that way of imagining the Middle East by focusing attention on a period deep in the past. That form of sacred knowledge and expertise faced growing challenges in the early twentieth century as expanding U.S. global interests, World War I, and the rise of the international oil industry began drawing the attention of strategists, journalists, and government officials to the contemporary Middle East. The demand for information about the modern Middle East was met initially by the old missionary hands and ancient Near East specialists, who parlayed their knowledge of the Middle East in the past into acknowledged authority on the present. They thus were able to extend the influence of an enduring Orientalist framework for imagining the region. World War II demonstrated the inherent weaknesses in that system of knowledge production and consumption, and in combination with the emerging Cold War led to calls for a new system for training specialists in and producing secular knowledge about the contemporary Middle East. As a consequence, there emerged between the end of World War I and the mid-1950s an informal and at times transnational network of increasingly professional individuals who shared a common interest in the contemporary Middle East, were paid to interpret the region for American audiences, and promoted the increasing institutionalization of the production of both sacred and secular knowledge about the region.

At least three separate evaluations of this new system for producing and consuming knowledge about the Middle East and its place in the international orientation of the United States appeared in the early 1960s. Fittingly, each assessment approached the topic from a different angle. The first, by Princeton social scientist and former State Department intelligence analyst Manfred Halpern, reviewed five recent publications and offered a scholarly inventory of the new academic field of Middle Eastern studies. There was, to be sure, a significant difference from the late 1940s, when so few scholars focused on the region. According to Halpern, who drew from a survey conducted by J. C. Hurewitz, across America over 400 academics taught courses dealing with the Middle East in some form by 1962. Nonetheless, significant gaps in knowledge remained and tensions within the field endured. Halpern pointed out that the Orientalist focus on texts and an unchanging Islam had been badly misplaced, but the newer emphasis on purely contemporary issues had missed the critical process of transformation. Moreover, while it was important to describe contemporary conditions, those descriptions needed to be read through a "more systematic framework of analysis." To do that, Halpern offered many suggestions, including investigating the relationship between forces internal and external to the region, comparative analyses that might either confirm or disprove a prevailing perception of Middle Eastern exceptionalism, an increased focus on the transformation of Islam over time, and the examination of aspects of Middle Eastern cultures, economies, politics, and societies that might be completely unrelated to religion.[43]

The second much briefer and breezier assessment appeared in the July/August 1965 issue of *Saudi Aramco World*, the in-house publication of the prominent oil company. Its author, journalist John Starkey, was more celebratory than Halpern. Starkey noted that Americans as a whole were much less confused about the Middle East than they had been in 1939, when a Baltimore businessman asked a visiting academic "can three hundred million Muslims really live in a *desert*?" Starkey commended "the efforts of American journalism, which has begun to take a sharper look at all of the formerly 'exotic' regions of the world," but credited most of the improvement in knowledge of the region to educators. The growth of Middle East studies had been all to the good, as it "contributed to a new understanding of the Middle East— of its history, its religion, its people, its hopes, aspirations and problems." Thus, according to Starkey, a Baltimore businessman of the mid 1960s would recognize that the prevailing image of the Middle East of a quarter century earlier "was not only false but dangerous."[44]

William R. Polk authored the third review. He was ideally positioned to survey the scene in fall 1965, having spent the previous decade working in academia or government, and at that moment freshly off to the University of Chicago to establish a new center for Middle East studies. He framed the issues more broadly than did Halpern or Starkey, and confronted head-on many of the problems presented by government use of scholarly expertise in support of policy. Polk acknowledged, for example, that government funding played a large role in determining research and teaching agendas in the university, and that the abstract knowledge produced by academics could at times appear far removed from the practical concerns of policymakers. He also recognized that U.S. policy in a variety of places, including the Middle East, had been highly problematic over the previous several years and accepted the fact that it was the scholar's obligation to point out such shortcomings. Yet there was one fundamental point that Polk acknowledged but never challenged. He never questioned the notion that despite all the tensions between academia and the government, the relationship needed to remain intact. Rather, he argued those tensions were critical to the success of the relationship. Polk noted, "Because Americans are now acutely aware of our newly assumed world-wide responsibilities and are dissatisfied with existing answers to dangerous international problems, it is in the area of foreign affairs where the academic community and the government attract and repel one another with the most vigor." As we will see later, the next generation of professional Middle East experts, particularly those within academia, would be much less comfortable with that premise.[45]

CHAPTER TWO

THE ALL-PERVADING INFLUENCE
OF THE MUSLIM FAITH

The Perils and Promise of Political Islam

In December 1948, Walter Livingston "Livy" Wright Jr. appeared as the discussion leader at a meeting of a Council on Foreign Relations "Study Group on the Moslem World." Wright came to the meeting from the academic and philanthropic circles of Near East specialists, having been president of Robert College in Turkey, a consultant to the Library of Congress, and chief historian of the War Department. By 1948 he had joined Princeton University's growing stable of scholars working on contemporary Middle Eastern affairs as a specialist on Turkey. Wright's purpose at the meeting was to present a broad overview of the state of Islam in the early postwar years. At the meeting, Wright noted that Islam "tells its followers what to believe, how to think, what to do. It is a complete way of life, a complete culture. Islam . . . is a seven day a week religion." He returned to the idea later in his remarks, stating, "Islamic culture is a seamless fabric—it covers the whole of the Moslem world."[1]

Wright was not alone, as other specialists also commented freely on Islam's allegedly homogenizing characteristics. Rom Landau, an expert on Morocco, offered a representative statement: "Whatever the racial and national differences between them, the Moslems form a more united religious body than do the followers of any other great religion." The 1952 intelligence report "Problems and Attitudes in the Arab World" elaborated on Landau's point. Despite the tremendous diversity of the Middle East, Islam still offered the single greatest unifying factor in the region. It provided "the vast majority of Arabs with common religious, political, social, legal, and economic symbols strong enough to enlist the loyalty of the majority of peasants, nomads, and artisans and to demand at least the outward obeisance of all politicians and many bureaucrats, traders, professional men, and students." A 1953 report from the Psychological Strategy Board, a Truman-era committee designed to coordinate the implementation of U.S. foreign policy, was more blunt: "No consideration of the traditional Arab mind is possible without taking into consideration the all pervading influence of the Muslim faith on Arab thinking."[2]

Given that members of the informal network of Middle East specialists and others believed that Islam determined the day-to-day behavior of its adherents, it should not surprise us that they worked to arrive at an operational understanding of the religion. To that end, the Department of the Army circulated a paper in 1955 justifying the study of religion—and Islam in particular—through the National Security Council. The paper noted that in recent years analysts had "studiously explored" the "politics, geopolitics, sociology, ethnology and to some extent the history and cultures of the peoples" in "various parts of the contemporary world." It asserted, however, "that the most important subject of all, namely, the religious situation as it bears upon all these other factors, has been curiously ignored." Such "neglect" seemed "all the more extraordinary when it is remembered that the religious beliefs and usages of any given people afford the surest key to their psychology, culture and historical conduct." The authors further emphasized the point, contending, "that the conduct of men, especially in moments of crisis, is very largely determined by what they believe. . . . If we can discover what men really believe, and how firmly they believe it, their behavior under given circumstances will become in some degree predictable."[3]

While the paper called for an investigation of the role of religions such as Islam in international affairs, it also recognized that doing so was not a simple task. Just defining "religion" presented a major obstacle. The paper put forth a broad definition: "any complex of beliefs concerning the nature of transcendent reality shared by any considerable number of human beings in any age or in any part of the world." Religion defined in this manner went well beyond institutionalized forms to include any number of ideologies or philosophies, perhaps even communism. The fact that "in nearly all parts of the contemporary world conflicting factors of religion . . . are at work, and frequently within the mind and imagination of the individual person" further complicated the study of religion. It therefore would be virtually impossible to distill different religious influences from one another, or religious influences from other philosophical or ethical influences. And if common perceptions of Islam's impact on its adherents were any indication, making such distinctions would be particularly difficult when studying that specific religion.[4]

Added to the conceptual obstacle that defining religion presented was the no less important logistical problem of finding people qualified to study non-Western religions like Islam. Even with the emergence in the 1940s and 1950s of centers to study the Middle East, few people in the United States could participate in such efforts. To deal with this shortage of specialists, the paper's authors did not intend to call on the Orientalists, which would have been the likely course of action just a decade earlier. Rather, they suggested that a group of army chaplains trained in comparative religion and "accustomed to working in close and intimate association without concern for denominational differences" would be best suited for the job. Yet another earlier (1954) report outlining a similar project for studying Islam showed why such an approach might prove unsuccessful. That report correctly pointed out that studying world religions and their impact on international affairs required substantial abilities, including an understanding of international politics, specific area expertise, and language skills that were well beyond the reach of the average army chaplain. The first step of any concerted effort to understand Islam and its international political implications would therefore be to train more people to help with the work. The 1954 paper called for the creation of training bases at established academic centers for Middle Eastern studies, such as the Johns Hopkins University School of Advanced International Studies, or at think tanks like the Middle East Institute with connections to both academia and the government. More detailed investigations would be possible only after this basic training infrastructure had been constructed.[5]

It is not surprising that the authors of these two papers believed it was essential to develop an operational understanding of Islam and its role in international affairs. Indeed, though the papers stated the point most explicitly, individuals imagining the Middle East had worked from that assumption for decades. The papers placed in bold relief the intellectual and logistical challenges that such an endeavor entailed and thus suggest the types of questions to be asked today about how specialists imagined Islam and its political implications at that time. What qualifications did they bring to their efforts to define Islam and its basic features? How did people understand the "modern trends in Islam," as one scholar titled a series of lectures he gave in 1945, and their potential impact on regional politics? More importantly for those interested in U.S. relations with the region, how did they comprehend the relationship between Islam and other significant international ideological and political forces such as communism, nationalism, and secular modernity?

This chapter addresses how the informal transnational network of academics, businesspersons, government officials, and journalists envisioned the Middle East through the sacred lens of Islam. It examines their efforts to produce knowledge about the religion that would help them develop an operational understanding of its role in regional and international affairs. We begin with a brief look at the years after World War I, when many observers and commentators believed religion was a clear source of tension in the Middle East and viewed Islam—the dominant religion in the region—as being at the center of those tensions. The emergence of Turkey as the secular successor to the Ottoman Empire in the mid-1920s served as a focal point for the expression of those concerns. Our attention then shifts to the 1940s and early 1950s, when specialists also developed parallel and sometimes competing interpretations of Islam that emphasized both traditional and modernizing forces in the region and portrayed a religion in crisis. Some observers worried that certain religious leaders might capitalize on this instability and use traditional aspects of what they argued was a "totalitarian" Islam to rally the Muslim masses to a violent anti-Western pan-Islamic movement. Coming on the heels of World War II and the emergence of the Cold War, such characterizations once again revealed the enduring belief that Islam itself was a source of conflict. By the mid-1950s, Cold War concerns led analysts to undertake more sustained studies of the relationships among Islam, communism, and nationalism in the Middle East. Initially focused on whether Islam provided an opening or a barrier to communism in the area, network participants eventually shifted their emphasis away from communism and the Cold War as they came to believe Islam warranted attention in its own right. By the mid- to late 1950s, however, a new force appeared on the horizon, a modern and potentially uncontrollable secular nationalism that specialists believed challenged Islam's position as the dominant political force in the region. In this new environment, some specialists and policymakers hoped the traditional religious movements they had previously feared might serve as a counterweight to the new forces animating the region.

Islam, Religious Conflict, and the Fall of the Caliphate

Even before World War I had ended, observers and analysts viewed the Middle East through the lens of religion. Americans had long conceived of the region as the "Holy Land," and religious tensions played a central role in late nineteenth-century Western European understandings of the "Eastern Question" or the "Sick Man of Europe." Such concerns were only heightened by the deaths of hundreds of thousands in intermittent bouts of horrible violence between Armenian Christians and Ottoman Muslims from the 1890s through the end of the war, and by the emerging concerns about interactions between Muslims and the increasing Jewish population in Palestine. Thus, by the time World War I came to a close, the emerging group of policy-oriented observers of the Middle East generally believed religion, and Islam in particular, played a crucial role in the region's political conflicts.

Concerns about religious conflict in the Middle East were evident in U.S. efforts at postwar planning. William Westermann, the lead Middle East specialist on the Inquiry and in the U.S. delegation to the Paris Peace Conference, brought these issues to the fore in his "Report on Just and Practical Boundaries for the Turkish Empire." There he contended that ethnic and linguistic differences were generally so blurred as to be ineffective for determining boundaries in the post-Ottoman Middle East. Instead, populations had divided along religious lines, and "determination" based on that criterion should therefore take precedence, supported by other factors such as economic, strategic, ethnic, and linguistic interests. In some cases, such as Syria's, those other factors should be used to overcome religious diversity and to promote national unity. Westermann suggested that boundaries in Palestine should "satisfy the aspirations for a national state" for Jews, but he also argued for international control of the area until negotiators could work out a peaceful resolution of competing ethnic and religious claims to the land.[6]

Nowhere were early post–World War I concerns about Islam more evident than in discussions of the emergence of a successor state to the Ottoman Empire in Turkey under the leadership of Mustafa Kemal. Kemal had commanded Ottoman forces at Gallipoli, and successfully led rebel Turkish forces in a two-year effort to regain control of parts of Anatolia from the occupying Greek, Italian, and French militaries. He built upon that success to begin taking control of the new Turkish state. He began in 1922 by implementing a new constitution that relieved the caliph of all temporal powers and limited the institution to the spiritual realm, declared Islam the official state religion, and allowed for at least a modicum of political openness through the election of a national assembly every four years, though Turkey effectively became a one-party state. Then, in mid-October 1923, he cajoled a provisional assembly to declare Ankara as the capital of an independent political entity, which would be announced before the end of the month as the new Republic of Turkey. Choosing to house the government in Ankara, home to a relatively homogenous Turkish population and the site of Turkish military headquarters during the war with Greece in 1921 and 1922, represented an important break with the Ottoman past when the seat of empire had been the much more diverse Constantinople. He abolished the caliphate altogether in 1924, and the provision regarding Islam was stricken from the constitution in 1928. Kemal implemented a new legal system based on German commercial laws, Italian penal laws, and Swiss civil laws, as well as more specific sociocultural regulations, in 1926. Traditional attire (such as the fez) was outlawed altogether or strongly discouraged (as was the veil), while polygamy was prohibited, and marriage and divorce became civil institutions and practices. Equally significant was his announcement in August 1928 that a new script based on the Latin alphabet would replace the classical Ottoman script based on Arabic letters and that Arabic could no longer be used in education or in public more broadly, including during the Muslim call to prayer. The policy not only attacked basic Muslim religious practices, but also had the effect of creating a clean break with the Ottoman past by making existing Arabic or Ottoman Turkish speakers essentially illiterate and creating a new generation of individuals beholden to the new Turkish state for their sense of national identity. By 1934, women had gained the right to vote and could serve in the assembly.[7]

Two articles by Sir Valentine Chirol, an influential British journalist who had been writing about the Middle East since Alfred Thayer Mahan coined the term for the region in 1902, and who represents the transnational nature of the emerging informal network of specialists, clearly reveal the dominant sentiments regarding Islam at this moment in time. Writing in *Foreign Affairs* in 1923 as Kemal was just beginning his efforts to transform Turkey, and when Kemal's path was not necessarily clear to outside observers, Chirol expressed concerns about a powerful Muslim regime in Turkey that were not even thinly veiled. He explained, "The resurgence of Turkey has focused attention on the Mohammedan world," and explored the impact such an event might have on British colonial possessions in India, home to a substantial Muslim population. He began his essay "Islam and Britain" by noting, "Islam alone of all the great religions of the human race was borne sword in hand. Islam has always relied on the sword." In the hands of Turks, who had "destroyed but never built," Islam "became a formidable danger to Western civilization" until the failed siege of Vienna in 1683. Ottoman decline from that point forward was the result of Turkish misrule, which generated resistance across the empire, while Islam itself retained a powerful hold over its adherents. As European powers become increasingly involved in Asia, they faced greater resistance from "the rigid orthodoxy of monotheistic Islam based upon the finality of the Koranic revelation down to the last vowel-point of the text revealed by Allah to Mohammed" than they did from any other source. Turkish resurgence in an age of European colonialism, newly formed nationalism, and Asian anticolonialism would only compound an "irreconcilable Mohammedan aversion to the West." Events in Turkey, India, Egypt, and elsewhere in the preceding years had "shown how easy it is to work up a Mohammedan populace into savage outbreaks against Europeans." Indeed, according to Chirol, a shared identity would "unite" all Muslims "for common and effective action against the West, when the renewal of Islamic militancy derives whatever vitality it really possesses from so many mutually conflicting forces and finds its chief expression in the sudden resuscitation of the Turk, who, even if he should agree to a superficial modus vivendi with the West, can no more than the leopard ever change his spots." Chirol was not alone in using such tones to describe Islam and Muslims in the early 1920s. In *Turkey, the Great Powers, and the Bagdad Railway: A Study in Imperialism*, Columbia University historian Edward Mead Earle wrote of "Moslem fanatics" seeking inspiration and tangible support for pan-Islamism from Germany during the decade before World War I. He implicitly connected America's enemy from the war with a force he clearly hoped would be overcome by the secular regime taking shape in Turkey at the time of his writing.[8]

Chirol revisited events in Turkey just one year later in another article in *Foreign Affairs* and assumed a distinctly different tone as he celebrated Kemal's pursuit of a secular Turkish nationalist agenda. He began "The Downfall of the Khalifate" by recalling the previous year's essay, where he "pointed to the grave portent that millions of Mohammedans, including Indian Mohammedans, were acclaiming [Turkey] as the invincible sword of the Faith, whilst other millions of Asiatics who are not Mohammedan were hailing her as the champion and spearhead of an Asian revolt against the West." From there, Chirol became much more upbeat, proclaiming, "An amazing thing has happened since then. Turkey of her own free will—for one must assume that the action of her present rulers is the expression of her will—has cast away the sword with which she had rallied the enemies of Western civilization to her support; she has abolished the Khalifate upon which she based her claim to the leadership of Islam; . . . She has proclaimed herself a Republic of a type at least nominally advanced and democratic." Chirol noted that "it was on national rather than on religious lines that [Kemal] appealed to Turkish patriotism" during the war with Greece. Chirol praised Kemal's early accomplishments, claiming, "Only an exceptionally capable and energetic administrator could have reorganized the Turkish army . . . after the Great War or could have galvanized into fresh life the exhausted forces of national resistance." Similarly, Kemal's conduct of the war against Greece "showed him to be a master of strategy."[9]

The war with Greece was significant for Turkey, but according to Chirol it was truly momentous for the rest of the Middle East and the broader Muslim world, as it was not clear where the world's Muslims would look for leadership. He was cautiously optimistic about the future, though his general opposition to the idea of a strong Muslim state shone through. Chirol warned, "Though Mustapha Kemal has abolished the Turkish Khalifate he cannot touch the Khalifate as an Islamic institution, which if disowned in Turkey must continue to subsist elsewhere." His best guess was "that Islam for a time will be split up, as it has been before, and even more than it has been recently, into a number of separate Khalifates." While Chirol was not sure where the caliphate might end up, his discussion of the possible replacements focused on the heads of emerging states—the king of Egypt, the king of Afghanistan, and the soon-to-be king of Saudi Arabia—and their potential conflicts with other states or Muslims in the Middle East. Thus, while the possibility of a renewed caliphate was worrying, for the time being it was "a prospect which need not disturb any European nation with large Mohammedan connections in its overseas dependencies." Moreover, in Chirol's estimation Islam could never be as dangerous as it was when unified under Turkish leadership, and implicit in his argument was the point that Europeans and Americans should be pleased to see Islam weakened and disunited.[10]

Chirol was upbeat about the prospects for Turkey, but there remained a hint of ambivalence in his assessment of Kemal that would characterize most specialists' analysis of powerful secular leaders in the region for decades: "Is the revolution which he has carried through the work of an enlightened social reformer, convinced that the regeneration of his country can only be consummated by freeing its people from the trammels of a narrow creed which blocks the way against all modern progress? Or has the intoxicating love of power turned his head and prompted him to destroy the Khalifate as the only danger that might threaten the dictatorship which he has built for himself on the ruins of the Sultanate?" To answer that question, Chirol responded, "Those who prefer to place the best construction on the Turkish dictator's policy contend that it really reflects a great psychological change in the mentality of a large majority of the Turkish people, who have been driven by the terrible ordeal through which Turkey has passed during the last twelve years and more to subordinate religious sentiment and interests to the more vital exigencies of national salvation." Thus, although Mustafa Kemal had not attained by the mid-1920s the status in the eyes of those interpreting the Middle East for U.S. audiences that he would by the 1940s and 1950s for his policies in Turkey, it is clear that experts found his authoritarian, secular national agenda appealing, and they began to consider him a model that they hoped the rest of the Middle East would follow.[11]

Islam, Tradition, and Modernity

While many specialists in the 1940s and 1950s believed Islam determined the personal behavior of all Muslims, another strain of thought stressed growing fissures within this supposedly monolithic, global Muslim community. To many observers, Muslims appeared to be caught in an identity crisis between tradition and modernity. The emergence of groups such as the Muslim Brotherhood—allegedly backward looking and devoted to traditional cultural, political, religious, and social practices—appeared to represent one vision for the Middle East. The more secular, modern, and increasingly Western-oriented Turkey seemed to exemplify a second, fundamentally different vision for the region. How analysts believed the United States should deal with the region was thus in part dependent on an assessment of which group or model they believed was ascendant at any given moment in time.

Specialists from a wide array of professional backgrounds thought the Middle East and the world of Islam were caught between tradition and modernity, but none articulated it more clearly and with greater intellectual rigor than Hamilton A. R. Gibb, the renowned British scholar of early Islam who shifted his focus after World War II to the modern Middle East and eventually became the director of Harvard University's Center for Middle Eastern Studies in the late 1950s. In 1945 Gibb delivered the prestigious Haskell Lectures in Comparative Religion at the University of Chicago, later published in monograph form as *Modern Trends in Islam*. The lectures took place early in

Gibb's transition to studying the modern period, and he had only just begun to think through how to move beyond traditional Orientalist scholarship. The lectures therefore still reflect the dominant Orientalist interpretation of a Muslim Middle East that had long been stagnant. Overall, Gibb argued the defining feature of Islam in the mid-twentieth century was a growing division between modernists and traditionalists. According to Gibb, the split first emerged at the end of the nineteenth century and had widened considerably, especially since World War I, after which the modern Western world had introduced massive and rapid technological, political, economic, and intellectual changes to a still medieval Middle East. Gibb believed Muslims were responding to such changes either by embracing modern secular nationalism or by turning toward "a violent assertion of the supremacy of the sacred law . . . the kernel of revolutionary Mahdism."[12]

Gibb's thesis that Muslims struggled to relate to a changing world drew on traditional Orientalist themes and gained wide adherence among those observers who identified Islam as the primary barrier to the acceptance of modernity in the Middle East. The young Harvard Middle East specialist William Polk relied heavily on Gibb's analysis and the idea of a long-stagnant Muslim world in his influential 1952 essay "What the Arabs Think." Polk claimed that because Islam was "at once a religion, a state, and a way of life," it was "difficult to make a convenient separation between secular and religious affairs." Moreover, Islam "had nothing comparable with the Protestant Reformation" and therefore remained "impervious to the secular ideas which have come into the modern Arab world." Government intelligence officers expressed similar views in the 1952 report "Problems and Attitudes in the Arab World." The people of the Middle East, the report claimed, responded to modernity within "a religiously-inspired way of life which, born in a static, pre-scientific, pre-national era, lack[ed] the institutions and perhaps the philosophical premises through which to revitalize its traditions." Robert Montagne, a French specialist on North Africa, made the point quite bluntly in a 1952 article in Foreign Affairs. "Islamic society," he stated, "clings too closely to mediaeval forms of thought and religion to be able to resume its forward journey." Between the late 1940s and the mid-1950s, conventional wisdom among academic, government, and media commentators suggested that Muslims were ill-equipped to deal with the changes they faced and thus were caught between tradition and modernity.[13]

The respected religious studies scholar Wilfred Cantwell Smith combined the different strains of this interpretation in his careful examination of Islam in the postwar Middle East. The Canadian Smith had been a graduate student at Cambridge University in the late 1930s and early 1940s working on a dissertation on Islam in twentieth-century India under the direction of Gibb, who was then at Oxford. It is clear that Smith, like J. C. Hurewitz, who was working on contemporary Palestine at the same time, was skeptical of the traditional Orientalist reliance on the founding texts and doctrines of early Islam to explain circumstances in the Middle East of the mid-twentieth century. Cambridge rejected Smith's thesis on Islam in contemporary India, thereby leading him to resume his graduate studies at Princeton after World War II. Smith moved between various Canadian universities and Harvard University for the remainder of his career. He contributed his own widely read book-length study of Islam in the modern world in 1957, but in October 1951 he published a short essay in *Foreign Policy Bulletin*, titled "The Muslims and the West." There, Smith emphasized the alleged total integration of cultural, political, and social life in the Islamic world and, as Gibb had, found Muslims struggling to reconcile modernist and traditionalist impulses. He also contended that the military defeat in the 1948 war with Israel, as well as widespread postwar economic problems, contributed to the cultural and political dislocation of Middle Eastern Muslims. In combination, Smith believed all of these factors had created a "spiritual crisis" throughout the Islamic Middle East.[11]

In asserting the existence of a spiritual crisis in Islam, Gibb, Polk, Smith, and others identified what they saw as two diametrically opposed groups vying for political and religious control in the Middle East. On one side were peasants, religious leaders, the urban poor, and segments of the rising middle and intellectual classes who had been educated within Middle Eastern educational systems. Members of these social groups were thought to be suspicious of Western influences and saw limited opportunities for advancement within the existing sociopolitical and economic structures. Moreover, the moral dislocation Muslims allegedly experienced living in a rapidly changing world suggested that religious principles must be reapplied in their strictest forms. According to one report from the Psychological Strategy Board, an organization created to develop, coordinate, and oversee U.S. foreign policy under President Truman, this group was "increasingly radical and revolutionary-minded in its thinking" and produced the leadership "of both the most extreme nationalist parties and of communist groups."[15]

The Society of the Muslim Brothers exemplified the discontented faction in the minds of many Middle East specialists in the 1940s and early 1950s.

The brotherhood formed in Egypt under the leadership of Hasan al-Banna, who at a young age developed a powerful critique of both secularization and foreign domination. He worked as a teacher in a state-sponsored school in the Suez Canal Zone town of Ismailia and formed the society in March 1928 when six laborers in the British camp sought his guidance to help restore Arab and Muslim dignity in the shadow of foreign domination. The society spread by collecting funds for constructing mosques and schools and for providing educational and social welfare services. It entered Cairo in 1932 and combined with other religious societies, some of which were controlled by Hasan's brother 'Abd al-Rahman al-Banna, while also connecting with reform-minded politicians, military officers, and civilian officials. The group opposed King Faruq and the Wafd, the country's leading political party, for forming a government that served British interests during World War II. The brotherhood thus emerged from the war as one of Egypt's most powerful political forces.[16]

Several circumstances led the society to even greater prominence after the war. Various political parties, a number of paramilitary groups, and the palace battled for control of an Egypt mired in economic, political, and social turmoil. The conflict over Palestine and the 1948 war between the Arab states and newly independent Israel only added to the chaos. The brotherhood stockpiled weaponry and trained members to fight against the British in Egypt or Jews in Palestine. After the society was implicated in several bombings and assassination attempts, the government declared it illegal in December 1948, arrested as many as four thousand members in seven months, and probably also organized the killing of Hasan al-Banna in February 1949. Despite these obstacles, the society remained powerful in Egypt in part because the government jailed members together and with other prisoners, allowing members to retain their preexisting relationships while at the same time building new ones. The group reappeared with legal standing after winning a lawsuit challenging the original dissolution decree and immediately resumed agitating for an Egypt free of foreign intervention and for economic, political, and social reforms without secularization. The society supported the Free Officers Movement that deposed King Faruq in 1952, but soon parted ways with the new secular government. Tensions between the brotherhood and the government climaxed in October 1954 when members attempted to assassinate Gamal 'Abd al-Nasser, leader of the ruling military junta. Nasser responded by arresting most of the group's leaders and one thousand members within a month.[17]

For academics, government officials, and journalists in the United States, the brotherhood's popularity and its antiforeign, pro-Islamic message seemed to confirm concerns that Muslims were emotional and violent. Fears that the society's polarizing rhetoric and use of violence would eventually destabilize the entire Middle East spread among observers. One 1947 intelligence report noted that "the post-war development of the Moslem Brotherhood Party, with its emphasis upon Islam and its extreme antipathy to foreign interference in the Arab world," was the greatest immediate threat to stability in Egypt and was also a significant factor in the wider Middle East. The CIA argued in 1949 that the brothers were "fanatically religious, ardently nationalist, violently anti-foreign, and terrorist in their methods." Similarly, Robert Montagne noted in his 1952 article in Foreign Affairs on "Modern Nations and Islam" that "the popular religious and anti-foreign movement . . . had under its control more than a million Egyptians." Moreover, the brotherhood's reliance on the "ignorant and emotional masses" suggested "terrorism has taken the place of political activity; and assassination has become a method of government, so much so that in three years a dozen statesmen of the older generation have paid with their lives for their courage and independent spirit."[18]

Few observers actually understood the larger ideology that motivated the brotherhood. Instead, most observers reflexively believed the group's desire to remain faithful to Islam automatically constituted an antimodern agenda. In actuality, the society maintained that modernization and reform could occur within an Islamic framework and did not require secularization. Indeed, the brotherhood's emphasis on religiously based modernization played a crucial role in the movement's rapid growth. It held great appeal for an emerging middle class of professionals, students, artisans, and merchants who accepted a modern lifestyle but remained faithful Muslims, as well as for urban laborers and rural peasants. Yet some commentators echoed earlier interpretations of an unchanging Islam, as Christina Phelps Harris, a scholar writing for the Hoover Institution, suggested as late as 1964 that "in spite of being a politico-religious movement born in the twentieth century, the Muslim Brotherhood in its motivation and religious objectives was an ideological throwback to the eighteenth and nineteenth centuries." The society, according to Harris, also faced a critical dilemma: it used megaphones, printing technology, and other modern tools to spread its ideology and gain converts, thereby undermining its supposedly antimodernist objectives. In this way such assessments of the Muslim Brotherhood fit nicely into and helped to sustain ways of imagining Islam and the Middle East that highlighted the tension between modernity and tradition that many participants in the informal transnational network of specialists saw as a central feature of the region.[19]

Like the larger discourse of which it was a part, the specialists' emphasis on the Muslim Brothers was in many ways misplaced and lacked nuance. To be sure, some brothers resorted to violence regularly enough to legitimize questions about whether such tactics were an explicit policy of the organization as a whole. But other groups in Egypt used similar tactics to pursue a variety of objectives. The primary difference between the society and those groups was the level of popular appeal; few organizations in the Middle East could reach as many people as could the brotherhood. Observers also emphasized the Egyptian branch to the exclusion of its sibling organizations in other countries. The society resorted to violence much more frequently in Egypt than it did elsewhere. In Jordan, for example, the society formed in 1945 to specifically address the Palestine situation and worked to achieve its objectives through reform of the established political structures of the state rather than through acts of violence. The brothers gained legal recognition and support from Jordan's king ʿAbdullah, who considered them an ally against communism and in the struggle over Palestine. Likewise, Hussein, ʿAbdullah's grandson and successor to the throne in the early 1950s, allowed the brothers to function in part because they provided social welfare services his own state apparatus could not.[20]

If the Muslim Brotherhood represented the discontented radical aspect of the "spiritual crisis" of Islam, as many specialists believed, a small but still growing group of mostly Western-educated, upper- and middle-class intellectuals who supposedly adhered to more secular principles symbolized what some commentators called the "progressive" side of the conflict. Though members in this group were allegedly still suspicious of foreign intervention, especially given the conflict over Palestine and Israel, they sought to modernize the Middle East by integrating Western technology and political principles into everyday life. Islam was to be utilized only as a guide for personal morality and decision making. Network members hoped this process would play out much as they believed it had in Turkey, which served as their preferred model—imperfect though it was—to achieve their sacred and secular vision for a new, modernized Middle East.[21]

Analysts in the 1940s were enamored of the reforms Kemal had instituted in Turkey, which two scholars characterized as engaged in its own "Operation Bootstraps" as it looked toward Europe, increasing westernization, and modernity. Reforms that extended beyond the political arena into the social and cultural realms and that were specifically designed to weaken and de-emphasize Islam received particularly high praise. Walter Livingston Wright, the Ottoman and Turkish affairs expert, indicated that reformers believed Islam was "the chief obstacle" to westernization. Kemal overcame that supposed obstacle by implementing the new legal codes in February 1926, which academics Lewis Thomas and Richard Frye contended "discarded the whole apparatus of High Moslem rule."[22]

While most specialists adhered to this fundamentally positive view of an increasingly secular Turkey, a series of papers presented by academics and policymakers at a Harvard conference on "Islam and the West" in July 1955 demonstrated that some observers offered more nuanced—though still quite positive—interpretations of Kemal's reforms and the role of religion in Turkish society. Rather than emphasize the complete break with the past that Kemal seemed to represent on the surface, they placed his rule in a long-term context of Ottoman reforms dating back more than a century. To be sure, Niyazi Berkes (a visiting scholar at McGill University's Institute of Islamic Studies) and Dankwart Rustow (then assistant professor of politics at Princeton) saw Kemal's policies regarding religion and secularization as radical. But for them, such actions were necessary to pull an independent Turkey once and for all out of the supposed long sleep from which the old Ottoman Empire had been struggling to emerge since at least the Tanzimat period of the mid-nineteenth century, if not earlier.[23]

Moreover, when a powerful movement emerged in the late 1940s and early 1950s to restore certain religious practices—voluntary religious education in elementary schools, the use of Arabic for calls to prayer, and the reestablishment of a theological faculty at the University of Ankara, for example—it seemed an appropriate and fundamentally democratic process for working through the role of religion in society. According to Rustow, perhaps eighty to ninety percent of the Turkish population consisted of "Secularists" or "Moderates." The former saw religion as the fundamental cause of Ottoman decline and an obstacle to improved education and westernization; the latter recognized Turkey as a fundamentally Muslim country but also held that Kemal's "reforms were necessary and salutary in their day but should be subject to some revision." One could therefore recognize and make some concessions to the "Clericalists," whom Rustow believed represented the remaining ten to twenty percent of the population and pushed for more far-reaching reforms. And Rustow happily reported that even the Clericalists "prefer to state their case in terms of liberalism and democracy. A free religious establishment, they now insist, is a corollary of secularism itself." In this way, the presence of individuals and groups promoting a greater role for Islam in Turkish society than many specialists might have wished, and the fact that they were dealt with through relatively open political processes, served as a further demonstration of the value of the Turkish model for the rest of the region.[24]

Thus, whether one celebrated the antireligious reforms that Kemal implemented or preferred the processes through which the Turkish people arrived at an acceptable compromise regarding the relationship between religion and the state, the Turkish experiment seemed to present intriguing possibilities for the remainder of the region. According to observers at the time, Turkey offered the best example of how the tension between modernity and tradition might be resolved in the Middle East. It is not a stretch, then, to claim that Lewis Thomas's and Richard Frye's characterizations of Turkey were broadly representative of how specialists in the 1940s and 1950s understood that country. They noted that Turkey was "certainly the most resolute, independent, and stable element and also unquestionably the most democratic and the most western element in a semi-oriental area of widespread political and economic unrest." Turkey's turn toward secular westernization made it "distinctly America's best bet in an important area." According to these efforts to imagine the Middle East, the further a country pulled away from Islam, the less "oriental" it became.[25]

During the first decade after World War II, members of the informal transnational network of Middle East specialists imagined Muslims stood at a crossroads. One route led to a possibly radical Islam that many analysts believed much of the population might find appealing. If the peoples of the region chose this road, however, they would continue to be guided by a mental map that could never lead them to modernity. The Middle East would proceed, as the State Department's Bureau of Intelligence and Research argued, without "a philosophical basis for assimilating Western objectives to its own" and would face innumerable challenges along the way. Furthermore, this path was likely to be most inimical to U.S. interests in the region. Yet, despite what many individuals believed were potentially brighter long-term prospects for U.S. interests, the other road—a secularized model of development along Turkish lines—also presented problems. Effecting the extensive changes necessary for still relatively small secular groups to dominate the

Middle East required time, so even in the best circumstances the supposed spiritual crisis would remain a formidable obstacle for the foreseeable future. In a short August 1951 article titled, "The Moslem World," *Time* offered a telling commentary on the perceived status of the religion in the mid-twentieth century: "Islam is poor, a sad fate for the only great religion founded by a successful businessman. Islam is divided and headless, a painful fate for a religion founded by a first-rate practical politician. Islam is militarily feeble, a disgrace to a religion that so eagerly took up the sword. Islam is intellectually stagnant, an ironic punishment for a religion which was founded upon an idea which for centuries carried the lamp of learning, and then, at the crisis of its history, deliberately turned its back upon reason as the enemy of faith."[26]

Totalitarian Islam

During the course of the remarks that Walter Livingston Wright made at the Council on Foreign Relations meeting with which this chapter opened, he also noted, "Islam is not a religion, as religion is conceived in the West. It is a totalitarian religion." When another member of the study group mentioned that "monolithic" might be "a better and less pejorative" adjective, Wright agreed, but noted that "he had chosen 'totalitarian' as being perhaps less subject to misinterpretation because of its currently wide usage." Wright's comment was not unique for that time period. Indeed, as Hamilton A. R. Gibb commented in *Modern Trends in Islam*, "Islam has often been described as a 'totalitarian' religion." But for Gibb, other religions, including Christianity, shared some totalitarian characteristics. What distinguished Christianity in Gibb's mind, however, was that it "suffer[ed] the assault of two new and deadly enemies: humanism and science," two forces which Gibb believed were only just beginning to impact Islam. Wright's, Gibb's, and others' use of "totalitarian" to describe Islam in the mid- to late 1940s reveals one of the ways Middle East specialists viewed the religion as a potentially threatening political force.[27]

Historian Benjamin Alpers argues that Americans in the 1940s and 1950s understood totalitarianism as one possible outcome of the transition from tradition to modernity, the issue at the very heart of the spiritual crisis that specialists believed engulfed the Middle East at that time. From the 1920s to the 1950s, "totalitarianism" evolved into a term used to characterize a variety of otherwise quite diverse ideologies or political movements in states that appeared to be in the midst of this transition, though it is unclear whether

Americans believed totalitarianism represented the embracing of or resistance to modernity. Alpers never considers that religion itself could be a wellspring of discourses about totalitarianism, nor does he address the Middle East or Islam in any substantive way, but he identifies several other features Americans ascribed to totalitarian regimes that help explain why observers of the Middle East found that word appealing as they imagined the region after World War II. First, he contends most Americans understood totalitarianism to be fundamentally antidemocratic. Second, common perceptions held that totalitarian regimes controlled the basic day-to-day activities of their subjects, left little room for individual choice, and thus subordinated individual desires to those of the state. A third prominent feature of totalitarian regimes that Alpers argues postwar Americans identified was a close relationship between emotional mass politics and a powerful dictator or small leading oligarchy, though it was unclear whether the masses created the dictator or vice versa. Finally, Alpers notes that Americans in the 1940s and 1950s believed totalitarian regimes were at base concerned with conquest, making them inherently confrontational and often violent. Using Alpers as a guide can therefore help us understand how and why analysts like Wright, Gibb, and others found "totalitarianism" such a compelling term in the late 1940s and early 1950s.[28]

Middle East specialists did tend to view Islam as antidemocratic, even though they occasionally acknowledged some potentially prodemocratic features of Islam. As the State Department's Philip Ireland noted at a Middle East Institute conference on Islam in the modern world in March 1951, "Islam has been the most successful of religions in eliminating barriers of race, color, and nationality." But Ireland later claimed that equally if not more powerful antidemocratic tendencies existed within Islam. The most important of these features was the division of the world into the Dar al-Islam (realm or house of Islam) and the Dar al-Harb (realm or house of war) and the adherence to a hierarchy that placed Islam above all other religions. Historically, that hierarchy had been implemented through the dhimmi system, in which members of recognized religious minorities, such as Christians and Jews, could practice their religion and live in relative freedom as long as they paid a separate tax. According to the State Department official, the reliance on Shariʿa law also presented an obstacle that Muslims needed to overcome if democracy was to thrive in the Middle East. Hence, as the earlier discussion of Turkey revealed, early post–World War II Middle East specialists believed that establishing a strong democracy probably required at least the temporary elimination of religious influences in public cultural, political, and social life. Once democratic practices were accepted and respected by the population as a whole, then some of those religious influences could be restored.[29]

Other aspects of how Alpers argues Americans understood totalitarianism in the 1940s and 1950s fit with common characterizations of Islam at that time. The opening to this chapter clearly demonstrates that most Middle East experts believed Islam determined the day-to-day behavior of its adherents. And though there was some disagreement as to whether the emotional or fanatical crowd created the dictator or vice versa, the belief that Islam—like other totalitarian regimes—promoted a particularly potent form of mass politics extended all the way to the top of the foreign policy establishment in the United States in the early postwar years. John Foster Dulles, Republican foreign affairs specialist and later secretary of state under President Eisenhower, on at least two occasions in the late 1940s compared the spread of communism in the twentieth century to the spread of Islam into Europe and North Africa a millennium earlier. Dulles indicated that the emotional appeal of both Islam and communism lay in the belief "that they can offer better terms than any others to the mass of mankind." Later, as U.S. concerns about events in Vietnam escalated in 1954, Eisenhower himself wondered aloud at a National Security Council meeting "whether it was possible to find a good Buddhist leader to whip up some real fervor" like that he believed had driven Muslim and Arab expansion "in the early Middle Ages." Amid widespread laughter, a council member "pointed out to the President that, unhappily, Buddha was a pacifist rather than a fighter." Eisenhower's musing and the response it generated demonstrated the common perception that the emotional Muslim masses supported particular types of leaders and the pursuit of conquests.[30]

Along these same lines, conventional wisdom also held that Muslims were especially susceptible to being controlled by dictators because the emotional masses could be stirred fatalistically to follow a leader that Allah had placed in power. According to early postwar specialists, the individual most likely to play that role was the mufti of Jerusalem, Hajj Amin al-Husseini, whom many early postwar observers believed to be not only the Middle East's most powerful man but also its most popular and dangerous. A colorful character who seemed to many specialists to possess all the requisite characteristics of a "fanatical" leader, the mufti garnered attention more for his dramatic appeal than his actual impact in the region. In fact, the case of the mufti suggests that the dominant discourses and assumptions about the region led specialists to single out a leader who posed little real threat and was actually declining in influence by the early 1950s.

Born Muhammad Amin al-Husseini in 1895 into an influential family that had held the position of mufti of Jerusalem (the city's leading Muslim legal expert on sacred law, although his opinions were nonbinding) for most of the nineteenth century, he studied at a Turkish government school and then at Al-Azhar University in Cairo, where he became interested in political issues and organized opposition to Zionist activities in Palestine. He outmaneuvered other members of the city's elite and convinced the British high commissioner to appoint him mufti in 1921 and later became the permanent president of the Supreme Muslim Council in Jerusalem, with control over the mosques, religious schools, orphanages, Shar'ia courts, and waqf funds in the city. As the most powerful Muslim in Palestine, he was aware of, and perhaps helped increase, tensions that led to a series of deadly confrontations between Jews and Palestinian Muslims in Jerusalem in 1929, and he enhanced his anti-Zionist credentials by joining the Arab Higher Committee during the Arab Revolt of the mid-1930s. Fearing arrest because of his increasing opposition to British policies in Palestine, the mufti fled Jerusalem in 1937 and settled in Iraq from 1939 to 1941, where he supported nationalists fighting British control throughout the Middle East. The mufti went to Iran in 1941 before heading to Rome and Berlin, where he negotiated with Mussolini and Hitler for mutual assistance against their common British enemy. After the war, he avoided arrest as a war criminal by British, American, and Soviet forces by seeking asylum in France, which accepted him but placed him under house arrest. While the British repeatedly urged the French to extradite him, and as underground Jewish groups plotted to kill him, the mufti disguised himself and under an assumed name boarded an American passenger plane for Cairo in 1946. He immediately began agitating against foreign involvement in Middle Eastern and Palestinian affairs. The mufti helped rally Arab forces to fight Israel when it came into existence two years later, only to witness their defeat in the wars of 1948 and 1949. His followers vented their frustration in July 1951 by murdering King 'Abdullah of Jordan, whom they believed had sacrificed Arab and Palestinian objectives for his own by annexing the West Bank with British backing in 1950. Organizing 'Abdullah's killing was the mufti's final substantive act on the Middle East stage.[31]

The mufti exemplified the tendencies that many journalists and other specialists believed characterized Muslims and that Alpers argues Americans thought were primary features of totalitarian states in the 1940s. Commentators labeled the mufti a "scoundrel," "an ambitious would-be dictator," "an extremist," a Nazi war criminal, and a murderer, and they regularly announced his "fanaticism." His escape from France in 1946 inspired a number of stories in American news periodicals, and both Newsweek and Life published feature articles about him after 'Abdullah's assassination in 1951. The Newsweek piece titled, "Behind the Turmoil in the Middle East . . . Stands the Sinister Mufti in Exile," argued, "The very title [the Grand Mufti of Jerusalem] suggested plots in the bazaars, knives clashing in dim mosques, pistols cracking in the hot sunlight. And the extraordinary fact was that the Mufti lived up to the implications of the title as a sort of arch-villain of the troubled Middle East." Continuing to sound more like a film script than a news magazine, the article referred to the mufti as a spider weaving a web of intrigue and murder around the region and suggested that nothing less should be expected of a man who had been a Nazi collaborator during the war. James Bell conducted a rare interview with the mufti and began the Life article by claiming, "The name of Haj Amin el Husseini . . . has been associated with assassination, riot, revolt and wars, both civil and religious, all through the Near and Middle East. As a Moslem leader, his activities have always been shrouded by the miasma of intrigue behind which he prefers to operate." The story linked the mufti with totalitarianism by focusing on how he justified his means—especially the connections with Nazi Germany and his use of mass politics—of pursuing his anti-Zionist ends. Bell concluded by emphasizing what he believed to be the mufti's significant power at a critical time: "What Haj Amin had said was one man's point of view . . . But it was one shared by thousands of important and millions of unimportant people in an extremely sensitive part of the world."[32]

Government and academic evaluations of the mufti were more restrained, though they still conformed to common American perceptions of the relationship between dictators and the emotional or fanatical masses that followed them into totalitarianism. Even the most temperate government assessments charged that the mufti was an "instigator" who "egged on" Muslims to use violence to promote change. The mufti also still appeared in these commentaries to possess a popular appeal across the Middle East that nobody else could match. According to the U.S. consul general in Jerusalem in 1948, "No Arab approaches the Mufti's stature in the eyes of Palestinian Arabs. He is the central figure on the Arab stage, and as in other days, his organization shows itself to be ruthless in the pursuit of its aims." His arrival in a city generated expectations of an "immediate uprising of [the] Arab population" that would likely turn violent. Loy Henderson, director of the State Department's Office of Near Eastern Affairs in September 1947, believed the mufti's presence and willingness to use violence operated as a brake on U.S. policies in favor of the declaration of an Israeli state. "If we press for a Jewish state," Henderson argued to the Secretary of State, "we shall undoubtedly weaken the position of the moderate Arabs . . . and strengthen that of the fanatical extremists. Just last week, for instance, one of the moderate Arab leaders was slain in Palestine by followers of the fanatical Mufti."[33]

Such analyses of the mufti and the wider political environment in the Middle East were only partially correct and generally overstated his influence. To be sure, he had been a crucial figure in prewar Palestine, and he remained the most significant Palestinian leader through the late 1940s, particularly among the refugees created by the 1948 Arab-Israeli war. His appeal beyond that point, however, never reached the levels that outside observers believed it did. His wartime efforts to assist Germany by spreading propaganda and promoting revolt against Britain achieved only minimal success. Moreover, he possessed wide regional popularity only briefly in the postwar period and was quickly surpassed by rising nationalist movements in Egypt and elsewhere. That Middle East specialists focused so intently on the mufti despite his declining influence thus further demonstrates how Wright and others viewed Islam through the lens of "totalitarianism" in the late 1940s and early 1950s.[34]

Finally, it is clear that regional specialists in the 1940s and 1950s understood Muslims as being fundamentally concerned with the spread of their religion and thus with confrontation and conquest. For the State Department's Philip Ireland, the primary goal of an explicitly Islamic state was "the extension of the true religion," while a political democracy pursued the "extension of tolerance." A 1953 Psychological Strategy Board report reached a similar conclusion. Trying to define a "psychological strategy program for the Middle East," board members found that "when Islam dominates it is regarded as the natural order of things; rule and authority exercised by non-Muslims is regarded as unnatural and an indication that Islam is weakening and must gather its forces and counterattack to regain its ordained supremacy."[35]

Using the term "totalitarian" to define the Middle East in the late 1940s therefore served a specific purpose. It drew explicit comparisons to World War II and suggested how to deal with such regimes in the context of the emerging Cold War. Conventional wisdom, solidified by wartime experiences with Germany and Italy, held that appeasing totalitarians would only allow them to grow stronger, and simply delay an inevitable moment of confrontation. In this context, Wright's reference to totalitarian Islam thus implied that Muslims were an aggressive people and the United States must be prepared to confront them.

Responses to Israel's emergence in the late 1940s only contributed to worries that a totalitarian Islam was inherently confrontational. According to some analysts, Israel's presence helped unify not only Palestinians but also many Muslims throughout the Middle East and around the world against U.S. and Western European influence in the region. Writing in the *New York Times Magazine* in 1948, Middle East correspondent Clifton Daniel argued, "The issue of Palestine might help to unite the Moslems against the West as it has served to submerge the feuds of the Arab states." Moreover, unity produced by a common hatred of Israel "obviously" could never be "used for positive action." Rather, it would only result in a "negative reaction — the casting off of ties and associations with the Western powers, rejection of Western ideas and revulsion against Western tutelage." French scholar Robert Montagne echoed Daniel's concerns, arguing in *Foreign Affairs* that the conflict over Palestine stimulated "an irresistible movement toward Islamic solidarity across national frontiers."[36]

The foregoing analysis reveals the problems with and contradictions in the ways members of the post–World War II informal transnational network of specialists interpreted Islam and its role in the international political arena. They drew on an Orientalist framework that emphasized an unchanging and monolithic Islam while also emphasizing the dramatic impact of externally driven change. Viewing Islam through the competing binary lenses of tradition and modernity in this way permitted experts to avoid coming to terms with many of the complexities that characterized Muslims and their world. Instead, specialists relied on the much more familiar discourse of totalitarianism, a discourse that carried with it implicit assumptions about the need to remain vigilant against the supposedly emotional and violent Muslim masses.

Islam and Communism

While many participants in the informal transnational network of specialists viewed Islam as a challenging political force in the Middle East, they were much less consistent in their assessments of its relationship to other significant global political forces. Would Islam serve as a bulwark against communism in the region, or would it facilitate Soviet advances? And how would Islam interact with or react to growing nationalist forces across the region? If, for example, Islam was incompatible with communism but was very compatible with nationalism, then it would be more important for the United States to address nationalist concerns than to worry about outright communist infiltration of the Middle East. These were critical questions to which academics, journalists, policymakers and others regularly turned their attention in the 1950s. Their efforts to understand the relationship between Islam and communism led to surprisingly new ways of imagining the roles that both forces might play in the world.

Though the Cold War began as a battle over the future of Europe, the Middle East factored into the conflict from the outset. Tensions surrounding the delayed withdrawal of Soviet troops in Iran in early 1946, Soviet pressure on Turkey for greater access to the Dardanelles later that year, and more general U.S. concerns about access to regional oil resources put the Middle East at the center of the contest almost immediately. Given that Middle East specialists and others focused so heavily on Islam when they imagined the region, it is no surprise that they began contemplating the relationship between religion and communism. No less a figure than the noted Soviet specialist and father of containment George Kennan weighed in on the topic. In March 1947, little more than two weeks after President Truman announced a substantial aid program for Greece and Turkey and issued an ideological declaration of Cold War against the Soviets, Kennan gave a talk at the National War College. Much of the speech was devoted to arguing why the Middle East was a national security interest and thus why the United States must do everything in its power to prevent the region from falling into Soviet hands. For part of the speech, however, Kennan tackled the complicated issue of the relationship between Islam and communism in the Middle East. His analysis drew on the emerging conception of Turkey as a model for a new Middle East and on common imaginings of the Middle East as a place dominated by an Islam that was timeless in nature.

Kennan generally supported the ideas behind the Truman Doctrine, particularly the notion that the United States should take over British responsibilities in Greece and Turkey. He believed the Soviets or Soviet-sponsored groups posed significant challenges to both countries. Looking at the Middle East more broadly, Kennan argued that the region "outside of Turkey, is in a delicate and precarious position." He worried that unstable governments across the Middle East were vulnerable, perhaps even to a growing number of communists "whose education has spoiled them for the darkness and squalor of life among the underprivileged, without giving them the where-withal to share the life of the wealthy few. Semi-educated, restless and neurotic, seeing little to lose and much to gain from social change, these people may come to constitute an energetic and incisive instrument of initial communist penetration."[37]

Kennan reached a different conclusion about the Soviet threat when he assessed other forces at play in the region. Though he expressed the afore-mentioned concern that communism could emerge from within the Middle East itself, he seriously doubted that the Soviet Union could devote enough resources without direct military intervention to dominate Muslims. For proof, he pointed to the problems the Soviet government encountered trying to establish and maintain authority in Central Asia, where Muslim control was strong but nowhere near as powerful as it was throughout the Middle East. Overall, Kennan found "it difficult to believe that an attempted ideological conquest of the Middle East by the Russians, effected without the use of large Russian military and police forces and by reliance principally on local elements, could prove successful or enduring." Moreover, Kennan continued, "if I ask myself in all honesty whether the Russians at the present stage of their development would be capable of changing the whole political character of that area, a character anchored in the experiences of so many centuries and centuries and millenniums, I am forced to answer that question in the negative." Thus, for Kennan, the presence of an essentially timeless Islam would prevent the spread of Soviet communism throughout the Middle East.[38]

Although Kennan did not think the Soviets could conquer the Middle East, he believed Americans would do themselves a great disservice by viewing such limited Soviet capabilities "with equanimity." Countering a Soviet attack would not be easy and would entail substantial costs. Bluntly assessing the situation, Kennan proclaimed that defending the Middle East after a Soviet incursion "would be a long and bloody process. A great deal that is useful and valuable would be lost in the course of it." Equally important in Kennan's analysis were the implications—or "by-products"—of such a struggle on the rest of the world. Not only would a Soviet challenge in the Middle East threaten oil supplies, it would have great "psychological effects" by "confirm[ing] the impression that the Western Powers were on the run and that international communism was on the make." Other movements, even noncommunist ones such as those inspired by Islam, might therefore draw inspiration from the situation and launch their own challenges to the United States and its allies.[39]

Kennan's piece is interesting and instructive because of how he explained U.S. interests in the region and the religious obstacles to the extension of Soviet influence there, but it is also useful because of how others responded to it. Kennan forwarded a copy of his speech to William Eddy, whose missionary roots and on-the-ground experience in the Middle East had allowed him to become perhaps the United States' premier regional specialist during and shortly after World War II. To be sure, many of Eddy's views aligned with Kennan's. Eddy replied in a letter to Kennan that he could not "imagine that anybody else will turn up with a statement as accurate or as convincing as yours." Moreover, Eddy agreed with Kennan's assertion that a disillusioned Arab intelligentsia provided a point of access for communist doctrine in the region but that the Soviets would find it difficult to assert control over much of the Muslim Middle East. But Eddy's response also suggested that he had even graver concerns about the potential for a Soviet incursion into the region than did Kennan. Eddy looked to the recent past and pondered the possibility that Soviet access to the Middle East might occur through other means and thus pose a more immediate danger. Thinking specifically of recent U.S.-Soviet relations, Eddy presented a different scenario: "It seems to me that the greater and more immediate danger is that the Arab world, including its orthodox leadership, if goaded too far by aggression on the pattern of the French in Syria or of the Zionists in Palestine, would form an alliance with Soviet Russia without accepting any Communist ideas or institutions. This could come about in the same way that we were strongly allied to Russia during the war, without at the same time modifying our rejection of Communist doctrines." Thus, in Eddy's analysis, the Middle Eastern masses, perhaps with the assistance or at the behest of the religious leadership, might overlook important ideological differences in order to align with the Soviet Union to mount a serious challenge to U.S. interests in the region.[40]

The question of whether Islam would serve as a barrier or an opening to communism in the Middle East assumed greater urgency among analysts as the Cold War unfolded and communist forces gathered strength in China, Vietnam, and Korea in the late 1940s and 1950s. The North African specialist Rom Landau noted in the April 1952 *New York Times Magazine* article "Peace May Be In Moslem Hands" that "the attitude of the Moslem countries toward the West might easily determine the future of every American, Britisher or Frenchman." A mere glance at the sheer size of the Muslim world in the mid-

1950s lent some credibility to that claim. A 1957 report issued by the Middle East experts on the Operations Coordinating Board (OCB), a group created by Eisenhower to oversee the implementation of U.S. foreign policy and to replace Truman's Psychological Strategy Board, indicated that the United Nations had eighty-one member nations in early 1957, of which sixteen had populations that were majority Muslim and thirty-two had a Muslim population of over 50,000. In all, there were well over 350 million Muslims, most of them living in newly independent states in Africa, Asia, and the Middle East.[41]

Specialists struggling to come to terms with the relationship between Islam and communism focused their investigations on the alleged compatibility or incompatibility of the basic features of the two forces. On the one hand, as the State Department's Philip Ireland pointed out in 1951, Islam's requirement that its adherents submit to Allah appeared to conflict directly with Lenin's denunciation of religion as "the opium of the people" and the Soviet Union's efforts to stamp out religious practices. Equally important, according to Ireland, the Qur'an's recognition of private property worked against communism's calls, at least in practice, for state ownership of property. Other analysts, such as the authors of the 1957 OCB report on Islamic organizations, followed suit by suggesting that Soviet and Chinese efforts to exploit Islam were encountering limited success. They believed communists could offer little ideological succor to such deeply religious peoples. That Islam, Christianity, and Judaism were "variations of a single ideology which includes the unity of God, the brotherhood of man, and the importance of submitting to the will of God for the purpose of establishing order in human affairs" also bred optimism among those who hoped Islam would serve as a barrier to communism. Based on this shared system of beliefs, the Muslim world and the United States "should be natural allies against atheistic communism."[42]

On the other hand, some specialists pointed to certain features that Islam and communism allegedly shared that might make the Middle East more susceptible to communist influence. Richard Frye, the associate director of Harvard's Center for Middle Eastern Studies in 1956, drew on the well-established imagining of Islam as a totalitarian religion to argue, "Islam is a rigid system, like communism, controlling all man's activities and even his thoughts." Though Frye was not convinced that Muslims would automatically welcome communism, he conceded, "The parallel between Islam and communism is valid insofar as both are all-inclusive, demanding more from their adherents than the church, or the state, or any other institution in the West does from its members." To Frye's mind, that meant U.S. policymakers and others had to figure out how to convince Muslims to work with them, as "Islam . . . alone" could stop communism in the Middle East. State Department Asian specialists made comparable assertions regarding the similarities between Islam and communism in their responses to the 1957 OCB report on Islamic organizations. When asked to comment on the report, they claimed that it drew a too simple comparison and placed "invalid stress on the incompatibility of Communism and Islam." Instead, the Asianists contended that "there is much historical evidence to suggest that this is not a valid premise," and that "the two have superficially much in common, and in areas where Moslems are not devout and orthodox the point of Communist atheism can be easily overlooked."[43]

The effort to investigate whether Islam signified an obstacle or an opening to communism in the Middle East never produced a clear consensus, but it did lead to a shift in how some observers of international politics thought about the religion and its role in the Cold War. To be sure, the 1955 army paper that called for increased focus on the role of religion in international politics, with which this chapter opened, relied in part on common explanations of why studies of Islam were necessary. The powerful Islamic resurgence occurring throughout much of the Middle East, the argument went, combined with strong internal divisions, extreme nationalism, and opposition to Western influences to create a dangerous situation. But the paper also provided other justifications for studying Islam. The report drew on underlying concerns about potential conflict between Islam and the West that were present in the late 1940s and early 1950s to argue that Islam had become "no less a world force than communism," and "strategists . . . must reckon with it as such." The scholar of Islam Wilfred Cantwell Smith made a similar point in 1957, arguing that Islam is "a powerful, profound and human force that must be faced with respect, even reverence." Fruitful relations with the Middle East would be possible only once "the West" recognized this fact. For these specialists, Islam—not communism—was the more important force with which the United States had to reckon in the region.[44]

Islam and Nationalism

While the debates over the relationship between Islam and communism were almost entirely a product of the Cold War, the concern with the relationship between Islam and nationalism was not. Indeed, as the discussion over the emergence of independent Turkey in the 1920s revealed, there had long been an interest in the relationship between religion and nationalism in the Middle East. That interest was compounded in the 1930s and 1940s by growing anticolonial sentiment, increasing foreign involvement in regional affairs, and the network participants' concerns about an Islam in crisis and that crisis's potential consequences.

By the early 1950s, at the heart of these concerns was what many observers believed was a growing Islamic revival, as Muslims sought to navigate their way through the spiritual crisis in which they were allegedly mired. John Badeau, who had been a missionary in Iraq and was in 1953 president of the American University in Cairo, contended that the religious resurgence in the decade and a half since 1939 was palpable. It was, according to Badeau, a "rebirth of religion as a social force, as a political party and as part of the organism of society." Religion was coming to the fore in situations that in other times or places might have evolved along more secular nationalist lines. Several factors, including opposition to foreign involvement, resistance to the new state of Israel, the absence of a clear secular nationalist movement in many places, and religion's ability to serve as a "common denominator" among all people of the faith regardless of class, education, or level of political awareness contributed to this Islamic resurgence. For Badeau, it remained to be seen whether or not Islam would be able to address all of these issues successfully, but he believed the process through which change played out would present certain challenges to the United States.[45]

Badeau and others found evidence for their claims that a resurgent religion dominated nationalist politics in the Middle East in an upsurge of calls for pan-Islamic unity in the late 1940s and early 1950s. These calls for unity also contributed to the widespread concerns regarding the totalitarian leanings of the religion. The so-called "reactionary" nature of most pan-Islamic movements, which supposedly sought to "remain isolated and insulated, with little cross-fertilization or intercultural exchange between them and the West," seemed particularly problematic. Revealing enduring Orientalist ideas about the unchanging nature of Islam, Princeton scholar and founder of the university's Near East studies program, Philip Hitti, argued that "pan-Islamism is backward looking," and "draws its inspiration from medieval concepts of life—it is anti-Western and anti-democratic." As such, it needed to be closely watched.[46]

State Department officials also grew worried about a possible symbiotic relationship between nationalism and religion as pan-Islamist movements manifested themselves in a series of international conferences between 1949 and 1955. Pakistan promoted the first few conferences, which brought together Muslim religious leaders (including the mufti of Jerusalem), youths, popular figures, and members of the political elite from Muslim states on an annual basis between 1949 and 1952. Pakistan supported the idea of pan-Islamic unity, and thus the conferences, because it wanted to convince the world's Muslims that it was a viable state. Pakistani intellectual Chaudhri Khaliquzzaman played the dominant role in organizing the conferences, putting so much effort into promoting Islamic unity that one State Department wit labeled him the "erstwhile organizer of Islam." According to at least one observer, the conferences spread feelings of unity and Islamic revival among Arabs and Muslims across the region. William Brewer of the U.S. embassy in Saudi Arabia noted, "It is true that such conferences and subsequent manifestoes stressing the religious unity of Islam have appeal here in view of Saudi Arabia's role as the Holy Land of Islam and the focal point of the annual Moslem pilgrimage to Mecca."[47]

Government Middle East specialists believed the conferences held the potential to create significant problems for the United States and closely monitored both the meetings and the reaction of the world's Muslims to them. The conferences usually included the passage of a number of vaguely worded resolutions on Islamic unity that committed the peoples and governments of Muslim states to very little, and therefore achieved minimal tangible results. Reporting on the 1951 World Muslim Conference, one staff member of the U.S. embassy in Pakistan cabled the State Department that even "the anti-Western, 'anti-imperialist' tenor of the Conference was considerably more subdued than the Embassy had anticipated. Observers are in general agreement that the Conference was much ado about little." Policymakers and other observers breathed a sigh of relief after each set of meetings.[48]

Even though the conferences claimed few tangible accomplishments, they generated enough fears about a politicized and potentially totalitarian Islam that by 1952 State Department Middle East specialists felt compelled to devise a policy for dealing with such initiatives. In early 1952, Pakistan issued yet another call for a meeting of Muslim states. The U.S. Ambassador in Turkey, former assistant secretary of state for Near Eastern, South Asian, and African affairs George C. McGhee, was both annoyed with and concerned about the recurring conferences. He requested official State Department guidance and the views of other chiefs of missions in the region about pan-

Islamic movements and meetings. In making his request, McGhee recognized that the idea of unity within the Middle East was not in and of itself a bad idea "if divorced from religion and based on solid [political], strategic, [economic] and cultural factors which [Middle East] countries obviously have in common." Moreover, the "principal disadvantage" of the Pakistani initiative was its "emphasis on Islam as [the] basis of proposed association." McGhee urged a policy of "influencing [Pakistan] and other countries interested in [an] association of [Middle East] states to abandon or subordinate [the] religious basis."[49]

The respondents to McGhee's inquiry almost unanimously opposed any efforts to promote religious unity in the Middle East and reflected an underlying belief in the inferiority of Islam and its institutions as well as the potential for future conflict. The U.S. ambassador in Kabul, George Merrell, agreed with McGhee that "any effort" to promote Middle Eastern unity on a "purely Islamic basis is unrealistic and bound to founder. Moreover there are certain positively disadvantageous aspects to this type of religious grouping including [the] connotation of religious intolerance and [the] support it [would] give to more fanatic anti-Western Muslim elements." Harold Minor, the U.S. ambassador in Beirut, argued that he could "not see value" in the Pakistani initiative, and that what was needed was something that would "bring stability, order, unity and social improvement to [the] [Near East] through [the] restoration of [an] occidental leadership position."[50]

Only two respondents to McGhee's call to discuss the issue of Islamic unity voiced even limited dissent. The first to do so was the staff of the U.S. embassy in Baghdad, which tried to deflate concerns about pan-Islamic unity by pointing to the widespread perception of Arab and Muslim ineptitude. The embassy staff contended that any effort to achieve Middle Eastern unity, whether based on religion, culture, politics, or economics, would fail to achieve any real success, so discussion of the entire issue was unnecessary. These committed Cold Warriors believed analysts and policymakers could better spend their time finding ways to promote the defense of the Middle East against the Soviet threat.[51]

Raymond Hare, the U.S. ambassador in Saudi Arabia, expressed more thoughtful reservations about McGhee's suggestions. As Teresa Thomas has pointed out, Hare was one of the first State Department employees to learn Arabic, which he began by becoming the only American graduate of a three-year program run by the French in the 1930s, and then completed his studies largely by teaching himself. He was also known as an expert at quietly getting his point across and working through the State Department bureaucracy, particularly through the medium of the carefully crafted cable. In addition to the six ambassadorial appointments Hare received in the 1950s and 1960s, he also served as both a formal and informal mentor to the growing body of regional specialists in the State Department, especially to those who came out of the Foreign Service Institute's Middle East training program, which he had helped implement. With respect to the religious unity movement in the region, Hare did not stand against his colleagues' opposition, though he could "see great possibilities in encouraging adherents [of] Islam as well as other religions in spiritual assertion against Communist nihilism." In most cases, however, he too believed it would be best to "keep politics and religion on separate but parallel tracks leading to [the] same destination." That destination, of course, was a secular, stable, anticommunist, pro-U.S. Middle East.[52]

The State Department ultimately concurred with McGhee and the majority of its operatives in the field, suggesting a policy that, if successful, would have been the ideal outcome in the minds of most observers of the Middle East at the time. The department pushed its representatives in the area to cautiously urge the leaders of the region's states to follow a path much like that Mustafa Kemal traveled in Turkey. The department's response, drafted by the head of Near Eastern affairs G. Lewis Jones and the head of South Asian affairs L. E. Metcalf, and sent under the signature of Secretary of State Dean Acheson, clearly articulated policymakers' preferences regarding religious movements in the Middle East: ". . . [The department] considers one of [the] best Ataturk legacies is Turks' firm policy of secular approach to both internal and [international] political relations. While it will require time to realize [a] comparable attitude [among] Paks, Afghans and [Middle East] States, [the department] considers emulation [of] this Turk policy [a] desirable objective."[53]

State Department wishes aside, proposals for pan-Islamic meetings continued to appear through the mid-1950s. In Jerusalem in December 1953, the Islamic Congress for the Palestine Question produced the strongest resolutions of any of the meetings. Its participants concluded that Muslims throughout the world were obligated to "work for the liberation of Palestine," that negotiating peace with Israel was a "treasonable act," and that worldwide "popular mobilization for the positive struggle" would replace "useless pacifism." Jordan and Egypt proposed conferences for 1954 and 1955 as well, although each of these encountered difficulties as the organizers appeared unable to arrive at a justification acceptable to the participants for why the conferences should even take place.[54]

While many analysts believed a revived Islam and rising nationalist forces existed in a symbiotic relationship that created the strongest political force in the Middle East through the early 1950s, that view began to change toward the end of the decade. The 1957 OCB report on Islamic organizations stated the conventional wisdom that nationalism provided "an outlet for numerous repressions and feelings" that were fundamentally Islamic in nature. Some of these supposedly Islamic aspects of nationalism were the "desire for material progress," the "reaction to Western domination," "nationalism as a fluctuating and sometimes temporary expedient . . . to free Muslim nations from colonialism," "the desire to capture lost glory," and the "use of Islam for political purposes." Asian specialist John Gordon Mein, however, issued a necessary corrective by making an obvious observation: "Nationalism and neutralism are characteristics of non-Moslem nations of Asia and Africa. Therefore the implication that these attitudes are an outgrowth of, or must necessarily be associated with, Islam does not appear valid." Continuing to view all expressions of nationalist sentiment in the Middle East as religious sentiment would therefore have given Islam too much credit.[55]

The emerging interpretation that Islam and nationalism were not necessarily the same or even mutually reinforcing led experts to reconsider Islam. It opened up the possibility that Islamic unity might not have been as perilous as specialists had believed just five years earlier, when State Department responses to pan-Islamic unity movements in the early 1950s demonstrated a clear preference for limiting Islam as a political force. The changing and highly nationalist political environment in the Middle East in the late 1950s combined with these new interpretations of Islam to lead some observers to begin to see Islam as a potential counterweight to nationalist forces.

The shift in approaches to Islam is evident in responses to the growth of secular Arab nationalism during the mid-1950s, particularly after Gamal ʿAbd al-Nasser and the Free Officers Movement rose to power in Egypt. Most Middle East specialists initially viewed the new Egyptian leader as an exemplar of the modernist, secular faith they promoted and hoped Egypt would follow a path similar to the one Turkey had taken a generation earlier. Nasser, however, pursued a pan-Arab nationalist course that opposed foreign intervention in the Middle East and promoted Cold War neutralism, an approach highlighted by his efforts to secure Britain's withdrawal from its base at Suez, the agreement for which was finalized in 1954. The United States supported those efforts, but Nasser's star dimmed significantly in the minds of U.S. analysts in 1955. In that year alone he negotiated a deal to procure arms from the Soviet Union, recognized China, and refused to participate in Project Alpha, a secret U.S.-sponsored plan to resolve the Arab-Israeli conflict. As a result, U.S. policymakers actively began searching for ways to isolate and undermine him.

Facing what they believed to be an increasingly intransigent secular Arab nationalist regime in Egypt, between 1956 and 1958 U.S. policymakers reversed their position on religious-based identities and unity movements in the Middle East. President Eisenhower searched for viable ways to counter Nasser's ambition and prestige in the region as U.S.-Egyptian relations soured in early 1956. Eisenhower thought building up a leader who possessed "mutually antagonistic personal ambitions" with Nasser might serve to limit the Egyptian leader's options. In a region where policymakers, academics, journalists, and businesspersons believed Islam played the dominant role in determining the thoughts and actions of Muslims, and where religion or communism seemed to present the only alternatives to nationalism, Eisenhower's choice was King Saud of Saudi Arabia. Just as U.S.-Egyptian relations worsened in spring 1956, Eisenhower noted in his diary that "Arabia is a country that contains the holy places of the Moslem world, and the Saudi Arabians are considered to be the most deeply religious of all the Arab groups. Consequently, the King could be built up, possibly, as a spiritual leader. Once this were accomplished, we might begin to urge his right to political leadership." Eisenhower continued to promote this policy for the next eighteen months. He noted to British minister of defense Duncan Sandys during King Saud's visit to the United States in February 1957 that, while Saud was "medieval in his approach," he remained the only available "'stone' on which to build." Eisenhower also reminded Saud of the king's "special position . . . as Keeper of the Holy Places of Islam" in an August 1957 letter intended to motivate Saud to work to help contain a Syrian move toward the left.[56]

Historian Salim Yaqub has shown how the initiative to build up Saud's stature as a religious leader to rival Nasser's secular appeal suffered from multiple problems. Eisenhower's assertion that Saud was responsible for protecting the holiest sites in Islam was correct, but the king's own lifestyle hardly epitomized what one might expect from a devoutly religious individual. Saud had at least 107 children, had accumulated massive wealth from oil exports, and spent his money freely and in any number of ways. Saud therefore had very little support outside of his own country and never should have been expected to rival Nasser for regional power. Saud did take his role as defender of Muslim holy places seriously, but that fact actually undercut friendly U.S.-Saudi relations. As negotiations continued through early 1957 regarding Israeli shipping rights through the Straits of Tiran and the Red Sea following the Suez Crisis of late 1956, Saud consistently expressed concern that Israeli transit rights would pose a threat to Muslim holy sites and the annual Muslim pilgrimages to them.[57]

In addition to the problems Saud presented for those hoping to use him as a religious counterweight to Nasser, the policy also revealed a fundamental contradiction in how U.S. policymakers and other experts imagined the Middle East in the late 1950s. Supporting a regime like King Saud's in Saudi Arabia could provide a measure of stability and control in an area of tremendous global significance, but doing so challenged important aspects of the enduring sense of sacred and secular mission that dominated American imaginings of the Middle East. Supporting Saud seemed to reject transformation in favor of what many analysts believed was a corrupt, ruthless, medieval Islam. Moreover, had the policy of elevating Saud to a legitimate contender for regional leadership succeeded, it might also have backfired if, as some specialists had long argued, the impact of Western nationalism and other influences were indeed responsible for the ongoing "spiritual crisis" in the Middle East. Conservative Muslims in Saudi Arabia or elsewhere in the region might have proved able to combine the ideology of nationalism with their drive for a return to a purified Islam—the exact outcome that Middle East specialists had been so concerned about in the late 1940s and early 1950s.

As Middle East specialists became aware of this contradiction, they gradually arrived at a general consensus in the late 1950s that the relationship between Islam and nationalism demanded closer attention than did the relationship between Islam and communism. Earlier attempts to create a usable interpretation of Islam's role in the world had foundered on these very issues. A 1958 Council on Foreign Relations study group on "The Middle East and Modern Islam," composed of the foremost regional specialists from academia, government, and the business world, arrived at a much more coherent interpretation. Participants in the group found that the relationship between communism and Islam had become secondary in importance. These individuals argued that the Middle East had demonstrated by the late 1950s that it was a powerful region in its own right and would not readily submit to foreign domination. Policymakers therefore needed to address the region in those terms, rather than simply in Cold War terms. Thus, the study group devoted most of its energy to exploring the many facets of the relationship between Islam and nationalism in the region.[58]

The study group's most significant conclusion was that in the struggle to dominate the Middle East, Islam had suffered a narrow and perhaps temporary defeat to modernity, inasmuch as modernity was expressed in the form of secular Arab nationalism. According to the group, a telling signal in this direction was that the constitution of the newly formed United Arab Republic did not acknowledge Islam as the state's official religion. In addition, the state, rather than religious institutions, now controlled the economic, political, and social environment in most places. Seeing secularism on the march, the study group therefore dismissed the threat of a pan-Islamic revolution. Group members still relied on well-worn imaginings of Islam as medieval, stagnant, and antimodern, and they also continued to assume Western and Islamic ideas were irreconcilable. But unlike their colleagues in the late 1940s and early 1950s, who feared that a pan-Islamic movement could be wedded to Western nationalism, specialists now argued that any movement seeking to combine Islamic revival with concepts of Western nationalism was doomed to fail. It would reflexively reject integration into an increasingly secular, modern, and interconnected world and thereby severely restrict its own economic and political viability. The same factors that caused the supposed crisis in Islam would therefore prevent a successful pan-Islamic revolution from taking place. As the final meeting of the study group on "The Middle East and Modern Islam" drew near in May 1959, one member wondered whether they had "been talking about the wrong thing all year." He concluded that they had not, for "it is something to have learned that Islam is not the central issue in the modern Middle East."[59]

That specialists concluded religion was no longer the central issue in the Middle East did not mean they now dismissed Islam as completely insignificant. To be sure, they still remained concerned about Islam and saw it playing a crucial supporting role in the region even though they believed secular nationalism had replaced religion as the dominant political force there. Islam's supposedly pervasive influence and emphasis on the community over the individual meant that it continued to provide the ideological buttress necessary to strengthen the appeal of secular Arab nationalism and to allow pan-Arabism to succeed. Alleged Islamic fatalism also appeared to support the aims of Arab nationalism by providing for the presence of "the strong man" in Middle Eastern politics. According to this line of reasoning, Muslims honored, respected, and followed especially charismatic or powerful leaders because Allah destined them to lead the community. And, even with the threat of a pan-Islamic revolution discounted, pan-Arabism still kept open the possibility that a united Middle East might threaten U.S. and Western interests. Moreover, and perhaps most importantly, the study group concluded that the Middle East needed a reformulated Islam to help moderate other forces in the region. Without it, the alternatives looked grim. According to Badeau, nationalism might grow unchecked until it succumbed to "the extremes of national hysteria or xenophobic emotionalism," or communism might yet emerge as an option for those "restless and vacant-minded intellectuals who have lost the foundations of their historic faith, yet seek something more effective than the uncertain tides of nationalism." These were some of the same concerns that sparked fears of totalitarian Islam nearly a decade earlier.[60]

Of course, some observers clung to older Orientalist notions of a confrontational religion in crisis and rejected altogether either the idea that Arab nationalism had replaced Islam as the defining characteristic of the Middle East or that nationalist and religious forces could not be combined into a powerful and antagonistic political force. Harold Hoskins, who like his cousin William Eddy came from a missionary and World War II intelligence background, and who was Director of the Foreign Service Institute in August 1958, submitted a memorandum to the State Department's policy planning staff in which he argued that religion was the "one basic problem in the Middle East." Regarding Islam specifically, he contended, "In reality, Arab nationalism is . . . a cloak for Mohammedanism." The State Department's Bureau of Near Eastern Affairs rejected Hoskins's analysis and generally tried to minimize the importance of religion. Hoskins's views, the bureau's William Rountree contended, were "based on the assumption that religion remains an important political factor in the area; we believe this to be less and less true." That specialists no longer equated Middle Eastern politics with Islam reflected the extent to which a more complex—even if still flawed—understanding of the region had come to challenge missionary and Orientalist frameworks by the late 1950s.[61]

Observers looked to the rise and apparent fall of Ayatollah Khomeini and a religious opposition movement in Iran in the mid-1960s for confirmation of their new interpretation that secular nationalism was overrunning Islam. Khomeini had a long history of resistance to the ruling monarchy, dating back to the 1930s and the days of Reza Shah Pahlavi. By the early 1960s, he had built up a following as one of the most respected religious leaders in Iran and drew large crowds whenever he spoke publicly. He first entered the consciousness of specialists and policymakers in June 1963, when he played a critical role in a series of anti-shah rallies that turned into massive riots. Khomeini was especially bothered by what he considered an antireligious reform program put forth by the shah, particularly those measures that promoted rights for women and made land owned by religious institutions subject to redistribution. The shah responded to the riots by calling out the military and by arresting Khomeini and his fellow clerics. The shah released Khomeini in spring 1964, only to have him renew his religious critique, add a highly nationalist, anti-American tone to it, and call for the shah to change his ways or face certain overthrow. Ultimately, Khomeini was rearrested and exiled to Turkey later that year, not to set foot on Iranian soil again until his victorious return during the 1979 revolution.[62]

Not many specialists acknowledged the presence of a powerful religious opposition movement in Iran in the early 1960s, and those who did generally dismissed it. The foremost Iran specialist in the United States, Princeton's T. Cuyler Young, seemed entirely unaware of the growing religious opposition. Young's January 1962 overview of "Iran in Continuing Crisis," published in Foreign Affairs, focused on the nationalist opposition to the shah's reign to the complete exclusion of the burgeoning religious movement. The unwillingness of State Department officials to take seriously the religious opposition also clearly indicated their belief that Islam was of decreasing importance in the region. Phillips Talbot, a long-time Middle East specialist, assistant secretary of state for Near Eastern and South Asian affairs, and chairman of a special government task force on Iran in June 1963, noted that due to the shah's response to the rioting, "religion as an active political force in Iran will have been dealt a mortal wound." Less than three weeks later, staff in the U.S. embassy in Iran claimed that "certainly no reactionary groups" could successfully oppose the shah, and that Khomeini and the religious leaders would "have to accept the full reform program." Even State Department Iran specialist John W. Bowling, who in hindsight appears most prescient for having recognized "rightist opposition" to the shah, devoted more attention to the wealthy, landed elite. Bowling generally dismissed the religious opposition in a March 1961 report as being driven by "very xenophobic religious leaders" or "religious fanatics . . . given to assassination as a means of political expression." He also downplayed the nationalist component of the clerics' message, pointing out that they had split with the Mossadegh nationalists over the issue of secularization, and he implied that they had therefore been irremediably weakened.[63]

Some specialists may have also considered the rise of Khomeini to confirm their interpretation that Islam's primary significance was its ability to support other political movements. The Khomeini example might have been read to have demonstrated that religion could, as the Council on Foreign Relations study group had suggested, amplify nationalist forces and thus remain in some measure an issue that U.S. policymakers would have to address. A 1965 State Department paper acknowledged that Khomeini's critique of U.S. involvement in Iranian affairs and his exile to Turkey "aroused dormant nationalist feelings" among the Iranian masses. At the same time, the State Department's belief that Khomeini represented "the point of view of traditional Iranian society" indicated that specialists still imagined Iran and the wider Middle East as being engaged in the struggle between modernity and tradition and had not yet worked through the alleged spiritual crisis. Finally, much as Nasser had in Egypt and other parts of the Middle East, Khomeini appeared to fill the "big man" role that the 1958 study group suggested Islam always made a fundamental need of the masses in the Middle East.[64]

IF ISLAM PROVED AN important aspect of how Americans imagined the Middle East through the nineteenth and early twentieth centuries, it came to play an even more critical role for members of the informal transnational network of Middle East specialists in the mid-twentieth century. As World War II drew to a close, members of that emerging network believed they had to understand Islam if they were to make sense of the region and its role in international affairs. Arguing that Muslims were caught between tradition and modernity and were enmeshed in a spiritual crisis, specialists used the concept of totalitarianism to think through the implications for the region and U.S. involvement there. These specialists looked more closely at the relationship between religion and communism in the late 1940s and early 1950s as the Cold War took shape, but they soon moved beyond their initial Cold War–oriented concerns and started to imagine Islam as a powerful force they had to reckon with on its own terms. Thus, as the network of specialists expanded from the mid-1940s to the early 1960s and began studying the religion more closely, a much more complicated and nuanced interpretation emerged that challenged the fundamental Cold War assumptions that had led to the more careful study of Islam in the first place. At the same time, however, many of these specialists also came to challenge their own views about

Islam's dominance as a political force in the Middle East. Instead, they began to see secular nationalism's superseding religion as the most pressing problem throughout the region.

Viewed in broader interpretive and methodological terms, the fact that specialists in the 1940s and 1950s focused so intently on Islam as a political force and as the path to understand the region as a whole suggests that scholars studying the relationship between the United States and Islamist movements in the Middle East today must widen their chronological focus. Most scholarship on the topic focuses on Iran in the late 1970s, a period one scholar has referred to as "America's first encounter with radical Islam," or on U.S. efforts to assist the mujahedeen fighting Soviet forces in Afghanistan in the 1980s. In fact, one can best come to terms with the surprise that Americans felt following the Islamists' victory in Iran not by seeing it as a movement that seemed to come out of nowhere, but rather by recognizing that specialists' efforts to understand Islam and its role in regional and international politics from the 1940s to the 1960s led Americans to believe that Islam was in decline. From the American perspective, the outcome in Iran was simply unimaginable.[65]

CHAPTER THREE

A NEW AMALGAM OF INTERESTS, RELIGION, PROPAGANDA, AND MOBS

Interpretations of Secular Mass Politics

On 14 November 1960, the Council on Foreign Relations convened the first meeting of a new study group on "Arab Foreign Policy." The group gathered to provide a forum for Charles Cremeans to work through material for a book he was writing on Arab nationalist foreign policy and its implications for the United States. Cremeans had a long background in Middle Eastern affairs, having moved to Egypt to teach in 1936 and eventually becoming a Middle East analyst for the CIA. The meeting was attended by the usual assemblage of specialists from academia, the business world, the government, and the media, though as one of the organizers noted, the group was "a bit heavy on the academic side, and it takes special talents to keep the professors in order."[1]

From the outset, the meeting took on a lively tone. The minutes suggest that the conversation ranged widely as the participants probed the boundaries of the topic and sought to define an agenda for the remaining meetings. Along the way, they offered some revealing general impressions on whether or not there even existed such a thing as Arab foreign policy, either as a unified policy representing the region as a whole or as an approach that was notably distinct from that pursued by newly independent states and their leaders elsewhere in the world. They also considered the relationship between the masses and various nationalist regimes, and they deliberated over whether they should focus on Egypt's Gamal 'Abd al-Nasser as the primary proponent of Arab foreign policy or on the region as a whole. So wide-ranging were their discussions that one member suggested that a better title might be "Why do the Arabs behave as they do?" Still other members cautioned that participants be as specific as possible in their analysis of this important topic. Cremeans himself was urged to distinguish "between a government's foreign policy and the people's attitudes about it." According to the minutes, "Mr. Cremeans agreed, noting that the image we have generally had in the past, one based on Western interests and conceptions, was inappropriate, and that Arab foreign policy was a new amalgam of interests, religion, propaganda, and mobs." The book that Cremeans ultimately published in 1963, *The Arabs and the World: Nasser's Arab Nationalist Policy*, was actually quite sympathetic to the Egyptian leader and to the broader cause of Arab nationalism, but his somewhat flip response to the earlier criticism and the broader discussion at that meeting hinted at some of the underlying ways in which the informal transnational network of Middle East specialists had come to understand not only nationalism, but mass politics more broadly, in the Middle East by the early 1960s.[2]

The previous chapter examined how academic, business, government, and media specialists saw the Middle East through the sacred lens of Islam. Here we take up the issue of how they understood secular mass politics in the region and focus specifically on interpretations of Turkish, Arab, and Iranian nationalist movements. Members of the nascent network first wrestled with the issue in the years between the end of World War I and the end of World War II, when they identified two different types of nationalist movements in the region. According to their analyses, the first type of movement emerged from the actions of particularly powerful individual leaders, such as Mustafa Kemal in Turkey, Reza Khan in Iran, and ʿAbd al-ʿAziz Ibn Saʿud in the Arabian Peninsula. The second, defined most effectively in George Antonius's *The Arab Awakening*, was understood to be the product of a growing middle- and upper-class anticolonial and intellectual movement. In both cases, specialists argued that the United States had long supported Middle Eastern nationalism they considered benign and hoped nationalism might bring about the fulfillment of America's sacred and secular mission in the region. In the 1950s, the emergence of two secular nationalist leaders—Mohammad Mossadegh in Iran and Gamal ʿAbd al-Nasser in Egypt—shattered the existing belief that nationalism was a benevolent force and led to the creation of interventionist policies designed to defend U.S. interests from "radical" nationalists. Much like the concerns expressed about "totalitarian" Islam, the network's analysis reflected unease about the connection between secular nationalist movements, their leaders, and the masses across the region. These more critical interpretations then generated a backlash in the late 1950s and early 1960s in which specialists began to reimagine secular Middle Eastern nationalism and its impact on the United States in more pragmatic terms, though there remained a deep ambivalence over the relationship between powerful leaders and the masses.

"The Awakening of the Nationalistic Spirit"

Early post–World War I observers of the Middle East were certainly well aware of the growing nationalist desires spreading across the region. They tended to equate such desires with a more general anticolonial sentiment also found in Asia, Africa, and Latin America, which they believed had drawn some inspiration from Woodrow Wilson's proclamations about the inherent right of peoples to self-determination. Thus, members of the Inquiry and the King-Crane Commission did not develop comprehensive interpretations of nationalism in the Middle East itself. From the mid-1920s through the mid-1940s, however, there did emerge two distinct models of understanding nationalism in the region, each of which recognized the importance of anticolonial sentiment but focused on other potential sources of and outcomes for nationalist movements. One model focused on individual leaders' creating nationalist movements, either secular or sectarian, around themselves in individual states. The emergence of independent Turkey under the leadership of Mustafa Kemal, the rise of Reza Khan in Persia, and the unification of the Arabian Peninsula under ʿAbd al-ʿAziz Ibn Saʿud were all interpreted in this manner. (Hereafter the Saudi king will be referred to as Ibn Saud.) The other model focused on the issue of Arab unity more broadly and emphasized its anticolonial and intellectual roots that allegedly took hold in Syria and Lebanon in the late nineteenth century. This model was articulated most powerfully in George Antonius's acclaimed The Arab Awakening, which was first published in 1938 and gained even more attention in the mid-1940s as analysts assessed the prospects for "Arab unity."

The first sustained recognition by U.S. policymakers and analysts of nationalism in the Middle East came during and immediately after World War I, as both the Inquiry and the King-Crane commission confronted the issue repeatedly, even if not always explicitly. Yet neither group seemed to consider seriously the notion that Middle Eastern nationalism might be generated from within the region. In their efforts to determine what to do with the holdings of the former Ottoman Empire, advisors such as George Louis Beer acknowledged the emergence of anticolonial nationalism in the Middle East and noted that Arabs might feel some vague sense of shared identity. Yet, as historian Lawrence Gelfand noted, members of the Inquiry believed these common sentiments were easily overcome by identities and affiliations to tribes and local communities. The only exceptions were the growing Jewish presence in Palestine, which was clearly understood and presented as a much more unified and motivated nationalist movement of European origin, and Egypt, which many interwar analysts believed had a longer history of promoting a separate identity. Moreover, if Beer's January 1918 paper on "The Future of Mesopotamia" is representative of broader views on the topic, the notion of Arab nationalism and its concomitant ideal of an independent Arab state were seen as premature. According to Beer, "Although of a distinctly virile and able stock, the Arabs are apparently still too uneducated politically for so extensive a project." Indeed, it was sentiments such as those that led to the implementation of the League of Nations mandate system in the Middle East.[3]

The activities and methods of the King-Crane commission, sent to determine public sentiment regarding the implementation of that mandate system, reflected a similar unwillingness to take seriously indigenous forms of Middle Eastern nationalism. The commission's goal "was to meet in conference individuals and delegations who should represent all the significant groups in the various communities, and so to obtain as far as possible the opinions and desires of the whole people." To that end, King and Crane crossed the region for six weeks in summer 1919, accepting petitions and hearing various groups express their desire to avoid being declared a mandate under French or British control. Yet the primary portion of the final report mentioned nationalism rarely and usually discussed it as a reaction to other forces. Nascent Arab nationalism was thus a response to Turkish rule, while budding Palestinian nationalism was a consequence of the growing Jewish presence.[4]

The one place where King and Crane did address nationalism at length was in a "Confidential Appendix" to the report, but there too the discussion tended to reflect a rather limited conception of Middle Eastern nationalism. For much of the appendix, discussions of nationalism appeared only as they related to other issues, and thus seem somewhat tangential or peripheral, though nonetheless revealing. For example, King and Crane identified many factors that they believed explained why there was far more desire for an American mandate (as opposed to a British or, worse, French mandate). Two were directly relevant to the issue of nationalism, and both referred implicitly to the enduring notion of a sacred and secular American mission in the Middle East. The first, "confidence in President Wilson as mainly responsible for the freedom of Syria," suggested that only outside powers could bring about and protect the independence of the Middle East. The second factor presented Middle Eastern nationalism in Syria as a product of the American missionary presence in the region. According to King and Crane, there was "a hearty approval of and desire for the extension of American education in the country. England has done little educationally for Syria. While France has done much, she seeks to denationalize the native peoples and make Frenchmen of them. America, especially through the Syrian Protestant College, has taught Syrian nationalism. The American training and the Anglo-Saxon literature and civilization, are regarded as morally superior to the French."[5]

It was in the final section of the appendix, titled "Syrian Nationalism, Pan-Arabism, and Pan-Islamism," where King and Crane tackled the issue most explicitly by offering their assessments of the various nationalist options they could see in the region, but even here the analysis offered little sense of the forces under which nationalism had emerged or might evolve as a movement. Most of the petitions they received, at least in Syria, "were nationalistic; that is to say, they called for a United Syria under a democratic constitution, making no distinctions on the basis of religion." The commissioners believed that most Muslims supported such an agenda, while Christians, according to King and Crane, appeared to be more skeptical of what they saw as a "new and feeble" Syrian nationalism. Looking at the region more broadly, King and Crane found it "hard to see" how a unified but decentralized Arab state with poor communications infrastructure "could be more of a danger to the world than the Turkey of which it formed a part." Any larger vision of pan-Arabism, especially one that might include North Africa, was "a mere dream." "Pan-Islamism" seemed an even less likely accomplishment. Moreover, even if such movements were to achieve some success, there would be little cause for concern. "If," the commissioners averred, "the European civilization has sufficient wisdom to avoid further extensive self-destruction, it can with the greatest of ease control the Moslem world, it is not necessary for those who labor to establish the League of Nations to contemplate the opposite possibility."[6]

While members of both the Inquiry and the King-Crane Commission imagined nationalist sentiments and mass politics in the Middle East as products of external actors, by the mid-1920s interpretations that considered different forms of Middle Eastern nationalisms in their own right began to emerge among analysts. One of these new interpretations emphasized the role of charismatic individuals around whom nationalist movements might coalesce. The shift in focus was initiated in part by the 1924 abolition of the Turkish caliphate. Historically, the caliphate had served as the political head of Islam responsible for defending the community's interests. Over the centuries the title had become increasingly symbolic as power accrued to local leaders, and claimants, dating all the way back to the late seventh century, competed for the position. Nonetheless, its abolition by Turkey, combined with the dismemberment of the Ottoman Empire completed by World War I and the implementation of the League of Nations mandate system, removed the final formal institution that unified much of the region. Moreover, in the eyes of the few individuals who might be called Middle East specialists at that time, the end of the caliphate and declaration of the Turkish Republic under the leadership of Mustafa Kemal presented the first real possibility for secular regimes to emerge in the region. Thus, regional specialists turned their attention to identifying those local leaders who could consolidate their power and begin to build political entities that might function in a modern international political world dominated by the secular nation state.

The previous chapter discussed specialists' response to Kemal and his reforms, so here we will focus on analysts' views of two other regimes: Reza Khan's in Persia (renamed Iran in the mid-1930s) and Ibn Saud's in the Arabian Peninsula. Reza Khan rose to prominence in Persia during World War I through the Cossack Brigade, a Russian-led military unit in northern Persia. With Russian troops withdrawn following the Bolshevik Revolution, British forces occupied the entire country and in 1920 reorganized the Brigade under British leadership, placing Reza Khan in command. He gradually amassed more power until 1926, when he proclaimed himself shah and founder of the Pahlavi dynasty. Though the autocratic Reza Shah was practically illiterate, he began a series of reforms designed to build a secular, modern national state independent of foreign control, which he consciously modeled on Kemal's Turkey. From the mid-1920s through the late 1930s, Reza Shah implemented a series of policies designed to limit the influence of Islam and to promote loyalty to the state. Thus, among other things, religious attire was forbidden or discouraged in favor of secular European dress, the French Civil Law Code and the Italian Penal Code replaced Shariʿa law, and Persian words replaced many Arabic and Turkish words and place-names. Women, who "were to be the mothers of the nation," were granted greater legal and educational rights.

In addition, from the late 1920s forward, Reza Shah worked to limit foreign influence in Persia by renegotiating trade agreements, eliminating foreign economic missions, and increasing domestic industrial output.[7]

Commentary on Reza Shah's reforms was not as plentiful as that on Kemal's, but it generally presented him as leading his country out of backwardness and into modernity. The work of Harvard University's Soviet specialist, Bruce Hopper, offers a good example. Writing of "the Persian Regenesis" in Foreign Affairs in 1935, Hopper argued Persia's "rebirth" was most striking because of "the suddenness with which it has occurred, the rapidity with which the process of slow atrophy has been reversed." Much of the credit for the turnaround went to Reza Shah, who "realized that independence, once it had been won, could not be maintained unless Persia put her house in order by adopting Western methods. His program of discipline has undoubtedly revitalized Persia." Hopper went on to chronicle Reza Shah's political, legal, economic, and social reforms, noting, "The most remarkable change of all is in the spirit of the country. Islam had long since ceased to represent enough of a binding force to assure national unity. The awakening of the nationalistic spirit demanded a release from its dead hand. The Shah travelled far and wide, preaching love of country and patriotism." Hopper concluded that the "pattern of 'great-man reform'" undertaken by Kemal in Turkey and Reza Shah in Persia was good for the two countries and for the region as a whole.[8]

Not all discussions of Reza Shah were so positive, however, as a 1936 dispute between Iran and the United States revealed. The broad context of the conflict centered on an extended effort undertaken by Iran to renegotiate its economic relationship with the United States as Reza Shah sought to reduce his country's reliance on imported industrial goods and build up Iranian industries. That process was concluding in 1935 and 1936, and as a consequence some newspapers in the United States included some minimal coverage of U.S.-Iranian relations. In doing so, however, certain publications included commentary that Reza Shah found disagreeable, the most notable example of which suggested that the Pahlavi dynasty did not have deep historical roots and argued that Reza Shah had once been "a stable boy." The shah and his representatives demanded the U.S. government punish the offending publications or at least force them to retract the statements, and the State Department finally elicited a retraction in one case. But Reza Shah found the retraction unsatisfactory and eventually recalled all Iranian representatives to the United States. Quickly growing frustrated with the protracted conflict, the

State Department made several references to the differences between how an autocratic ruler such as Reza Shah and the leader of a democracy such as the United States could handle such a situation. Along the way, however, U.S. officials tried to placate Reza Shah by highlighting their admiration of and support for his dramatic reform program.[9]

The other leader to whom specialists looked as a focal point of rising nationalism in the Middle East from the mid-1920s to the mid-1940s was Ibn Saud in the Arabian Peninsula. The Saud family had aligned with the religious leader Muhammad Ibn 'Abd al-Wahhab in the late eighteenth century to conquer Mecca by 1803, before being defeated by Egyptian forces working for the Ottoman government. Ibn Saud brought his family out of exile in Kuwait in the early twentieth century and engaged in a series of military campaigns to reconquer much of the Arabian Peninsula by the mid-1920s. In doing so, he relied on a group of devout Wahhabis—known as the ikhwan, or the Brothers—who believed that the Qur'an, Shari'a law, and the Hadith (the recorded sayings and activities of the prophet Muhammad) should govern the behavior of all individuals and the state. By 1926, Ibn Saud had taken control of much of the Arabian Peninsula, and in 1932 he proclaimed the Kingdom of Saudi Arabia.[10]

Scholar Hans Kohn, whose reputation grew primarily from his work on nationalism, assessed Saud's achievements and the challenges that remained before him in a 1934 article in Foreign Affairs. Kohn saw Saud as the ultimate victor in a conflict among several figures for supremacy, demonstrating that he "was the real leader and statesman of Arabia." Saud's control was an "effort to improve the economic and cultural situation of the nomad and to make possible a stable government, a permanent governmental structure." The process of exerting control and building state institutions meant "a new outlook opened before Ibn Saud. And through his strong personality and his understanding of the essential currents of contemporary history a new Arabia was born." Saud had used the forces of Wahhabism to create a new nation-state, but his challenge was now "to divert the religious enthusiasm of his followers into modern social activity. Arabia has not only to organize, but also to enter the complex civilization which, having originated about two hundred years ago in Western Europe, is now on the way to becoming universal since the World War." In short, according to Kohn, Saud was in the process of making Wahhabism "flexible and adaptable to modern conditions" through his own strong personality, via technological advances, and by creating new economic opportunities. Saud was thus well on his way to becoming "the undisputed lord over a strongly organized, united and cautiously but firmly modernized Arabia."[11]

Kohn was not the only specialist to write so favorably of Ibn Saud's prospects in Saudi Arabia, as others sang his praises even just within the pages of *Foreign Affairs*. Joel Carmichael, whose primary focus was Islam and the Soviet Union, published "Prince of Arabs" in July 1942. Carmichael described Ibn Saud as "growing up into a gigantic, swaggering buck with inexhaustible physical vitality, an indomitable will to power, and a determination to restore the ancient luster of his family and take the rule of the land into his own hands." As an adult, Ibn Saud "was a full-blooded giant, a combination of uncompromising ruthlessness and capricious generosity which made him the idol of those who clung to him." In asserting his control over the Bedouin tribes, Ibn Saud "had brought about a qualitative change in desert affairs," and "in spite of its apparent atavism" his "religious revival was the beginning of a westernizing movement." In an era in which "any Power of world stature" should be "interested in the welling-up of the Arab national spirit," it was important to recognize that "in the waste expanses of the Arabic-speaking world Abdul Aziz Ibn Saud, despite his country's remoteness, looms up as a tower of strength."[12]

These interpretations of Ibn Saud, Mustafa Kemal, and Reza Shah suggest two key points beyond what they tell us about specialists' understandings of Middle Eastern nationalism between World War I and World War II. The first concerns what these observers saw as the evident tension between sacred and secular politics in the Middle East and enduring concerns about Islam. Kohn implied nationalism and religion were incompatible; the achievement of modern nationalism in the Middle East—an admirable objective in his mind—required the people of the area to move beyond religion. He thus tried to demonstrate that religion was merely a tool that Ibn Saud used to rise to power: "Ibn Saud is a pious Muslim, but he is far from being narrow-minded and fanatic, and the dominant idea of his life never was Pan-Islamism; from the beginning he has been an ardent Arab nationalist." Under Ibn Saud's guidance, Wahhabism was "becoming flexible and adaptable to modern conditions. Ibn Saud teaches his Wahhabis moderation alike towards non-Wahhabi Muslims and non-Muslims," with the implication being that Wahhabism, and Islam more broadly, would eventually be weakened as an institution. Speaking at a conference more than fifteen years later, Kohn made explicit a point he left implicit in the mid-1930s: "Nationalism is primarily . . . a secular movement. Nationalism . . . can only come in a secularized society."

Notably, Kohn no longer referred to Saudi Arabia as a modern nation in 1952, reserving that designation for only Israel and Turkey among Middle Eastern states.[13]

Second, by emphasizing Ibn Saud as the focal point of Saudi nationalism, Kohn and others contributed to an emerging tendency to highlight particular individuals as a way of understanding specific cultural, political, or social forces in the Middle East. Observers saw individual leaders like the mufti of Jerusalem, Mustafa Kemal, Reza Shah, and Ibn Saud as exercising inordinate control in Middle Eastern affairs, able to inspire the people who followed them to tremendous achievements, be they good or bad. That tendency to focus on specific individuals and their ability to connect with the Middle Eastern masses would become even more powerful in the 1950s and 1960s, and in many ways endures to the present.

At the same time that some specialists were focusing on the role of individual leaders in building nationalist movements in specific countries, others were beginning to interpret Middle Eastern nationalism as a broader region-wide drive toward "Arab unity." Rather than seeing individual leaders as the wellspring of such movements, these analysts instead looked to the development within intellectual circles of theories of regional nationalism overlaid by rising mass discontent with foreign rule and a shared sense of cultural identity. Not all of the analysts agreed on whether this drive toward Arab unity was good or bad, or on its prospects for success. Nonetheless, such an interpretation built upon the vague understandings of Middle Eastern nationalism that were evident in the work of the Inquiry and the King-Crane Commission.

The scholar and archaeologist David Hogarth was one of the first to articulate this regional approach to understanding Middle Eastern nationalism. For Hogarth, language rather than land or religion formed the centerpiece of Arab identity: "all societies whose mother tongue is Arabic, whatever they be racially, are more or less conscious of integral community with an Arab world." This broad Arab community might be divided between its "Asiatic and African" components, with the former feeling a much deeper sense of community than the latter. The heart of this Asiatic Arab community was in Syria. It was there, according to Hogarth, that "the idea of Arab nationality was first born within the memory of a living generation chiefly through the influence of returned emigrants, which was enforced by that of such home-keeping Syrians as had attended, or been affected by, the Western schools established and maintained in the East by America and the Latin peoples. All of these Syrians had imbibed and assimilated ideas of self-determination, even before President Wilson gave them expression and currency." The new "movement for 'Arabia-for-the-Arabs' . . . found sympathizers in all denominations. Though inspired and supported to some extent by Moslems who resented the eclipse of the race that had founded and led the Faith, and who used its sacred tongue, the movement was not at the first, and is not today, essentially Islamic, much less pan-Islamic." This intellectual movement came to resonate with the Syrian and Arab masses as the French brutally exerted their authority as they implemented their League of Nations mandate following World War I.[14]

Yet Hogarth did not believe Arab unity could actually be achieved in a political sense even within a single country such as Syria. For it to succeed would require that the people of Syria and the rest of the Middle East overcome their local identities, which Hogarth thought impossible. "Syrian towns," Hogarth contended, "feel little sense of community even with one another; and if anyone could get self-government, it would care little what might become of the rest." Local identification with town, district, or, more prominently, tribe, was simply too strong to be overcome by a larger national or Arab identity. Hogarth acknowledged that the situation looked different in "peninsular Arabia," where "a remarkable Arab [Ibn Saud]" enlisted a powerful and motivated fighting force to unify the area. But he suggested that these accomplishments were only temporary, that "these assets contribute better to the making of Arab Empire than to its retention." Wahhabi "zealotry" could not "be sustained at heat," and as things stood the empire itself depended "on the character and energy of one man who is little likely to be succeeded by any one at all his equal." Moreover, Wahhabism had little appeal outside of the peninsula and could not be used as an ideology of expansion without fundamentally altering the basic nature of a broader Arab identity. Thus, while one might "trace here and there and now and again some sign of common policy and action," there was "no sign that now or in the future . . . Moslems will, or can, unite forces in a common effort to prevail again as their first Caliphs prevailed."[15]

While Hogarth identified the sources of the likely failure of Arab unity in the overwhelming power of local identities, George Antonius articulated a more optimistic and more widely accepted interpretation of the rise of Arab nationalism as a combination of elite intellectual and mass politics that might succeed if only the great powers would let it. Published in 1938, The Arab Awakening: the Story of the Arab National Movement went through three printings its first year, was reissued in 1946, and then went through several subsequent reprintings. Post–World War II State Department officials involved in Middle Eastern affairs were well acquainted with the book, as were their colleagues in Europe. Indeed, the British Foreign Office ordered all consuls in the Middle East to read it. Halford Hoskins, former Director of the Middle East Institute and a Near East specialist working for the Library of Congress, remarked in his own 1954 work that Antonius's book was "in a class by itself." Similarly, the young scholar and future policymaker William Polk noted that The Arab Awakening was "one of the best books on the nationalist period." Hoskins and Polk, as well as other commentators on Middle Eastern affairs, relied heavily on Antonius's interpretation of the rise of Arab nationalism in their own assessments of the region in the early postwar years. Thus, The Arab Awakening played a crucial role in defining the basic boundaries within which Americans imagined Middle Eastern nationalism in the early decades after World War II.[16]

George Antonius drew on years of personal experience of living and working in the Middle East when he wrote The Arab Awakening. Born in 1891, Antonius was of Lebanese descent and grew up in Alexandria, Egypt. There, he attended an English school before heading off to study at King's College, Cambridge. Antonius worked with the British in the administration of their League of Nations mandate in Palestine from 1921 to 1930 before joining Charles Crane's new Institute of Current World Affairs in New York City as a Middle East specialist. Antonius published The Arab Awakening, his only work, while a fellow of the institute and dedicated it to his patron, Crane. George Antonius died just four years later at the age of fifty-one.[17]

There are few records that reveal why the book gained such a following among officials, businesspersons, journalists, and a new generation of U.S. Middle East specialists after the war, but it is possible to offer some speculative explanations. One reason had to be the pride of place Antonius gave to nineteenth-century American missionary and educational experiences in the Middle East and his apparent affirmation of Western European and U.S. ideological and intellectual superiority. According to Antonius, Arab nationalism would not have developed to any significant degree if Western European and, more importantly, American missionaries had not imported Western ideas to the region. Antonius believed the lessons the Arabic-speaking American missionaries and their French counterparts taught, as well as some of the basic logistical and technological changes they helped implement, proved critical to what he called the "intellectual effervescence" from which he argued Arab nationalism emerged. Learning about the ideals of the American and French revolutions and about the development of modern nation-states, Antonius contended, planted the ideological seed out of which future nationalist movements in the region sprouted. Moreover, the missionary schools emerged just a few years after a series of reforms undertaken by Muhammad Ali in Egypt and Syria had established government-sponsored schools to educate at least a few hundred students every year. These reforms, combined with the installation of Arabic-language printing presses, which existed only in Cairo and Constantinople before the 1830s, further expanded opportunities for education and allowed for the transmission to the masses of the burgeoning nationalist movement.[18]

Antonius's emphasis on language, rather than Islam, as the strongest force for unity in the region was the second possible reason The Arab Awakening did so well. Antonius argued that the combination of the new state schools, printing presses, and American missionary schools contributed to the rebirth of Arabic itself, which he claimed had "degenerated" during almost four centuries of Ottoman control of the area. During the last few decades of the nineteenth century and the first decade of the twentieth, students coming out of the missionary schools formed literary societies that relied on the Arabic language as the means through which Arabs and other Muslims could recapture both figuratively and literally—their past glory. The process of linguistic rebirth, Antonius believed, gained momentum following the Young Turk Revolution in 1908 and continued to build right up to World War I. Although Antonius identified ethnicity and shared cultural and social traditions such as religion as important components of Arab nationalism, language emerged as the rallying point of opposition to Ottoman rule and as the dominant feature of a nascent Arab nationalism. Antonius therefore fundamentally challenged the notion that Islam was the dominant force in the Middle East and the idea that Arab nationalism was really just a guise for a religiously based nationalism. Such an interpretation, combined with the emphasis on American missionary contributions, spoke directly to Americans' sense of sacred and secular mission in the region.[19]

Finally, by presenting the Arab nationalist cause as mass support of a movement led by educated, intelligent, and rational men with limited objectives, Antonius challenged stereotypes of Arabs as militant, emotional, and irrational that supporters of Arab independence might have found disagreeable. He introduced members of the Hashemite family in the Hijaz (Husain, Faisal, and 'Abdullah) as the chosen leaders of a unified Arab nationalist movement and showed them dealing with British policymakers to secure the postwar independence of a single unified Arab state. The Arab Revolt of 1916 appeared in his presentation as the outcome of a groundswell of mass Arab resistance, undertaken with British support, to longstanding Turkish oppression. Similarly, Faisal was a leader who personified the Arab cause, heroically led it throughout the war, and stood ready at the conclusion of hostilities to open a new era in Arab history. Antonius noted, "The War was won, and for the first time in its history the Arab national movement stood abreast of its destiny . . . The area of the Turk's defeat was precisely the area of Arab aspirations, and its frontiers coincided exactly with those defined by the Sharif Husain as the natural limits of Arab independence." Antonius's interpretation of the rise of Arab nationalism thus appeared as the direct counterpoint to the prominent belief that Islam was a totalitarian religion.[20]

Antonius furthered his argument by suggesting that responsibility for the failure of the movement rested on British and French authorities, rather than with the Arabs. The British interfered with destiny and delayed the achievement of Arab aspirations by pledging pieces of the same land to multiple parties in the 1915 Husain-McMahon correspondences, the 1916 Sykes-Picot Agreement, and the 1917 Balfour Declaration. In exchange for accepting the implementation of a mandatory system throughout much of the Middle East, Arab nationalists received British and French promises of independence at some future date. Antonius contended that the independence Arabs received was very different from what they believed they had been promised. The Arabs had been seeking a unified Arab state for several decades, but instead received delayed independence for several separate states. Increasing violence in the 1920s and 1930s, Antonius claimed, was therefore an understandable, albeit admittedly unfortunate, attempt by Arabs to bring attention to the "injustices" and the "moral violence done to them" during several decades of European involvement in the region and by increasing Jewish immigration to Palestine. Antonius argued forcefully against the postwar settlements: "It is beyond all doubt certain that the post-War handling of the Arab question led directly and inevitably to explosions which would not have happened but for that so-called settlement. Thousands of lives, millions of treasure and incalculable moral suffering and damage would have been avoided."[21]

Antonius possessed keen analytical skills and was a gifted writer, but The Arab Awakening was and remains flawed in numerous ways. The balance Antonius attempted to strike between historical analysis and political advocacy was particularly discomforting for later readers. He did a marvelous job, in recounting a century of Arab history, of tying together disparate themes, events, and peoples in an engaging manner. In doing so, however, Antonius intended to convince British, American, and European elites and policymakers that a unified Arab nationalist movement was "destined" to succeed, and that the only reason it had not done so yet was because outside powers continually thwarted it. To that end, he exaggerated both the extent of Ottoman oppression and the strength and unity of the Arab nationalist movement. The rule of Abdul Hamid in the late nineteenth century was, for example, a period "which, for its tyranny and corrupt abuse of power, has scarcely been surpassed in history." Similarly, Antonius proclaimed the 1916 executions of twenty-two Arab political prisoners by Ottoman rulers in Syria to be a "holocaust," a choice of words that would have been indefensible had he written the book in the mid-1940s rather than the mid-1930s. With the exception of Egypt, a country Antonius largely exempted from his analysis because he believed it had a longer nationalist history, he never entertained the idea that different participants in the Arab nationalist movements might have had more parochial or selfish interests in mind when they issued the nationalist call. According to Antonius, the Hashemites were just as concerned with independence in Iraq or Syria as they were with independence in the Hijaz. As William Cleveland has pointed out, Antonius therefore considered the post–World War I settlements a threat to both the "independence" and the "unity" of the region.[22]

In accepting Antonius's interpretation of "the Arab awakening," contemporary specialists overlooked a number of issues that more recent scholarship has tried to address. Primary among these was Antonius's emphasis on the early Lebanese and Syrian literary societies and their impact on later nationalists. Albert Hourani made clear in his 1981 retrospective on The Arab Awakening that there were in fact very few connections between the two groups. That The Arab Awakening generally lacked the typical scholarly conventions of footnotes and a bibliography only compounded the reader's unease, as many of Antonius's claims were unverifiable. His close contact with and access to a number of the actors about whom he wrote, on both the Arab and British sides, further forestalled those who might have wanted to challenge his interpretation of the rise of the Arab nationalist movement.[23]

Yet, despite these many problems, specialists in the 1940s and early 1950s accepted Antonius's interpretation of the rise of Arab nationalism. They also emphasized and modified certain themes to fit post–World War II regional and international contexts that made Middle Eastern nationalism even more politically charged than it was when Antonius wrote *The Arab Awakening*. Postwar specialists believed, for example, that historically Middle Eastern nationalist movements had been isolated and had thus remained focused only on ridding themselves of foreign involvement; now, however, the nationalists might see themselves as part of a much broader worldwide anticolonial movement. As early as 1945, members of the Coordinating Committee of the Department of State argued in a paper originally drafted by department Middle East specialists that Americans as a whole must realize "that these [Middle Eastern] countries are jealous of their political independence" and "are cynical regarding western imperialism." Analysts in the CIA elaborated on the same point three years later. In a report titled, "The Break-Up of the Colonial Empires and Its Implications for US Security," they acknowledged that nationalist movements and the process of decolonization in Africa, Asia, and the Middle East were playing increasingly larger and more powerful roles in shaping local, regional, and international politics. The report argued that "intensely nationalistic" peoples in the Middle East and Asia "tend to unite in opposition to the Western European powers on the colonial issue and to US economic dominance." This notion of a shared colonial experience led to a sense of common purpose. "As a result," the report stated, "there has been a tendency toward the formation in the UN and affiliated bodies of a so-called 'colonial bloc,' whose members have already brought colonial disputes into the UN and will likely take the lead in attempting in this manner to hasten the liberation of further colonial areas." Post–World War II members of the informal network of specialists clearly believed Middle Eastern nationalists were key players in this new, global anticolonial movement.[24]

Postwar specialists modified Antonius's interpretation in a second way by focusing on extensive cultural, economic, and social changes taking place in the region and their impact on regional nationalism. Few specialists seemed better qualified than Bayard Dodge to articulate this theme. Dodge came from a missionary background and first visited the Middle East with his twin brother Cleveland in 1910, following their graduation from Princeton. He returned to the region during World War I to learn Arabic and to aid in postwar relief efforts. In addition, Dodge's great grandfather had been an original member of the Board of Trustees of the American University of Beirut, one of the oldest and best known American missionary schools in the Middle East. In fact, Bayard Dodge had himself served as president of the institution from 1922 to 1948. Dodge noted in a 1949 meeting of a Council on Foreign Relations study group on the Muslim World that "modernism has wrenched the people from prejudice and stagnation to radicalism and initiative. The change has been too rapid to be healthy." When asked to elaborate on this point later in the meeting, Dodge "replied that the Pan-Arab movement [described by Antonius] had been such a total failure that it had resulted in bitter disillusionment." Hence, according to Dodge's analysis, the "Arab awakening" had been unable to address successfully many of the changes taking place throughout the region and to achieve independence, so people were pushing for an even more powerful nationalist movement.[25]

Americans more generally gave even more attention than did Antonius to the conflict over Palestine as a driving force behind Middle Eastern nationalism in the postwar period. Many Americans—Middle East specialists or not—were keenly aware of the ever-increasing tensions that existed between Arabs and the growing number of Jewish immigrants to Palestine. The events of World War II in Europe and the early postwar Jewish drive to create a national homeland in Palestine only heightened that awareness. According to most specialists, the conflict over Palestine helped define not only Middle Eastern nationalism, but also the broader regional political landscape, as the declaration of an independent Israeli state and the subsequent war between Israel and its Arab neighbors illustrated. That war created approximately seven hundred thousand Palestinian refugees, produced greater Arab concern about an expansionist Israeli state, and threw into question control over some of the area's vital water resources. By the late 1940s, the conflict over Palestine assumed a key role in defining Middle Eastern nationalism in ways that Antonius, despite his many gifts as a historian, writer, and political advocate, could not have foreseen in the late 1930s.[26]

Finally, postwar Middle East specialists highlighted what they perceived as a long history of favorable U.S. dealings—of which the American missionary experience Antonius emphasized was only a part—with the region, its peoples, and their nationalist movements. Loy Henderson, head of the State Department's Office of Near Eastern Affairs in 1945, noted that there had been a "traditional American attitude of benevolence toward Arab nationalism." He continued, "The American Government has traditionally viewed with sympathy the attempts of the Arab people to reestablish their independence and play a more prominent role in world affairs." Others, most notably William Polk and anthropologist Hans Kohn, stressed the impact that Woodrow Wilson's Fourteen Points and the idea of self-determination had on Middle Eastern nationalists. Similarly, E. A. Speiser's early postwar assessment of U.S. involvement in the Near East emphasized that although

U.S. policies did not always indicate it, the United States was "genuinely committed to the goal" of Arab independence. In making this argument about a history of American encouragement of Arab nationalism, Henderson, Polk, Kohn, and Speiser reflected the extent to which observers and commentators had internalized and expanded George Antonius's argument about traditional U.S. support of Middle Eastern nationalist movements.[27]

In the years immediately following World War II, members of the informal transnational network of Middle East specialists from across the different professions drew on the influential ideas of George Antonius to imagine Middle Eastern nationalism as one significant by-product of Western European and U.S. involvement in the region since the mid-nineteenth century. They identified nationalism as a growing force based in both elite intellectual politics and mass politics, but they did not perceive it as a threat. On the contrary, American observers, believing Arab nationalism had been nurtured by the spread of liberal democratic ideals, imagined it in positive terms. Antonius's emphasis on language, as opposed to a religion with which many Americans were generally uncomfortable, as a unifying nationalist force encouraged specialists' comfort with Arab nationalism in this period. In short, early post–World War II specialists saw U.S. support for the emergence of secular nationalist movements in the Middle East as bearing the potential to bring about the achievement of America's sacred and secular mission in the region.

The Mass Politics of "Old Mossy" and "Hitler on the Nile"

Though a modified form of Antonius's rendering of Middle Eastern nationalism was the more widely accepted interpretation immediately after World War II, many network participants would combine it with their focus on charismatic leaders and a growing emphasis on mass-based politics to arrive at an interpretation that posited Middle Eastern nationalism as a less benign force during the 1950s and 1960s. The emergence of two nationalist leaders caused specialists to return to the earlier emphasis on the role of charismatic individuals who possessed the ability to build powerful movements around themselves. The first challenge came from Mohammad Mossadegh in Iran, whose nationalist policies appeared to threaten U.S. and British interests there and led most observers to begin to question whether Middle Eastern nationalism was a positive force. Regional specialists and high-level policymakers alike arrived at paternalistic, dismissive imaginings of Mossadegh that helped set the stage for his removal in a CIA-sponsored coup in August 1953. The second challenge was issued by Egyptian leader Gamal 'Abd al-Nasser, whom many observers initially viewed quite favorably before they developed a more paternalistic outlook that paralleled the approach to Mossadegh and relied on a similarly dismissive discourse to delegitimize the younger, military-trained leader. Between 1955 and 1958, moreover, policymakers assumed an increasingly aggressive stance and sought to isolate Nasser and Egypt to prevent the spread of what they perceived to be a radical nationalist ideology that appealed to the Arab masses. Mossadegh and Nasser forced both policymakers and area specialists to confront a nationalism they understood only vaguely. What resulted was a new way of imagining Middle Eastern nationalism that portrayed it in much more radical and potentially dangerous terms than had previously been the case. In addition, this new interpretation of Middle Eastern nationalism rejected, at least temporarily, the secular, authoritarian, nationalist model that specialists previously believed had worked so well under Mustafa Kemal in Turkey.

Because Mossadegh was Iranian, he did not automatically fit into Antonius's interpretation of the origins of Arab nationalism, but the broader context of the Cold War, decolonization, and regional change was the same, so the network's modifications to Antonius's interpretation still applied. Mossadegh was the central figure in a protracted crisis that pitted a constellation of international actors against several quite diverse Iranian participants from 1951 to 1953. On one loosely aligned side were the British government, international oil concerns, and various members of the U.S. government. On the Iranian side were a variety of nationalists, religious fundamentalists, and communist sympathizers. In between sat the ruling monarch, Muhammad Reza Shah Pahlavi, who rose to power during World War II when British and Soviet occupying forces ousted his father, Reza Khan, due to fears that he was too close to Nazi Germany. The shah, seeking to maintain his rule and the dynasty his father established, sided more with the British and the Americans than he did with the other Iranian participants in the conflict. In spring 1951, the Iranian parliament (the Majlis) elected Mossadegh prime minister with the explicit mandate to implement a resolution nationalizing the British-owned Anglo-Iranian Oil Company (AIOC) and to promote Iranian nationalism and independence. The weak shah saw few options if he wanted to retain any of his power and signed the nationalization bill into law. The British were already seeking to lessen internal Iranian opposition to their presence in the country by negotiating a new oil agreement, and they reacted angrily to the act. Also concerned about the precedent that acceptance of national-ization would set for other British interests in the region, they immediately began looking for ways to undermine Mossadegh. Truman administration officials certainly did not agree with the seizure of AIOC and did not possess particularly favorable views of Mossadegh. Nonetheless, they responded in a manner they believed demonstrated American support for Middle Eastern nationalism by being more sympathetic to Iranian calls for greater control over and more profits from internal oil production. Indeed, the United States explicitly rejected British calls to overthrow Mossadegh and instead pushed the British to negotiate a more equitable oil agreement along the lines of a fifty-fifty profit sharing agreement that was becoming an industry standard at the time. That policy would be overturned within months of Eisenhower's arrival at the White House.[28]

Mossadegh was approximately seventy years old in the early 1950s and had extensive experience in Iranian nationalist politics. He came from the estab-lished Persian elite and was Western educated, although not by the Ameri-can missionaries of whom Antonius wrote. He had been active in Iranian politics since at least 1906 and was one of the country's most vocal nation-alists. He worked hard to open up the political system as well, which fur-ther endeared him to the general population. Mossadegh also possessed an extraordinary charisma equaled only by his sense of dramatic flair, both of which he used on his domestic constituency and foreign diplomats alike. He could be both charming and dismissive, or appear completely calm at one moment and driven by emotion the next. He was unafraid to change politi-cal courses rapidly, even at the cost of embarrassing foreign leaders, if doing so promoted the nationalist cause or enhanced his legitimacy in the eyes of his fellow Iranians. None of these traits, however, enabled him to deal with an economic crisis that resulted from a British blockade on Iranian oil, be-hind which the close-knit international oil industry united to great effect. He also faced an increasingly powerful Iranian communist party (the Tudeh, or "masses" party). As Mossadegh's internal support weakened in 1953, the newly elected Eisenhower administration feared that rising communist influ-ence would lead to greater instability and the prospect of a larger Soviet role in Iran. Eisenhower reversed his predecessor's position and began looking for alternative ways of dealing with Mossadegh. The end finally came in Au-gust 1953, when the CIA implemented Operation TPAJAX to overthrow Mos-sadegh and return power to the shah, who had temporarily fled the country.

Mossadegh was imprisoned for three years before being placed under house arrest until his death in 1967.[29]

Contemporary and postcrisis assessments of Mossadegh by policymakers, journalists, and academics reflected a paternalistic attitude characteristic of their larger outlook on Middle Eastern nationalism. Most American and British officials found "Old Mossy" (as they referred to him) to be a formidable political foe, but they also believed he was ignorant of the modern world and emotionally unstable. George McGhee was the assistant secretary of state for Near Eastern affairs and represented the Truman administration in negotiations with Mossadegh in 1951. In his memoirs, McGhee referred to Mossadegh as "an intelligent man and essentially a sincere Iranian patriot," but he was simply unable "to understand the facts of life about the international oil business," regardless of how much McGhee tried to instruct him in such matters. Similarly, the editors of the Middle East Journal, in their postcrisis commentary, painted a picture of an inept leader who little understood the game of power politics. "Evidently," they argued, "Mossadegh did not understand the 'facts of life' in regard to the organization of the oil industry and his 'playing with fire' with the Communists failed to 'smoke out' any assistance or sympathy from the United States." Such frequent references to "the facts of life" suggested that analysts and policymakers did not consider Mossadegh to be politically mature, and that it was the responsibility of American negotiators to educate him.[30]

These paternalistic views were not limited to assessments of Mossadegh's supposed political ineptitude, as they influenced numerous other perceptions of the Iranian leader as well. As historian Mary Ann Heiss has demonstrated, U.S. and British officials portrayed Mossadegh as eccentric, feminine, weak, childish, and immature. The statements of Loy Henderson—U.S. ambassador in Iran from September 1951 to December 1954 and one of several Americans who negotiated with Mossadegh—certainly support Heiss's assessment. Following a July 1952 meeting with Mossadegh, Henderson found it discouraging that the United States appeared to have to rely on someone "so lacking in stability and clearly dominated by emotions" to resist communist advances in Iran. Henderson also referred to Mossadegh as "someone not quite sane" who had to be "humored rather than reasoned with." Moreover, because of Mossadegh's "silly exaggerations and extravagances it seemed almost useless to talk further."[31]

In addition to viewing Mossadegh through a paternalist lens, Americans grew increasingly concerned about his wide appeal among Iranians and the extremism and instability they believed his brand of popular nationalism and mass politics fomented. In October 1951, Loy Henderson in some ways contradicted his later assessment of Mossadegh as "not quite sane" and unable to be "reasoned with" by identifying him as a "shrewd" political leader who understood and manipulated the "emotions and character" of the Iranian people. Just as significantly, Mossadegh seemed driven by an "almost megalomaniac desire to act as champion of people in struggle for 'independence.'" Middle East specialists on the National Security Council also worried about the instability they believed Mossadegh's nationalist movement generated. He rode to power, they argued, on a "political upheaval" that "heightened popular desire for promised economic and social betterment and . . . increased social unrest." Halford Hoskins offered a scathing review of Mossadegh and his type of nationalism in 1954, labeling Mossadegh a "rabid nationalist" who ruled "practically with dictatorial authority" and pushed "his program of nationalism to extreme limits." By the end of the crisis, Mossadegh "had become a prisoner of the intense nationalism that he himself had done so much to create. Once committed to a fanatical course, he was unable to return."[32]

The popular press also reflected this more negative way of imagining Mossadegh's brand of Middle Eastern nationalism. *Time* magazine led the way, naming Mossadegh its "Man of the Year" for 1951. Writing in the midst of the crisis, the magazine's editors initially characterized Mossadegh in fairly balanced terms as "in some ways the most noteworthy figure on the world scene. Not that he was the best or the worst or the strongest, but because his rapid advance from obscurity was attended by the greatest stir." What made Mossadegh even more significant, at least to the editors of *Time*, and probably to policymakers and other regional specialists as well, was that this seemingly incomprehensible old man somehow represented something much larger than himself or Iran. As the authors continued to justify their choice, they grew increasingly negative, stating that "the stir was not only on the surface of events: in his strange way, this strange old man represented one of the most profound problems of his time. Around this dizzy old wizard swirled a crisis of human destiny." *Time* was "sad to relate" the accompanying story, which presented an image of a childish, irrational, and even crazy leader who was as likely to appear in public in his pajamas as he was to faint at the conclusion of an important speech. Furthermore, Mossadegh could not be trusted to understand the drastic consequences "his grotesque antics" might have for the Middle East and the wider world. Other important publications like the *New York Times*, the *Washington Post*, *Newsweek*, and the *Wall Street Journal* joined *Time* in portraying Mossadegh in this way.[33]

Thus, while members of the informal transnational network of specialists professed tolerance of early postwar manifestations of nationalism in the Middle East, their responses to Mossadegh revealed a much less accommodating attitude. Portrayals of Mossadegh as an eccentric and inept leader who relied on emotional mass support indicated movement away from George Antonius's view that Middle Eastern nationalism was benign and constructive. Instead, drawing on their experience with Mossadegh, Americans began to imagine Middle Eastern nationalism as a force they had to resist, especially given their Cold War fears of possible Soviet advances in the region and the belief that unchecked developments in Africa, Asia, and the Middle East could have a dramatic impact on the great powers themselves.

As Mossadegh's challenge was receding into memory, a new nationalist leader with much wider regional appeal appeared in the figure of Egypt's Gamal 'Abd al-Nasser. At thirty-four, Nasser was one of the senior members of the revolutionary Free Officers Movement that emerged from the military to overthrow King Faruq in July 1952. Nasser and his peers in the Revolutionary Command Council (the title assumed by the Free Officers after the revolution) pledged to solve all of Egypt's problems when they assumed power. They hoped to rid Egypt of foreign domination, combat the Jewish presence in Palestine, provide political stability, reduce rampant poverty, and promote economic development. In *Egypt's Liberation: The Philosophy of the Revolution*, an account of the Free Officers' rise to power that Nasser wrote with the assistance of his close friend, confidant, and soon-to-be editor of the semiofficial *al-Ahram* weekly, Mohamed Heikal, Nasser revealed that he and his colleagues lacked a clear sense of how to address Egypt's problems. Instead, the inexperienced group of new leaders was guided only by a set of vague ideas and principles. First, and most obviously, each participant in the Movement felt a strong sense of Egyptian nationalism that manifested itself in a keen desire both to move beyond the arbitrary rule that characterized King Faruq's reign and to remove any remnants of colonialism, particularly as exemplified by continued British control of a military base at Suez. Second, and closely related, Nasser and his colleagues quickly became aware of and helped to stoke broader regionwide anticolonial and Arab nationalist sentiments. This notion of a broader movement for Arab unity meshed nicely with Nasser's own beliefs that the only way to defeat Israel would be through united Arab action and that most Arabs faced similar economic, political, and social problems that were in part a product of a shared colonial experience. Pan-Arab unity would allow all Arabs to attack those problems in unison. Third, Nasser believed that any nation that hoped to make its way through the postwar world had to modernize. That meant Nasser wanted to reap the benefits of recent scientific and technological advancements, which might provide the key to development in Egypt. The emphasis on modern technology further implied that Nasser needed and wanted updated weaponry for the continuing conflict with Israel.[34]

Nasser's efforts to promote economic, political, and social modernization through these methods presented the young leader with two serious political problems. Egypt had limited financial resources with which to pay for new technology, which meant Nasser needed foreign aid to advance his agenda. The reliance on foreign aid presented a direct conflict with the other stated goals of Arab and Egyptian nationalism, especially the anticolonial desire to limit foreign intervention in the Middle East. Furthermore, the combination of the Revolutionary Command Council's ideas — Egyptian nationalism, pan-Arab nationalism, and modernization — led Nasser to promote a secular view of Egyptian society. That evolving vision of a modern, secular Egypt battled not only with the conservative views of the Muslim Brotherhood in Egypt, but also with traditional monarchies in power in Iraq, Jordan, and Saudi Arabia.

Despite these obvious contradictions and problems in Nasser's evolving vision, most observers initially held him in high regard. Government specialists responded particularly favorably to the youthful and inexperienced Nasser. They believed he confronted similar internal pressures and was driven by the same concerns that motivated Mossadegh in Iran, but they initially saw in Nasser a responsible individual, which they did not see in the Iranian leader. They hoped Nasser might lead Egypt successfully through the difficult transition from colony to independent state to developing nation. G. Lewis Jones, counselor in the U.S. embassy in Egypt in 1955, remarked that "however wrong or right his ideas may be, Nasser displayed . . . sincerity, honest devotion to his principles and a sense of leadership which must be rare among heads of state in [the Middle East]." Jones's peers shared this view. Parker Hart, one of the State Department's first Arabists, its director of the Office of Near Eastern Affairs, and ultimately Jones's successor as counselor of the U.S. embassy in Egypt, commented during a March 1955 trip to Egypt that "my appraisal of Nasser personally rises with each meeting . . . [He is] basically the best Egypt has had in our lifetime." A few days after returning to the United States, Hart reaffirmed his earlier estimation. He could "not quarrel with a good assessment of Nasser . . . I would agree that he is a strong and intelligent man of a caliber not readily found in the area. He is indeed about the best we could hope for in Egypt at the present moment." Even Raymond Hare, U.S. ambassador to Egypt as U.S.-Egyptian relations began to spiral downward in 1956, recalled years later that he originally considered Nasser a "young Egyptian patriot . . . of more than usual vigor of thought and also sensitivity." [35]

Journalists and other observers shared these favorable early impressions of Nasser. New York Times correspondent Robert Doty followed Nasser's career for several years after the 1952 revolution. Doty described Nasser in 1954 as "a strong-willed, selfless and icily intelligent man who in a little more than two years has grown from a conspirator into a statesman commanding the respect of veteran Western politicians and diplomats." That neither Nasser nor any of his close advisors had been involved in any "financial or personal" scandals during their first two years in power "set him apart from the average Middle East political leader." Assessing Nasser's impact on Egypt in mid-1954, the academic and future appointee as ambassador to Egypt Richard Nolte concluded that "the revolutionary regime had made an excellent start toward its objective of making Egypt strong, free and respectable: a beginning all the brighter by contrast with the moral and economic bankruptcy of the preceding era." Even in late 1954, as the Egyptian revolution seemed momentarily to run out of steam and to succumb to political infighting, former president of the American University in Cairo and later President Kennedy's appointment as U.S. ambassador to Egypt, John Badeau, wrote that Nasser's leadership remained "the best hope for Egypt's future." [36]

Within just a few years of Nasser's 1952 ascent to power in Egypt, he developed a vision of his country's and the broader Middle East's role in international affairs that differed dramatically with how specialists and policymakers viewed the world. An arms deal Nasser signed with Czechoslovakia (serving as a Soviet proxy) in 1955 first generated concern among policymakers and indicated that U.S.-Egyptian relations were headed for difficult times. Earlier that year, Israel retaliated for numerous small-scale raids by Egyptians and Palestinians on Israeli territory and citizens by launching an attack on Gaza. Over thirty Egyptian soldiers died in the Israeli raid, which emphasized to Nasser that his primary enemy was Israel, not the Soviet Union. American Cold War concerns therefore carried little weight with Nasser over the next several years. The raid also demonstrated to Nasser Israel's obvious superiority in military weaponry and training over Arabs. In short, Nasser believed he needed help fast. With the United States unwilling to deal, Nasser turned to the Soviet Union. Historian Steven Spiegel noted that the conclusion of the 1955 arms agreement forced U.S. policymakers to recognize that some leaders "might *choose* to deal with the Kremlin." The deal with the Soviets, however, left most U.S. observers and policymakers believing Nasser had little concern for Western interests and would willingly jeopardize them to pursue his own. President Eisenhower recalled in his memoirs that he believed at the time the arms deal "greatly increased danger of a major outbreak of violence in the area." Nasser's recognition of the People's Republic of China in May 1956 appeared to further confirm these concerns that he had turned to the East.[37]

Nasser's turn to the Soviets also suggested that he and his country were undergoing a significant ideological and political change, which deeply concerned policymakers. His pursuit of a neutralist course in the Cold War worried those policymakers who viewed the world according to stark Manichaean dichotomies. In the eyes of moralistic policymakers like Secretary of State John Foster Dulles, neutralist leaders were but one step away from Soviet domination, and their policies served as an indication of newly independent peoples' ignorance, immaturity, and weakness in the international political arena. Dulles gave voice in June 1956 to prevalent feelings about neutralism and nonalignment, which he argued had "increasingly become an obsolete conception and, except under very exceptional circumstances, it is an immoral and short-sighted conception."[38]

Considering Cold War neutralism from a Middle Eastern or Arab perspective, however, reveals that nonalignment was really the logical outcome of the more general anticolonial nationalism so prevalent in Africa, Asia, Latin America, and the Middle East in the 1950s. Formerly colonized peoples had experienced the worst a Western European–dominated international economy and political system had to offer, and they were not voluntarily going to place themselves under the domination of either the Soviet Union or United States and its allies, many of which had been former colonial masters. Neutralism was therefore a rejection by newly independent peoples of both the old colonial world order and the new Cold War world order. It was a statement of their desire to control their own destinies. In what became a popular refrain throughout the Middle East, Nasser made the point to John Foster Dulles during the secretary's 1953 trip to the region: "I must tell you in all frankness that I can't see myself waking up one morning to find that the Soviet Union is our enemy. We don't know them. They are thousands of miles away from us. We have never had any quarrel with them. I would become the laughing-stock of my people if I told them they now had an entirely new enemy, many thousands of miles away, and that they must forget about the British enemy occupying their territory. Nobody would take me seriously if I forgot about the British." Nasser did not become part of a wider and more clearly defined neutralist movement until he attended the Bandung Conference of Asian and African states in April 1955, but his statement to Dulles nonetheless reflected his vision of an alternative world order. Nasser tried to convey his sense that nonalignment was a creative movement and sought to confront directly the negative connotations U.S. policymakers attached to the word "neutralism" by referring to his nation's position in world affairs as one of "positive neutralism." But the Cold War blinders U.S policymakers like Dulles wore in the 1950s prevented them from recognizing that some countries and their leaders might actually have legitimate reasons for not wanting to be allied too closely with either of the primary Cold War combatants. Even educator, philanthropist, and future U.S. ambassador to Egypt John Badeau, who was generally more sympathetic to Nasser and recognized the nationalist motivations behind his pursuit of neutralism, argued in late 1955 that such a goal was an "illusory hope."[39]

Nasser's apparent unwillingness to cooperate with a top secret American initiative to negotiate a comprehensive peace between Egypt and Israel further worsened U.S. policymakers' impressions of him throughout 1955 and into early 1956. The plan, codenamed ALPHA, was intended to turn Nasser away from the Soviets and back toward the West by resolving the Arab-Israeli conflict. U.S. policymakers believed that an Egyptian peace with Israel would mean that Nasser would not need weapons, would set the stage for a broader regional peace agreement, and would thus lead both Nasser and the rest of the Middle East away from the Soviet Union. The plan went through several iterations, but generally contained the following components: American support for Egyptian preeminence among Arab states; U.S. funding for the building of a dam at Aswan, as well as support for broader regionwide development programs; Western-financed renovations of the Suez Canal, including possibly digging a wider and deeper canal that would be under undisputed Egyptian control; permanent resolution of disputes over borders and sovereignty over Jerusalem; a peace treaty that would include mutual security pledges and possibly an internationally guaranteed collective security arrangement; and American financial and political assistance for settling and/or compensating Palestinian refugees.

Both the United States and the Britain invested a great deal of energy in the proposal, with British foreign secretary Anthony Eden making the initial pitch to Nasser in February 1955. U.S. ambassador to Egypt Henry Byroade followed up with Nasser later that spring, and Dulles publicly announced the plan in August. Ongoing clashes along the Egyptian-Israeli border, along with Nasser's decision to negotiate the Czech arms deal, consistently thwarted U.S. efforts. President Eisenhower made one final effort by sending one of his most trusted advisors—Robert Anderson—to pitch the plan to Nasser and Israel's David Ben-Gurion on multiple occasions in early 1956. While both Nasser and Ben-Gurion listened to Anderson politely and intently, none of the three was willing to take the necessary steps to achieve peace. Anderson negotiated with one eye on the presidency, both in terms of the upcoming election in which Jewish Americans would have a loud political voice and in terms of his own prospective run for the office in 1960. Nasser claimed he was willing to negotiate but dragged his feet on territorial and refugee issues. Ben-Gurion used frequent offers to meet personally with Nasser to good political advantage. He forced Nasser, who could not agree to such a proposal without placing his political legitimacy and his life in serious danger, to reject all such proposals and, with them, any hope for peace. The result was that Anderson and his superiors viewed Nasser as "a complete stumbling block" in the negotiations, and they placed the blame for the failure of the initiative squarely on his shoulders.[40]

Criticism of Nasser within wider U.S. political circles, such as Congress, increased dramatically just as the U.S. government took up discussion of an Egyptian request to help finance construction of the Aswan Dam in the first half of 1956. Although most members of Congress were likely unaware of Project ALPHA and the Anderson mission, several disgruntled legislators expressed their unhappiness about Nasser's willingness to deal with the Soviets and his recognition of Communist China. They opposed any financial assistance packages the Eisenhower administration might consider for Egypt. One senator implicitly related Nasser and his ambitions in the Middle East to those of Hitler in Europe two decades before: "We have gone far enough toward appeasing Mr. Nasser." Little did that senator know how much more explicit and prevalent such comparisons would be over the coming years, beginning with the Suez Crisis of late 1956.[41]

As domestic opposition to Nasser grew in early 1956, U.S. policymakers turned more dramatically away from him and, in the process, helped spark a major international crisis later that year. Nasser's arms contract with the Soviets, his recognition of the Chinese Communists, and his alleged unwillingness to deal on the Arab-Israeli conflict convinced Secretary of State Dulles that Nasser was a growing threat to U.S. interests in the Middle East. Dulles therefore decided in July 1956 to withdraw an earlier U.S. pledge to help finance the Aswan Dam. Nasser likely already had devised plans for the nationalization of the British- and French-owned Suez Canal Company and used the opportunity presented by Dulles's decision to seize the canal on 26 July. The British and the French immediately developed contingency plans for military action to reassert their control over what they considered a vital waterway and to deal a severe blow to Nasser. President Eisenhower repeatedly made clear that he disagreed with Nasser's actions, but did not think they justified a military campaign or other serious attempts to undermine him, so the United States sought a peaceful resolution of the crisis. The British and the French grew impatient, however, and with Israeli collusion, attacked Egypt in late October. The United States responded by exerting pressure on the British and French to quickly withdraw from Egypt. The crisis was over by the end of the year, except for the withdrawal of Israeli troops and the reopening of the Suez Canal.[47]

Throughout the crisis, Nasser appeared a hero to many people in the Middle East, but U.S. policymakers, journalists, and other specialists imagined him to be a much more dangerous individual than they previously had. In late July, shortly after Nasser seized the canal, the Joint Chiefs of Staff took the position that he "must be broken." Secretary of State Dulles was even more critical, seeing Nasser's nationalization of the Suez Canal as part of a carefully designed plan to dominate the Middle East and "to reduce Western Europe to subservience to Arab control." President Eisenhower, like the *Time* editors who chose Mossadegh as 1951's "Man of the Year," also saw Nasser as someone who represented larger forces at work. The president argued that Nasser "embodie[d] the emotional demands of the people of the area for independence and for 'slapping the white Man down,'" and that going after Nasser would only help "spread his influence progressively, to the detriment of the West through the Middle East."[43]

An evaluation of Nasser prepared in the midst of the Suez Crisis by a special Middle East policy planning group made up of regional specialists in the State Department and the CIA revealed what was quickly becoming conventional wisdom regarding Nasser and Arab nationalism. Analyzing the Egyptian leader and his presumed objectives, the group recognized that Nasser's early actions left "room for divergence" in interpreting his motives and goals, but more recent actions pointed "clearly to the conclusion that Nasser is an international political adventurer of considerable skill with clearly defined objectives that seriously threaten the Western world." Reevaluating Nasser's earlier policies in this light led analysts to conclude that the Egyptian leader was "guided by the objective of building as much personal power as possible." If that were the case, Nasser would not have been "a leader with whom it [would have been] possible to enter into friendly arrangements of cooperation or with whom it would [have been] possible to make any feasible accommodations." Even William Polk, who became a harsh critic of U.S. policymakers in the post-Suez period, believed Nasser promoted "hostile ideologies."[44]

The language of some commentators, from journalists up to the president, revealed more worrisome assessments of Nasser and his movement. Some comments from 1956 hearkened back to just a few years earlier, when postwar fears of a revitalized Islam peaked and observers worried that the mufti of Jerusalem might emerge as the leader of a confrontational, "totalitarian" Islam. Eisenhower himself made such an assertion about Nasser in a 12 August meeting with the congressional leadership. There, the president explicitly compared Nasser's writings to Hitler's *Mein Kampf*. Even individuals who believed such comparisons were inaccurate assisted those who viewed Nasser through this lens. Two days after Eisenhower made his remark, the State Department's Office of Intelligence and Research submitted a three-page comparison of Hitler and Nasser, presumably for the use of those who hoped to equate Nasser with Hitler. The authors of the paper believed such comparisons were too simplistic and urged others to avoid making them, though that was "not to say, of course, that anyone cannot take the various items and for propaganda purposes simply state similarities. To help such a person we have at least contributed a break down. But I do think it is our business to point out that such a person would be wrong and would expose himself to informed rebuttal."[45]

By imagining Nasser as the totalitarian leader of an uncontrollable and insatiable mass Arab nationalism, policymakers were able to justify a new policy toward the region and, in the process, equated Middle Eastern nationalism with the perceived Soviet threat. In early January 1957, shortly after the Suez Crisis subsided, Eisenhower went before a joint session of Congress to request authorization for the use of any means necessary, including force, to protect Middle Eastern states against "aggression from any nations controlled by International Communism." Eisenhower relied on the anticommunist consensus that dominated American political thinking in the 1950s to connect Arab nationalism and communism. Doing so ensured that he gained wide congressional and popular support for policies designed specifically to counter Nasser's growing influence in the region.[46]

Nasser's actions through 1957 and early 1958 further convinced policymakers that Arab nationalism was a dangerous force. Nasserist forces in Jordan tried unsuccessfully to overthrow King Hussein in spring 1957, leading Eisenhower to deploy the U.S. Sixth Fleet in the eastern Mediterranean. The situation in Syria grew even more serious. As leftist forces there drew closer to the Soviet Union, U.S. policymakers renewed a covert plan, originally developed in 1956 as Operation Straggle, and renamed Operation Wappen, designed to support moderate forces in a coup attempt. The Syrian leadership got wind of the plot, sparking a crisis in U.S.-Syrian relations that rapidly escalated to draw in not only other countries of the region such as Turkey, Saudi Arabia, and Iraq, but also the Soviet Union. In this instance, U.S. policymakers actually relied on Nasser to reduce tensions, only to encounter the unintended consequence of the formation of the United Arab Republic between Egypt and Syria in early 1958.[47]

Policymakers' fears of Arab nationalism peaked in July 1958 as nationalist forces in Iraq overthrew one of the most pro-Western regimes in the region. On 14 July, 'Abd al-Karim Qasim led a revolt of young military officers, much as the Free Officers Movement had pursued its own revolutionary course in Egypt six years earlier. The revolt quickly spread throughout the country and led to the assassination of King Feisal, Crown Prince 'Abd al-Ilah, and former prime minister Nuri Said. Fearing destabilization elsewhere in the region and convinced that Nasser had sponsored the coup, Eisenhower and Dulles relied on the congressional support provided by the Eisenhower Doctrine and sent 14,000 troops into Lebanon while the British sent forces into Jordan. Responding to these events on 23 July 1958, Secretary of State Dulles characterized "Arab nationalism as a flood which is running strongly. We cannot successfully oppose it, but we can put up sand bags around positions we must protect." One week later, Dulles made a similar remark, referring to Arab nationalism as "an overflowing stream—you cannot stand in front of it and oppose it frontally, but you must try to keep it in bounds." Dulles's comment reflected the realization by U.S. policymakers and other observers of the region that Middle Eastern nationalism was a powerful and dynamic force that they needed to understand and to which they had to respond. Coming on the heels of aborted U.S.-backed coup attempts and efforts to isolate Nasser in the Middle East, the deployment of Marines under the auspices of the Eisenhower doctrine and Dulles's comments were the final indicators that policymakers, and members of the informal network of specialists, had long since rejected the assertions of a decade earlier that Middle Eastern nationalism was a benign force. Moreover, the experiences with Mossadegh and Nasser issued a fundamental challenge to the enduring sacred and secular American mission in the Middle East.[48]

Rethinking Arab Mass Politics

While policymakers in the mid-1950s imagined Nasser as the head of an ever more confrontational nationalist movement, dissenting voices arose among some regional specialists, particularly among those within the academic segment of the informal network, and among those situated at the boundaries between the specialists and policymakers. From the end of the Suez Crisis through 1958, dissenting individuals called for a searching reassessment of U.S. interpretations of and policies toward Middle Eastern nationalists. The historical moment surrounding the Iraqi coup of July 1958 presented these dissenters with an opportunity to voice their concerns more loudly and to reimagine nationalist forces in the Middle East. While the dissenters also viewed nationalist movements as more challenging and potentially problematic than they may have a decade earlier, they called for a more nuanced understanding that they believed would lead to a less strident and more accommodating approach.

Although academic specialists dissented from policymakers for many reasons, there were two fundamental concerns at the heart of their critique of the response to Nasser in the mid-1950s. First, some specialists believed policymakers needed to take more seriously the people of the Middle East and their interests. John Badeau, for example, argued that the United States, Britain, and France would never reach a reasonable settlement during the Suez Crisis as long as they considered only their interests to the complete exclusion of any Egyptian interests in the Canal. Egypt, Badeau claimed, had as much reason for concern about the canal, as it was "a major economic resource located on the soil of Egypt and made valuable because of the country's strategic geographical position." Because of Suez's value, Egypt was just as worried about its falling under foreign control as the British, French, and Americans were about its coming under Egyptian control.[49]

More powerful, however, was the argument that policymakers needed to recognize the various ways in which the United States had contributed to Middle Eastern nationalism, though academic specialists did not necessarily agree on the nature of those contributions. J. C. Hurewitz blasted U.S. policymakers as the Suez Crisis drew to a close in December 1956 for bouncing between extreme views of Nasser and the Revolutionary Command Council. He drew on the Turkish example, though he only mentioned the generation before Kemal took over, to criticize policymakers for believing "that the Egyptian 'Young Turks' who had seized power in 1952 could do no wrong," and for "assuming that, because the [military] junta was pursuing an enlightened policy at home, it would as a matter of course pursue a cooperative policy abroad in its relations with the West." That favorable assessment and the policies it sustained, Hurewitz argued, "contributed inevitably to building up Abdel Nasser as a great leader and popular hero everywhere in the Arab world." Had policymakers been more circumspect in their early appraisals and taken a more "vigorous stand" against the Egyptian leader earlier in the relationship, they might have "reduc[ed] Abdel Nasser to size" long before the Suez Crisis ever developed. Policymakers therefore might not have felt compelled to move to the opposite extreme in their post-Suez imaginings of Nasser.[50]

Hurewitz and fellow academic and future State Department employee William Polk also saw U.S. policies in the region contributing to the rising tide of what had come to be called "radical nationalism" in potentially more dangerous ways as well. Policymakers' unwavering commitment to pro-Western leaders who helped maintain Western domination of oil resources alienated large portions of the population concerned with eliminating foreign involvement in the Middle East. In addition, these policies had created "lone giants," such as Iraq's Nuri Said, who supported the United States and Western Europe but who did not permit the establishment of any governing structures or leaders that would remain once the giant fell from his political heights. And Polk, at least, was reasonably certain Said would fall at some point.[51]

Polk also saw the United States' contributing to the rise of nationalist forces in a manner similar, though not identical, to that expressed in George Antonius's interpretation of the initial emergence of Arab nationalism. As Antonius had, Polk looked to Western education as a critical factor in the rise of Middle Eastern nationalism, but not in the intellectual manner that Antonius emphasized. Polk identified an emerging younger generation of men and women "who grew to adulthood under Western domination; [who] are directly or indirectly Western-trained, and [whose] ideals are much more like ours than were those of the older generation" of Middle Eastern nationalists. According to Polk, this new generation viewed nationalism in much more expansive terms and held it more dearly than their predecessors did. He argued, "What was to the older generation a loosely worn cloak of nationalism is to [the younger, westernized generation] a skin; not only is there a more intense dedication to nationalism but there has also been a certain discernible shift away from the simple self-determination concept of nationalism toward a greater concern with domestic problems." Nasser, as the voice of Arab nationalism, represented this restive younger generation.[52]

While Badeau, Hurewitz, and Polk led the charge from outside the government for a more nuanced response to nationalist forces in the Middle East, a similar and in some ways more powerful effort was being waged in the halls of Congress. There, Arkansas senator J. William Fulbright challenged the antinationalist emphasis of U.S. policy in the Middle East. Fulbright lacked the knowledge of a Middle East specialist, but as a member of the Senate Foreign Relations Committee he was as well or better informed than most policymakers on the intricacies of the Middle East.

Fulbright's opposition to U.S. policy concerning Arab nationalism was the product of several different influences and reflected multiple strains in his complex and often surprising foreign policy thinking. First and foremost, Fulbright was a foreign policy "realist," which meant he believed U.S.–Middle East relations needed to be premised upon a clear calculation of American interests. For Fulbright, the hard realities of power governed international politics. In practical terms, this meant he was a committed Cold Warrior, although not of the ideological anticommunist sort. He saw U.S.-Soviet tensions emerging out of a typical great-power conflict and supported containment of the Soviet Union on these grounds. Although Fulbright was a firm believer in popular participation in domestic politics, he felt leaders had an obligation to educate an ignorant and sometimes prejudiced populace in the intricacies of international affairs. The distinction between popular ignorance and popular understanding, in his mind, came down to whether or not people had personal experience with and reasonable knowledge about specific issues. Americans knew the economic, political, racial, or social situation in their own town, county, or state, but the international arena was different. National leaders had more experience with and knew more about the rest of the world, so Fulbright believed foreign policy was better left to them.[53]

Fulbright's upbringing and adult life in Fayetteville, Arkansas, also impacted his views of U.S.–Middle East relations and Arab nationalism. He was a man of his time and place—the Jim Crow South—and although he claimed not to oppose integration on principle, according to one of Fulbright's biographers, "the blacks he knew were not equal to whites." Fulbright considered racial tension to be part of the historical and the contemporary environment of the South. His and his fellow Southerners' attitudes existed within a democratic society, so he did not think they could be altered through legislation forced on them from other parts of the country. Nationalist revolutions in the Middle East, like Southern racism, were local issues in which the United States had little right to intervene, especially when to do so might jeopardize important interests. Similarly, Fulbright believed that revolutions resulted in violence and repression, just as resistance to southern racism had, because the systems being challenged were so entrenched and required "a shattering of the old social fabric and an attempt, often unsuccessful, to create alternative social values and institutions." According to Fulbright, most Americans had virtually no experience with social revolutions, but they had little appreciation for this fact.[54]

Fulbright's reading of his state's post–Civil War history further legitimized nationalist revolutions in his mind. He believed that Arkansas underwent much the same sort of economic exploitation after the Civil War that the colonized areas of the world endured throughout the nineteenth and twentieth centuries. Outsiders came into the state to exploit its natural resources, especially bauxite, at enormous profit, leaving little for the people of Arkansas. The poor peoples of the world were using means—revolutions and the nationalization of foreign business interests in particular—that Fulbright found completely understandable to fight a "cold war" against the world's rich consumer nations. In this way, Fulbright's thinking about revolutions differed significantly not only from contemporary foreign policy thinkers, but also from his predecessors in American history, most of whom had been ambivalent at best, and downright hostile at worst, toward revolutionary movements.[55]

Lastly, Fulbright was firmly committed to the idea of U.S. internationalism. He came away from three years as a Rhodes scholar at Oxford University and several months of travel around Europe convinced of the utility of international cultural exchange in the effort to promote worldwide peace and understanding. Within months of winning election to the Senate in 1944, Fulbright proposed the legislation that still funds the travel of American academics abroad and brings foreign scholars to the United States. His basic belief in building connections between peoples also undergirded a strong commitment to collective security, the United Nations, and extensive U.S. involvement in world affairs. Combined with his ideas regarding race, this meant Fulbright saw U.S. participation in world affairs, particularly in areas like the Middle East, in both morally and racially superior terms.[56]

As a member of the Senate Foreign Relations Committee, Fulbright challenged policymakers and their consensus-driven ideas regarding U.S.–Middle East relations. His first serious critique of U.S. Middle East policy took place in February 1956, after Secretary of State Dulles testified about the state of world affairs before the Senate Foreign Relations Committee. Fulbright argued that Dulles, in presenting Soviet foreign policy as a colossal failure, imagined a world situation fresh out of "a midsummer dream" that bore little resemblance to the realities of world power at the time. "Does the dramatic and vigorous entry of Russia into the once forbidden zone of the Middle East represent a setback for the Kremlin," Fulbright asked rhetorically, and then answered emphatically, "It does not." That attack on Dulles was only a precursor of what was to come, however, as Fulbright's opposition to the secretary of state and U.S. policy in the Middle East grew over the next two years.[57]

Fulbright's assessment of Dulles appeared almost as a mirror image of U.S. policymakers' critiques of Mohammad Mossadegh and Gamal 'Abd al-Nasser from earlier in the 1950s. Just as the two Middle Eastern leaders had allegedly relied too much on emotions, both their own and those of their followers, Fulbright contended that Dulles too frequently let his own emotions overwhelm reason, especially when it came to the issue of anticolonial nationalism in the non-Western world. The senator later recollected that he "was appalled by Dulles's sanctimonious moralism. I thought he was an extreme ideologue . . . All his talk about 'liberation' as against 'containment' offended me—and he didn't liberate anybody. I think his piety and self-righteousness were what was most offensive." Fulbright thought Dulles's penchant for equating anticolonial nationalism with communism led him to a further and potentially more damaging error: working against revolutionary movements and thus alienating their followers when in the long run they might have been turned toward the United States. Such an error, Fulbright believed, helped create the context in which the 1956 Suez Crisis occurred.

In early 1957, Fulbright sought to discredit Dulles by pushing through a motion that established a subcommittee of the Senate Foreign Relations Committee to study the background of U.S. policy that led up to the Suez Crisis. Frustrated by stringent secrecy requirements that prohibited him from publicizing critical documents, and overwhelmed by the amount of material the State Department sent to him, Fulbright called off the inquiry within just a few months on the grounds that it could serve "no useful purpose."[58]

When Fulbright reported back to the Senate on his investigation in August 1957, he took Dulles to task for misreading Arab nationalism. He criticized Dulles not only for hastily and inappropriately withdrawing the U.S. offer to help finance the Aswan Dam, but also for generally misunderstanding the economic and political situations in Egypt and the broader Middle East. Fulbright concluded that "our policy was influenced too much by emotion and not enough by hardheaded realities," and that "the ill-considered decision to withdraw" the aid offer resulted in serious damage to European economies and to U.S. relations with England and France. The Suez Crisis therefore heightened the level of danger in the Middle East by reducing U.S. influence and increasing Soviet influence.[59]

Fulbright delivered his most vitriolic assault on Dulles and U.S. policy toward the Middle East in the aftermath of the 1958 Iraqi coup. That event was the culmination of a series of happenings—including the launching of Sputnik in 1957 and Vice President Nixon's tour of Latin America in May 1958—that left Americans in a state of shock. Fulbright found U.S. policy "inadequate, outmoded, and misdirected" and the leadership of those responsible for that policy to be either "weak and desultory" or "impetuous and arbitrary." He highlighted a host of problematic policies, many of which had direct bearing on U.S-Middle East relations. Such policies, Fulbright argued, were based on a set of misconceptions that placed the U.S. "indiscriminately in the role of the defender of the status quo throughout the world." In conclusion, Fulbright called for "a fresh, new, uncommitted look . . . at the mistaken policies we have been following, and which have led us into our present impasse."[60]

The Iraqi Revolution in July 1958 brought to a head the disagreements over how to interpret and respond to Nasser specifically, and Arab nationalism more generally. Initially, policymakers viewed the coup in Iraq through the same lens they had been using since 1955, seeing the event as yet another example of Nasser's supposed adventurism and desire to dominate the entire Middle East. It was not long, however, before Nasser and Qasim were clearly at odds, raising the question of whether Nasser had ever been involved in the coup. To some observers, however, whether or not Nasser was involved was irrelevant. It was much more important to recognize that the United States had to come to terms with nationalist forces in the Middle East. Just two weeks after the coup, and with the extent of Nasser's involvement still unclear, regional specialists on the National Security Council began to discuss whether the United States should "make serious efforts now to reach an accommodation with radical Pan-Arab nationalism of which Nasser is the symbol."[61]

Salim Yaqub has argued persuasively that while U.S. policymakers gave some consideration to reaching an accommodation with Arab nationalism in spring 1958, it was really in the weeks and months after the Iraqi Revolution that they shifted course dramatically. He suggests that policymakers began to reach out to Nasser in late summer and early fall even as they remained skeptical of his ambitions in the Middle East. The result, according to Yaqub, was that by late 1958 the United States "was left with an essentially negative—not to say paralyzed—Middle East policy: opposed to Nasser, and opposed to opposing him." The situation only improved as a rift emerged in Nasser's relations with the Soviet Union, at which point U.S. policymakers came belatedly to realize that Nasser and his supporters might actually serve to resist communist subversion in the region.[62]

A close examination of how members of the informal network of specialists and other critics of U.S. policy imagined Middle Eastern nationalism from late 1957 through 1958 supports Yaqub's findings, but it also suggest a broader circle of debate and influence that extended beyond the narrow boundaries of actual policymakers. Indeed, the criticisms of policymakers' understanding of and responses to Middle Eastern nationalism that Badeau, Hurewitz, Polk, and Fulbright leveled began by late 1957 or early 1958 to generate a clear set of policy prescriptions. The most explicit attempt to influence policy came from William Polk and Richard H. Nolte, who coauthored an article published in *Foreign Affairs* in July 1958, the same month as the Iraqi Revolution. They argued that U.S. policymakers needed to do a better job of identifying American objectives in the region. Specifically, they suggested, "a clear distinction should be made between objectives and the means to achieve them and between essential objectives and those that are merely desirable." Polk and Nolte believed that focusing on the minimum essential objectives rather than on the maximum desirable objectives would allow the United States to accept more of the nationalist agenda. It might also mean that Middle Easterners would not always see the United States as supporting the status quo and reflexively opposed to any nationalist objectives. John Campbell, director of political studies for the Council on Foreign Relations, proposed a similar definition of U.S. interests in his 1958 book, *Defense of the Middle East: Problems of American Policy*.[63]

Inside the government, the National Security Council was given the task of figuring out how policymakers might best rethink U.S. policy toward the Middle East in general, but especially with respect to Arab nationalism. The ideas contained in a draft report bore a striking resemblance to those laid out by Campbell, Polk, and Nolte. Like the three specialists, the National Security Council began by suggesting that policymakers needed to distinguish clearly between "primary" U.S. interests and objectives in the region and "secondary" concerns. Primary interests included preventing the spread of communism and maintaining Western European access to Middle Eastern oil. Everything else was of secondary importance. Once the initial step of defining the minimum primary interests that policymakers needed to protect was taken, it became much easier to distinguish between what policymakers might recognize as legitimate and illegitimate forms of nationalism in the Middle East. According to this line of reasoning, if the nationalist agenda threatened a primary interest, then it must be opposed. If, however, it threatened a secondary interest, it might be possible either to avoid addressing the problem or to accommodate the nationalists. Using this criteria, the National Security Council then suggested that "the elements of Arab nationalism which we must accept as legitimate and appropriate may be described in terms of Arab aspirations for: a) Independence and dignity; b) the right of self-determination; c) the right to choose a policy of neutralism in the East-West struggle; d) social reform and economic progress; and e) equitable arrangements with respect to their oil resources."[64]

The work of Polk and Nolte, Campbell, and the National Security Council all revealed an effort not only to reassess U.S. policy toward Nasser, but a concern with Arab nationalism more broadly. But policymakers and specialists who hoped to reach an accommodation with "radical" Middle Eastern nationalism first had to try to understand it better, an effort that fit into a larger project of increasing policymakers' knowledge of nationalism more broadly. According to Gordon Gray, Eisenhower's special assistant for national security affairs, a subset of the National Security Council considered undertaking an official study of nationalism. Such a study seemed necessary due to the "sparseness of literature on the subject" and the fact "that in almost every country we were concerned with these days the question of nationalism seemed to be a key question but that it appeared to mean one thing in Communist China, another in the Near East, and still another in the Latin American countries." Of course, not all policymakers believed nationalism warranted such careful attention, and they preferred taking a much harder line against Nasser and other similar nationalists. Some government officials even hinted that assassination would be the most productive policy. The CIA, however, did not advocate this course, as it believed nationalists like Nasser would play even more prominent roles in the future. Gordon Gray later noted, "The CIA view was certainly not to assassinate, but embrace [Nasser], you see. Because they thought he was the wave of the future and we better jolly well get on with the wave of the future." Riding the wave of the future, however, necessitated a fundamental reimagining of Arab nationalism and policymakers' responses to it.[65]

That was precisely what William Polk hoped to do in December 1958 when he revisited the events of the previous summer and undertook a broad regionwide analysis of "the Lesson of Iraq." There, he proposed not only a new understanding of Arab nationalism, but of the issue of mass Arab politics as a whole, its proponents, and the general terms of how the United States should respond to it. According to Polk, Arab nationalism could no longer be understood simply as a political movement to pursue national independence; rather, it was a movement to address numerous complaints and issues that originated in both internal and international developments. There were "bursting new expectations from life, expectations which have resulted both from increased contact with the outside world and from the internal improvement at home." The rising middle class, a product of increasing oil revenues, better educational opportunities, and the possibilities presented by technological advancements, expressed and grasped onto these expectations most powerfully. Yet there continued to exist, in Jordan for example, a class of people "incapable of performing the semi-complex functions required even by the simple economy." Bridging the gap between these two groups, while also meeting the expectations of the middle class, presented enormous challenges. The best prospect was to support governments that were willing to address these questions. Otherwise, "if these governments do not evolve politically, if they continue to want to ride the airplane of Western-style progress and yet retain paternalism, they cannot avoid losing the loyalty of their subjects." Polk still believed specialists and policymakers had to ask themselves a very basic question: "What, in effect, do we want from the Middle East?"

Once that question was answered, then it would be possible to address the demands of the masses through the careful application of U.S. aid and support for forward-thinking governments. In this way, Polk also sought to re-center U.S. involvement in the Middle East on the pursuit of its sacred and secular mission in the region.[66]

The attempts to reimagine Arab nationalism and to delineate acceptable and unacceptable forms of it are noteworthy in several respects. The legitimization of neutralism and the implicit decoupling of Arab nationalism and communism, which had been linked in policymakers' thinking throughout the mid-1950s, were certainly striking. According to these reimaginings of Arab nationalism, a fundamental shift had taken place as a result of the demise of "conservative nationalism" in the Middle East. Specialists outside the executive branch now believed policymakers needed to reconsider what they found to be an acceptable level of Soviet and communist involvement in the region. It was now only "desirable" to oppose and limit Soviet influence, but it was "essential" to prevent Soviet domination of a Middle Eastern country. As Raymond Hare, U.S. ambassador to the United Arab Republic, noted in October 1958, "I assume we now have no illusions re possibility of denial of area to Soviets in terms in which we used to think few years ago. Soviets are already in area massively and problem is how contain their advances short of actual domination."[67]

Equally as significant as the placement of neutralism on the list of legitimate nationalist concerns were the important omissions from the list. Presumably, everything that was not explicitly identified as a legitimate nationalist concern was by implication deemed illegitimate. Notably, the Arab-Israeli conflict was not on the list of legitimate interests, though the National Security Council report defined seeking a resolution to the conflict as a desirable secondary objective. Placing the issue within this category made it possible for policymakers to deemphasize it. Yet, by not recognizing any nationalist claims against Israel as legitimate, Polk, Nolte, Campbell and the National Security Council also suggested that Israel deserved separate consideration, and implicitly acknowledged strong U.S. ties with the Jewish state.

These late-1950s reimaginings of Arab nationalism and of mass politics more generally were written into a new version of the primary document guiding U.S. policy toward the region, "NSC 5820/1: U.S. Policy Toward the Near East." In fact, the major point of that document was to stress the need for finding ways to reach an accommodation with nationalism as the dominant force in the Middle East. Reimagining Arab nationalism thus provided the basis for a policy initiative toward Nasser, discussed here more fully in chapter 4, that stressed areas of common interests such as promoting development over areas of opposing interests like the Arab-Israeli conflict.[68]

Policymakers' efforts to find new, less confrontational, and less paternalistic ways to respond to nationalist forces in the Middle East appealed to even the harshest critic of previous policy in the region. In August 1959, Senator Fulbright found hope in the fact that Americans "seem to have matured somewhat in our understanding of the strong drives of Arab nationalism. We seem finally able to distinguish between Arab nationalism and communism." But U.S. policy still needed to "become something more than a series of ad hoc measures designed to cope with periodic crises." The only way to accomplish that objective was to treat "each of these sovereign states on an adult and realistic basis, rather than suggesting the presence of a political vacuum in the Arab world. We must take into account the full capabilities of the Arabs themselves." Finally, Americans had to adopt a more pragmatic, less ideological vision of the Middle East. "This is what we wish to see," Fulbright proclaimed, "not representative government necessarily in our pattern — not economic growth necessarily in the America pattern — but essentially we want to see men and women able to govern themselves and improve their standards of living."[69]

Fulbright was correct, at least in part, that U.S. policymakers and regional specialists were by the late 1950s and early 1960s developing a more nuanced interpretation of Arab nationalism and demonstrating a keen desire to come to terms with a significant challenge to U.S. interests and power in the area. The 1960–61 Council on Foreign Relations Study Group on Arab Foreign Policy, with which this chapter began, reflected this new approach. The group took great pains to understand the local motivations driving Arab nationalist foreign policy, especially as Nasser practiced it, and also recognized that Arab nationalism represented a broader form of mass Arab politics. Although group members did not question that Nasser remained the most powerful and important Arab nationalist leader, they did acknowledge that they could no longer assume that he spoke for all Arab nationalists. Similarly, when NSC 5820/1 was revised in the summer of 1960, the new version gave significantly less attention to nationalist forces in the region. G. Lewis Jones, assistant secretary of state for Near Eastern and South Asian affairs, noted in the cover letter he attached to the document when he sent it to Acting Secretary of State C. Douglas Dillon that "the introduction has been rewritten . . . to lessen the previous paper's stress on the threat of radical pan-Arab nationalism."[70]

The reimagining that took place in the late 1950s and early 1960s did not, however, suggest U.S. policymakers had reached a long-term living arrangement with either Arab nationalism itself or with mass politics more generally in the Middle East. Such initiatives did not eliminate entirely the paternalistic and dismissive attitudes that characterized the earlier thinking of both area specialists and policymakers toward nationalist leaders like Nasser and Mohammad Mossadegh. Indeed, even as the United States started to reach out to Nasser in the late 1950s, President Eisenhower argued that such a policy change was justified because Nasser had "grown up a little." Similarly, as the initiative to retain a working relationship with Nasser continued into the Kennedy and Johnson administrations, White House Middle East specialist Robert Komer noted in 1963 that Nasser might be "the one major Arab leader who may make sense," but even he could "succumb to hysteria."[71]

These efforts also continued to reveal an overall discomfort with mass politics in the Middle East more generally, and specifically in the ability of a charismatic leader like Nasser to manipulate the masses seemingly at will. Nowhere was this point more evident than in a series of four intelligence assessments of Nasser and Arab nationalism that were completed between June 1961 and September 1965. Each of the reports acknowledged what they referred to as "Arab particularism," by which they meant that each Arab state and population had its own concerns and motivations that would prevent the regionwide unification of either movements or countries. But each assessment also argued in some form that, as the 1961 report's opening statement read, "militant nationalism will continue to be the most dynamic force in Arab political affairs, and Nasser is very likely to remain its foremost leader and symbol in the foreseeable future." It was, they argued, Nasser's ability and willingness to speak beyond the particularist concerns to the common wishes and demands of the Arab masses that made him so effective and thus so challenging for specialists and policymakers alike. It was also what suggested for the authors of the 1965 report the ultimate threat and dilemma presented by Nasser, Arab nationalism, and Middle Eastern mass politics: could such forces be used in a manner to promote democracy, or would they lead the Middle East inevitably toward totalitarianism? Regarding Nasser, they concluded he had "gradually established governmental control over almost every aspect of Egyptian life. The pervasiveness of that control . . .

would seem to undermine his hopes to bring a democratic, socialist society to Egypt." Failure to relinquish some control would mean that Nasserism would tend toward "totalitarian rule, and his professed aims will remain mere slogans."[72]

AS THE EVIDENCE PRESENTED here demonstrates, it is possible to identify three broad phases in American efforts to imagine Middle Eastern nationalism between 1918 and the late 1960s. Shifts from one phase to the next were prompted by developments in the region itself, as American observers responded to its political dynamics. In the first phase, which spanned from the end of World War I to the early 1950s, members of the informal transnational network of Middle East specialists were aware of emerging nationalist forces in the region. Initially, their interpretations of "the awakening of the nationalistic spirit" stressed American missionaries' role in rousing it and portrayed it as a benign and welcome force. Yet the emergence of leaders like Mustafa Kemal and Reza Shah Pahlavi, among others, as well as broadly based nationalist movements, required more complex interpretations. One new interpretation emphasized the role of prominent and charismatic individuals who were successfully building movements around themselves, while another focused on the intellectual and anticolonial origins of Middle Eastern nationalism. Both interpretations suggested an increasingly important political role for the Arab masses, though both also left that role undefined. At this point, most Americans concerned with the region continued to see nationalism in positive terms, even suggesting it could assist in the process of sacred and secular transformation.

In the early and mid-1950s, specialists and policymakers came to imagine Middle Eastern nationalism in much more negative terms, framing it in a discourse of radicalism, equating it with Soviet communism, and working to isolate it. The rise of Mohammad Mossadegh in Iran, and later Gamal ʿAbd al-Nasser in Egypt, demonstrated that Middle Eastern nationalism was much more complicated than it had seemed even just a few years earlier, and that it might be far more challenging than U.S. policymakers and specialists had imagined. In both instances, specialists and policymakers came to fear the power of the individual to appeal to the Middle Eastern masses and therefore utilized paternalistic discourses to delegitimize both the leaders and their nationalist aspirations. In assessments from the late 1940s and early 1950s that reflected similar concerns about totalitarian Islam, network members disparaged the masses who succumbed to such leaders as blind followers of potentially totalitarian dictators.

When the regional context changed once again, American understandings of nationalism entered their third phase. In mid-1958, when U.S. interests in the region appeared to be in significant danger, regional specialists and policymakers alike once again reimagined Arab nationalism, its place in regional affairs, and its significance for the United States. In doing so, they concluded that rather than firmly opposing Arab nationalism, it was best for the United States to try to maintain contact with nationalist leaders like Nasser. A deliberate engagement with such leaders would help redirect their energies toward less radical ends and encourage them to contain mass politics. As the next chapter demonstrates, the primary form that redirection would take was to reemphasize America's sacred and secular mission in the Middle East by promoting the controlled transformation of the region's economic and social foundations.

CHAPTER FOUR

WHAT MODERNIZATION REQUIRES OF THE ARABS . . . IS THEIR DE-ARABIZATION

Imagining a Transformed Middle East

In September 1969, the State Department's Bureau of Intelligence and Research forwarded a lengthy research paper to the secretary of state. Thirty-one pages long, "The Roots of Arab Resistance to Modernization" sought to explain why "the Arabs of the Near East [were] failing to fulfill their aspirations to become modern men, as the term is understood in Europe and the Western Hemisphere." The paper contended that "the cause does not lie in external forces, as is frequently rationalized, but in internal ones that lie at the very core of the Arab system of social relationships and values." Social relationships in the Middle East were allegedly dominated by the competing forces of authoritarianism, which promoted conformity, inhibited religious reform and independent thinking, and created atomism, through which strict adherence to clan or family-based identities prevented loyalty to larger identities, except those based on religion. Traditional Islamic and Arab thought and value systems supposedly perpetuated these forces. Nowhere was it more evident than in "The Failure of Arab Education as an Instrument of Modernization," a topic of eight pages of the report. The education system, the report claimed, could not advance modernization because it emphasized memorization and the prestige of attendance over learning critical thinking and other problem-solving skills. In short, Arabs could not live up to western standards of modernization because of who they were, their social relationships, and their cultural and religious practices.[1]

The paper concluded that there was little cause for optimism that the Middle East would modernize in the near future. The people of the region were "not successfully coping with the problems posed by modernization. The cause clearly lies in the fact that the society is saturated with values and social and intellectual attitudes that produce dysfunction in the modern institutions and techniques that are borrowed from abroad." The secular nationalists had in some cases succeeded in challenging Islam's dominance, but had not been able to build within the populace sufficient loyalty to individual states, a sense of "patriotism," to overcome the prevailing atomism. Secular national and "revolutionary" states might build some loyalty, but that loyalty was typically given either to the individual leader, such as Nasser, or to a vague notion of change that was pursued "at too fast a pace and by ineffective methods because [the revolutionary leaders] do not understand that the problem is one of strong and deep forces in Arab Islamic culture that are inimical to modernization in the Western sense." Change was occurring, but it was "much more rapid in the material than in the non-material sphere. It is in the latter, however, that the key to true modernization lies." The first sentence of the final paragraph of the paper encapsulated the prevailing view: "What modernization requires of the Arabs, in effect, is their de-Arabization."[2]

This chapter places the informal transnational network of specialists' analyses and frustrations of the late 1960s—exemplified by the State Department's 1969 report and evident in many other sources—in the context of half a century's worth of sacred and secular efforts to imagine and achieve a transformed Middle East. Those efforts began in 1918, a year members of the Inquiry and the King-Crane Commission believed provided a unique opportunity to bring change to the Middle East. They therefore promoted U.S. involvement in a proposed series of League of Nations mandates to supervise the transformation of the Middle East into a set of modern nation-states. The failure of the United States to join the League of Nations, however, meant that from the late 1920s through the late 1940s the pursuit of America's sacred and secular mission through a policy of liberal developmentalism was left to the private sector, particularly U.S. companies involved in the nascent Middle Eastern oil industry. Our attention then shifts to the late 1940s and early 1950s, which marked two key developments. First, the rise of new social science methodologies and concepts led to new efforts to measure literacy rates, population growth rates, poverty rates, disease rates, and more, which were then used to classify the peoples and places of the Middle East in a larger international hierarchy of development and underdevelopment. Second, beginning in the late 1940s, the U.S. government assumed more direct responsibility for trying to bring about a transformed Middle East, while also hoping to prevent revolutionary change across the region. That effort peaked from the late 1950s to the mid 1960s, when policymakers implemented new social scientific modernization theories in U.S. relations with countries such as Egypt and Iran. Our focus then turns to "The Roots of Arab Resistance to Modernization," as we revisit that document from the perspective of fifty years of failed efforts to achieve the Middle East that the network of specialists and policymakers imagined U.S. involvement in the region would bring into existence.

Big Oil and Liberal Developmentalism

To be sure, a strong desire to transform the Middle East animated the activities of many nineteenth-century Americans who operated in the region. Missionaries and philanthropists pursued educational and health care initiatives, while veterans of the U.S. Civil War advising the Egyptian military in the 1870s imagined themselves as the leaders of a great civilizing endeavor. But as they had when trying to come to terms with Middle Eastern nationalisms, policymakers, strategists, academics, businesspersons, and journalists in the interwar period first linked desires to transform the region to expanding U.S. interests there. Immediately after World War I, members of the Inquiry and the King-Crane Commission, as well as other commentators, believed the implementation of the League of Nations mandates presented a unique opportunity to enact sweeping reforms across the region. Yet the United States refused to participate in the mandate system, leaving the private sector to step in.[3]

During and immediately after World War I the perceived need to transform the Middle East had a significant impact on how specialists and policymakers thought about postwar planning. Specialists working for either the Inquiry or its successor, the American Commission to Negotiate Peace, regularly commented on the "backward" nature of the Middle East and the supposed benefits that association with Western Europe or the United States would bring. Historian and Inquiry and Commission member George Louis Beer argued that all of Mesopotamia required "drastic regeneration from the very foundations up." Egypt, which had been under British control since 1882, constituted an exception to this general rule, as it had "for a full generation enjoyed the benefits of an honest and enlightened administration." Beer credited the British with, among other things, creating an atmosphere in which Egypt improved its irrigation systems along the Nile, significantly increased its population, expanded foreign trade, solidified its national finances, and began to expand land ownership. Beer did recognize that British rule in Egypt also engendered resistance, but in general he accepted the words of Lord Cromer, the highest-ranking British official in Egypt for twenty-four years, who argued that the enlightened British imperialist was "in truth always striving to attain ideals, which are apt to be mutually destructive—the ideal of good government, which connotes the continuance of his own supremacy, and the ideal of self-government, which connotes the whole or partial abdication of his supreme position." Cromer, according to Beer, had always limited the size of the British staff, sacrificing "full efficiency . . . in pursuance of the principle that Egyptians must themselves be led to learn by experience the problems of government."[4]

Assessing the situation in Egypt through a British, rather than Egyptian, lens led Beer to become one of the earliest proponents of a mandatory system to administer the holdings of the defeated German and Ottoman empires. Beer believed the war had "created a clean sheet" by eliminating many preexisting political relationships between Europe and the Middle East. Moreover, according to Beer, "in general, the Arabs welcomed the British conquest as a relief from grievous oppression" practiced by their former Turkish overlords. But Beer did not think the people of the Middle East were ready for independence and instead suggested that there must be an intermediate step between Turkish control and full independence. Elaborating further on his plan, Beer argued, "Under modern political conditions, apparently the only way to determine the problems of politically backward peoples, who require not only outside political control but also foreign capital to reorganize their stagnant economic systems, is to entrust the task of government to that state whose interests are most directly involved." These statements make Beer appear to be an apologist for European imperialism, but he was also attuned to rising anticolonial sentiment around the world and attached what he considered a necessary—even if condescending and paternalistic—caveat to any system in which outside powers might exercise control over or pursue increasing economic penetration of the Middle East. Any such system must include "clearly defined provisions to protect the natives from exploitation. . . . The native must be protected from his own ignorance and cupidity by strict land laws. The capitalistic penetration must be rigidly supervised and controlled, so that the result of Mesopotamia's reclamation may not be merely a vastly large population scarcely elevated from its former state of penury and a considerable accession of wealth to London, New York, Paris, and Berlin."[5]

The King-Crane Commission found Arabs to be less pleased with British (or French) conquest than Beer imagined, yet the group's report revealed many of the same ideas about the region and its peoples that governed Beer's thinking. The report's discussion of Syria offers a good example of some of the underlying assumptions driving American imaginings of the Middle East of the future. Syria was "a place of such strategic importance, politically and commercially, and from the point of view of world civilization," King and Crane stated, it was "imperative that the settlement here brought about should be so just as to give promise of permanently good results for the whole cause of the development of righteous civilization in the world. Every part of the former Turkish Empire must be given a new life and opportunity under thoroughly changed political conditions." The final demise of the Ottoman Empire, brought about by the war, created a situation rich with possibilities. It gave "a great opportunity—not likely to return—to build now in Syria a Near East State on the modern basis of full religious liberty, deliberately including various religious faiths, and especially guarding rights of minorities. It is a matter of justice to the Arabs . . . that an Arab state along modern political lines should be formed. While the elements are very various, the interests often divisive, and much of the population not yet fitted for self-government, the conditions are nevertheless as favorable as could be reasonably expected under the circumstances to make the trial now." To that end, King and Crane determined that it would be best to assign Syria as a mandate of the League of Nations, to be carried out by a Western European power that would literally create a new state. According to their report, King and Crane believed the governing power under which Syria would serve its "tutelage" must "be characterized . . . by a strong and vital educational emphasis," through which it could "train the Syrian people to independent self-government as rapidly as conditions allow." That process would entail "forming gradually an intelligent citizenship" and "a large group of disciplined civil servants," ensuring "complete religious liberty . . . and the rights of all minorities," and bringing "the new state as rapidly as possible to economic independence as well as to political independence."[6]

The report's language regarding the need for the people of the Middle East to undergo a period of "tutelage" is striking if not entirely surprising, but equally important is the explicit claim that political modernity could only be achieved by first establishing religious liberty. King and Crane justified this assertion by noting, "to begin with division of territory along religious lines is to invite increasing exclusiveness, misunderstanding, and friction." A generous reading of such language suggests that King and Crane were concerned about preventing possible clashes based on religious identity, particularly given the attacks on Armenians in the preceding decades and the rising tensions between Jews and Arabs in Palestine. But even such a favorable reading must acknowledge a second argument implicit in the statement: the belief that the road to political modernity travelled through a weakened Islam, the dominant religion in the region.[7]

Beer's writings and the King-Crane report articulated the belief that the Middle East needed to undergo fundamental transformation, but they did so in support of a mandatory system in which the United States ultimately never participated. From the early 1930s to the early 1950s no individuals or organizations did more to promote the American mission to transform the Middle East than did U.S. oil companies. In doing so, they benefitted from and exemplified the ideology of "liberal developmentalism," which posited that the processes of national growth and development that took place in the United States was an appropriate model for Africa, Asia, Latin America, and the Middle East. Since the 1890s, U.S. policymakers and businesspersons had, in the words of historian Emily Rosenberg, emphasized "equal trading opportunity, open access, free flow, and free enterprise" to promote development along American lines. The government's role was to ensure a stable and open environment for the growth of American business interests. In the Middle East, U.S. policymakers and businesspersons remained steadfastly committed to this liberal developmental model as they negotiated U.S. involvement in oil development during the interwar period. Private sector investing was intended to guarantee American businessmen equal access to oil resources in areas nominally controlled by or under the influence of other powers. Private investors were to provide valuable foreign capital to the region and expose local business and government leaders to the American, capitalist, open-market economic system. And as the oil companies themselves grew more involved, the infrastructure they built and the resources they brought into specific countries were supposed to bring tangible progress and uplift the peoples of the region.[8]

The oil companies possessed their greatest latitude to pursue this model from the mid-1930s, when Standard Oil of California began exploring its Saudi Arabian concession, until the early 1950s, when the U.S. government turned away from liberal developmentalism as its preferred method of transforming the Middle East. The Saudi concession was cemented by a substantial loan from the company to Ibn Saud, and from the outset carried with it an assumption that the company would be involved in major infrastructure projects such as road building. On the U.S. side, policymakers preoccupied in the immediate post–World War II years with the larger international arena believed liberal developmentalism in the Middle East and elsewhere offered numerous advantages over a more active government role. First and foremost, it allowed the government to devote its limited resources to the areas it deemed most important, which during this period of emerging Cold War tensions were Western Europe and Japan. Second, reliance on the private sector also maintained an informal U.S. presence that policymakers did not believe (albeit incorrectly) indigenous peoples concerned about colonialism could mistake for any kind of imperial ambitions on the part of the U.S. government. Third, policymakers thought private sector investing might also help integrate developing economies into the increasingly connected global economy more quickly and fully than would direct U.S. government assistance. Finally, if private sector investing achieved these three objectives, it might also achieve a more important fourth objective: making U.S. interests in the Middle East more secure in the face of the alleged Soviet threat. For all these reasons, Truman administration officials made supporting the private sector and trade development the focus of early postwar economic assistance programs.[9]

If the U.S. government was willing to work through the private sector to pursue its interests in the Middle East, companies such as ARAMCO, the American conglomerate in charge of the Saudi Arabian oil concession and the largest private U.S. foreign investment in the mid-twentieth century, were happy to oblige. A commissioned company history, written in the mid-1950s but unpublished until the late 1960s, and the reminiscences and records of early employees offer a window through which we can see how these assumptions and attitudes influenced ARAMCO in imagining its role in the Middle East in the 1930s and 1940s.

Discovery! The Story of Aramco Then, authored by noted novelist and naturalist Wallace Stegner, offers a look into how ARAMCO employees saw the Middle East. Stegner spent two weeks in December 1955 in Saudi Arabia, researching a history of the early years of ARAMCO that the company had commissioned earlier that year. He submitted the 80,000-word manuscript four months later, in March 1956. Stegner and ARAMCO then engaged in a long-running dispute over the nature of the book, which went unpublished until ARAMCO released an edited version in chapter-length installments in their in-house publication *Saudi Aramco World*, between January/February 1968 and July/August 1970. The book focused on the period from 1933 to the end of World War II, the years of exploration and early production when the American community was still relatively small and intimate, and before the effort took on a large, multinational corporate feel.[10]

In recounting the early years of U.S. involvement in the Saudi oil industry, Stegner argued that the company and its employees had played a transformational role in Saudi Arabia. He consistently wrote of the oilmen who brought "change," "social and economic revolution," and "the nervous needs of the 20th century into contact with the undeveloped possibilities of a land older than Abraham," a "timeless" place "little interested in innovation." According to Stegner, "These were the days . . . when Saudi Arabia's astonishing push toward modernization began, the days when a revolution of things began in eastern Saudi Arabia. For whatever they may think of the nations which produce and possess them, whatever distaste they have for their beliefs, their dress and their politics, no people in history has been able to resist for half an hour the things that people like this small contingent of geologists bring with them. The Saudis were no different." The geologists "were attendants at the birth of a world." Concluding the work, Stegner wrote of the early ARAMCO employees as "missionaries — missionaries of what they would vaguely describe at a time when the phrase was still hallowed — as the American way of life." Their "missionary zeal" kept them involved in any number of projects — mapping, construction, agriculture, land reclamation, water conservation, public health, education — that were all "part of the contribution Americans tended to make wherever they went, whatever the implications." In the process, these industrial missionaries "were building something new in the history of the world: not an empire for plundering by the intruding power, but a modern nation in which American and Arab could work out fair contracts, produce in partnership, and profit mutually by their association." But, in Stegner's view, "they had made a contribution more significant than any of the gadgets adopted by the Arabs or any of the skills and resources the Arabs had newly learned. They had begun a transformation of a state of mind."[11]

The nostalgia and romanticism with which Stegner wrote of the early years of ARAMCO were also captured in a May/June 1984 issue of *Saudi Aramco World*, published to celebrate "the 50th anniversary of the search for Saudi Arabian oil." The special issue included pieces written based on interviews with several of the first American employees in Saudi Arabia and, it is no surprise, told stories of adventure, complicated cross-cultural contact, perseverance, privation, and a shared sense of mission. There were also a number of assumptions—some readily apparent, others hidden—within these recollections of everyday life in what the employees clearly considered to be a backward land. Some employees, for example, hinted at the impact of technology such as airplanes, cars, surveying equipment, or even the most basic distance-measuring and directional equipment. Other authors, such as John Starkey in his remembrance of Karl Twitchell (one of the individuals who negotiated the Saudi concession in the early 1930s), explicitly discussed the issue of transformation. Starkey noted that a Saudi publication eulogized Twitchell "as the man 'who first lifted the lid on Saudi Arabia's treasure box of natural riches.'" Starkey put a finer point on the sentiment, adding, "But the process of rapid growth and modernization that he helped set in motion is probably his most enduring memorial." Thomas Barger, a geologist who arrived in Saudi Arabia in December 1937 and later became chairman of the board of ARAMCO, captured all of these assumptions in the closing line of his essay. It was, he noted, "an enormous satisfaction to grow up with a society which is in rapid change and to do what you can to help."[12]

Of course, we do need to inquire whether Stegner's book and the employee reminiscences published years after the fact accurately reflect what ARAMCO employees fully believed, or if some of what they stated was essentially a marketing ploy. William Eddy—the son of missionaries, a World War II intelligence officer, the first U.S. ambassador to Saudi Arabia, and in 1948 an ARAMCO employee who also worked for the CIA—wrote that year to a family member about a plan to try to convince Arab leaders of the benefits of allowing U.S. and British companies to control the regional oil industry. The letter is worth quoting at length, as Eddy explicitly acknowledged that there was an element of deception in ARAMCO's efforts: "We are preparing a documentation of the idea which I have proposed briefly in the enclosed memorandum, to be translated into Arabic and 'planted' by Arab friends in the hands of members of parliaments of Arab countries, etc. It must be written as though an Arab were writing. The idea will be to describe the tremendous development in Arab lands which can take place in the next few years by private capital, British and American, if the Arabs will encourage such development instead of taking sanctions against companies: the hundreds of millions of dollars which will be invested in construction, payrolls, goods and services, without a cent of cost to the Arabs since the companies take all the financial risk. The royalties and benefits to the Arabs, on the other hand, will arm them economically to withstand expanding Zionism, and give them a bargaining point with the Powers who MUST have oil from the Near East and will therefore have to cooperate with the Arabs." The letter reveals multiple ways in which businesspersons involved in the Middle East imagined the region and their role in it during the relatively early years of involvement. It is clear that they saw Arab leaders as relatively unsophisticated individuals who could be duped by cunning and allegedly superior Americans and Europeans. It also suggests, however, that they believed the theme of transformation offered the most plausible grounds on which the oil companies could make their case.[13]

Robert Vitalis has argued, and the *Discovery!* volume and Eddy letter would both seem to confirm, that ARAMCO worked assiduously to create a "myth" in which it "acted more generously and less exploitatively than enterprises of other nations," and that this myth is fundamentally interconnected with a larger myth of American exceptionalism and benevolence in the world. Such myths, in Vitalis's analysis, necessarily overlook the implementation in Saudi Arabia of common race-based business practices that originated in the resource industries (particularly mining) in the Jim Crow American south, anti-immigrant American southwest, and Central and South America. Thus, ARAMCO employees brought to their efforts to transform the Middle East all the assumptions and attitudes about race, the superiority of the United States, and the inferiority of Islam and the people of the Middle East that were common to their time and place. Moreover, Vitalis points out that ARAMCO, like many resource mining companies around the world, engaged in construction projects—railroads, docks, highways, etc.—that were necessary costs of doing business in a particular place; the business could not thrive without them. All of ARAMCO's claims about working for the transformation of Saudi Arabia were, according to Vitalis, mere pretense, the product of elaborate myth production.[14]

But Vitalis leaves underexamined one central point in his otherwise excellent analysis of the relationship between ARAMCO, the Saudis, and the U.S. government: why did this myth hold such broad appeal for audiences in the United States? The pretense worked because it fit within an already widely accepted way of imagining the Middle East and the U.S. role there. Americans had imagined themselves as benevolently transforming the Middle East in some form or another for decades. Indeed, that was the central point behind the implementation of the policy of liberal developmentalism. In this way, the acceptance of the ARAMCO myth about its role in Saudi Arabia was a crucial piece of the broader American sense of mission not only in the Middle East, but around the world.

While liberal developmentalism endured as a prominent approach to U.S. involvement in much of the world through the first half of the twentieth century, it was not implemented without resistance. Some government Middle East specialists adamantly opposed this approach to transforming the region. They argued that bilateral private sector developmentalism might be good in theory, but it was subject to the whims and interests of businessmen. It was therefore inconsistent over time and uneven within countries, to say nothing of the region as a whole. In October 1945, Under Secretary of State Dean Acheson sent a memorandum capturing the concerns of State Department Middle East specialists to Secretary of State James Byrnes. Acheson pointed out that U.S. economic officers in the Middle East were unhappy with policymakers' unwillingness to involve the federal government more fully in the promotion of Middle Eastern development. According to Acheson, regional economic specialists "repeatedly complained that it is impossible to execute any consistent long-range economic program on which the local governments can rely unless the authority of the executive branch extends further than writing diplomatic notes and making loans on a strictly commercial basis." Of course, those who opposed liberal developmentalism did not challenge the underlying assumptions of the sacred and secular mission that the Middle East needed to be transformed and that the United States should pursue policies to achieve that goal. Indeed, the debate focused entirely on the means to achieve that end, not on the end itself.[15]

Attempts to allow liberal developmentalism to work in Iran between 1947 and 1951 seemed to confirm such concerns that the approach was not capable by itself of transforming the Middle East and provided ammunition for its critics. U.S. policymakers relied on oil consultant Max Thornburg, who had worked for ARAMCO in the late 1930s, to serve as their "chosen instrument" to promote economic development in Iran. Thornburg believed that economic change must precede political change and that U.S. businesses could participate by using profits for development projects, promoting foreign investment, and generally contributing to a stable economic base. He also believed that the United States would benefit from further involvement in foreign markets and from relieving local social and political pressures through economic means rather than seeing them released through destabilizing revolutions. Thornburg pursued his vision in Iran by working with reformers in the Iranian government, by promoting the development of businesses following American lines and managerial models, by helping to institute a seven-year economic plan, and, most importantly, by working toward a renegotiation of the existing contract between the British and the Iranians regarding the Anglo-Iranian Oil Company. He believed all of these steps were necessary if Iran were going to develop economically, politically, and socially.[16]

Liberal developmentalism failed under Thornburg's guidance in Iran for several reasons. Politically conscious Iranians were already concerned about excessive foreign involvement in their country, and having a foreign businessman involved in Iranian economic planning only heightened that sensitivity. Thornburg himself was also a problem, as he worked his way into the local political scene and occasionally operated at cross-purposes with Truman administration officials and policies. Moreover, Iran was mired in political turmoil in the late 1940s and early 1950s, with various groups from across the political spectrum vying for power under the shah's monarchy. Thornburg added one more ingredient to the mix by placing himself between those groups and working with reformers. The Korean War and increasing Cold War tensions also caused the Truman administration to pursue a more active line on its own, as policymakers grew concerned that while their attention was focused elsewhere the Soviets would advance into Iran. Linda Wills Qaimmaqami has argued that, taken as a whole, these factors suggest that Thornburg bears some responsibility for the oil nationalization crisis that dominated Anglo-American-Iranian relations from 1951 to 1953. Regardless of the accuracy of that assessment, the Iranian and Saudi Arabian experiences revealed liberal developmentalism's limitations as a means of achieving America's sacred and secular mission in the Middle East.[17]

Defining Underdevelopment

The increasing exposure of Americans to the Middle East through involvement in the growing regional oil industry and the World War II military presence produced wide-ranging and almost reflexive commentary from observers remarking on the apparent underdevelopment of the region. American observers of the Middle East had long believed the region to be a backward, desolate place. As we have seen, commentaries from late eighteenth-century captives in North Africa, mid-nineteenth century missionaries in what are today Lebanon, Syria, and Turkey, and late nineteenth-century travelers to the "Holy Land" were filled with statements about widespread disease, poor sanitation, and grinding poverty. None of these characteristics were unique to the Middle East at the time. By the mid-twentieth century, however, increasing American exposure to and involvement in the Middle East combined with new forms of social scientific knowledge to lead observers to make increasingly specific claims about what plagued the region. No longer did it suffice to speak in general terms of a backward people. Instead, specialists looked to quantifiable and supposedly objective measures like literacy rates, agricultural output, and population growth rates as indicators of what came to be called Middle Eastern underdevelopment.

In some cases, a brief summary was all that was required. A 1945 State Department memorandum for President Truman argued that the "peoples of the region remain for the most part ignorant, poverty-stricken and diseased," while a July 1950 State Department paper declared the Middle East "economically immature" and "extremely 'underdeveloped.'" Likewise, the scholar J. C. Hurewitz, writing for a Council on Foreign Relations study group in 1952, noted that "most of the independent states are . . . politically immature," the "primarily agrarian" economies were "primitive" in nature, and much of the region's population was "disease-ridden and illiterate, despite the considerable progress since World War I."[18]

In other cases, commentators drew on new forms of social scientific expertise and went to greater lengths to convey the extent of the problems they believed confronted people in the Middle East. Hedley Cooke, the former U.S. consul in both Palestine and Turkey, and consultant for Middle Eastern issues to the Economic Cooperation Administration, outlined a multitude of concerns in *Challenge and Response in the Middle East: The Quest for Prosperity, 1919–1951*. According to Cooke, economies throughout the region were woefully insufficient, as were health and sanitation conditions. There was dramatic population growth and, with the exception of Islam, the existing social structures did little to create any form of a unified society or community within individual countries or across borders. The University of Pennsylvania Near East specialist E. A. Speiser did not present quite as lengthy a catalogue of the region's problems in *The United States and the Near East*, but he still devoted two out of ten chapters to these issues.[19]

Yet no commentator utilized new social scientific expertise to define so powerfully and to describe so vividly Middle Eastern underdevelopment and poverty as did British agronomist Doreen Warriner. Warriner took great pains in her 1948 monograph *Land and Poverty in the Middle East* to establish the distance separating her European and American readers from her Middle Eastern subjects. She opened her study by painting a bleak and graphic picture of daily life in the region: "Near starvation, pestilence, high death rates, soil erosion, economic exploitation—this is the pattern of life for the mass of the rural population in the Middle East. It is a poverty which has no parallel in Europe, since even clean water is a luxury. Money incomes are low . . . but money comparisons alone do not convey the filth and disease, the mudhuts shared with animals, the dried dung fuel. There is no standard of living in the European sense—mere existence is accepted as the standard." Warriner proceeded to examine the situation in five separate parts of the region (Egypt, Palestine, Transjordan, Syria and Lebanon, and Iraq). In Egypt, the peasant lived in conditions of "unrelieved horror." "The fellaheen are physically wretched," she argued, "and judging by the statistics of rural crime— the extraordinarily high murder rate—they are morally degenerate also; this is hardly surprising, since they are an almost slave population." And though circumstances in Egypt seemed particularly bad, peasants elsewhere in the region fared only marginally better. Warriner concluded her study with three primary recommendations for improving the lot of the Middle Eastern peasant: fundamentally reforming existing land tenure systems and a peasant-landlord relationship that promoted a certain fatalism among the rural poor; gradually shifting to mechanized agriculture; and promoting more comprehensive agricultural planning within and across state borders to improve irrigation techniques and to prevent soil erosion.[20]

Other specialists quickly hailed Warriner's book as not only one of the best works on Middle Eastern socioeconomic systems, but as one of the best on the region as a whole. The young Middle East specialist William Polk, who drew heavily on Warriner for his own vivid description of the Middle Eastern peasant's existence, referred to Warriner's work in his "What the Arabs Think" (1952) as "one of the best and most honest books on the area." Other academic specialists seconded his assessment. The bibliography to a volume of essays edited by social scientist Sydney Nettleton Fisher labeled Land and Poverty in the Middle East one of two "basic and competent studies" on " 'The Villager' of the Middle East." Similarly, J. C. Hurewitz found that Warriner "incisively" analyzed land tenure issues and agricultural economics in the Middle East. Even as late as 1965, seventeen years after Land and Poverty in the Middle East was published, Polk still found its unsparing descriptions of the peasant condition throughout the Middle East "shocking and powerful."[21]

Such representations of the Middle East often correctly argued that the economic, political, and social structures in the Middle East did not provide for the needs of the region's population. Two world wars and a global depression hit the area very hard. World War I brought about several hundred thousand deaths and forced significant disruptions in trade, both within the region itself and with Europe. Just when the region began to recover in the mid- to late 1920s, the Great Depression drove down prices and inhibited global trade. The decrease in European imports helped stimulate some local industrial growth, but the lack of substantial funds for investment limited expansion. Then, just as signs of another recovery appeared, world war again interrupted the process. Another decline in international trade and the limited availability of crucial imports such as fertilizer once again hindered growth. The cumulative result was little net gain in such development indicators as per capita income and gross domestic product throughout the first half of the twentieth century. In Egypt, for example, per capita income stagnated from 1913 through World War II, while Turkey's gross national product grew at an average annual rate of just 0.6 percent from before World War I through World War II.[22]

The regional political situation was only marginally better than the economic circumstances. World War I brought about the final demise of the Ottoman Empire, long the dominant political structure in the region, and the implementation of a European-dominated League of Nations mandatory system. The 1920s and 1930s did see the emergence of a few independent states (initially Egypt and Turkey, and later Saudi Arabia and Iraq), though both Egypt and Iraq were ruled by conservative monarchs and remained under heavy British influence. The mandate system seemed to offer more in the way of the continuation of European imperialism than it did for future Middle Eastern independence. Rarely did the ruling powers, be they monarchs in the independent states or the British and French in the mandate areas, work to establish political and economic systems that responded to the needs of the general population.[23]

Americans trying to explain what made the Middle East the way they imagined it to be in the mid-twentieth century tended to look past such explanations, however, and instead identified several broad causes originating from within the region itself. Conventional wisdom among specialists of the period held that the Middle East's geography and climate exercised inordinate influence. The desert was dry, dangerous, and unforgiving, and supposedly did much to determine the basic constraints within which the peoples of the region existed. As former Library of Congress ancient Near East specialist Halford Hoskins noted in 1954, "With respect to the principal features of the physical environment of the Middle East area itself, about the only major generalization that will apply is that the area is dry. . . . Probably no other circumstance, and possibly no other combination of circumstances, has exerted as much influence on the human elements which have moved into the area in the course of centuries as this single fact of prevalent desiccation." The desert had "set group against group in struggles for the possession of the watered lands," and "shaped and circumscribed the cultures now regarded as indigenous to the area." Warriner, too, analyzed annual rainfall amounts and the size and quality of arable land to emphasize the basic limitations that climate and geography placed on the possibilities for agricultural development in the Middle East. Finally, Kermit Roosevelt—grandson of Theodore Roosevelt, historian, World War II intelligence agent, and later a key participant in the 1953 CIA coup in Iran—spent the first two substantive chapters of a 1947 book discussing the impact of climate and geography on the making of the contemporary Middle East and its problems.[24]

A second explanation for the imagined backwardness of the Middle East revolved around the notion of "the long sleep," a concept soundly rejected by more recent research but that factored prominently in Orientalist scholarship of the early to mid-twentieth century. This line of analysis suggested that a dynamic Islamic and Arab civilization expanded quickly and broadly out of the Arabian Peninsula following the death of the prophet Muhammad, but that Arab complacency by the mid-thirteenth century led that civilization into decline. The sack of Baghdad by Genghis Khan's grandson Hulagu Khan in 1258 was the harbinger of centuries of stagnation, decline, and foreign domination first as the Ottomans and later as Europeans exercised control throughout much of the Middle East. The prevalent belief was that the Middle East of the early to mid-twentieth century was only just emerging from this long sleep.[25]

Observers identified a third explanation in the social structure of the Middle East, particularly among its Arab Muslim population. Analysts combined several different features—the most important being a history of tribal and nomadic societies and great distinctions between the wealthy and the poor—to argue that the dominant forms of social organization in the region inhibited economic and political growth. William Polk stated the point succinctly in his 1952 essay titled, "What the Arabs Think": "Society in the Arab world—excluding the proud desert nomads who form only a small percentage of the total population—resembles a flattened pyramid. At the top are a few thousand immensely wealthy merchants and landowners; then comes a narrow layer of middle-class, largely Western-educated professionals and technicians; and finally, the vast mass of landless or nearly landless peasants.

Separating the upper two groups from the lower is an incredible gulf in education, ways of life and standards of living." Such analysis not only placed Middle Eastern underdevelopment within the context of the region's socioeconomic order, but also suggested particular ways of correcting the problem. It was hoped that improved educational and economic opportunities, as well as increasing urbanization, would overcome the structural flaws in the Arab and Middle Eastern social system, and thereby eliminate, over time, the problem of regional underdevelopment.[26]

Specialists located yet a fourth cause of the problems in the Middle East in the nature of the people themselves. Observers did occasionally acknowledge positive character traits among Arab Muslims. One CIA report, for example, recognized that "external politeness is greatly valued," that "Arabs are very sensitive to bad manners or rudeness," and they were "noted in ordinary transactions for simplicity and honesty." Yet American Middle East specialists were much more likely to imagine the people of the region through a slew of more negative or derogatory characterizations. Indeed, the same CIA report labeled Arabs as "non-inventive and slow to put theories into practice; they find it hard to depart from traditional methods. They often seem to Europeans to be incompetent and lazy, lacking in constructive ability, and skillful mainly in avoiding hard work. Contempt for manual labor is common both to Bedouin and to townsmen, particularly the upper class." In addition, the report claimed, "the Arab will evade the spirit while observing the letter of the moral obligations which he recognizes," while Arabs as a group displayed "a remarkable capability for intrigue, and their loyalty is tempered by time serving; on occasion they commit astonishing acts of treachery and dishonesty."[27]

Underlying many of these explanations was a fifth assumption: a basic concern that Islam itself was the problem. Chapter 2 examined how specialists viewed Islam as a totalitarian religion that controlled how all Muslims thought and acted, and thus limited adherents' conceptions of their own individual and political possibilities. A similar argument was applied to socioeconomic issues. According to Polk, all peasants were "bound by a common cultural tradition and a similar historical development" that acted "as a frame of reference for modern Arab thought." Moreover, the peasants' ability to find "some comfort from Islamic fatalism" allowed them to tolerate such a meager existence.[28]

Many specialists and policymakers believed the post–World War II period brought new opportunities to alter these regional circumstances and, with these opportunities, the potential for uncontrollable revolutionary change. The war signaled the end of European hegemony and with it the demise of colonialism in the Middle East. The very principles for which the war had been fought—self determination, freedom from want, and free and open trade—suggested to the peoples of the Middle East that the United States would support newly independent states in their quest for fundamental change in the existing economic, political, and social orders. Even before World War II ended, a State Department group of regional specialists studying alternatives for postwar U.S. economic policy in the Middle East argued that the region would "remain one of the principal testing grounds of the ideals for which the war is being fought . . . The countries of the Middle East are weak and in a state of intense readjustment—political, social and economic."[29]

What remained unclear to American observers, however, was which group—the peasant masses or a new rising urban middle class—would drive that readjustment. According to Polk, the peasants were "so bound by the fetters of poverty, ignorance and disease . . . that they have been unable to show many signs of political life. To date they have expressed almost no political thought, as they have been unable to do more than barely keep alive." But that was no guarantee that the peasants would continue to remain quiescent. Polk continued, "Surely if there ever was a group which fitted Karl Marx's phrase about a group having nothing to lose but its chains, it is the fellaheen. The peasants gain some comfort from Islamic fatalism, but they have no stake in the present order and could not but gain by any conceivable change." For the time being, all that prevented the peasants from rising up was their daily struggle for existence, but it was unclear how long that would continue to be the case: "To talk to them in terms of democracy or freedom is to mock them; for them the basic question is life or death—not how life can be led. Thus, they say little; yet they act as a sort of brake on the political thought of the other groups and constitute a big question mark about the political future of the area."[30]

Polk believed the peasants might hold the key to the future of the Middle East, but he and other members of the network also thought that increasing exposure to Western lifestyles, living standards, and technologies, as well as greater educational opportunities, created a "revolution of rising expectations" among the urban middle classes. Some analysts emphasized the impact of Western films and the images they presented of a better lifestyle, or the influence of people returning to the Middle East from the United States. Polk, for example, argued that "the *Arabian Nights* were nothing compared" to the images of life in the United States conveyed by comparatively wealthy returning immigrants and Hollywood films like *Mr. Blandings Builds His Dream House*. Others focused on the creation during the previous few decades of a new, educated middle class of urban workers and intellectuals seeking to modernize the Middle East. According to this line of argument, the members of this new class had grown restive and were beginning to agitate for a fundamental social reordering that would overturn the existing conservative elite leadership. This apparent revolution of rising expectations therefore gave calls for fundamental change even greater resonance.[31]

By the late 1940s or early 1950s, then, most members of the informal network of specialists agreed that the peoples of the Middle East were embarking on an era of dramatic and broad-based revolutionary change, though they were not sure whether that change would be driven by the peasant masses or by a new urban middle class. Either way, popular discontent with the economic, political, and social states of affairs in the region appeared to be increasing rapidly. That dissatisfaction, combined with the perceived new opportunities presented by the fundamental global changes wrought by World War II, convinced members of the network and policymakers that the Middle East was wrapped up in a revolution of rising expectations. Tired of years of privation, the arguments went, the masses were rising up to overturn the domestic and international social and political classes that had enforced and maintained such terrible conditions. "Social revolution," a 1951 draft National Security Council study argued, "may be impossible to prevent." It remained to be answered, however, whether such revolutionary change would push forward and ultimately fulfill America's sacred and secular mission or if revolutionary change and American interests would contradict each other and work at cross-purposes.[32]

Pursuing Transformation While Controlling Revolutionary Change

The prospect of revolutionary change meshed nicely with the American sense of mission in the Middle East, but members of the network and U.S. policymakers believed that a variety of global concerns forced them to find some way to try at least to control the change. The overall importance of the region and its resources to the global arena was reason enough for the United States to attempt to intervene, as Middle Eastern oil and trade routes would be crucial to the rapid postwar international economic recovery that U.S. policymakers desired. The process of decolonization also promised further instability that might be limited or prevented if the United States could somehow assist newly independent states in the region to become economically and politically viable. Finally, as tensions between the United States and the Soviet Union increased after World War II, policymakers and members of the network became more concerned that an unstable Middle East provided fertile ground for Soviet involvement. For all of these reasons, maintaining good relations with the countries and peoples of the Middle East meant dealing in some manner with the issue of revolutionary change.

Analysts focused much of their attention on the complicated objective of how the United States might pursue change throughout the Middle East while at the same time ensuring political and ultimately social stability and order. Doing so would not be easy, as any attempt to promote moderate reform necessarily carried with it the possibility of unleashing uncontrollable change. The participants in a Near East chiefs of mission conference in 1950 posed the question clearly. "The problem," they stated, "is to introduce into Near Eastern political and social systems a compelling degree of liberal thought and desire for social justice without forcing a too rapid change of the existing order which might create an opportunity for communism to develop rapidly."[33]

Policymakers and specialists alike drew on deeply ingrained notions of American exceptionalism, magnanimity, and moral superiority as they imagined their country's playing a transformational role in the Middle East. According to these arguments, the United States had a long history of beneficent involvement in the region. Secretary of State Cordell Hull noted in 1942 that, because of "a century of American missionary, educational and philanthropic efforts that have never been tarnished by any material motives or interests," the United States held "a unique position in the Near East" and enjoyed "widespread goodwill" throughout the region. Similarly, when the chiefs of mission of four U.S. legations in the Middle East met with President Truman in November 1945, they argued that the United States' "moral leadership" was internationally recognized. People in the Middle East and around the world were waiting for Americans to decide if they were "going to follow through after their great victory or leave the field."[34]

Such statements also reflected uncertainty about what principles should guide the United States as it simultaneously sought to promote transformation and control change. It was clear to network members that the United States should pursue some change to protect its own interests in the region. If policymakers carelessly pursued those interests to the exclusion of any concern for the local inhabitants, however, Middle Easterners might abandon their favorable view of the United States and begin thinking of the country in much the same way as they did Britain and France, their current and former imperial masters. In October 1945, the head of Near Eastern affairs at the State Department drafted a memorandum to remind his superiors, including President Truman, that uplifting people of the region must remain an important part of the equation if the United States were to fulfill its sacred and secular mission in the Middle East. "If we are to serve our higher long-range political, economic and strategic purposes," opined Gordon Merriam, "our activities in the Near East must be based upon the political, educational, and economic development of the native peoples and not merely upon the narrow immediate interest of British or American economy." At the same time, though, too much emphasis on uplifting the peoples of the Middle East would have recalled memories of the "White Man's Burden" ideology that animated imperialist endeavors in the late nineteenth and early twentieth centuries. The United States therefore needed to walk a fine line between its competing interests in pursuing change in the Middle East.[35]

Government Middle East specialists were the first to argue strongly that promoting economic development offered the best chances of bringing controlled change to the Middle East. Even as World War II concluded in Europe, State Department Middle East specialists made the case that economic development would address problems of decolonization and possible postwar tensions between the United States and the Soviet Union. A May 1945 report on U.S. economic policies in the Middle East contended that "improvement of economic conditions and raising of standards of living" would "assist in removing economic discontents and thereby lessen the possibility that these countries will be hauled and pulled by the USSR on the one hand and by Great Britain on the other." Shoring up local economies and increasing standards of living would deprive the Soviets of the disenchanted masses on which the global communist movement supposedly relied, while also assisting the transition to independence. State Department papers prepared during the 1947 "Pentagon Talks" between U.S. and British officials put the point even more forcefully. The U.S. participants argued that "a general increase in the economic prosperity of the peoples of the Middle East, as broadly distributed as through the masses of the population, is most desirable if not essential. It is needed as a basis for internal stability and security of the area, and to reduce the danger of revolutionary developments and communist penetration."[36]

State Department Middle East specialists repeatedly asked their superiors to implement a comprehensive program to provide development assistance to the Middle East. In August 1945, Near Eastern Affairs Division Chief Gordon Merriam called for the creation of a focused development program for the Middle East, funded with approximately $100 million annually. In early June 1946, Director of the Office of Near Eastern and African Affairs Loy Henderson made another appeal for a concerted and comprehensive development assistance program. Henderson's proposal called for the allocation "of at least $120,000,000 for construction and development loans to Near Eastern countries without demanding excessive assurances that every cent loaned will be repaid in dollars." Such an allocation, Henderson believed, would make it possible for the United States to reap important political rewards. Finally, in June 1950, Assistant Secretary of State for Near Eastern, South Asian, and African Affairs George McGhee once again floated the idea of a focused development program for the Near East and South Asia as "a major step in the formulation of our post-ERP [Marshall Plan] foreign economic policy."[37]

High-level policymakers' responses to these proposals revealed their early opposition to using government aid to promote development in the Middle East. They rejected two of the three proposals outright, with almost no discussion. According to Under Secretary Dean Acheson, Secretary of State Byrnes responded bluntly to Merriam's proposal in October 1945, stating simply, "This cannot be done at present." Henderson's proposal was dismissed almost as quickly. Less than three weeks after Henderson submitted his request, Director of the Office of Financial and Development Policy George Luthringer and Assistant Secretary of State for Economic Affairs William Clayton rejected it, claiming that using loans in such a political manner was "undesirable." Only McGhee's proposal received further investigation, and even it appears to have been overshadowed by events in Korea and elsewhere, and never to have received formal acceptance or rejection.[38]

The failure of liberal developmentalism and dramatic Cold War developments combined in the late 1940s to lead policymakers to shift their emphasis toward direct foreign aid to bring about controlled change in the Middle East. The first step in this direction was the British decision to stop aiding pro-Western governments in Greece and Turkey, both of which U.S. policymakers believed were coming under increasing communist pressure. As a result of the British withdrawal, in March 1947 President Truman requested $400 million from Congress for assistance to Greece and Turkey. In making that request, Truman also proclaimed his nation's willingness to provide support "through economic and financial aid which is essential to economic stability and orderly political processes" to those countries "resisting attempted subjugation by armed minorities or by outside pressures." The president thereby assumed for the United States the mantle of global defender against communism as well as other forms of economic, political, and social instability. The Truman administration followed up its commitment to foreign aid by announcing the Marshall Plan for European economic recovery later in 1947.[39]

This transition to direct foreign aid brought U.S. policy more in line with what government Middle East specialists wanted, but with the exception of increased funds for Turkey the policy did not immediately bring significantly more aid to the region. Policymakers were generally more concerned with European and Japanese economic recovery, and were thus prepared to devote much of the available resources to those areas. Moreover, Congress and the general public were not yet ready to pursue an open-ended foreign aid policy that required full-scale commitments throughout the non-European world. As a result, President Truman and his advisors relied on more limited efforts to transfer the ideas and perceived benefits of the Truman Doctrine and the Marshall Plan to the Middle East and elsewhere.

In the late 1940s and early 1950s, therefore, technical assistance—known more popularly as Point Four—became policymakers' preferred method of promoting development and stability and addressing the revolution of rising expectations throughout the Middle East and elsewhere. In the fourth point of his 1949 inaugural address, Truman emphasized the rewards that Americans and non-Western peoples might reap from the simple act of providing relatively inexpensive aid in the forms of technical advisors and the sharing of scientific advances and technology. "For the first time in history," Truman claimed, "humanity possesses the knowledge and skill to relieve the suffering" of peoples in the underdeveloped areas of the world. The "more vigorous application of modern scientific and technical knowledge" in these areas would not only "help the free peoples of the world, through their own efforts, to produce more food, more clothing, more materials for housing, and more mechanical power to lighten their burdens." It also provided the "key to greater production," which in turn was the "key to prosperity and peace" in the United States and around the world.[40]

In addition to the new Point Four program, policymakers began two other aid initiatives that related directly to the Middle East in the early 1950s. The first was the Mutual Security Program, created by Congress in 1951. The program was intended to coordinate through the Mutual Security Agency all U.S. foreign aid programs, including economic, military, and technical assistance. Under the provisions of the Mutual Security Program, President Truman appointed Edwin Locke Jr., a banker with experience and business connections in the Middle East, to coordinate all U.S. aid to the area. The second aid program related specifically to the Arab-Israeli conflict, and appropriated funds for the United Nations Relief and Works Agency for the Palestinian refugees created by the 1948–1949 war between the Arab states and Israel. The original allocation was $250 million, the majority of which was supposed to be spent over three years for economic development, employment, and resettling refugees in Arab states.[41]

Many specialists welcomed Point Four and the broader aid initiative for the Middle East, but they also recognized that it would likely produce only limited results. Well before Truman announced Point Four in 1949, Doreen Warriner argued in *Land and Poverty in the Middle East* that the achievements of technical assistance would be minimal. Technical assistance would not fundamentally alter land tenure systems or overall social structures that she believed inhibited regional transformation and needed to undergo fundamental, yet carefully controlled, change. Only much more significant amounts of capital could begin to address this type of issue and generate dramatic improvements throughout the region. Afif Tannous, a Middle East agricultural specialist of Lebanese descent who worked in the U.S. Department of Agriculture, made a similar point in 1951. He argued that Congress clearly had altruistic motives in mind when it agreed to support technical assistance, and Point Four would certainly benefit the Middle East as much as any other region. Tannous contended, however, that "the crying need of the Middle East cannot be filled through technical aid, capital investment, and economic development alone . . . The solution lies in economic development that is conceived and achieved for one sole purpose: *the emancipation and welfare of the people*." The only way to achieve such an objective in the primarily agrarian economies of the Middle East was to promote fundamental land reform. The Library of Congress Near East specialist and first head of the Middle East Institute, Halford Hoskins, focused more narrowly on the specific issue of technical assistance and what it might offer the region. Hoskins did see Point Four assistance providing tangible results of measurable value, particularly in the area of water development. He also argued, however, that any realistic assessment of the value of Point Four for the Middle East had to take into account the "character and extent of underdevelopment" throughout the region. Because of the region's climate and the limited natural resources available for industrialization, Hoskins argued, the Middle East might not have been "capable of extensive improvement beyond present levels" simply through technical assistance. In short, Warriner, Tannous, Hoskins, and others believed technical assistance was a start, but that it was only a start, and a notably meager one at that.[42]

The prediction proved correct that Point Four and other early U.S. foreign aid programs in the Middle East would be of limited value. To be sure, the $150 million provided to Turkey under the Truman Doctrine helped strengthen that nation as a U.S. ally. Point Four allocations for the rest of the Middle East were relatively small, however, with only a few small projects undertaken in the early 1950s. The United States did provide the $250 million to benefit the Palestinian refugees, but much of that money went for basic relief measures such as food, clothing, and housing rather than the development and resettlement projects for which it was originally intended. The broader initiative was also characterized by bureaucratic infighting both in Washington and in the field. The attempt to coordinate all regional aid programs under the direction of Edwin Locke Jr. also failed. He, his superiors in Washington, his colleagues in the field, and the leaders of the Middle Eastern states the United States was supposed to be assisting could rarely agree on the nature of specific aid programs. Locke resigned less than a year after taking the job, and his position went unfilled for the remainder of the Truman Administration. Then, as the previous chapter outlined, the first few years of the Eisenhower presidency were characterized by an emphasis on military assistance and collective security arrangements. It would therefore not be until the late 1950s that America's sacred and secular mission to transform the Middle East would again take center stage.[43]

The Rise of Modernization Theory

During the late 1950s, the pendulum swung once again to development as the best means to control revolutionary change in the Middle East. The growing criticisms of security-based U.S. foreign aid programs coming from inside and outside the informal network of specialists coincided with a broader reassessment in academic and policymaking circles of how the United States might pursue controlled transformation not only in the Middle East, but also in Africa, Asia, and Latin America. Policy-oriented social scientists devised an overarching framework—commonly referred to as modernization theory—that presented revolutionary change as a process that could be understood, pursued, and controlled through the application of American social science expertise and U.S. foreign aid. As policymakers rethought U.S. policy in the Middle East following the Iraqi Revolution in 1958, specialists from across the network—but particularly in academia—and the new modernization theorists had their greatest opportunity to pursue their own secular mission to transform the Middle East.

The roots of what emerged in the mid-1950s as modernization theory had been growing in several different academic disciplines, most notably sociology, political science, and development economics, since the 1930s. The driving intellectual force behind modernization theory in the mid-1950s was the belief that utilizing an integrative approach combining insights from a variety of academic fields offered the best means of understanding and controlling revolutionary change. Following this line of investigation, modernization theorists related the process of economic development to the broader political and social transformations they believed were taking place in specific countries as well as in the broader global arena. Three different studies of modernization, two of which dealt with the Middle East directly, revealed the diverse intellectual approaches to modernization theory and emphasized the idea that societies undergoing revolutionary change needed to be understood as single entities with economic, political, and social components.[44]

In 1958, sociologist and Middle East specialist Daniel Lerner published *The Passing of Traditional Society*, which proved to be the dominant text relating modernization theory to the Middle East. Lerner, true to his sociological roots, was deeply concerned with explaining modernization in terms of how people lived their lives. He searched for ways in which a "modernist inspiration" or "a rationalist and positivist spirit," supposedly characteristic of Western European or U.S. educated elites in the region, became dispersed among wider populations. Lerner argued that there were four key components of a modernizing society: the degree of urbanization, literacy rates, media consumption (how many people listened to radio, how many people were aware of different parts of the world, etc.), and the population's general level of empathy (the ability of individuals to imagine themselves in someone else's position).[45]

Lerner used results from a series of surveys conducted throughout the Middle East in the early 1950s by the Bureau of Applied Social Research at Columbia University to construct a theory of modernization based on these four criteria. Voluntary urbanization constituted the first phase in the transition from a traditional to a modern society. Once urbanization reached approximately 10 percent of the population, literacy rates would begin to rise significantly until urbanization reached 25 percent, at which point literacy would increase independently of the rate of urbanization. Twenty-five percent urbanization, combined with continually rising literacy rates and a concurrent increase in the level of consumer, economic, educational, and informational desires of the population, would then lead to the creation of a significant mass communications infrastructure, including radio and newspapers. Finally, when people could listen to the radio or read newspapers, they would become more familiar with the wider world and demonstrate a much greater capacity for empathy. Lerner's model, based on this step-by-step process, suggested that the level of modernization in a specific country could be quantified and charted simply by looking at these four characteristics of the nation's general population.[46]

Lerner then utilized these criteria and relied on the same survey results to analyze and rank the extent of change in six Middle Eastern societies racing toward modernity. While none of the six had yet achieved full "modernity," Turkey and Lebanon appeared to have made the greatest strides. Lerner argued that even though Lebanon scored higher than Turkey on several indices and was thus "more modern," the larger population in Turkey and the more rapid process of modernization that had taken place there made it "more dynamic" and suggested it was undergoing a more "balanced" modernization.[47]

Egypt and Syria presented more problematic cases in Lerner's estimation. Egypt had to overcome the greatest natural obstacles to modernization of any country in the Middle East, limited arable land and significant population growth rates, and was undergoing an extremely unbalanced modernization process. Egyptian urbanization had moved beyond optimum levels (25 percent) and had surpassed Turkey's by 1950, but Egyptian literacy rates ran well behind Turkish rates. Lerner observed that "to match Turkey's urbanism-literacy ratio, Egypt would require over 400% more literates than it had." Rather than ponder whether such findings invalidated his model for modernization, Lerner instead concluded that Egypt was caught in a "vicious circle" of poverty, small strides toward modernization, population growth, and more poverty. As Egypt had, Syria had made some strides toward modernization, but it too faced its own vicious circle. Instead of the natural obstacles of limited arable land, poverty, and population growth that confronted Egypt, however, Syrians faced a number of social and political problems. The most significant of these obstacles was continual political instability, which resulted in part from the country's great religious and ethnic diversity, an underdeveloped economy, and an "underparticipant population."[48]

Of the six countries Lerner ranked in his study, Jordan and Iran had the farthest distance left to travel on their journey from being traditional societies to becoming modern societies, and there was little cause for optimism that their development would speed up anytime soon. Jordan's problems stemmed, according to Lerner, from its "desert universe" and tribal social order, as well as the conflict over Palestine. Because of that conflict, the "desert fief suddenly found itself cast in the role of a modern nation" with a population that increased significantly with the addition of 700,000 refugees during the 1948–49 Arab-Israeli war. It was very difficult in these circumstances for Jordan to establish any sort of economic, political, or social stability that would allow the process of modernization even to begin, much less to advance in any meaningful way. Lerner believed modernization in Iran was nonexistent because of a confluence of issues. Nearly continuous foreign involvement prevented strong domestic institutions from taking root, while the population was too dispersed to promote urbanization, which was supposed to kick-start the whole modernization process. Moreover, in Lerner's analysis, Iran's social and economic structures promoted apathy among the population, and the political system tended toward extremism.[49]

While Lerner explored the social components of modernization in the Middle East, his associate at Massachusetts Institute of Technology's Center for International Studies, the economic historian and later high-ranking Kennedy and Johnson administration official Walt Rostow analyzed the economic aspect of change in *The Stages of Economic Growth: A Non-Communist Manifesto* (1960). Rostow was never heavily involved in the study of Middle Eastern affairs and he tended to group the Middle East with Africa, Asia, and Latin America in his explanations of global economic change. Indeed, few of his writings from the mid-1950s through the mid-1960s, the years when modernization theory achieved its greatest impact, have much to say about the Middle East specifically. Nonetheless, as the most influential articulator of modernization theory, Rostow helped to establish the broader context within which modernization theorists writing on the Middle East operated. In addition, Rostow did assume some responsibility for U.S. policy toward the Middle East. He worked as a consultant to the Eisenhower administration and played a crucial role in developing a response to the Iraqi revolution of 1958. He went on to become the director of the State Department's Policy Planning Council under President Kennedy, and he ultimately served as President Johnson's special assistant for national security affairs. His ideas therefore warrant attention.[50]

Rostow developed an argument about revolutionary economic change that was, in the words of historian Diane Kunz, "simple and comforting." *The Stages of Economic Growth* was intended for "an intelligent non-professional audience" and made the process of development seem deceptively easy. Each country only needed to move through a basic five-step program: (1) beginning as a traditional society, (2) developing the preconditions for takeoff into self-sustained growth, (3) taking off into self-sustained growth, (4) driving to maturity, and finally (5) arriving at the age of high mass-consumption. Rostow contended it was "possible to identify all societies, in their economic dimensions, as lying within one of [these] five categories." The process would, of course, take some time to work itself out in each case, but all the evidence suggested that the complete transition, from being a traditional society to being one in an age of high mass-consumption, should take no more than sixty years. Rostow argued that a fundamental shift in attitudes, from the static "pre-Newtonian," traditional ideas to the realization that economic progress was "a necessary precondition for some other purpose, judged to be good," was needed to propel a nation through the three necessary generations of change. That change in attitude would then give rise to a similar shift in economic behavior that would lead to increased savings and investment rates. The desire "to exploit the fruits of modern science," made manifest by the new attitudes and economic behavior, would also be accompanied by a significant political change—the creation of a centralized national state.[51]

Rostow believed it was possible to kick-start economic change in traditional societies through contact with what he identified as more advanced societies. Reminiscent of George Louis Beer's reading of the British presence in Egypt in the late nineteenth and early twentieth centuries, Rostow's *Stages* held that European colonialism had previously allowed for such contact to take place and had therefore initiated the requisite shift in attitudes by exposing traditional societies to modern technology and everything it could accomplish. In addition, according to Rostow, colonial powers also typically invested enough money in infrastructure, commercialized agricultural, and the exploitation of natural resources to provide a head start for colonized peoples when they finally achieved independence. Rostow acknowledged that the shift in attitudes that colonialism supposedly initiated often played out in different ways, most notably by helping to sustain the drive for independence throughout the colonized world. With decolonization in full force by the late

1950s, Rostow found it necessary to promote other ways of providing a similar stimulant. He called for the prudent and rational application of U.S. and Western European foreign aid in the postcolonial world to fill the void created by decolonization. Rostow thereby proffered an interpretation that stressed the benefits accrued rather than the negative effects of colonialism and active U.S. involvement throughout the post-1945 world.[52]

While Lerner emphasized the social aspect of revolutionary change in the Middle East and Rostow analyzed economic components of the process, political scientist Manfred Halpern tried to understand the political aspect of modernization in *The Politics of Social Change in the Middle East and North Africa*. Halpern spent ten years in the State Department, much of it in the Division of Research and Analysis for the Near East, South Asia, and Africa, before joining the faculty at Princeton in 1958. There he worked in the Program in Near Eastern Studies and the Center for International Studies while also serving as a consultant for the RAND Corporation. Halpern was less concerned than Rostow and Lerner with laying out an overall model of modernization and instead explored what the process of Middle Eastern social change meant in political terms for the peoples and states of the region and the rest of the world. Of the three works, Halpern's presented the most comprehensive picture of modernization and its problems in the Middle East.[53]

Halpern divided his book into five parts, which he believed "define[d] the scope of the Middle Eastern and North African transformation." The first part hearkened back to enduring conceptions of Islam as the determining factor in Middle Eastern life and examined the breakdown by modern forces of the traditional, religiously centered way of life that Halpern contended had dominated the region for thirteen centuries. "The cumulative growth of ideas, production, and power generated outside the Islamic system," Halpern argued, "has penetrated that system and is tearing apart its repetitive pattern of balanced tensions. A system connecting man, God, and society is falling apart, and the new forces are still too far out of balance, sometimes even out of touch, with the old and with each other to constitute a stable and resilient new pattern." That, in turn, suggested the second aspect of social change in the region: the establishment of a new social system and new values to replace the old social structure. Here the roles of the traditional classes, such as peasants and landlords, and the relationships between them were being redefined, while new social classes like an urban middle class and a growing working class emerged.[54]

These processes of class redefinition and emergence gave rise to a variety of new ideologies that fundamentally challenged the basic premises of the traditional society, and out of which the people of the region created new "instruments of political modernization." In what Halpern considered the third component of political and social change in the Middle East and North Africa, no less than seven new political ideologies appeared—reformist Islam, neo-Islamic totalitarianism, communist totalitarianism, nationalism, democracy, authoritarianism, and socialism—that defined the range of Middle Eastern political opportunities. According to his or her social station, a member of a new and redefined class could rely on one of these ideologies to provide structure and an agenda for political change, the fourth step in the overall process. Entities participating in this new era of political opportunity included the army, political parties, trade unions, and the civil bureaucracy.[55]

For Halpern, however, this wealth of alternatives for ideological and political affiliation raised a number of significant national, regional, and international problems and contradictions that hindered the process of social transformation and created a role for the United States to play. The process of working through these problems, of recognizing that they entailed "revolutionary consequences at home [in the Middle East] and abroad," constituted the fifth aspect of political and social change in the region. The threat of instability was the most significant of these problems with local and global implications. Halpern therefore argued that the United States should "recognize the full scope of the revolutions now transforming the Middle East and to help all its nationalists cope successfully with rapid social change."[56]

Taken together, the ideas of Lerner, Rostow, Halpern, and other modernization theorists had tremendous appeal for regional specialists and policymakers concerned about revolutionary change in areas such as the Middle East. Modernization theorists and the policymakers they influenced believed studying nations as organisms with fundamentally related economic, political, and social components provided a single interpretive framework through which to understand the numerous challenges such nations faced. Specifically, modernization theory suggested a straightforward solution to the problems of decolonization and development, and in the process made them seem manageable. One could easily plot a newly independent country's position on Lerner's or Rostow's modernization continuum by looking at a few objective factors such as urbanization or literacy rates, the types of goods a country produced, or the rate of savings and investment. Policymakers then only had to decide how the United States might best intervene to push forward economic development or social transformation. Lerner's and Rostow's theories suggested that the rational application of American social science expertise and U.S. and Western European funds would lead to the final accomplishment of America's sacred and secular mission of transforming the Middle East, and at last integrate the region's people into the international economy and political arena as close allies of the United States.

Second, by making the economic and societal challenges Middle Eastern states faced appear manageable, Lerner and Rostow suggested a means of controlling revolutionary change by engaging it. They assumed societies like those in the Middle East were undergoing economic, political, and social change. Rostow argued that national economies moving through the stages of growth were part of larger societies in transition from tradition to modernity, a process Lerner analyzed. Halpern also articulated this notion, although he complicated Lerner's and Rostow's ideas of managing development or social transformation by analyzing the destabilizing consequences of the process. Social change caused a powerful sense of disorientation among the general population and could potentially lead it down a path toward political radicalism. It was important for the United States to do what it might to prevent such an occurrence.

A third area in which modernization theory appealed to members of the network and policymakers was in its ability to address fears that the process of revolutionary change led to increased opportunities for Soviet or communist penetration of the Middle East. Rostow viewed communism as "a kind of disease which can befall a transitional society if it fails to organize effectively those elements within it which are prepared to get on with the job of modernization." But if that transitional process could be appropriately managed, a problem that Rostow called "the central challenge of our time," then political instability would be much less likely to occur. Transitional states that followed an American or Western European model of economic development, or those that moved through the transition from tradition to modernity most quickly, would be much less radical and pose far fewer threats to U.S. interests throughout the world. In this way, Lerner, Rostow, and Halpern all implied that Americans should remain confident in their nation's model of development and the policy of opposition to the Soviet Union.[57]

In their quest to make revolutionary change more manageable, however, modernization theorists created models that were too rigid and relied too heavily on U.S. and Western European experiences. With the exception of Halpern, who recognized the many different paths that social transformation could take, they assumed that all societies moved along the same linear path, and that such a path was measurable and predictable. Modernization theory also generally could not account for leaders who pursued their own agendas. Despite Rostow's best wishes, and as U.S.-Egyptian relations in the 1960s would demonstrate, foreign aid intended to promote development was intimately linked with other issues. How well the leaders of different states got along, the actions of foreign leaders, and politicians' beliefs that foreign aid was given only with the expectation of receiving something in return all impacted the extent to which the United States could manage revolutionary change in the Middle East and elsewhere. Moreover, many people in the Middle East and elsewhere who had devoted their lives to fighting foreign involvement in their home countries saw the United States' reliance on modernization to control revolutionary change as synonymous with promoting "westernization."[58]

These problems demonstrated some of modernization theory's many weaknesses, but perhaps the greatest challenge grew out of the realization that no clear correlation existed between the application of U.S. development aid or social science expertise and the actual achievement of America's sacred and secular mission in the Middle East. As early as 1960 a subcommittee of the National Security Council reported that the United States "carries on its foreign economic programs without benefit of an ideology or even a coherent theory about the relationship between assistance, development and international politics." The report went on to argue that U.S. aid programs arose "from a variety, even a confusion, of generalized objectives — economic, military, humanitarian, and others." Even Manfred Halpern recognized this very serious problem in U.S. foreign aid programs, noting at a 1961 conference on Iran "that we have no theory of political and social change to complement our theory of economic development . . . We have only an ad hoc approach to revolution — capitalizing on the breaks where we find them." Perhaps *The Politics of Social Change in the Middle East and North Africa* was an attempt to address that issue.[59]

Testing Modernization Theory in the Middle East

Modernization theorists gained influence on policymakers, who were themselves looking for alternative approaches to U.S.–Middle East relations following the tension-laden years of the mid-1950s, and began by the end of that decade to impact U.S. policy and attempts to transform the Middle East. The Iraqi Revolution of 1958 presented a limited first opportunity for theorists, but events in Egypt and Iran proved more indicative of both the appeal and limitations of modernization theory. The influence academic members of the informal network of specialists exerted over U.S. policy in the region was greatest from the late 1950s through the mid-1960s and blurred the line between the network and policymakers.

In order to appreciate fully the effort to transform the Middle East through the application of modernization theory, however, it is first necessary to acknowledge and make explicit a key point regarding a basic transition that took place in U.S. foreign economic policy during the Eisenhower administration. Burton Kaufman has convincingly argued that the Eisenhower years witnessed a fundamental change in U.S. policymakers' attitudes both to promoting change abroad and to dealing with a variety of pressing international economic and political concerns. Kaufman suggests that with certain important exceptions such as the Truman Doctrine, the Marshall Plan, and the relatively small-scale Point Four programs, postwar U.S. policy had been to emphasize "trade not aid" as a means of getting U.S. dollars abroad and promoting international economic growth. The liberal developmental approach discussed above certainly fit that model with respect to the Middle East. According to Kaufman, however, that policy shifted as the Soviet Union began providing financial aid packages to countries in Africa, Asia, Latin America, and the Middle East beginning in the mid-1950s and as U.S. policymakers became convinced that economic growth and development could only be pursued on a regionwide basis that required significant public financial support to complement trade. Thus, a virulently anticommunist Eisenhower administration looked to combine "trade and aid" as it began to promote comprehensive development schemes abroad. To do so meant relying on regional specialists and the new ways of defining underdevelopment and measuring change discussed earlier in this chapter, and thus created an environment in which the emerging modernization theorists could thrive.[60]

The July 1958 Iraqi Revolution presented modernization theorists, network members, and policymakers their first opportunity to employ their ideas to try to pursue controlled transformation in the Middle East. President Eisenhower later stated that he was convinced that "only improvement of living standards could bring stability to the Middle East." He therefore turned to an old World War II friend, Time-Life executive C. D. Jackson, to prepare a speech for an early August address in which the president would lay out before the United Nations the U.S. response to the events in Iraq. Jackson had been in charge of psychological warfare operations in Europe under Eisenhower's command during the war, and assumed the post of the president's special assistant for psychological warfare when the general moved into the oval office. Jackson, in turn, drew his own longtime friend Walt Rostow into the drafting process. Rostow took over from there, working virtually around the clock for several days to put together a speech that highlighted the need for the people of the Middle East to focus on modernization and development.[61]

The speech that Jackson and Rostow composed represented the rise of modernization theory as the preferred method of trying to engage and manage revolutionary change in the Middle East and thus to achieve America's sacred and secular mission of transforming the region. Eisenhower instructed Secretary of State John Foster Dulles and Jackson that discussion of the specific crisis should be limited to a single paragraph, and that the remainder of the speech should make suggestions that revealed both the "practical" and "idealistic" nature of U.S. foreign policy. Given such great leeway, Jackson and Rostow wrote a speech that reasserted the principle of U.S. government assistance for Middle Eastern development. The speech's major initiative was a proposal for an Arab development institution, to be run by the coordinated efforts of the various Middle Eastern states and the United Nations. This new institution would utilize funds provided by the states in the region and by private institutions and other nations — including the United States — that were willing to participate. The concept of a separate Arab development bank or institution had been bandied about since at least 1954, although other events had always prevented policymakers from moving beyond initial explorations of the idea. The 1958 proposal never reached fruition, but it did state the U.S. government's basic commitment to modernization in the Middle East. Even though the 1958 proposal was stillborn, it provided a critical precedent for more elaborate attempts to employ modernization theory to transform the Middle East in the late 1950s and early 1960s.[62]

A brief review of U.S.-Egyptian relations during that period reveals the serious obstacles modernization theorists faced as they applied their ideas to that country. As chapter 3 demonstrated, a political revolution had already taken place in Egypt by the time modernization theorists had their opportunity. Through the mid-1950s, policymakers tried isolating Egypt to control Nasser's regime and the revolutionary change it promoted. The events in Iraq led policymakers and members of the network to rethink that policy and to look for alternative ways to control revolutionary change by engaging Egypt. This reevaluation of U.S. policy toward Egypt and the turn back to Nasser rested on a reassessment of the Egyptian leader, as U.S. policymakers and network members came to realize that he was never as dominant as they had portrayed him to be. Yet, even if Nasser was not as strong as was originally believed, he was clearly powerful enough to harm U.S. interests in the region, which meant it might be better for the United States to try to maintain some form of positive contact with him. Policymakers were therefore trying to limit the effects of revolutionary change and redirect its energy in Egypt, rather than trying to prevent it altogether. At the same time, however, strong domestic support for Israel constrained members of the network and policymakers as they tried to apply modernization theory to Egypt. A Congress that firmly supported Israel simply would not permit extensive aid to Egypt if any money appeared to be diverted in a manner that might prove harmful to Israel. Because of these two factors, members of the network and policymakers could therefore use aid to promote modernization in only very limited ways.

The first steps to engage Egypt were small, and utilized the existing "Food for Peace" concept as the foundation for a much larger policy initiative toward Nasser. The "Food for Peace" program originated with Public Law 480, which provided for the subsidized sale to foreign countries of surplus U.S. agricultural products, with payment accepted in local currency. After helping to pay for the cost of maintaining legations in recipient countries, the proceeds from the sales could be used to provide grants or loans back to the same country that purchased the surplus goods. The United States initiated limited P.L. 480 assistance to Egypt in 1955, but it was curtailed (with the exception of minimal aid to relief agencies) from 1956 to 1958 when U.S.-Egyptian relations soured. The United States began a more substantive P.L. 480 aid program in 1959 in the hope that it might provide an opening to Nasser. Nasser's simultaneous decision to improve U.S.-Egyptian relations also contributed to the expansion of the program. According to historian William Burns, Nasser instructed his ambassador in Washington, Mustafa Kamel, to "do anything you can to repair U.S.-Egyptian relations." Kamel then suggested to U.S. policymakers that Egypt might be willing to put issues of serious difference between the two countries "in the icebox" if the United States were willing to do the same. In all, P.L. 480 aid constituted 73 percent ($294.6 million out of $404.8 million) of all U.S. aid to Egypt between fiscal years 1955 and 1961, $239 million of which was given between 1959 and 1961.[63]

Rather than simply using food aid as a token connection to Nasser, modernization theorists in the Kennedy administration wished to use it more broadly to promote development. Doing so was in keeping with the Kennedy administration's emphasis on the "new look" of long term, country-wide development schemes and the concept of a "development decade." Policymakers hoped to achieve the short-term objective of allowing Nasser to devote resources to internal modernization by providing more food aid. If Nasser responded appropriately to the food assistance by reducing anti-American and anti-Israeli rhetoric, then the United States would consider more substantial aid packages. A series of amicable letters from Kennedy to Nasser were supposed to pad the initiative, with the possibility of an invitation for a formal state visit by Nasser held in reserve. As Walt Rostow noted in June 1961, the objective of the initiative was "to strengthen the foundations for [Nasser's] independence and to build up a whole range of more intimate human contacts with his people." The United States pledged $118.74 million in P.L. 480 aid in the first five months of the initiative (July–November 1961) and considered several other forms of assistance. Kennedy and Nasser also exchanged several letters, although Kennedy never issued the invitation for a state visit to the Egyptian leader.[64]

The highpoint of the aid initiative came in 1962, when policymakers undertook an action program they considered a significant step forward in overall U.S. policy toward Egypt. The United States was already evaluating a number of separate Egyptian aid requests, totaling several hundred million dollars. Policymakers believed that if they could fund all or most of those projects and combine them into a single aid package it might create the opportunity for an even larger opening to Nasser. Were Nasser's responses to such a package to indicate that he too wanted to turn over a new page in U.S.-Egyptian relations, then the two sides could begin high-level talks concerning a wide-ranging development consortium to which the United States might contribute. White House Middle East specialist Robert Komer made clear in a December 1961 memorandum outlining the expanded initiative that getting Nasser heavily invested in improving U.S.-Egyptian relations would not resolve the main issues of contention. It might, however, convince him to continue focusing on internal development and to resist promoting the revolutionary change that threatened U.S. interests elsewhere in Africa and the Middle East.[65]

The effort to engage revolutionary change in Egypt initially seemed quite successful. The United States agreed to several Egyptian requests, including rescuing Nubian monuments from areas that would be flooded by the Soviet-funded building of the Aswan Dam. President Kennedy also sent an economic planning consultant, Harvard economist and Walt Rostow acquaintance Edward Mason, to Egypt to evaluate its development plan. Chester Bowles, Kennedy's special advisor on the third world, met with Nasser in Cairo in February 1962, and Nasser's minister of the economy, Abdel Kaissouni, visited Washington in April of that year. The initiative to invest more heavily in Nasser even led to the signing in 1962 of a three-year P.L. 480 agreement to last through 1965. Things seemed to be proceeding such that, in May 1962, Komer wrote, "Bearing in mind that we are engaged in a long term effort to overcome an ingrained UAR heritage of suspicion of the West, it seems to be going reasonably well. The important thing is not to let the inevitable minor irritants which will crop up deflect our strategy." [66]

One of those "minor irritants" arose in Yemen in the fall of 1962, and it ultimately derailed the U.S. action program and revealed some of the problems of relying on modernization theory to engage Egypt. A succession crisis followed the death of the Imam Ahmed bin Yahya, the longtime leader of Yemen. That crisis led to a coup in which the royalist successor was overthrown and fled to Saudi Arabia, where he quickly received support. Nasser saw an opportunity to extend his influence into the Arabian Peninsula and to challenge the Saudi royal family, so he lent his support to the republicans who engineered the coup. The situation rapidly deteriorated into a state of near war between Saudi Arabia and Egypt, as Nasser sent nearly seventy thousand troops to fight Saudi-funded and -supplied Yemeni royalist forces. The British and the Soviets sent in their own operatives, and the Saudis requested U.S. assistance. The United States recognized the Yemeni Arab Republic as the legitimate government in December 1962 but, in a thinly veiled warning to Egypt to stay out of Saudi Arabia, informed all parties that it would defend its interests in and around the Arabian Peninsula. The United States put forth multiple peace or withdrawal initiatives, and occasionally won Egyptian and Saudi acceptance, only to have the conflict reescalate. The alleged Egyptian use of chemical weapons on Yemeni royalist opposition forces only weakened support for Egypt among U.S. policymakers and already skeptical congressmen. [67]

Yemen was only the initial irritant, however, as numerous other issues further undermined U.S.-Egyptian relations in the mid-1960s. Nasser became less willing to keep the Arab-Israeli conflict "in the icebox" while the United States began to engage more openly in arms sales to Israel. Moreover, President Johnson never maintained the amicable relationship with Nasser that Kennedy had, and grew increasingly impatient over Nasser's perceived intransigence in Yemen and protests over Israel. Economic assistance programs dwindled as relations worsened. When the Kennedy-era three-year wheat deal expired in 1965, a new one was negotiated, but it covered only six months and was not renewed. Predictably, when tensions between Egypt and Israel heightened to all-out warfare in 1967, U.S.-Egyptian relations reached their low point. Nasser believed the United States played a critical role in assuring an Israeli victory in the Six Day War, and broke off formal diplomatic relations with the United States. He attempted to reestablish them only after a new president was elected in 1968.[68]

Historian William Burns has noted that "for Lyndon Johnson, diplomacy was essentially an extension of the game of national politics. As an instrument of diplomacy, food aid was bound—in the Johnsonian scheme of things—by the cardinal rule of national politics: never do something for nothing." But Johnson was no different in this regard than his predecessors with respect to development assistance to Egypt. The primary objective behind implementing modernization theory in U.S.-Egyptian relations had always been to limit Nasser's nationalist agenda and his willingness to promote revolutionary change throughout the region. Eisenhower and his subordinates made clear that they linked U.S. food aid to changes in Egyptian policies, such as progress on the conflict with Israel or the strengthening of pro-Western and anti-Soviet connections. The "action program" undertaken during the Kennedy years had its own "wait and see" moments, and even though it did not obligate Nasser to move forward on peace with Israel, it was predicated on Nasser's willingness to leave the issue "in the icebox." To be sure, Johnson's expectations were set at a higher threshold, he stated them much more explicitly, and he showed even less patience when they went unmet, but he was not establishing a new precedent when he politicized U.S. aid to Egypt.[69]

Overall, the U.S. reliance on modernization theory and development assistance to engage and manage revolutionary change in Egypt should be judged a partial success from both specialists' and policymakers' perspectives. Food aid addressed an important need in Egypt in the early to mid-1960s, and allowed Nasser to devote other resources to internal development. The United States supplied approximately $997 million of P.L. 480 food aid to Egypt from 1958 to 1966, and at times provided more than half of Egypt's net supply of wheat. The food aid therefore made available a sizeable sum of money that Nasser used to push forward his first five-year development plan. The sectors of the economy most significantly affected were electricity, construction, and communications, all of which grew at double-digit annual rates from fiscal year 1959/60 to 1964/65. Overall, the gross domestic product grew at an average annual rate of 6.1 percent, or 3.5 percent adjusted for the 2.6 annual population growth rate. Modernization theorists must have been pleased with these results. Likewise, policymakers welcomed warmer U.S.-Egyptian relations, even though they proved difficult to maintain over the long term. Robert Komer, who as a White House Middle East specialist under Kennedy and Johnson served as a bridge between the network and policymakers, said as much in July 1963. "I hate to sound defensive," Komer stated, "but even I confess that staying on even keel with slippery UAR hard. It seems to involve one prickly issue after another . . . Do all realize that we've never been in a better position in [the] Arab world: we're on reasonably good terms with revolutionary Arabs, yet without losing our old clients. This is right where we want to be, despite pain and strain involved in staying there."[70]

Modernization theory and development assistance could never overcome, however, the wide gap between the long-term objective of socioeconomic transformation and short-term political concerns. Those policymakers and specialists who supported the action program for Egypt readily recognized that it would never lead Nasser and U.S. policymakers to agree on Israel, conservative monarchies in the Middle East, or pan-Arabism. They did hope it would build the foundation for a relationship that could withstand those differences and help Egypt change in a controlled manner. When neither Nasser nor U.S. policymakers could any longer keep those issues "in the icebox," U.S.-Egyptian relations immediately soured, and the effectiveness of modernization and development assistance suffered. The difficult interpersonal relationship between Johnson and Nasser further compounded the problem by making each leader more willing to read the actions of the other in a negative way. Implementing modernization theory required patience and could not bridge the gap between the short- and long-term outlooks.

Some individuals recognized these contradictions at the time. William Gaud, who as the Agency for International Development's assistant administrator for the Near East and South Asia was responsible for overseeing the implementation of the aid program in Egypt, later recalled his opposition to the program. The United States entered into the 1962 agreement, Gaud lamented, "over my dead body — that is a slight exaggeration — very much over my objections." According to Gaud, the three-year deal gave away too much: "We bargained away our leverage and as soon as Mr. Nasser got his three-year agreement under his belt, he embarked on a whole series of political activities which were inimical to us, and it was much harder for us to cut off the food to his people who needed it badly when we had an outstanding agreement than it would have been if we had had a series of short-term agreements, and each time when we negotiated the new short-term agreements, we had the opportunity to exercise influence." Gaud believed major differences existed between how the Agency for International Development and the assistant secretary of state for Near Eastern and South Asian affairs viewed the program, differences largely due to politics. Gaud remembered that the assistant secretary "and his people were strongly in favor of the three-year agreement for political reasons. We were strongly against it. We, in AID, were strongly against it because we didn't think it made sense. The UAR program, ever since I have been here, is essentially a political program rather than an economic development program. We do things in that program which we hope will help the UAR's economic development, and we do things which we believe make sense. But essentially, the reason that we have a program in the UAR is political, and the primary purposes that we are trying serve are political." For Gaud, if the goal was long-term economic development, then the political considerations had to be set aside and an enduring commitment made, but if the primary concerns were political, then short-term deals that allowed the United States to exercise nearly continuous leverage would be more useful. A politically based three-year deal served neither purpose, and in Gaud's mind was unlikely to succeed on either count.[71]

The use of modernization theory as a means of engaging revolutionary change received a fuller test in Iran, but it still exhibited some of the same weaknesses it displayed when applied to Egypt. The context in Iran differed significantly from that in Egypt in the late 1950s and early 1960s. Unlike Egypt, Iran was a U.S. ally that produced significant amounts of oil and shared a border with the Soviet Union, so analysts and policymakers worried even more about any potential instability. U.S. policymakers also hoped to prevent in Iran the overthrow of a conservative and generally pro-U.S. monarchy by revolutionary forces from below, whereas in Egypt the revolution had already occurred and the objective was to limit or redirect its energy. The shah of Iran was also on reasonably good terms with Israel, so there was much less domestic resistance to U.S aid to Iran than there was regarding Egyptian aid. Taken together, these differences meant policymakers could draw on modernization theory's idea of a national organism made of political, social, and

economic parts and use different types of aid and influence much more liberally to try to manage change in all three areas.

Observers expressed grave concerns about the discordant rates of political
and social change in Iran on the one hand and economic change on the other.
T. Cuyler Young, the nation's preeminent academic specialist on Iran at the
time, noted in his 1962 article "Iran in Continuing Crisis" that Iranians had
no faith in a corrupt political system and electoral process. And more serious
issues lay behind this almost continuous political crisis. Young argued that
Iran was "at a relatively advanced stage in that total social revolution which
presently engages most of the non-Western world." Unlike numerous other
countries around the Middle East and elsewhere, Iran actually had undertaken a development program that in Young's estimation had been "remarkable, if not indeed spectacular during recent years." But he also believed the
success of economic development actually made it more difficult to control
revolutionary change, as potentially more serious problems loomed if the
economy proved unable to keep growing or if political and social reform remained incommensurate with the economic growth that had taken place.
John W. Bowling, the State Department desk officer in charge of Iranian affairs, made a similar argument. Bowling noted that the shah's existing efforts
at economic development and rural reform had created a variety of opposition groups. Leftists, moderate nationalists, conservative elites, and the religious leadership all challenged the shah's grip on power, and large portions
of the peasantry, especially those who were landless and faced the harshest consequences of the shift to mechanized farming, also felt alienated. In
addition, the shah refused to share power and was obsessed with building
up Iran's military for use against internal resistance forces. Bowling warned
that "a combination of circumstances in the future, leading a combination of
opposition political elements and disaffected members of the security forces
toward an attempt to overthrow the regime cannot be discounted, and will
probably increase over the long run if present political trends continue."
President Kennedy shared these concerns and, following a teachers' strike in
early May 1961, had the National Security Council create a special Iran task
force comprised of Middle East specialists and representatives from various
government departments.[72]

U.S. policy toward Iran in the early 1960s, built upon these concerns, reflected the ascendance of modernization theory as the primary method of
engaging and managing revolutionary change. The United States had main-

tained an aid program in Iran since the CIA restored the shah to power in August 1953. Much of that assistance had been military or security oriented, and was intended to stabilize the shah's regime. While the United States continued to provide the military hardware and training that sustained the shah's repressive regime, the direction of the larger aid program shifted dramatically in the early 1960s. Unlike in Egypt, however, the new focus was not only on providing aid for economic development. Rather, policymakers emphasized social and political reform alongside economic development. Over time, in fact, the economic component of modernization, especially that derived from U.S. economic aid, became of secondary importance. The United States was able to decrease its development aid program in Iran dramatically because by 1965 Iran was taking in $750 million annually in oil revenue.[73]

A May 1961 proposal from the International Cooperation Administration incorporated Daniel Lerner's emphasis on communications and the human component of modernization and was designed to convince Iranians to bring about controlled economic, political, and social transformation in their country. Following the shah's appointment of reform-minded Ali Amini as premier during a May 1961 teachers' strike, the proposal suggested that television might be used to "teach development economics to strengthen the new premier." The U.S. government was to create a "30 to 50 hour 'course'" that outlined the path of economic transformation that the United States, England, Japan, and other transitional states such as Formosa followed. One of the program's objectives would be to promote a top-down approach to modernization whereby wealthy landowners would willingly give up land for redistribution to poor peasants. The series would have the authority of top-notch economic historians to demonstrate the validity of the approach, and it would be constructed so that it might be used in other countries as well. The proposal revealed modernization theorists' emphasis on secular models of development, as the product was intended to be a one-size-fits-all, do-it-yourself, fifty-hours-to-modernization video. It also belied modernization theorists' distinct urban and elite bias, as television had been introduced in only two Iranian cities and only about 300,000 people had access to it by 1961.[74]

The proposal met with resistance as it moved up the policymaking chain, but even its critics revealed their basic acceptance of modernization theory. Assistant Director of the Bureau of the Budget Kenneth Hansen commented on the proposal for then deputy special assistant to the president for national security affairs, Walt Rostow. Hansen argued that the proposal's author had good intentions, but incorrect facts about Iran. The problem in Iran was not yet land redistribution, which would be necessary down the road, but land tenure. Trying to convince wealthy land-owning Iranians to give up some of their possessions at this point was moving too fast. In addition, Hansen argued that the United States should not assume such an obvious role in domestic Iranian affairs. Doing so smacked of the "usual 'do-it-for-them' philosophy." Instead, it would be better to provide the new premier, Ali Amini, with background assistance so he could put together his own video. Thus, Hansen concluded the proposal was a good idea, but that it needed modifications and the timing was not quite right. He might also have recognized the limited prospects for success of a plan expecting 300,000 of Iran's wealthier citizens to watch fifty hours of instruction on how to forfeit significant amounts of their own wealth so as to modernize their country along lines that might not be applicable in their context.[75]

The shah of Iran probably never heard about that specific proposal, but he did hear and eventually succumb to frequent urgings from American policymakers that he needed to undertake political modernization to avoid being swept away by revolutionary change. Kennedy administration officials used a series of meetings with the shah's representatives in Washington, D.C., and Iran to state repeatedly their desire to see the shah solidify the position of his country as a modernizing, forward-looking and U.S.-oriented state. The way to do so, they argued, was to engage and manage revolutionary pressures by implementing programs that would change Iranian economic, political, and social institutions and systems in a controlled manner. Both Kennedy and Vice President Johnson made the case to the shah directly when he visited the United States in April 1962. Johnson reiterated the point when he toured Iran in August of that year. These urgings, combined with numerous uprisings in Iran in 1961 and 1962, finally led to a series of anticorruption and agricultural reforms. The shah was not committed to these reforms, but members of his government implemented them and forced him to accept them as faits accomplis. The shah soon recognized that he needed to undertake his own reform program if he had any hope of maintaining control, and proclaimed a "White Revolution" in January 1963. The program entailed land reform, privatization of industry, women's suffrage, and literacy promotion.[76]

The shah's U.S.-backed modernization scheme promoted controlled change, but it also generated extensive opposition across Iranian society. The shah did little for the middle classes, which he viewed as his greatest opposition, and which he intentionally neglected, and also refused to open up the political system in any meaningful way. The *bazaari* merchant class, the rural and urban poor, and the leftover Mossadegh nationalists all resented the ways in which the shah's program undermined them. But the White Revolution's most articulate critics, and those able to generate the widest support, came from the religious leadership. Of these, the most popular was Ayatollah Ruhollah Khomeini, who played a crucial role in leading a series of riots in June 1963 that the shah's forces brutally repressed by killing thousands. Khomeini believed the Shah's program threatened to weaken unalterably Shi'ite Islam and the foundations of Iranian society by promoting westernization and permitting American imperialism.

By the late 1960s, the shah emerged triumphant, at least temporarily, in his battle with U.S. policymakers on the one hand and his internal opposition on the other, and ended his modernization program. He toned down the criticism from the religious leadership by exiling Khomeini, who went first to Turkey, then Iraq, and eventually landed in Paris. The shah's maintenance of his repressive and well-equipped security forces kept internal dissent under wraps. Continuing economic expansion, based on increasing oil revenues and an economy growing in its own right, earned the acquiescence of some portions of the population to the shah's reign. Greater instability in the Middle East in the mid- to late 1960s then convinced U.S. policymakers that the shah was a pillar of strength in the region. They therefore came to rely on him more than ever to protect U.S. interests in the area. Reliance on Iran came with a price, however, which Lyndon Johnson and Richard Nixon gladly paid after June 1967 by granting the shah carte blanche to purchase almost any military equipment he wanted. The shah used his new power and increasing freedom of action to crack down even more forcefully on the opposition. Of course, the short-lived and Pyrrhic nature of the shah's victory revealed itself in the late 1970s when Iranians, under the guidance of the religious leaders, overthrew the shah and welcomed Ayatollah Khomeini back from exile.

Much like the Egyptian case, an analysis of U.S. policy toward Iran from the late 1950s through the mid-1960s reveals the limitations of modernization as a means of bringing about controlled transformation. The application of modernization theory in Iran resulted in some outcomes that members of the informal network of specialists and policymakers considered favorable. The shah embarked on the White Revolution that brought real but controlled change to some parts of the Iranian economy and society. But just as it failed to apply to Nasser in Egypt, modernization theory could never account for the outlook and desires of the leaders of the states to which it was applied. The shah's continuous emphasis on military aid and the maintenance of his regime dramatically undercut not only the potential effectiveness of his reforms, but alienated much of the population. Modernization theory also relied on long-term growth and change to ameliorate the plight of the masses in countries where it was applied, but it offered little to address the people's or policymakers' concerns in the short term. Thus, when Khomeini and his fellow religious leaders incited the masses, modernization theorists who believed in the primacy of U.S. and Western European models of development, society, and politics had few solutions to propose. Therefore, Iran too demonstrated that modernization was of limited value as a means of achieving America's sacred and secular mission of transforming the Middle East.

THE INABILITY OF THE United States to find any satisfactory means of transforming the Middle East by the late 1960s led to considerable frustration on the part of many members of the informal network of specialists and policymakers. It was within this context that the State Department's Bureau of Intelligence and Research completed "The Roots of Arab Resistance to Modernization" and forwarded it to the secretary of state in summer 1969. Revisiting that document after reviewing fifty years of U.S. efforts to transform the Middle East offers at least three critical insights.

First, the document is stunning in its reflection of the relationship between the production of knowledge and the exercise of power as it argued for the "de-Arabization" of Arabs. The report's authors relied heavily on some of the most widely respected academic specialists in the United States: Gustave von Grunebaum, Hamilton A. R. Gibb, Richard Nolte, and Kenneth Cragg all featured prominently in the footnotes. Yet the report's authors also drew from English-language publications by Middle Eastern scholars and journalists in an obvious attempt to give their thesis greater credibility. In this sense, the report offers a clear indication of the dominant assumptions of the era among members of the informal transnational network of specialists as they imagined the Middle East of the past, present, and future.

Second, the authors of the document demonstrated a striking inability or unwillingness to examine either their assumptions about the universal applicability of modernization or westernization—two terms they explicitly and purposely used interchangeably—or the many flaws inherent in the different ways the United States and its agents had pursued that goal in the Middle East over the preceding half century. They made no effort to consider whether or not the United States should be engaged in such a project, or to ask if the premises underlying modernization theory or its predecessors were sound. Indeed the exact opposite was the case. When the authors of the paper acknowledged conflicts or contradictions between what they termed "the fundamental assumptions behind . . . modern-type institutions" and "the Arab-Islamic tradition and value system," the default solution was "de-Arabization" rather than the questioning of those assumptions. Such a failure to question their own assumptions or to imagine limits on U.S. power and the United States' ability to implement change anywhere in the world is even more shocking when one considers that the document was written in 1969, when it was clear that policymakers holding similar assumptions about Asia had led the country into a quagmire in Vietnam.[77]

Finally, the document is more revealing than perhaps any other single source of the ways in which the different themes discussed throughout this book had become integrated into a comprehensive framework of meaning through which members of the informal transnational network of specialists had come to imagine the Middle East by the late 1960s. According to the authors of the document, it was necessary to understand Arabs' inability to modernize as part of the region's international political significance, a point driven home by the June 1967 war. Islam once again assumed a prominent role, allegedly exerting undue influence in cultural, economic, political, and social affairs and serving as a limiting factor on Arab efforts to modernize by sanctioning both authoritarian and atomistic forces across the region. The secular nationalists sought to combat Islam's impact, but failed because their success would have entailed shattering the basic tenets of Arab identity. Thus, "ambivalence" became "the hallmark of the 'modern' Arab," a result "of the incompatibility of Arab-Islamic and Western-secular culture." Those Arabs who overcame this ambivalence, who became "modernized (i.e., Westernized)," either suffered isolation at home or emigrated "to the West where different conditions prevail." The consequences of the failure to achieve broad-based modernization were significant: regional states were not able to pursue "independent foreign policies in their own interests," and economic, political, and social reform programs could be implemented only "piecemeal." Perhaps most significantly, failure meant a lack of "progress toward a resolution of the Arab-Israeli conflict" and subsequent military disaster, to which we now turn.[78]

CHAPTER FIVE

A PROFOUND AND GROWING DISTURBANCE . . . WHICH MAY LAST FOR DECADES

The Arab-Israeli-Palestinian Conflict and the Limits of the Network

William Eddy was closely connected to the Middle East for much of his life. Born to missionary parents in Lebanon in the late nineteenth century, he maintained a family home there and returned regularly even when working in the United States. When World War II began, Eddy reenlisted in the Marines, with which he had deployed in Europe during World War I, and worked as an intelligence officer in North Africa and the Middle East. After the war, he served as the first U.S. minister to Saudi Arabia and then returned to Washington, D.C., to work in the State Department. He officially resigned from the government in October 1947 to protest increasing U.S. support for the creation of a Jewish state in Palestine, to which he was adamantly opposed. He then went to work for ARAMCO as the head of its in-house research and intelligence division, though he remained in frequent contact with both the State Department and the CIA.

A prolific report writer and letter writer to family, friends, and professional acquaintances, Eddy sent his assessment of the current state of the Arab-Israeli-Palestinian conflict to Joint Chiefs of Staff Chairman General Alfred Greunther in January 1949. As one might expect, given Eddy's background and political views, much of the report was critical of Israel, though parts also criticized Arab leaders and states. He believed the creation of Israel "by force" was "a long-range disaster" that had "solved nothing," in part because there were no clearly established and internationally recognized boundaries to the new state. Instead of the possibility of peace, the region was "faced with the almost certain prospect of a profound and growing disturbance by Israel which may last for decades."[1]

Eddy's report, and that quotation in particular, is revealing for several reasons. To be sure, he stated his opposition to Israel more bluntly than did many of his fellow specialists, but his views broadly represented the general sentiments of a generation of regional experts — the leftover missionaries and Orientalists who dominated the informal network in its early years from the end of World War I through the period immediately after World War II. He was also obviously correct that the Arab-Israeli-Palestinian conflict would endure for decades. But the final quotation also symbolizes, unbeknownst to Eddy, the impact that conflict would have on the informal network itself over the coming decades. There certainly existed some disagreement among network participants, or between the network, policymakers, and the broader public, over the precise nature of U.S. national security concerns in the Middle East, over the role that Islam might play in U.S.–Middle East relations, over the extent to which nationalist movements threatened U.S. interests in the region, and over whether revolutionary change should be contained or promoted in the region. Such disputes were really quite small, however, and only rarely did they rise to the level of actually challenging network members' ability and authority as interpreters of the Middle East for American audiences. That was not the case with the Arab-Israeli-Palestinian conflict, about which certain segments of the U.S. population, high-level policymakers, and influential political advisors felt very strongly. That single fact made this issue in many ways much more challenging for those academics, businesspersons, government officials, and journalists responsible for creating a usable framework of meaning through which Americans might understand the Middle East and their nation's role there.

This chapter differs slightly from its predecessors in that it not only investigates the ways in which a particular issue — the Arab-Israeli-Palestinian conflict — fit into the evolving framework of ideas through which members of the informal transnational network of specialists imagined the Middle East between 1918 and 1967, but also examines some of the very real internal and external challenges to the network and the views it promulgated. From World War I through the mid-1930s, interest in the growing conflict in Palestine was intermittent, and most analysis emerged either from government officials at moments of crisis, from pro-Zionist commentators, or from British specialists who were much more invested in the issue due to Britain's possession of the League of Nations mandate for the area. As early network participants from the United States devoted more attention to the issue beginning in the late 1930s, many of the old Near East hands and Orientalists inside and outside the government resisted the expansion of the Jewish presence in Palestine. In doing so, they found themselves in conflict with high-level policymakers, their closest advisors, and politically powerful pro-Zionist private citizens in what some would call "the battle for Palestine." President Truman's decisions to support the creation of and recognize a new Jewish state constituted a stinging defeat for these segments of the network and, as early as the late 1940s, revealed the limits of its influence when politically powerful portions of the public became interested in Middle Eastern affairs. It was left to a younger generation of specialists that for the most part came of age professionally after 1948 to try to recover from that defeat and rebuild the informal network's authority by accepting Israel's existence and seeking to carefully manage the Arab-Israeli-Palestinian conflict through the 1950s. Central to the informal network's emerging framework of meaning was a keen desire to resolve the Palestinian refugee problem, which many participants identified as the single most destabilizing issue in the region. Those efforts met with failure in the 1960s, as the United States became fully engaged in an escalating Arab-Israeli arms race that reflected Cold War rivalries, and as the Palestinians developed powerful political forces that had to be reckoned with and considered important actors in the conflict in their own rights. The 1967 war made the failure on the issue complete, as it highlighted specialists' inability to come to terms with the conflict and revealed profound fractures within the network itself.

Imagining a Jewish Palestine

Between World War I and the late 1930s, interest in the conflict in Palestine was growing, though also episodic. From the start, the debate was defined in part by early participants in the emerging informal network of specialists, but more significantly by a wide array of politicians, policymakers, and a variety of other activists, many of whom spoke out in favor of creating a Jewish state in Palestine. Thus, from the very earliest stages of U.S. involvement and interest in the issue, there were significant limits to the emerging network's ability to exercise authority and retain its credibility with respect to this issue. We begin with a brief discussion of initial efforts to make sense of the issue by the Inquiry, the King-Crane Commission, and the State Department's Near Eastern Division, the latter two of which ultimately opposed

Zionist efforts. The focus then shifts to those Jewish activists from Britain and the United States who worked proactively through the 1920s and 1930s to pressure key political figures and policymakers to imagine a future Jewish state in Palestine. These activists highlighted the region's status as the Holy Land, a place of significance for Christians, Jews, and Muslims, and emphasized Judaism's historical role in a broader Judeo-Christian civilization. Yet these Zionist advocates also drew on the enduring and evolving sense of sacred and secular knowledge and mission that helped define the broader framework of meaning through which many Americans imagined the Middle East. Underlying it all, however, was a growing concern both among those who supported and those who opposed the creation of a Jewish state in Palestine about escalating levels of violence in the region.

The growing tensions in Palestine drew the attention of policymakers, what few specialists there were at the time, and other interested observers in the years surrounding the end of World War I. The tensions immediately suggested some significant potential problems for the United States in the Middle East. When President Wilson requested a declaration of war from Congress in April 1917, he explicitly exempted the Ottoman Empire, an ally of Germany, in an attempt to protect U.S. business, missionary, and philanthropic interests across the Middle East. Within weeks, Britain began working through well-connected Jews like Louis Brandeis—Supreme Court justice, head of the Zionist Organization of America, and one of Wilson's close friends—to secure the president's acquiescence before ultimately issuing the Balfour Declaration in November 1917. That statement not only proclaimed support for "the establishment in Palestine of a national home for the Jewish people," but also committed the British to "use their best endeavours to facilitate the achievement of this objective, it being clearly understood that nothing shall be done which may prejudice the civil and religious rights of the existing non-Jewish communities in Palestine, or the rights and political status enjoyed by Jews in any other country." Just two months later, however, Wilson began to articulate his notion of self-determination, an idea many independence-minded Arabs found appealing as they looked toward a postwar and post-Ottoman future, but that seemingly ran counter to U.S. support for the Balfour Declaration. Moreover, members of the U.S. missionary community in the Middle East, some of whom were also close friends of the president, openly expressed their support for Arab independence in 1918 and 1919. Even as World War I was coming to a close, battle lines were already being drawn over the future of Palestine.[2]

As was the case with other World War I–era aspects of U.S.–Middle East relations, efforts to develop a comprehensive understanding of the Palestine issue and to resolve these tensions in the U.S. approach were hampered by the general absence of specialist knowledge about the region. Two basic features characterized the work of the Inquiry, the first group to really tackle the problem. First, like much of the rest of the Inquiry's work on the Middle East, the reports on Palestine were deeply flawed. One report on the history and impact of Zionism was so bad that it elicited an extensive critique from David Hunter Miller, a well-known lawyer in his early forties who specialized in financial issues and international law, and who was placed on the Inquiry to keep track of its finances and because he could write well. According to Miller, the report was "absolutely inadequate from any standpoint and must be regarded as nothing more than material for a future report." He went on to evaluate not only the content (or absence of it), but also the basic structure and writing of individual paragraphs. Second, the Inquiry's work on Palestine presupposed a particular outcome of the conflict. According to historian Lawrence Gelfand, virtually all of the reports that dealt with Palestine in any meaningful way assumed that a Jewish state of some form would come into existence. Even reports that called for international control of the region once the war was over made references to "the Zionist State" in Palestine.[3]

The King-Crane Commission displayed a more nuanced understanding of the growing conflict over Palestine, in part because its members actually spent two weeks in Palestine speaking directly with participants on both sides. The commissioners included in their final report several pages on the issue, where they explored both Arab and Jewish proposals. Ultimately, they recommended that Jewish plans for the region be scaled back significantly, as it became clear during "the Commission's conference with Jewish representatives, that the Zionists looked forward to a practically complete dispossession of the present non-Jewish inhabitants of Palestine, by various forms of purchase." Such a policy would, King and Crane declared, violate the Balfour Declaration's requirement that the rights of non-Jews in Palestine be maintained. Moreover, it also ran counter to President Wilson's assertions that such problems should be solved and the solutions agreed to by all parties concerned. Finally, King and Crane hinted at future problems in Palestine, noting that violence offered the only means for Zionist ambitions in Palestine to be fulfilled, as Arab opposition was "intense and not lightly to be flouted."[4]

By 1922, Palestine had once more become an issue of national political discussion as both the House of Representatives and the Senate considered resolutions expressing support for the Balfour Declaration. Congress had first taken up the issue in 1919, when, according to historian David Schoenbaum, "some three hundred members declared their support." In 1922, representatives of the Zionist Organization of America in Massachusetts and New York met with Senator Henry Cabot Lodge and Representative Hamilton Fish, respectively, and requested that they each sponsor resolutions that would formally state U.S. support for the Balfour Declaration. Before submitting their resolutions for consideration, both Lodge and Fish solicited a response from the State Department. As historian Lawrence Davidson has noted, Secretary of State Charles Evans Hughes replied "that he had 'no objection' to such a resolution, and even went so far as to suggest wording for the text." Both resolutions ultimately passed, though Hughes made sure the final text substituted "favors" for the word "supports" to characterize the U.S. position regarding the creation of a Jewish national home in Palestine, and President Harding signed the joint resolution in September 1922.[5]

On its face, Hughes's statement that the State Department would not oppose the 1922 resolutions may not seem particularly interesting, but closer examination reveals that it ran counter to what appeared to be U.S. policy regarding Palestine in the early 1920s. Once the League of Nations assigned the Palestine mandate to Britain, State Department officials had one primary concern: securing a treaty with Britain that would guarantee U.S. trading rights and protect existing U.S. interests in the region, which the head of Near Eastern affairs in the State Department, Allen Dulles, referred to in a May 1922 memorandum as a "question of real concern." Because the United States was not a member of the League of Nations, Dulles and his colleagues at NEA could not be sure that U.S. interests would be secure against threats from any direction, be they Arab, Jewish, or British, without such a treaty. Moreover, once the mandate had been assigned, Dulles and his colleagues in Near Eastern affairs considered any issues extending beyond the security of U.S. interests in Palestine to be internal to the mandate itself and therefore exclusively British concerns. Thus, at least until such time as a treaty could be finalized (it was signed in 1924), Dulles argued "that the Department should avoid any action which would indicate official support for any one of the various theses regarding Palestine, either Zionist, anti-Zionist, or the Arabs."[6]

While Dulles and his colleagues sought to retain what they considered a traditional definition of U.S. interests in Palestine that did not include explicit recognition of the Jewish presence there, by the mid-1920s there emerged a powerful effort to build among policymakers, policy-oriented individuals and potential donors in the United States a broader base of support for the Zionist cause. The original wartime effort to win U.S. endorsement of the Balfour Declaration was premised on the belief that a Jewish state in Palestine could only be realized through a British victory in the war, which in turn required U.S. assistance. Following the war and the assignment of the mandate to Britain, Jewish immigration to Palestine increased, and with it the desire for greater financial resources and more political support from the United States for an eventual Jewish state. The demand for greater support heightened through the 1920s and 1930s as U.S. immigration laws tightened and discrimination increased across Europe. Passage of the 1922 resolutions might have suggested it would be relatively easy to achieve those goals, but other factors hinted that it might be more difficult. One key indicator was that, due to internal squabbles, membership in the Zionist Organization of America declined precipitously from approximately 175,000 at the end of the war to approximately 25,000 just a decade later. Smaller membership rolls presented at least the specter of less financial support coming from the United States, as well as a weakened ability to pressure U.S. politicians and policymakers. Moreover, just because many congressmen looked favorably upon the Jewish cause did not mean all Americans did, as anti-Semitism remained a concern in the United States and became an even greater problem during the 1930s, when many down-on-their-luck or nativist Americans considered business-savvy or immigrant Jews yet another challenge to their own economic well being.[7]

As pro-Zionist activists worked to build support in the United States, they drew on a number of themes already present in the way Americans were imagining the Middle East. Historian Irvine Anderson has argued that two influential interpretations of the Bible emerged by the early twentieth century, both of which assisted Zionist objectives in Palestine. One relied on a "liberal historical/critical viewpoint" in which the Bible contained "profound theological truths about the sovereignty of God and the moral precepts by which we should live," but did not read the Bible "as factual history." The second was a "fundamentalist literal/prophetic view" in which the Bible was read as "the inerrant word of God." The former did not commit its adherents to supporting the Zionist cause, but it did suggest that Jews had a historical place in the Holy Land and thus made their return to Palestine seem a reasonable proposition. Meanwhile, the latter interpretation predicted a "Second Coming of Christ and the End Times" following the return of Jews to the area of ancient Israel, and thus required support for the Zionist cause.[8]

Zionist advocates then combined the generally accepted Jewish connection with the Holy Land with the enduring yet consistently evolving desire to redeem and transform the region. Within this context, Leonard Stein published one of the most effective efforts to make the Zionist case. Stein was a British Zionist and served for most of the 1920s as the political secretary for the World Zionist Organization, and he therefore serves as a good example of the wide array of voices speaking out on the issue that extended well beyond the typical early members of the emerging informal network of specialists. Stein laid out a broad agenda in "The Jews in Palestine," published in April 1926 in *Foreign Affairs*. The article provided a brief history of the Jewish presence in Palestine and the origins of the British mandate and then sought to define the precise nature of that mandate and to identify certain features of it that distinguished it from other British and French mandates in the Middle East. There were two crucial differences according to Stein. First, there were no clear provisions, indications, or criteria to suggest when the Palestine mandate should end and an independent state emerge. Second, there existed within the mandate "Holy Places" for three religions but the directions for administering control over and access to those religious sites were ambiguous at best. Elsewhere in the article, Stein noted what he saw as the primary Jewish accomplishments in Palestine and the significant obstacles that remained. Ultimately, he argued in measured tones for the continued expansion of the Jewish presence by suggesting that eventually both Jews and Arabs could overcome their apparent animosity toward one another.[9]

What mattered most in Stein's article, however, was how he worked to convince others to imagine a Jewish Palestine by drawing on the enduring senses of redemption and transformation to make the Zionist case and to articulate a vision of an increasingly peaceful coexistence between Arabs and Jews in Palestine. To be sure, Stein was not the first to make these arguments, but he did so in a manner that presented a Jewish Palestine as the natural modern extension of both a sacred and secular Western civilization in the Middle East. He contrasted a future Jewish-controlled "Western Palestine" with an Arab dominated "Eastern Palestine" by imparting that "if they are encouraged to drift apart, Western Palestine will be a torso, and Trans-Jordan [Eastern Palestine] will, more probably than not, be consigned to something like permanent stagnation." Further, Stein suggested that only a Jewish Palestine could really bridge the gap between modern Western civilization and a backward Muslim world: "If there is a new Palestine in the making, it is the Palestine which faces westwards to Europe as well as eastwards to Arabia and

Iraq." From there, Stein worked to establish the precise ways in which Jewish Palestine was becoming a bastion of modernity in the Middle East, contending that increasing urbanization and economic output indicated "that Palestine is going through what may almost be called an industrial revolution," and that it was likely "to become the main industrial centre of the Middle East." From the growing industrial and agricultural output flowed schools and the broader "development of Palestine as a whole." Stein believed that "what is growing up in Palestine is a vigorous and many-sided Jewish society, which has its weaknesses as well as its virtues, but which has in any case its distinctive tone and color." While much hard work remained, the next, most important step was for the "lingering suspicions" of Arabs to be "gradually disarmed," after which Jews might be "regarded as welcome neighbors from whom there is much to be gained." It was up to the Arabs to accept Jews as Palestinians whose role was "to civilize Palestine, not from without, but from within."[10]

Deadly violence between Jews and Palestinians in August 1929 called into question this vision of peaceful coexistence that Stein and others had articulated. Tensions had been brewing since at least 1927 as an economic downturn in Palestine combined with continuing Jewish immigration to create intense competition between Arabs and Jews for what few employment opportunities existed. Those tensions were then exacerbated beginning in late 1928 by growing Jewish demands for greater control of the Wailing Wall, which Muslims considered part of the Mosque of Omar, and held to tightly. Existing agreements permitted Jews to worship at the Wailing Wall, but denied them the right to take any actions such as adding structures or affixing anything that might serve as a precedent for making future claims for greater access or control. Orthodox Jews challenged these previously acknowledged limits by constructing a screen to separate men and women worshiping at the Wall that also happened to block an access path connecting to a Muslim neighborhood. Muslim complaints to British authorities resulted in the deployment of police forces to remove the screen. Tensions over the Wall and its surrounding areas continued into 1929 and finally boiled over in late August. By early September, the violence had spread beyond Jerusalem and 133 Jews and 117 Arabs had died, with another 339 and 232, respectively, wounded.[11]

Initial Zionist responses tried to build sympathy by portraying the violence as another in a long line of deadly attacks against Jews specifically or conducted by Muslims against helpless minorities. Writing in Foreign Affairs in early 1930, British Zionist Henry Nevinson overlooked any possible Jewish role in the violence and instead suggested, "Our horror and sympathy would be moved by the slaughter and violation of so many human beings for the most part helpless and unarmed. For the massacres of Jews in Palestine at the end of August were marked by the same brutal ferocity as were the pogroms of Russian Jews under the Tsars or the slaughter of Armenians by the Turks under the Red Sultan and under the Young Turks at Adana, and later in northern Anatolia." He urged his readers who might desire the end of either the British mandate or the Jewish presence in Palestine to recall that for all properly educated Christians "the history and geography of Palestine were far more familiar to us all than our own," and to remember "with what feelings" such people "regard the Holy Land. It is their 'spiritual home.' They will not abandon it again to Moslems without a struggle. The spirit of Crusaders stirs among us." As Stein had, Nevinson extolled the virtues of the Jewish settlers carrying on this crusade in Palestine, their working the land and building cities, their growing the economy and improving health conditions. The contrast with Arabs was remarkable, and revealed a "clash of two races, of two civilizations, the eastern and the western, and that clash lies at the root of all the present woe."[12]

Some Americans might have found Nevinson's portrayal of the events of 1929 as the result of a clash of civilizations unobjectionable, but it was not necessarily the best way to convince U.S. policymakers to imagine and support the creation of a successful Jewish state. Moderate Zionist voices like that of the lawyer, well-connected Democratic Party operative, and future Supreme Court justice Felix Frankfurter therefore returned to the ideas Stein had emphasized half a decade earlier. In "The Palestine Situation Restated," published in April 1931, Frankfurter recalled the defiled and desolate Palestine of Mark Twain's *Innocents Abroad* and contrasted it with a transformation "nurtured by the most tenacious hopes and traditions of the Jewish people." While Frankfurter acknowledged that "clashes and conflict are the staple of the press," he hoped to redirect Americans' attention to "the organic life of a new civilization [that] has been steadily unfolding in Palestine since 1920." The Jewish presence was critical to that new civilization, but Jewish practices did not define Palestine in its entirety; rather, according to Frankfurter, Jews and Arabs were "collaborating in the thousand intimacies of their common life as builders of a new country."[13]

Frankfurter presented an optimistic view of the future, but he was neither naive nor oblivious to tensions in Palestine. Unlike Nevinson, who did not confer any legitimacy on Arab concerns, Frankfurter acknowledged nationalist sentiments among Arab Palestinians and instead suggested that responsibility for any continuing problems between Jews and Arabs fell on the British for improperly administering their mandate in Palestine. Frankfurter contended the British had tried too hard to balance their mandate both to promote the creation of a Jewish national home and to protect the rights of other peoples in Palestine. He chastised those who argued that Jewish advances in Palestine necessarily came at the cost of the Arabs, and instead suggested that British administrators had failed "to counteract mischievous misrepresentation and to educate the Arab masses to a true perception of the amelioration of the Arab's lot through Jewish enterprise." He singled out for specific criticism Lord Passfield, who issued a white paper in 1930 that raised serious questions about Jewish labor and land acquisition practices, and thus suggested Jews were exploiting Palestinian economic vulnerabilities. Frankfurter accused Passfield of interpreting the situation in a manner that "employed the safeguards in the Mandate for the protection of the non-Jewish communities of Palestine to read out of the Mandate all substantial meaning from the Mandatory's duty towards the establishment of a Jewish national home." That point led Frankfurter to an even broader assertion: peace in Palestine could only come "when the Mandatory—and more particularly its Administration in Palestine—abandons the negative role of umpire and assumes the creative tasks of the Mandate." Frankfurter had countered the prospect of seemingly unending conflict and appealed to potential supporters by offering a vision of a better future in Palestine for both Arabs and Jews.[14]

Frankfurter's plea to British and U.S. policymakers, and other interested parties, to look beyond the violence and to focus on more effective administration of the mandate so as to build a more amicable relationship between Arabs and Jews might have been mildly plausible in the early 1930s, but it became unsustainable as tensions escalated by the middle of the decade and broadened to include the British themselves. Jewish immigration to Palestine increased dramatically through the early 1930s in response to Hitler's ascension and growing discrimination in Germany and across Europe. As a consequence, the Jewish National Fund, the organization responsible for acquiring land in Palestine, stepped up its land purchases. Such purchases could only be used by Jews or for the benefit of Jews, and thus resulted in a greater number of evictions of landless Palestinian peasants. By April 1936, not only had Arab protests expanded across all of Palestine, but they were much more unified and organized, and ultimately took the form of a general strike. The British were thus under the greatest pressure they had yet experienced to limit Jewish immigration and land purchases. It was no longer possible to suggest that Arab-Jewish relations were improving and that Arab resistance consisted of occasional, random outbursts of violence. The conflict of the mid-1930s revealed once and for all the ultimate contradictions that existed within the Balfour Declaration's commitment to the creation of a Jewish national home in Palestine and the pledge to protect the rights and privileges of non-Jews residing there. The British were unable to maintain the fiction that they could achieve both objectives, a fact which British policymakers were forced to confront when rumors circulated that a commission investigating the situation (the Peel Commission) might recommend the termination of the mandate and the partition of Palestine, which it did in fact do in July 1937.[15]

The environment of 1936 and 1937 led Zionists to redouble their efforts to win over policymakers and potential supporters in the United States, and in the process established two important precedents for the future. First, the urgency of the moment meant that the ability to exercise pure political power overshadowed earlier arguments about redeeming the Holy Land or uplifting Arabs. Zionists in the United States bombarded the State Department with requests that it depart from its traditional policy of noninvolvement and pressure British policymakers by reminding them of the depth of interest that American Jews, and the U.S. government by extension, took in Palestine. U.S. diplomats formally rejected such pleas at first, but before long began pursuing "informal" and "unofficial" conversations with their British counterparts. As the release date for the Peel Commission's report approached, the Secretary of State formally reminded the British of the 1924 Treaty, which not only cemented U.S. economic rights in Palestine but also committed the British to consult with U.S. officials should any change to the mandate call into question the security of U.S. interests. The British protested that the Peel recommendations had no impact on U.S. interests and that consultations were therefore unnecessary. Nonetheless, the change in approach established the second precedent, as it was the first instance in which the State Department defined the Jewish presence in Palestine as a U.S. interest worthy of official protection.[16]

The Peel Commission's recommendation to partition Palestine was never implemented, as the outbreak of war in Europe created a fundamentally different environment for the debate over Palestine. British policymakers were wary of alienating Arabs and sending them into the arms of Germany and Italy, while they also recognized that Zionists had little choice but to accept almost any policy Britain might pursue in Palestine. In 1939 the British released a white paper that promised an independent Palestinian state within ten years and capped Jewish immigration at 15,000 per year for the next five years, with any immigration after that subject to Arab approval. Predictably, neither Jews nor Arabs in Palestine or elsewhere were pleased. Zionists correctly noted that the white paper, if implemented, meant the end of the dream of a Jewish Palestine, as the cap on immigration determined that they could never outnumber Arabs there. Therefore, during the war and after, as Britain, the new United Nations, and the rest of the world community debated how to handle the situation, Zionists promoted any and all means of legal and illegal Jewish immigration to Palestine. Arabs, meanwhile, saw the white paper as an improvement over previous policy, but had been hoping for full independence and worried about what might happen while it was delayed for another decade. Continued Jewish immigration during and immediately after the war only heightened such concerns. This new environment, combined with two new precedents for how policymakers and other interested parties in the United States might imagine the situation in Palestine and the U.S. role there, helped set the stage for a decade-long "battle for Palestine." That battle was waged in the minds of specialists, policymakers, and other interested Americans on both sides, but also in a very real policymaking sense, particularly as news of the Holocaust began to trickle out of Europe.

Before moving forward, however, it is important to acknowledge that while the focus to this point has been on the efforts of a variety of pro-Zionist voices operating outside the emerging informal network of regional specialists, there were some voices of opposition both inside and outside that emerging network. As we have seen, members of the State Department's division of Near Eastern affairs saw U.S. support for the Jewish agenda in Palestine as a direct challenge to extant U.S. interests in the region. Moreover, from the very beginning, there existed some Jewish opposition to the Zionist cause, premised largely on the belief that Judaism was a religion, and not an ethnic, national, or racial identity. As such, these non-Zionist Jews argued, their coreligionists could live within the borders of any state that would ensure fair and just treatment and therefore did not need a state of their own. Finally, some Arab Americans attempted to counter the Zionist narrative of Holy Land redemption, transformation, and the uplifting of Palestinian Arabs. That effort emphasized the challenges that expanding Jewish immigration to Palestine presented for the Arabs who lived there, called attention to the competing imperatives of the Balfour Declaration, and argued that the imposition of a largely European, Jewish population in Palestine constituted the denial of Palestinian self-determination. When Arab Americans presented these arguments to the State Department or other policymakers, they were met with either noncommittal replies or requests to assist efforts to seek peace and reconciliation between Jews and Arabs in Palestine. As the contest for the future of Palestine intensified between 1938 and 1948, these and other anti-Zionist voices would seek to counter increasingly powerful pro-Zionists voices.[17]

The Battle for Palestine

The period from the end of the 1930s to the declaration of the independent state of Israel on 14 May 1948 witnessed an increasingly bitter and vitriolic intellectual and policy battle over the future of Palestine. An ever-widening array of participants from inside and outside the emerging informal network of specialists took part. Many of the old missionary hands and Orientalists inside and outside the government, along with members of the growing oil industry in the Middle East, strongly resisted the idea of large-scale Jewish immigration to Palestine and an independent Jewish state there. Their opposition resulted from a variety of concerns: the desire to protect growing U.S. oil interests in the area; apprehension about the international and regional postwar political environments; long-standing worries about the U.S. image and role in the Middle East, especially as defined by missionary and philanthropic efforts to transform the region; and doubts about the basic character of Arab and Muslim peoples. A small though powerful group of ideologically committed anti-Zionist Jews joined these early network members in their resistance to the creation of a Jewish state in Palestine. On the opposite side of the debate were a variety of politically engaged and powerful groups and citizens that sought to redefine and expand U.S. interests in the region to include the Jewish presence in Palestine. In addition, once news of the Holocaust began to surface, Zionists could draw on an extremely powerful moral argument that had broad appeal in wider America. Once mobilized, these groups presented a combined force the Near Eastern Division, the missionaries and Orientalists, and the vocal anti-Zionist Jews proved unable to counter effectively, particularly as the battle intensified and became more acrimonious between 1945 and 1948. As a consequence, the missionary and Orientalist hands, along with government members of the informal network, suffered a humiliating defeat on the future of Palestine. They endured harsh and personal criticisms that caricatured their positions, and in many cases they abdicated or were pushed out of their roles in the policymaking process on the issue.

The late 1930s redefinition of U.S. interests that began with the debate over the Peel Commission recommendations not only added the Jewish presence in Palestine to the list, but also put a greater emphasis on U.S. oil interests in the region, and thus brought to light an enduring conflict that has defined—at least in part—how Americans have imagined the Middle East ever since. Many early members of the network, particularly within the State Department's Division of Near Eastern Affairs, its Office of Near Eastern and African Affairs (created in 1944 to oversee Near Eastern Affairs and two other divisions), and the growing regional oil industry, were extremely worried that the conflict over Palestine threatened U.S. oil interests throughout the area. Most of those interests were in areas controlled by Arabs opposed to the creation of a Jewish state in Palestine, a fact that led State Department employees in Near Eastern affairs to warn their superiors about the potential dangers inherent in a policy of support for the expanding Jewish presence in Palestine. Wallace Murray, director of the Office of Near Eastern and African Affairs, warned Under Secretary of State Edward Stettinius in October 1944 that U.S. support of Zionist objectives in Palestine "would seriously prejudice our ability to afford adequate protection to American interests in the Near East." Murray believed one country presented particular difficulty, as the U.S. position regarding Palestine would "have a very definite bearing upon our relations with Saudi Arabia and upon the future of the American oil concession in that country." Like Murray, individuals in the oil industry were also worried about how Saudi Arabia, which held the largest oil reserves in the world and the largest U.S. oil concessions in the region, would react to U.S. recognition and support of Israel. James Terry Duce, an executive with ARAMCO, relayed to the State Department in late May that King Ibn Saud of Saudi Arabia was threatening to retaliate against the company. The king, Duce argued, "may be compelled, in certain circumstances, to apply sanctions against the American oil concessions . . . not because of his desire to do so but because the pressure upon him of Arab public opinion was so great that he could no longer resist it." Fortunately for Duce and his oil industry peers, Ibn Saud never followed through with his threat, as he quickly realized that any sanctions he imposed on concessions would only decrease profits from the sale of Saudi Arabian oil and endanger the Saudis' evolving relationship with the United States. None-theless, such fears were very real for government and business participants in the network and led them to question U.S. support for the new Jewish state.[18]

The redefinition of U.S. interests extended beyond oil, as specialists were also keenly aware of the wider international political arena and, like most other Americans in the mid- to late 1940s, viewed the Soviet Union with ever more circumspection and worry. Many specialists in the mid-1940s quickly became committed Cold Warriors, and even at this early date saw the conflict over Palestine within the larger context of the evolving Cold War. Loy Henderson, U.S. ambassador to Iraq during the war and Wallace Murray's successor as director of the State Department's Office of Near Eastern and African Affairs from 1945 to 1948, internalized and articulated these fears about the expansion of Soviet influence in the Middle East more than any of the World War II–era government officials dealing with the region. Henderson spent a decade on Soviet affairs and living in the Soviet Union before he became involved in Middle Eastern affairs. His experience convinced him that the Soviet Union was a dangerous and expansionist country, and he wanted above all to prevent any increase in Soviet power around the world. He made a veiled reference to these concerns in an October 1946 memorandum to Dean Acheson. Backing a Jewish state, Henderson argued, would "lead the Arab and Moslem World to look elsewhere than toward the West for support." Henderson reiterated the point more explicitly in a September 1947 memorandum in which he laid out his opposition to a proposed U.N. plan to partition Palestine into separate Arab and Jewish states: "The attitude which we assume towards the Palestine problem . . . may have far-reaching effects upon our relations with the peoples of the Near East and with Moslems everywhere. It may greatly influence the extent of success or of failure of some of our efforts to promote world stability and to prevent further Soviet penetration into important areas free as yet from Soviet domination." For Henderson, the emerging clash between the United States and the Soviet Union provided the larger context he believed the contest over Palestine needed to be placed in and handled. In his view, U.S. policymakers should do nothing with respect to Palestine that would offer the Soviets any potential advantages in the Middle East.[19]

Some government specialists also believed U.S. support for the expanding Jewish presence in Palestine undermined the positive image that the United States had developed throughout the region over the preceding decades, and thus jeopardized not only immediate U.S. interests but also the enduring sense of sacred and secular mission in the region. According to these individuals, a century's worth of educational, missionary, and philanthropic involvement had built up a deep reservoir of good will, at least among educated Middle Eastern elites, toward the United States. Supporting the Zionist position on Palestine would rapidly drain that reservoir. Loy Henderson pointed out to Acting Secretary of State Dean Acheson in October 1945 that if the United States "should continue to press for the mass immigration of Jews into Palestine at this time, on humanitarian or other grounds, much of the work done in the Near East in recent years in building up respect for, and confidence in, the United States and in increasing American prestige, will be undone." Gordon Merriam, Henderson's subordinate as head of Near Eastern Affairs, made a similar point in a May 1946 memorandum to Acheson. Merriam noted that American educational and philanthropic interests, which "constituted a sheet anchor in the Middle East" when the United States was "militarily weak," would all be threatened by Arabs who had given "every indication of the intention to resist" Jewish immigration to Palestine.[20]

Finally, government participants in the network also brought stereotypes and concerns about the basic character of Arab and Muslim peoples to their analyses of the conflict over Palestine. It was not fondness for Arabs that led Loy Henderson to oppose a Jewish state in Palestine; he never held Arabs in especially high regard. Rather, Henderson considered Arabs to be "childlike" and "fanatical extremists" who would gain energy from U.S. support for a Jewish state in Palestine. Similarly, some government Middle East specialists equated the conflict over Palestine to a physical or mental illness afflicting Arabs. Gordon Merriam concluded in December 1946 that "the Palestine question and the related question of the future of the Jewish DP's [Displaced Persons] form an open sore, the infection from which tends to spread rather than to become localized." Middle East specialists in the CIA made a similar point in a late 1947 report, "The Current Situation in Palestine." Palestine, they argued, was significant largely because of the "psychological problem posed by irreconcilable claims of Arabs and Jews for hegemony over the country." According to these analysts, Arabs and Palestinians were responsible for perpetuating that problem. Following up in February 1948, just four months after the initial assessment and three months before the declaration of Israeli independence, agency Middle East specialists placed the onus for escalating violence in the area squarely on Arab and Palestinian shoulders, while also highlighting the problems of religious and nationalist extremism. Arabs would continue to violently resist the U.N. Partition Plan, passed by the General Assembly in November 1947, because "to the masses, the fight has become almost a religious tenet; to the governing classes, it has become a political creed which they dare not forsake."[21]

The State Department's Middle East hands concluded that, all things considered, support for a Jewish state in Palestine would foolishly place the United States in an untenable position. Again, Henderson's voice was both powerful and representative on this point. He argued in September 1947 that the U.N. plan would be "unworkable" because the logistics of building a partitioned state would require "Arab-Jewish friendship and cooperation." In the absence of that cooperation, which had been nonexistent in recent years, the plan would require outside enforcement. That meant the United States would need to commit more "force, materials, and money" than it could possibly afford at a moment of growing tension with the Soviet Union. Implementation of the plan, with the United States unable or unwilling to commit the resources necessary to enforce it, Henderson feared, would only serve to "guarantee that the Palestine problem would be permanent and still more complicated in the future."[22]

Of course, Near Eastern Affairs was not the only site of resistance to the creation of a Jewish state in Palestine in the mid to late 1940s, as many of the remaining missionary hands and Orientalists also stood in firm opposition. Two of the most prominent individuals to do so were William Eddy and Kermit "Kim" Roosevelt. Eddy had spoken openly about his opposition to a Jewish state in Palestine, and it was in late 1947 that Eddy resigned from the State Department, where he had been head of its in-house intelligence branch. While he did keep consulting with the CIA and State Department, he never reconciled himself to either the existence of Israel or to U.S. support for it, and continued to write and speak in opposition to both until his death in the early 1960s. Roosevelt, who was the grandson of President Theodore Roosevelt, had been a wartime OSS agent in the Middle East and had taught Middle Eastern history at Harvard and Berkeley. He too was unequivocal in his opposition to U.S. support for a Jewish state in Palestine, which he believed worked against U.S. interests in the region. After the declaration of independent Israel in 1948, Roosevelt joined, and served as the executive director of, the Committee for Justice and Peace in the Holy Land, an organization whose mission was to promote fair treatment of both Palestinian refugees and Palestinian Arabs within Israel.[23]

Just as Zionist activists from outside the network worked to define the debate over Palestine, there were vocal non-Zionist or anti-Zionist Jewish organizations that opposed the creation of a Jewish state in Palestine. The

American Jewish Committee, which Edward Tivnan has called "the most prestigious Jewish organization" in the United States until the early 1940s, and the American Council for Judaism (ACJ) both resisted the creation of a Jewish state in Palestine. Both were listed among the groups who were formally to be presented in 1946 with the final report of the Anglo-American Committee of Inquiry on Palestine, which had been designed to investigate whether or not the British, with American and U.N. support, should permit the immediate admittance of 100,000 Jewish immigrants to Palestine. Of the two groups, the ACJ worked more actively against the creation of a Jewish state in Palestine, and thus serves as a useful illustration of the highly political nature of this specific issue.[24]

Historian Thomas Kolsky has identified the ACJ as "the only American Jewish organization ever formed for the specific purpose of fighting Zionism and opposing the establishment of a Jewish state in Palestine." The ACJ was formed in 1943 by leading anti-Zionist, Reform American Jews, and with the support of New York Times publisher Arthur Hays Sulzberger. Elmer Berger, the group's chief ideologue, claimed the ACJ's stance on Palestine was premised on the belief that being Jewish was a religious identity, and not a national or racial identity. Members of the ACJ therefore adhered to the idea that there should be established in Palestine "a democratic political structure in which neither religious faith nor ethnic derivation would be a deterrent to full participation in the national polity." That opinion drew support among wealthy Jews who had done well in the United States and thought of it as a perfectly acceptable home for people of their religion, occasional episodes of anti-Semitism aside.[25]

The ACJ worked closely with government officials involved in Middle Eastern affairs who resisted the expanding Jewish presence in Palestine between the end of World War II and the declaration of Israeli statehood in May 1948. One high-ranking member of the ACJ, George Levison, had extensive government contacts, including Dean Acheson (first an assistant secretary of state, then undersecretary of state, and ultimately secretary of state), Loy Henderson, and Kermit Roosevelt. The ACJ was the only one of eight American Jewish groups contacted by the State Department to fully support the recommendations of the 1946 Anglo American Committee of Inquiry, among those recommendations the immediate admittance of 100,000 Jewish refugees to Palestine and the creation of a U.N. trusteeship that would eventually become an independent, binational state. In fact, the ACJ was instrumental in convincing the State Department to seek out non-Zionist points of view throughout the mid-1940s and remained a faithful ally of government specialists throughout the battle for Palestine.[26]

Standing opposite the government specialists, the old missionary hands, Orientalists, and the ACJ were a growing number of politically engaged and powerful groups specifically concerned with the issue of the Jewish presence in Palestine and working hard to secure U.S. government support for the cause. The Zionist Organization of America had been a powerful voice in American politics since Louis Brandeis served as the group's leader during World War I. It was joined by a number of other groups during World War II, benefiting from the rapid shift in the U.S. Jewish community from a generally ambiguous position on Palestine to one of strong Zionist support, a shift caused by news of the Holocaust in Europe. The American Zionist Emergency Council coordinated pro-Zionist demonstrations and lobbying efforts, and achieved remarkable success between 1945 and 1948 with letter-writing campaigns for Jewish and non-Jewish organizations alike that flooded State Department, White House, and congressional mailboxes with calls for the establishment of a Jewish state in Palestine.[27]

Wartime appeals for official U.S. support for the Zionist cause still relied on earlier arguments about achieving the transformation of Palestine through the expansion of the Jewish presence there, but these appeals also added two other arguments intended to alter how people imagined the conflict. The first of these arguments sought to counter claims that protecting U.S. interests during the war necessitated support of Arabs by emphasizing that the Jewish presence in Palestine was not just a U.S. interest, as Zionists contended in 1937, but could in fact prove central to winning the war, especially in the Middle East. In this line of reasoning, opening up Jewish immigration to Palestine during the war would create an environment in which, as one memorandum proposed, "the power of the Jewish economic machine" could prove an ally in fighting the war. Historian Lawrence Davidson has also suggested that Zionists contended that Jewish opposition to Hitler was absolute, while the Arab position was more ambiguous, and, moreover, that "to the extent that the Allies were fighting for a more civilized world, the Zionists, and not the Arabs, were their natural allies." So, Zionists suggested, supporting the Jewish presence in Palestine was the best option, regardless of whether one focused on the immediate goal of winning the war or the more distant issue of the nature of the postwar world.[28]

The second argument—premised on a moral obligation to permit Jews a state of their own—was not in itself new, but was given greater meaning by the Holocaust. As early as January 1942, Chaim Weizmann, the public face of the international Zionist movement, laid out in *Foreign Affairs* all the familiar positions regarding Jewish uplift and transformation in Palestine and the potential military and financial contributions to the war effort from a mobilized worldwide force of Jews. He then added that the increasingly violent and deadly persecution of Jews in Europe necessitated the immediate opening up of unlimited immigration to Palestine and the creation of Jewish state. As news of the Holocaust became more well known from 1943 onward, that moral imperative and the associated guilt for not having done more to save European Jews grew more powerful and touched a chord with broader America. To be sure, the conflict over Palestine was not a burning issue among the American populace at the end of World War II, but the vast majority of those who cared about the issue clearly supported the Jewish presence in Palestine. According to public opinion poll data, only 55 percent of Americans "followed the discussion about permitting Jews to settle in Palestine" in December 1945. Six months later, just 50 percent of poll respondents had "heard or read about the Jewish migration into Palestine." Yet, of those people who were aware of the issue, 76 percent in the December 1945 poll and 78 percent in the May 1946 poll supported Jewish immigration. An October 1947 poll concerning the potential for conflict in Palestine returned similar results. Of the 36 percent of the respondents who claimed to support either Jews or Arabs if the conflict led to war, twice as many favored the Jews.[29]

While it is important to consider how both anti-Zionist and pro-Zionist factions tried to imagine the future of Palestine, and to consider the impact of those imaginings on wider America, it is critical to realize that, ultimately, the battle for Palestine was really a contest for political power and the mind of the president, and it was one in which pro-immigration and pro-Zionist groups generally—though not always easily—won throughout the 1940s. President Franklin Roosevelt deferred to the British, who controlled Palestine through their League of Nations mandate, for most of his first two terms in office, but he was ideologically predisposed to support Jewish immigration to and the creation of a national home in Palestine. He assumed a more active pro-immigration role in the late 1930s and early 1940s, and frequently hosted American Zionist leaders such as Rabbis Steven Wise and Abba Hillel Silver at the White House. His relationship with Wise and Silver notwithstanding, Roosevelt remained concerned primarily with winning the war and did what he thought necessary to achieve that objective by trying to postpone any firm policy decision on Palestine until the war was over. He therefore hoped to mollify both Arabs and Jews with seemingly contradictory statements. He met with Wise and Silver in March 1944, and gave them permission to state that the United States had "never given its approval" to the 1939 British white paper limiting Jewish immigration to Palestine, and that "full justice will be done to those who seek [a] Jewish national home." Coming on top of congressional efforts to pass resolutions challenging the 1939 white paper, the statement by Wise and Silver generated a storm of protest from Middle Eastern governments and U.S. representatives in the region. Roosevelt then authorized Secretary of State Cordell Hull to instruct the U.S. representative in Saudi Arabia to inform Saudi King Ibn Saud that "no decision altering the basic situation of Palestine should be reached without full consultation with both Arabs and Jews." When Roosevelt and Ibn Saud met in February 1945, the king informed Roosevelt that "the Arabs would choose to die rather than yield their lands to the Jews," to which the president responded that "he would do nothing to assist the Jews against the Arabs and would make no move hostile to the Arab people." Roosevelt died soon after, leaving Truman to navigate his way through these conflicting statements.[30]

Truman was less concerned with wartime expediencies than was his predecessor and was even more inclined to favor an expanding Jewish presence in Palestine, although he was not without his own internal conflicts over the issue. Historian Michael Cohen has labeled Truman a "refugee Zionist," meaning he believed Jewish immigration to Palestine was morally appropriate because of the extent of Jewish suffering historically and in Europe during the war. Truman also knew that supporting the Jewish presence in Palestine might win him crucial votes—especially critical in New York—in what was sure to be a difficult election in 1948. He was unwilling, however, to put his country's credibility or any of its soldiers on the line to create a Jewish state by force, and he recognized the very real problems that support for the Jewish presence in Palestine created for the United States throughout the Middle East. Moreover, as important as Truman considered the issue of Palestine to be in 1946 and 1947, there were a number of even more pressing international issues that he had to handle at the same time. Events in Europe, Greece, Turkey, and Iran all weighed heavily on his mind at various points, making his involvement in the Palestine issue intermittent for most of the first two years of his presidency. Finally, Truman disliked the amount of pressure he felt from pro-Zionist quarters outside his administration, remarking on several occasions that he found satisfying Jews to be an impossible task. Thus, even though Truman agreed with the idea of expanding the Jewish presence in Palestine, he was, as Democratic Party foreign policy operative and Kennedy-era Secretary of State Dean Rusk later remarked, "a little schizophrenic" about the issue.[31]

Nonetheless, Truman overcame his "schizophrenia" to work consistently against the advice of regional specialists in the State Department in support of the expanding Jewish presence in Palestine, as domestic and international tensions over the issue came to a head between 1945 and 1948. In a meeting with Wise barely a week after assuming office, Truman discussed Palestine and expressed concern that the "striped-pants boys" at the State Department "did not care enough about what had happened to thousands of displaced persons who were involved." Later, on 31 August 1945, Truman conveyed his support for the admission to Palestine of 100,000 European Jewish refugees to British prime minister Clement Atlee without informing the State Department. That same day, Gordon Merriam and Loy Henderson sent Secretary of State James Byrnes a memorandum outlining why they believed such a policy was problematic. Then, after the joint Anglo-American committee inquiring into the situation of the Jewish refugees and their possible entrance into Palestine issued its report in 1946 finding in favor of admission and recommending the creation of a U.N. trusteeship leading to the independence of a binational state, Truman supported the recommendation over State Department objections. Finally, on Yom Kippur and just weeks before midterm congressional elections in fall 1946, Truman reiterated his belief that the refugees should be allowed entrance to Palestine and stated that the American public could accept the partition of Palestine into a Jewish and an Arab state.[32]

The tension between Truman, his White House advisors, and Zionist advocates on one side, and government Middle East specialists and their supporters on the other, intensified through 1947. In late August, the U.N. Special Committee on Palestine released a majority report recommending partition of Palestine into separate Jewish and Arab states and a minority report recommending a single state with Jewish and Palestinian components. Henderson and his colleagues rejected the majority report recommending partition for the same reasons they had opposed the expanding Jewish presence all along. They saw U.S. support for a Jewish state violating the principle of self-determination, threatening significant U.S. interests in the Middle East, and creating a situation of dangerous instability and opportunity in the region upon which the Soviet Union might capitalize. Truman demanded that the U.S. delegation to the United Nations support partition despite these objections, but he also followed State Department recommendations by ordering U.S. officials at the United Nations to stand aloof and not to try to influence the votes of other countries. Some evidence suggests at least two of Truman's closest advisors — Clark Clifford and David Niles — disregarded that order and worked behind the scenes without the State Department's knowledge to convince as many as seven initially undecided or opposed delegations to vote for partition, thus ensuring the two-thirds majority required to pass the plan.[33]

The conflict between government Middle East specialists and the White House and its pro-Jewish supporters climaxed in the six months between the vote for partition and the actual declaration of the independent Israeli state in May 1948. Specialists in Near Eastern affairs continued to search for ways to undercut the partition plan and to reassert themselves in the policymaking process, including resurrecting and promoting an alternative plan for a U.N. trusteeship leading to a binational state in Palestine. At the same time, Truman became exasperated with American Jews, who went to great lengths to pressure him to support partition. In February and March 1948, Truman actually gave verbal approval to the State Department's plan for trusteeship, but only if the United Nations voted not to implement the partition plan. State Department officials saw an opening and, without consulting the White House, had the U.S. ambassador to the United Nations announce on 19 March that the United States supported trusteeship rather than partition. Truman found out about the policy by reading the next morning's papers and confided to his diary: "This morning I find that the State Department has reversed my Palestine policy. There are people on the 3rd and 4th levels of the State [Department] who have always wanted to cut my throat. They've succeeded in doing it." Truman reluctantly stood by the announcement, but in early April he bypassed the State Department and contacted Chaim Weizmann to reassure him that the United States would immediately recognize an independent Israel as long as the United Nations did not vote for trusteeship, which it never did. Truman was true to his word to Weizmann, granting Israel de facto recognition eleven minutes after it declared independence.[34]

The creation of Israel, and the U.S. role therein, served in certain respects as a defining moment for the older generation of specialists that had dominated the emerging informal network between World War I and the end of World War II. Some members had their personal and professional reputations tarred with charges of anti-Semitism. President Truman, who remarked in his memoirs that some Near East specialists were "inclined to be anti-Semitic," was one of the most prominent individuals to level the accusation.

Such assessments of Loy Henderson and his colleagues caricatured their positions, which were based on reasonable readings of the Middle Eastern and international contexts. The recollections of Parker Hart, one of the first State Department employees who could speak Arabic, and who had opposed the creation of Israel, nicely capture the sense of betrayal that this generation of specialists felt after 1948. Hart noted that government Middle East specialists were "scandalized by what happened in 1948." Specialists felt they "had made a tremendous effort to lay the ground for good relations with the Arabs, and all of a sudden, when [the United States was] in good position, all of our hopes were dashed."[35]

There were also career implications for several individuals who had spoken against the creation of Israel. William Eddy left formal government service in late 1947 because of his opposition to U.S. policy. Henderson was up for reassignment in 1948, but his appointment as U.S. ambassador to Turkey was blocked in the Senate, so he was posted instead to India. Still others decided to retire within a few years or voluntarily switched out of Middle Eastern affairs. It certainly seems plausible that there existed a chilly environment in the late 1940s that may have led some government specialists to bite their tongues, rather than openly express opposition to U.S. policy toward Israel.[36]

Yet we must also be careful not to overstate the professional consequences of 1948. Hart, who had first served in the Middle East in Saudi Arabia in 1944, continued to work on regional issues for two more decades and even served as assistant secretary of state for Near Eastern and South Asian affairs in the late 1960s. Henderson moved from his exile in India to the U.S. ambassadorship to Iran from 1951 to 1954 and in that position oversaw the U.S. overthrow of Mohammad Mossadegh in 1953. Three other individuals who had been considered some of the most strident opponents to the Jewish cause in Palestine, and whom Dean Acheson would later refer to as "the three Arabs" — Harold Hoskins, William Eddy, and Kermit Roosevelt — remained influential voices for several more years. Even though Eddy resigned from government service, never reconciled himself to the notion of Israel as a permanent fixture in the Middle East, and spoke and wrote openly in opposition to U.S. policy toward the Arab-Israeli-Palestinian conflict, both the CIA and the State Department regularly consulted him in the late 1940s and early 1950s on other regional issues. Roosevelt joined Henderson in Iran in 1953 as the primary CIA operative in the overthrow of Mossadegh. Nonetheless, with the exception of Hart, Roosevelt, and perhaps a few others, most of the old missionary hands, Orientalists, and members of Near Eastern affairs who opposed the creation of

Israel were nearer the ends of their careers in 1948 than the beginnings. It would therefore be up to a new generation of specialists who would come of age professionally after 1948 to imagine the Middle East with an enduring Arab-Israeli-Palestinian conflict as one of its primary features.

Reasserting Authority and Managing Conflict

Historian Peter Hahn has argued that between 1945 and 1961 U.S. policymakers found themselves "caught in the Middle East" as they sought to secure U.S. interests in the region. Policymakers walked a fine line as they worked to deny the Soviet Union inroads into the Middle East, to retain access to Middle Eastern oil, and to maintain positive relations with all sides, while they also tried to lessen the violence of the Arab-Israeli-Palestinian conflict. In doing so, however, U.S. policymakers were never able to achieve their goals and ended up alienating all parties.[37]

Much the same can be said about the members of the informal network of Middle East specialists during the period from the late 1940s through approximately 1960. While there certainly were exceptions like William Eddy, most specialists during this period acknowledged that they had little choice but to accept Israel's existence, and they immediately began trying to reassert some authority on the issue, both among policymakers and Americans more generally. They did so, however, within complex domestic, international, and regional political environments that imposed significant constraints and defined how they imagined the Arab-Israeli-Palestinian conflict. The wider American audience drew on a series of shifting cultural constructions to imagine Israel as a reliable Cold War ally in a dangerous and unstable region of the world. Meanwhile, in the policymaking arena, the Truman administration remained generally supportive of Israel, but was not afraid to contest specific Israeli actions or policies. The Eisenhower administration did not feel the same political obligations to American Jews the Truman administration did and proved even more willing to confront Israel, though the Eisenhower administration also recognized certain limits on its policy options. Finally, network participants were committed Cold Warriors and were therefore worried about the potential opportunities the Arab-Israeli-Palestinian conflict presented for the Soviet Union. They were particularly worried about the continuing high level of violence between Arabs and Israelis, but were also concerned about the fate of more than 700,000 Palestinian refugees created by the war between Israel and its Arab neighbors in 1948 and 1949. Indeed, most specialists saw the refugee situation as the key to reducing violence and ultimately to resolving the crisis as a whole. In these contexts, a new generation of members of the informal network of specialists—many of whom entered the profession after 1948—imagined an enduring conflict that they believed the United States should try to manage, while minimizing the United States' own direct involvement so as to limit potential threats to U.S. interests. These new specialists were confronted by pro-Israeli forces working to build a close policy relationship between the United States and Israel. Those pro-Israeli forces increased their power through the 1950s and exerted tremendous pressure on network participants and others who opposed close U.S.-Israeli ties.[38]

Specialists seeking to play an important role in defining how Americans imagined the Arab-Israeli-Palestinian conflict between 1948 and 1960 encountered what historian Michelle Mart has characterized as a "dramatic discursive transformation of Jews and Israel in American popular culture and politics." These new cultural constructions recalled attempts from the 1920s and 1930s to present Israel as a potential U.S. ally in the region and the Jewish presence in Palestine as transforming the Middle East. Now, however, they portrayed Israel as a budding Cold War ally and a modern, Western democratic outpost in a distinctly traditional and undemocratic Middle East. In this transformation, the portrayal of Jews both in the United States and Israel switched "from [one of] curious minorities to [one of] kindred spirits and reliable allies in the Cold War." The application of a traditional gendered discourse constituted the key method through which Israel and its citizens became so closely identified with the United States. That discourse portrayed the United States as a country where "men were dominant, 'masculine,' and took responsibility for women." Playing out in the international Cold War arena, the discourse portrayed the United States as "a masculine country that took responsibility for other, 'weaker' nations." Over time, Israel moved into this discourse, shifting from being seen as "weak," and perhaps even cowardly, to becoming strong, heroic, and responsible like the United States. In doing so, Israelis became accepted not only as Cold War allies, but "as insiders, as similar to Americans, to be judged by similar political and social ideals: Israelis would not have been seen as insiders if they had not measured up to an image of traditional masculinity." Films, journalists' reports, and literary works all contributed to and reflected this discursive transformation.[39]

Mart's analysis emphasizes gender, but it suggests that other discourses based on race or ethnicity might also have promoted a strong sense of shared identity between Americans and Israelis in the 1950s. Historian Michael Hunt has identified a clear pattern of thinking in which racial hierarchies, where lighter-skinned peoples ranked progressively higher than dark-skinned peoples, were a critical component of a U.S. foreign relations ideology. Clearly some members of America's Middle East network believed race mattered. They drew distinctions — sometimes derogatory and sometimes not — between how white and nonwhite peoples acted in and interpreted the world. A 1950 State Department report on the military capabilities of the Arab states and Israel argued that Israelis were "for the most part of European extraction and differ greatly from the peoples of the surrounding Arab states in temperament, outlook, energy and approach to their problems. Their approach is essentially western." By contrast, "people of Arab stock" lacked competence in government, were "beset by internal bickerings," and would only "make good mercenaries."[40]

Sacred and secular discourses also influenced how specialists and other Americans imagined Israel. Many specialists, to say nothing of the more general American populace, had a difficult time understanding Islam and how it fit into the world arena, especially with respect to local and international politics. Specialists much more easily understood Judaism as part of their own religious heritage, a fact which Zionists in the 1920s and 1930s and supporters of Israel after 1948 relied on as they sought to build a close relationship with the United States. Similarly, the strong sense of a secular American mission helped strengthen U.S.-Israeli bonds. By the mid-1950s, Israelis were focused on building a militarily secure state that would be economically and politically viable. From the point of view of many specialists and network members, Israelis focused on development while Arabs had not moved beyond religion and radical mass politics and their minds and energies were still focused on confronting irrational anticolonial concerns.[41]

Sociocultural discourses, whether they were based on gender, race, sacred ideas, or secular values, helped form perceptions of the Arab-Israeli conflict during the decade after Israeli independence. Reinforced in films, literary works, and even within the network itself, these discourses provided support to those actors seeking to strengthen the U.S.-Israeli relationship. In this way, pro-Israeli discourses contributed to a domestic political atmosphere unlike any surrounding other issues on which network members worked.

A brief look at two organizations opposed to strengthening U.S.-Israeli ties illustrates the political impact of these new cultural discourses. The ACJ had resisted the creation of a Jewish state in Palestine and allied itself with government members of the network in the mid-1940s. The creation of Israel in 1948 removed the ACJ's raison d'être, so the group shifted its focus to promoting strong democratic processes in Israel and preventing the growing Jewish lobby from exercising undue political influence in the United States. The ACJ wanted to limit Israeli influence and financial demands on American Jews and to ensure full participation in the Israeli government for those Palestinians living within Israel. The argument against Israeli influence was premised upon the notion that Israeli law sought to establish among Jews around the world an assumed, and perhaps even obligatory, second national loyalty. The ACJ was particularly critical of the Law of Return and the Nationality Law, which permitted Jews anywhere in the world to "return" to Israel and granted them immediate citizenship. The ACJ argued that these laws interfered in the internal affairs of other states and violated international law. Moreover, according to the ACJ, those and other Israeli laws granted rights to citizens of other nations that were denied to non-Jewish residents of Israel, thereby making Israel, by definition, either racist or theocratic.[42]

The first two years of the Eisenhower administration saw the zenith of the ACJ's ability to reach high-level policymakers after the creation of Israel. Between 1948 and 1952, the Truman administration was generally more concerned with issues that related only indirectly to Middle Eastern affairs and Arab-Israeli tensions, and members of the ACJ assumed the administration was pro-Israeli anyway. Dwight Eisenhower, however, agreed to meet with ACJ members early in his tenure, in April 1953, which led to an amicable relationship between the council and the government over the ensuing two years. Elmer Berger cultivated a good working relationship with Assistant Secretary of State for Near Eastern, South Asian, and African Affairs Henry Byroade, convincing him to serve as the guest speaker at the ACJ's annual conference in May 1954 despite the expected backlash from pro-Israeli voices.[43]

The ACJ's access to the halls of power and to government members of the network declined precipitously in late 1954 and early 1955. Byroade moved to Cairo to become the U.S. ambassador to Egypt, while Eisenhower and Dulles moved nearer to Israel because of growing concerns about increasingly close ties between the Soviet Union and Egypt and the potential threats those ties posed in the Middle East. Nonetheless, the ACJ continued to try to influence policymakers, hoping to convince them to take a firmer line with the Israelis. The group met with less and less success. Lucius Battle, the State

Department's executive secretary for Near Eastern affairs, explained why the ACJ was no longer welcome and revealed the growing acceptance of a strengthening U.S.-Israeli relationship. Battle remarked that while the ACJ was "the most active anti-Zionist group in the country," and had "articulately expressed" its concerns to the State Department for several years, its attitudes "reflect a socio-psychological problem for the most part beyond the range of practical government action."[44]

The controversial American Friends of the Middle East (AFME) also demonstrates the impact of widely accepted cultural constructions of Israel as a budding U.S. ally. The AFME was formed when individuals associated with educational, missionary, and philanthropic interests in the Middle East approached journalist Dorothy Thompson following her 1950 visit to the region to study the refugee problem. They hoped she would be able to use her influence to build an organization to help Americans become more familiar with Middle Eastern issues, particularly the Palestinian cause. The result was, according to the State Department, "a private institute—non-political—whose aim [was] to present 'correct information' to the American people concerning the Middle East." The group held annual conferences, sponsored individuals for an exchange program between the United States and the Middle East, provided a news clipping service, and offered financial support for art exhibits and the construction of cultural and information centers. Initially the AFME was surprisingly successful, adding over three hundred new members in its second year (1952–53), and another six hundred the next. The AFME's financial resources grew just as rapidly. Beginning with a little over seventy-five thousand dollars in the 1951–52 fiscal year, the AFME's operating budget was nearly half a million dollars by 1953–54 and one million dollars in 1959–60, and remained in that range through 1967. Dorothy Thompson remained president of the board of directors and chairman of the national council of AFME through 1956, although Garland Evans Hopkins (formerly editor of the *Christian Century*) handled the organization's day-to-day affairs.[45]

Just as the ACJ had, the AFME enjoyed an amicable working relationship with the State Department in the early 1950s, particularly with the Middle East specialists working in Near Eastern affairs. State Department employees frequently participated in AFME-sponsored events, and official U.S. media outlets in the Middle East, such as the Voice of America, gave more favorable and fuller coverage to the AFME than they did to other organizations concerned with regional affairs. Indeed, the AFME carried enough weight in the State Department to be able, over an extended period, to reach the ear of

Secretary of State Dulles, either through meetings or occasional letters. That such a relationship originally went unquestioned is not surprising, given that a 1967 article in the *New York Times* revealed the AFME was one of a number of organizations the CIA covertly funded to help build ties between the United States and other parts of the world.[46]

To some observers, the AFME appeared to quickly abandon its original mission and to assume a pro-Arab position in the conflict with Israel. By 1953, the group's third year in existence, the State Department faced the question of whether it should continue providing full coverage of the organization's activities, particularly when AFME's public statements increasingly conflicted with official U.S. policy in the region. The AFME's position was not helped by the fact that some of its most well-known participants and members of its National Council—such as Elmer Berger—were also members of the ACJ or, as in Kermit Roosevelt's case, had at least openly opposed the creation of Israel. By 1955, respect for the AFME had declined to the point where one State Department wit referred to the organization as the "American Friends of the Arab East." In 1956, Dorothy Thompson's editors at Bell Syndicates informed her that her affiliation with an organization they believed to be blatantly pro-Arab threw her journalistic objectivity into question, and they forced her to choose between her position with them and the presidency of the AFME. Thompson succumbed to the pressure and resigned from the AFME. The organization's influence steadily declined from that point forward, and it eventually changed its focus to helping students from the Middle East gain entrance to colleges in the United States and financing small agricultural and business training missions to the region. In the 1970s, the AFME changed its name to AMIDEAST (America-Mideast Educational and Training Services, Inc.) to reflect its new mission.[47]

Within this cultural and political context, members of the informal network of specialists emphasized two key issues as they attempted to reassert their authority as the primary interpreters of the Arab-Israeli-Palestinian conflict. Just as they had been before the creation of Israel, most members of the network were tremendously concerned after 1948 that the conflict promoted dangerous instability and threatened U.S. interests throughout the Middle East. They were particularly worried about continued high levels of violence between Arabs and Israelis. The Arabs resented their defeat in the 1948–1949 war, and technically remained at war with the Jewish state. In addition, Arabs launched raids against Israeli towns, villages, and military outposts on an almost continuous basis, increasing the financial and human costs for Israelis.

The Israelis developed a method of retaliating in which they deployed massive military force to strike violently at the country from where the raids came. The first Israeli military venture of this sort, undertaken at Qibya in October 1953, left dozens of Arabs dead. A similar raid on Gaza in February 1955 left over thirty Egyptians dead and, as chapter 3 suggested, precipitated Nasser's turning to the Soviets for weapons. Rebukes from the United States and censures from the United Nations did little to stop either the Arab raids or the stinging Israeli retaliations. As Halford Hoskins noted in his 1954 overview of the region, "The main current in the trend of events in the Middle East since the early months of 1949 has been the continuation of the Arab-Israeli war by other means."[48]

In response, network members promoted a two-pronged approach to this aspect of the conflict. First, they suggested that Israel accept its position as a fundamentally Middle Eastern, rather than a fundamentally Western, state. Israel's economic viability depended, at least to a certain extent, upon access to regional and international markets, without which it never would have been able to provide for its growing population. Moreover, the face of that population was changing considerably. By the mid-1950s, most immigrants to Israel were coming from other parts of the Middle East, rather than from Europe or the United States. According to John Campbell, the "increasingly 'eastern' complexion" of Israel's population meant that Israeli society was in some ways adopting traditions and ways of living that placed it squarely within the Middle East, rather than as a Western outpost in the Middle East. As one commentator noted, "Israel, transformed by its recent Arab and African immigration into a nation which will soon no longer be of predominantly Western origin, may come to look and feel less different from Egypt than it does today. In fact, the less Israeli leaders stress the Western character of their state and the less Americans speak of Israel as a bastion of Western democracy—phrases which remind Egyptians of previous servitudes to the West—the more hope there will be for stability in this area."[49]

Network participants urged Israel to pursue a more accommodating policy toward its Arab neighbors as part of accepting its place in the Middle East. The most forceful and visible articulator of this idea was Henry Byroade, the assistant secretary of state for Near Eastern, South Asian, and African affairs who spoke sternly to Israelis in a speech before the Dayton, Ohio, World Affairs Council in April 1954. His words are worth quoting at length both for their bluntness and their clear statement of the network's general position: "To the Israelis I say that you should come to truly look upon yourself as a

Middle Eastern state and see your own future in that context rather than as a headquarters, or nucleus so to speak, of worldwide groupings of peoples of a particular religious faith who must have special rights within and obligations to the Israeli state. You should drop the attitude of the conqueror and the conviction that force and a policy of retaliatory killings is the only policy that your neighbors will understand. You should make your deeds correspond to your frequent utterance of the desire for peace." A more accommodating policy toward the Arab states would, Byroade and other proponents argued, make it possible over time for Israel to connect its economy to those of other Middle Eastern states. Integrating Israel into the economic and political fabric of the region would in turn reduce the potential for continued instability and violence in the area. It also meshed nicely with the broader, enduring, sacred and secular American mission in the Middle East.[50]

The second prong of the network's approach to reduce violence was to urge Arabs to accept Israel as a neighbor. Indeed, Byroade was just as blunt toward the Arabs in his 1954 speech as he was toward the Israelis. He pushed the Arabs to recognize that Israel was a permanent state and to begin looking for ways to move beyond the conflict: "To the Arabs I say you should accept this state of Israel as an accomplished fact. I say further that you are deliberately attempting to maintain a state of affairs delicately suspended between peace and war, while at present desiring neither. This is a most dangerous policy and one which world opinion will increasingly condemn if you continue to resist any move to obtain at least a less dangerous modus vivendi with your neighbor." Following such a policy, Byroade contended, would have numerous benefits for Arabs. It would allow them to improve their image in the world, especially in Western Europe and the United States. And network members believed that a more reasonable approach to the conflict with Israel would remove a major source of regional instability and calls for revolutionary change, while also allowing leaders of Arab states to devote more resources to much needed modernization and development, and thus speed the process of transformation.[51]

As the debate in the mid-1940s over Palestine and the fate of the ACJ and AFME demonstrated, however, network members also had to consider the growing domestic political power of pro-Israeli forces when constructing a framework of meaning regarding the Arab-Israeli conflict. By the mid-1950s, these forces exerted nearly continuous pressure on Congress, the State Department, and the White House to tie the United States ever more closely to Israel. "The Lobby," as it became known over time, tried to convince policymakers, legislators, and even average Americans that the United States needed to support Israel unequivocally. The government of Israel also exercised extensive influence over lobbyists in the United States.[52]

Regional specialists, especially those within the government, were keenly aware of the Israel lobby's power. According to then State Department Middle East specialist Edwin Wright, Henry Byroade received a phone call the morning after he delivered his 1954 speech urging Arabs and Israelis to be more accepting and accommodating of each other. On the line was Nahum Goldmann, president of the World Jewish Congress and the founder in 1954 of the Conference of Presidents of Major American Jewish Organizations (or President's Conference). Goldmann and Byroade knew each other, so Goldmann asked "Hank" if in fact he had made the speech Goldmann read about in the California papers. Byroade answered yes, to which Goldmann allegedly replied, "We will see to it that you'll never hold another good position." The story cannot be verified beyond Wright's account, and Byroade later became ambassador to Egypt, but even if the story is apocryphal it reflects government Middle East specialists' keen awareness of the political power of pro-Israeli lobbying forces.[53]

As concerned as network members may have been about domestic political pressures, it was events in the Middle East that ultimately ended their hopes of managing the conflict by promoting an Arab-Israeli rapprochement and thereby reducing the violence. When Israel colluded with Britain and France to invade Egypt during the Suez Crisis of 1956, it ended any possibility of peace in the short term. Nasser became less flexible in the aftermath of Suez, and instability in Syria, Lebanon, Jordan, and Iraq over the next two years precluded any other viable options for pursuing peace.

The network's other main area of concern as members imagined the Arab-Israeli-Palestinian conflict in the 1950s was the refugee issue, which appeared to be the fundamental problem needing a solution before progress on other fronts might occur. Over 700,000 Palestinian refugees were either forced out of their homes or fled them under duress during the 1948–49 war. These refugees were one of the main legacies of the conflict. The exodus was a humanitarian crisis on multiple levels. The United Nations, largely with U.S. funding, hastily constructed camps to house the refugees and provided at least a minimal level of relief aid. Most of the refugees had been farmers or had worked in markets, so few in the camps had jobs or any means to pay for goods. In addition, the longer refugees remained in the camps, the larger their numbers grew, which only compounded humanitarian problems. Moreover, the refugees remained in limbo as long as the Arab states and Israel obstinately refused to resolve their differences.[54]

Specialist assessments of the refugee crisis reflected a combination of basic humanitarian concern and a sense that the crisis somehow fit with enduring images of Arabs and Muslims as backward, emotional, and lazy. Georgiana Stevens, who had been a wartime Middle East specialist and worked as a journalist and consultant on Middle Eastern affairs, claimed that by the early 1950s most "adults in these camps" were "becoming professional refugees, without hope or desire to work again." The loss of home and property combined with bleak prospects for the future to cause "an uncounted number among the older generation" to "become psychotic." Moreover, according to some estimates, less than half of the refugees were even in the camps. The remaining refugees lived on city streets in Egypt, Jordan, Lebanon, and Syria, and were ineligible to receive U.N. relief assistance. Their presence, in the words of Don Peretz, was a "burden" that "weigh[ed] down the economy and social and political structure of every Arab state where they live," thereby preventing those states from improving their own citizens' lives.[55]

The longer the refugees' status remained unchanged, the more analysts believed the crisis provided the Soviet Union with an excellent opportunity to spread communist influence throughout the Middle East. Stevens claimed the situation was "made to order for Communist agitators." The camps themselves obviously provided sites with sizeable destitute populations through which commentators feared communist ideas might easily spread. According to Stevens, communist propaganda fed "the hopes of idle, homesick people" by suggesting that Western powers promoted resettlement of the refugees only to use them in future military operations. The Soviets therefore urged the refugees to resist resettlement "by marching en masse to their former homes." Network participants asserted that such claims helped foment the idea that the West, and the United States especially, was responsible for the plight of the Palestinian refugees and in turn suggested that Palestinians and Arabs should work against U.S. interests in the Middle East whenever possible.[56]

Drawing on their understanding of the broader conflict, of the refugee issue specifically, and of domestic political concerns, network members initially promoted an economic approach to the crisis. First, they accepted Israel and its domestic supporters' argument that repatriation of significant numbers of refugees to Israel was for the most part impossible. Jewish immigrants had taken up residence in most of the homes vacated by the Palestinians, and much of the land had either been taken over for Jewish farming or cleared for the construction of new settlements. The Palestine that the refugees left behind no longer existed and could not be recreated. The solution therefore appeared to be financial compensation for the refugees' losses and economic assistance to any countries that would resettle large numbers of refugees within their borders. In the early 1950s, the United Nations authorized the expenditure of $200 million for such purposes, the majority of which was to be provided by the United States, but only a fraction of which was actually used.[57]

As the refugee crisis defied all efforts to resolve it in the 1950s, government Middle East specialists and network participants searched for alternatives that would build on preexisting plans but that might present greater hope for success. With that goal in mind, they developed a much larger effort beginning in 1961 to resolve the refugee issue. The plan emerged out of the State Department's Office of Near Eastern Affairs and combined a number of recommendations made over several years. The chief component of the plan was to offer each refugee a choice of repatriation as a citizen of Israel, resettlement in an Arab country, or resettlement in a non-Arab country. An explicit assumption behind the plan was that few if any of the refugees would actually choose repatriation. The plan also generally adhered to the United Nation's December 1948 General Assembly Resolution 194, which stated in part that refugees who wished to return should be allowed to and those who chose not to return should be compensated for their losses. The State Department suggested running the plan through the United Nations' Palestine Conciliation Commission (comprised of the United States, France, and Turkey) in order to invest more countries in the effort. Joseph Johnson, head of the Carnegie Endowment for International Peace, was selected to serve as the United Nations special representative responsible for negotiating the details of the plan.[58]

The approach of at least some network participants and policymakers to the Johnson Plan reflected the network's basic acceptance of an increasingly close, special U.S.-Israeli relationship by the late 1950s and early 1960s. Most observers quickly recognized that the plan had very little chance of success, largely because Israel demanded ultimate control over the repatriation of any refugees, but network members continued to push it forward. Some individuals, such as President Kennedy's White House Middle East specialist Robert Komer, continued to do so because they believed neither the United States nor Israel should bear responsibility for the plan's failure. Instead, as Komer argued on several occasions, the Arabs would find some way to kill the plan and should "take the onus" for its collapse. Komer therefore urged his colleagues to remain committed to the plan, and tried to convince the Israelis to publicly state their willingness to continue discussing the option. All the while, he believed the plan had little chance of success and counted "on Arab hotheads to begin reacting and thus sharing the blame." Thus, if the plan would not work, at least its failure should not damage either U.S. or Israeli prestige.[59]

The Johnson plan also revealed one of the central weaknesses in how specialists and policymakers imagined the Arab-Israeli-Palestinian conflict through the mid-1960s. Even though they realized the refugee problem was one of the central issues in the conflict, they did not recognize the refugees themselves as real participants in the conflict. Instead, the plan and its supporters portrayed the refugees as a problem for the Arab states and Israel to resolve using U.S. money, or suggested that Nasser or other Arab leaders could control the refugees. Network members and policymakers therefore neglected to account for the interests and concerns of perhaps the most crucial group involved in this aspect of the conflict and therefore proved completely unable to address the concern, expressed by some intellectuals among the refugees, that agreeing to compensation and resettlement would be to concede much more than just access to former land holdings in Israel. Accepting resettlement would have been a firm denunciation of a nascent Palestinian nationalism that had been growing since the early twentieth century, and to which the original U.N. resolution on the partition of Palestine into two independent states had brought energy and at least a minimal level of international recognition.[60]

By the late 1950s and early 1960s, members of the informal network of specialists had grown frustrated as no progress had been achieved on either the refugee issue or promoting better relations between Israel and the Arab states. They concluded that the regional environment of the late 1950s was not conducive to resolving the Arab-Israeli-Palestinian conflict. John Campbell of the Council on Foreign Relations expressed network frustrations succinctly, stating that "no policy can be built on the expectation of early settlement of the basic issues in the conflict." By 1961, this belief had become so central to the network's understanding of the conflict that Charles Cremeans, writing after wrapping up a Council on Foreign Relations study group on Arab foreign policy, claimed that "it may be a mistake to think of this as the kind of problem for which a solution can be found, except in the processes of history." The council's discussions on the topic were generally even more pessimistic, with members of the group arguing that the conflict consisted of so many problems on each side that it would take years to work through them all. Then, even if the tangible problems could be solved, significant attention and energy would have to be devoted to altering Arabs' and Israelis' attitudes toward and images of each other. In the face of such obstacles, the best the network could hope for was to maintain the status quo and prevent the outbreak of any new crisis, especially as the Middle Eastern arms race escalated and the refugee problem continued.[61]

Escalation and Disarray

While members of the informal network of specialists became more accepting of what was becoming a special relationship between the United States and Israel, their efforts to manage the Arab-Israeli-Palestinian conflict and to imagine a peaceful resolution to it became even more difficult as tensions increased through the 1960s. An escalating regional arms race in which both the Soviet Union and the United States participated, the emergence of powerful Palestinian political movements, and the 1967 war forced network participants to reconsider their earlier attempts to manage the dispute. Perceiving the conflict to be more complex and intense than they had previously, and seeing clear indications that the 1967 war cemented the U.S.-Israeli special relationship, the network found itself in disarray over the issue. Network efforts at management had failed, so participants believed it was necessary to push for a settlement. Yet, with more parties to the conflict, a stronger U.S.-Israeli relationship, and Israel's occupying Arab and Palestinian lands, an early resolution of the conflict seemed an even more distant possibility.

More than any other issue, the question of whether or not the United States should sell arms to Israel forced observers to recognize the strengthening U.S.-Israeli special relationship and the difficulty of maintaining the status quo through a balanced approach to the conflict. Most specialists and policymakers generally opposed direct U.S. arms sales to any parties in the Arab-Israeli-Palestinian conflict for fear they would only heighten the level of violence and further destabilize the region. Traditional U.S. policy had been not to participate in a Middle East arms race and to sell only limited numbers of unsophisticated, defense-oriented weapons to the region ever since the United States joined Britain and France in issuing the Tripartite Declaration to that effect in May 1950. The situation changed in the mid-1950s, when the

French, generally but not always with tacit U.S. support, became the primary arms supplier for Israel.[62]

Several factors led network members and policymakers to reconsider the question of arms sales in the late 1950s and early 1960s. Nasser's purchases of Soviet arms from 1955 on, as well as Soviet sales to Syria and Iraq in the late 1950s, presented the specter of increasing communist influence in the Middle East. These sales also put increasing pressure on Israel, and increased pressure on the United States from the Israel lobby, to match Arab weapons procurements. In addition, policymakers and network members became concerned about Israeli nuclear ambitions when it was discovered in September 1960 that the French had helped construct a large reactor at Dimona. That same year, Israel requested HAWK (Homing All the Way Killer) missiles. HAWKs were the most sophisticated surface-to-air anti-aircraft missiles in production in the late 1950s and early 1960s. Israeli leaders were concerned about Soviet sales of jet fighters to Egypt, and desired the missiles to counteract Egypt's military advances. Direct sales of conventional U.S. weapons therefore appeared less dangerous and might have been used as an incentive to prevent Israel from going nuclear.[63]

Policymakers initially opposed the HAWK request, but as discussions dragged on into 1961 and 1962, and as Israel and its American friends exerted more pressure, they began to reconsider, which forced network members inside and outside the government to confront what constituted a fundamental change in U.S. policy toward the Middle East. Specialists certainly wished to avoid selling HAWKs to Israel, not least because such sales made the job of maintaining stability and reasonable relations with Arabs more difficult. The sale would also be a qualitative leap in the Middle East arms race, and specialists hoped to avoid making the United States responsible for such a change. Yet network participants also subscribed to the same Cold War mindset that dominated policymakers' thinking, and believed that the introduction of Soviet arms into the Middle East meant the United States had to be prepared to act in kind. Providing the missiles would not only have made sure that Israel was equipped to defend itself against any Arab attack; it would also have provided a small measure of U.S. military security against the Soviet Union in the Middle East. Thus, by mid-1962, specialists across the network were reconsidering their earlier opposition, and only urged policymakers to delay the sale until the latest possible moment. Specialists wanted to be sure that some attempt would be made to convince Arabs and Israelis that arms limitations provided a better long-term measure of security and, assuming such an effort would fail, that Egypt had actually deployed new weaponry that placed Israel at a comparative disadvantage. They also hoped to avoid selling arms that could be used for immediate domestic political benefit in an election cycle. The network lost out on the last issue as the United States agreed to provide the HAWKs in September 1962, right before midterm congressional elections.[64]

The two-year debate in the early 1960s over the HAWK missile sale was but a precursor to a much more serious and sustained discussion of an escalating and increasingly dangerous Arab-Israeli arms race in the mid-1960s. A series of Arab summit meetings in 1964 and 1965 resulted in the creation of the United Arab Command (UAC), which provided for the unification under Egyptian control of Arab military forces and required each state to contribute to the common defense. The Egyptians turned to the Soviet Union for weapons, and urged other states to do so as well. The Arab summits also led to the creation of a new organization, the Palestinian Liberation Organization (PLO), designed to speak and fight for the cause of the refugees. Further complicating the regional situation, this new organization was funded by the Arab states and operated out of Jordan, which contained the largest refugee population of the Middle Eastern states. The PLO therefore issued a fundamental challenge to the control of Jordan itself.

The combination of these occurrences presented a massive problem for Jordan's king Hussein and, concomitantly, for U.S. policymakers and regional specialists hoping to manage the Arab-Israeli-Palestinian conflict. Other Arab states, particularly Egypt, pressured Hussein to buy Soviet arms to meet his commitment to the UAC. Hussein, however, preferred to deal with the Americans, who had long supported him as a conservative monarch and a force for stability within the region. Hussein also believed he would benefit from arms purchases because they would increase his ability to control the Palestinians in his country. U.S. policymakers delayed deciding on Hussein's request as long as possible, but by early 1965 realized that he would soon have to turn to the Soviets to meet his obligations to the UAC and to maintain control in Jordan. Failure to provide the weapons would, policymakers believed, enhance Soviet prestige throughout the area, further strengthen Nasser at a time when he was becoming increasingly bellicose toward both the United States and Israel, and seriously weaken one of the United States' few allies in the region.[65]

The idea of selling arms to an Arab country, especially one that bordered

Israel, did not sit well with Israel or Jewish Americans and required extremely delicate handling. At a minimum, U.S. officials had to inform the Israelis in advance and convince them not to oppose the sale. More likely, a deal would have to be arranged whereby, in exchange for quietly acquiescing to U.S. arms sales to Jordan, the Israelis would receive at least an equal amount of weapons. The way network participants and policymakers handled the situation reveals both a shifting view of the Arab-Israeli-Palestinian conflict and some of the painful contortions policymakers made as they became more aware of the complexity and escalating tensions of the conflict.

Convincing the Israelis to accept the arrangement was no easy task, and it required two separate missions. The first mission, undertaken by National Security Council and White House Middle East specialist Robert Komer in mid-February 1965, was informational only, an opportunity to lay the basic groundwork and allow the Americans and the Israelis to feel each other out. It took four days and revealed that any follow-up mission would be incredibly complicated. The two men that President Johnson appointed to seal the deal in late February and early March were Komer and former New York Governor, Democratic Party politico, and U.S. foreign policy operative W. Averell Harriman. Harriman was under secretary of state for political affairs and ambassador at large, and was a logical choice for such a mission. He was one of the country's most respected statesmen, had provided a number of diplomatic services ever since World War II, and as the former governor of New York he possessed tremendous political capital with American Jews. His only drawback was that his prestige made it very difficult for him to travel without great publicity.[66]

Komer was a more intriguing, and also more problematic, choice. Komer was a Middle East specialist, but because he also worked on a variety of other issues that extended beyond the Middle East he should be considered as existing on the edge of the network. Nonetheless, he serves as a good indication of the complexity of views that existed within the broader network by the mid-1960s, as he held a series of seemingly contradictory positions. Like many other specialists, he sought to balance U.S. support for Israel with the protection of other U.S. interests in the region, which meant he was often perceived as "pro-Arab." He later recollected that President Kennedy took "great pleasure in matching his White House Jew, [White House counsel and contact with Israel and the American Jewish Community Myer] Feldman, against his White House Arab, Komer." President Johnson expressed similar sentiments, albeit in his typically blunt manner: "Komer you're a

God-damned Nasser lover." Even some fellow government specialists made similar observations. State Department Middle East specialist John Jernegan remarked to Under Secretary of State George Ball that "Komer was about as tough on the Jews as anybody," which he was. Komer found the Israelis annoying and difficult to deal with, and did not enjoy being treated as though Americans were, in his words, "a bunch of damn illiterates." He found this tendency especially bothersome when the Israelis were difficult on an issue within his area of expertise, such as intelligence estimates of the military balance in the Middle East. He therefore did not hesitate to oppose the Israelis, or their White House contact Feldman, on arms requests when he believed a fair analysis revealed the Arab states did not pose a credible threat to Israel's existence. He particularly disliked and complained about Israeli "propaganda campaign[s]" of public statements and leaks to the press, which always resulted in greater domestic pressure on the White House to increase aid to Israel.[67]

Despite these positions, Komer readily accepted the U.S.-Israeli relationship and did what he could to protect it, even when he appeared most sympathetic to the Arabs, and this position was representative of the basic outlook of most network members by the mid-1960s. Komer was one of the main movers behind the policy in the late 1950s and early 1960s of using aid to maintain ties to Nasser, but not because he had strong feelings for Nasser or other Arabs. Rather, Komer believed the United States needed to protect its interests in the Middle East—including Israel—and thus had to achieve a modus vivendi, even of a limited nature, with the man he saw as "Mr. Big" in the Arab world. When it became clear in 1963 that dealing with Nasser was achieving limited results, Komer backed away from a policy he had acknowledged from the start would be difficult and uncertain even though there were two years remaining on the existing agreement for U.S. wheat sales to Egypt. Just as Komer supported aid to Nasser, he helped finalize the 1962 HAWK missile deal with Israel. He also played a crucial role in arranging a covert deal in 1964 whereby Germany agreed to transfer weapons it already owned to Israel, with the United States agreeing to replenish German weapons stores, though Germany backed out of the deal when the details were made public. Komer's pragmatic approach to the Arab-Israeli-Palestinian conflict becomes even more noteworthy when one considers that he was Jewish, a fact that he tried so hard to hide that not even President Johnson knew. When Johnson was conferring with Under Secretary of State George Ball about whom to send with Harriman, he noted that Komer's "disadvantage is that he is not

Jewish." Ball responded to the president that Komer was in fact Jewish and "had disqualified himself from Arab ambassadorships" on those grounds.[68]

Government Middle East specialists pledged their measured support for the new arms sales as Komer and Harriman headed to Israel. In January 1965, Roger Davies, the director of the Office of Near Eastern Affairs, and Phillips Talbot, the assistant secretary of state for Near Eastern and South Asian affairs, met with Secretary of State Dean Rusk and Under Secretary of State George Ball. Both Davies and Talbot expressed reservations that selling arms to Jordan would be a clear violation of traditional U.S. policy and would open the door for more Israeli and Arab requests. In February, however, Talbot emerged from the annual Near East Chiefs of Mission Conference with a slightly different perspective. According to Talbot, the "views expressed by all Ambassadors reflected sober concern that protection and promotion of U.S. interests in [the] Near East [was] becoming increasingly difficult as [the] Arab-Israel conflict moves toward what some of them believe could be early climactic stage." All the ambassadors also agreed, however, that in such a context, U.S. interests were "best served by proceeding with [the] Jordan arms offer," even though they realized doing so would also necessitate selling arms to Israel. The sale of arms to Jordan would, at least in the minds of the ambassadors, prevent the loss of almost the entire Middle East to the Soviet Union.[69]

Government Middle East specialists' support for arms sales to Jordan and Israel reflected a broader recognition that the policy of conflict management they suggested in the 1950s had not worked. It was becoming easier to procure arms from a variety of sources, so the policy of avoiding arms sales only seemed to lessen U.S. influence in the Middle East. Two ambassadors even suggested that the United States open up arms sales to any willing purchaser in the Middle East, even if the possible outcome was almost immediate warfare. Middle East specialist and U.S. ambassador to Lebanon Armin Meyer argued that "perhaps an early bloodletting would not be too bad an alternative," as it might preclude a more serious clash later and could force the Arabs and Israelis to resolve the conflict. In this construction, an arms race was problematic but might be worthwhile if it could move the conflict to a new stage while allowing the United States to maintain influence in the region and outdo the Soviet Union.[70]

In the end, Komer and Harriman were able to offer the Israelis enough incentives, including direct purchases of U.S. weapons, to convince them not to oppose arms sales to Jordan. The United States was thus able to maintain its influence in Jordan. That influence, however, came at the expense of an escalating arms race in the Middle East that could not help but contribute to future tensions in the region and lead to later conflicts. The approach of both the network and policymakers to the question of direct arms sales, moreover, reflected their new understanding of the Arab-Israeli-Palestinian conflict as one of the most important, and potentially one of the hottest, Cold War battlegrounds.

As they had been during the escalating arms race, network participants were forced to reimagine the Arab-Israeli-Palestinian conflict with the emergence of viable Palestinian resistance movements. The Johnson plan for resettlement symbolized the conventional wisdom on the refugee issue through the early 1960s, but by 1963 at least one specialist was calling for a fresh look at the problem. Don Peretz had spent over a decade studying the refugee problem as a consultant to the United Nations, the U.S. government, and other organizations, and was the world's foremost expert on the issue at the time. Peretz took a decidedly different and, as it turns out, very prescient stance on the problem in an article published in *Foreign Affairs* in April 1963. To be sure, he agreed with some aspects of the dominant interpretation of the Arab-Israeli conflict and the refugees' position in it. He believed the refugees constituted one of the most destabilizing forces in the Middle East and that the Palestinian exodus was a terribly traumatic event for those who endured it. He also agreed that the refugees faced serious economic problems that required significant projects and resources over the short and long term to overcome. Finally, he concurred with his fellow network participants that a resolution of the Arab-Israeli-Palestinian conflict was not in sight and that the conflict therefore required careful management. There, however, is where Peretz's agreement with his peers ended.[71]

The fundamental point of departure was that Peretz believed the basic nature of the refugee "problem" had changed. Most members of the network, policymakers, and even Arabs and Israelis focused on the issue of Palestinian repatriation to Israel or resettlement in other Arab states and compensation by Israel for lands and goods lost. Peretz was more intimately familiar with the problem than anyone else, however, and emphasized the need for a solution to the problem that granted Palestinians their own political identity. He contended that framing the problem in terms of repatriation, instead of resettlement and compensation, "depends on assumptions which no longer seem relevant." Those assumptions ignored the fact that "nearly 40 percent of those now classified as refugees [in the early 1960s] have never been in their homeland." The original refugees had produced more than 400,000 more during fifteen years in the camps. This new generation of Palestinians knew of their homeland only through the stories their parents told them and what they learned of their history in schools. They were clearly identified as outsiders in the Arab states and were defined by the United Nations as refugees. While these Palestinians loathed Israel, the solution for them was not repatriation or resettlement; rather, it was a political entity that they could call Palestine, a state that would match the identity they so obviously felt and imagined. The Arab-Israeli-Palestinian conflict, and particularly the refugee aspect of it, seemed even more difficult than most commentators conceded. In addition to significant economic resources, resolving the conflict also required a separate piece of land for Palestinians that would encapsulate political identity in the nation state.[72]

It was not until late 1965 that events in the Middle East led other members of the network to recognize the Palestinians as an independent political entity and fall in line with Peretz's thinking. The formal creation by the Arab League of the PLO in 1964 certainly gave network participants reason to begin taking the Palestinian refugees more seriously. The CIA noted in December 1965 that the formation of the PLO represented the "frustrations of more than a million refugees from Israel." More important, however, was the creation of al-Fatah, an independent organization that received funding from wealthy Palestinians living in the Persian Gulf and was willing to use violence and terrorism to pursue its own agenda. Al-Fatah offered the Palestinians an organization that was unafraid to strike at the Israelis, conducting raids from bases in Jordan, which bore the brunt of Israeli reprisals. Even though specialists now acknowledged Palestinian refugees as independent actors in the Arab-Israeli-Palestinian conflict, most network members considered the refugees and their new organization to be political nonentities. According to William Dale, reporting from the U.S. embassy in Israel, al-Fatah members were "fanatics" whose only goal was to destabilize the situation. When some individuals tried to compare the PLO and its subsidiary, the Palestine Liberation Army, to other guerrilla groups in places like Vietnam, the refugee groups were dismissed as a "largely paper organization struggling for status."[73]

Specialists' general neglect of the Palestinians as a viable political force changed dramatically after the 1967 war, as Palestinians now appeared as a third crucial participant in the conflict, along with Israel and the Arab states. The benefit of hindsight made it easy for network members to identify refugee activities, especially those of al-Fatah, as a central cause of the war itself. Moreover, the network's new conventional wisdom suggested that the complete failure of the Arab states to address the refugees' concerns, and the failure to prevent the creation of more refugees and a subject Palestinian population during the 1967 war, had left Palestinians entirely disillusioned and ready to fight for themselves. Don Peretz even noted in a 1970 *Foreign Affairs* article that since the war Palestinians had "created a new identity" for themselves. "Increasingly," Peretz argued, " 'Palestinian' is identified with the commando warrior rather than with the downtrodden displaced person." Combining this argument with his earlier assertion that the Palestinian refugee issue needed to be framed in political rather than economic terms, Peretz and other members of the network suggested that any resolution of the conflict had to include the Palestinians as direct participants in discussions, rather than merely as the subject of talks. The fact that hundreds of thousands of refugees were now under direct Israeli rule made including the Palestinians even more necessary, almost as much for the Israelis as for the Palestinians.[74]

In addition to confirming Peretz's earlier identification of a new Palestinian role in the conflict, the 1967 war also led network members to view the Arab-Israeli-Palestinian conflict as increasingly difficult to resolve. A resolution not only had to include the Palestinians and the Soviets; it had to force both the Arabs and the Israelis to move forward. The 1967 war was more humiliating for the Arabs than the 1948–49 war, even if, as at least one network participant believed, the Arabs would never admit it. Many members of the network grew concerned that the Israelis' convincing victory left them complacent and even less willing than before the war to take their Arab neighbors seriously. In an October 1970 assessment of the conflict and efforts to negotiate a settlement, John Campbell characterized the Israeli view: "if the Arab states will not negotiate peace, then let them suffer the consequences of the absence of peace." That view was, according to Campbell, buttressed by Israelis' confidence that the Arabs could, in their words, "never" reverse the military balance of power in the conflict.[75]

In the minds of Americans and U.S. policymakers, the war generated the favorable image of a Jewish state in Palestine as a venerable U.S. ally in a troubled region, an image first presented in the 1930s and then buttressed through powerful cultural constructions between 1948 and 1960, and an image that now made it more difficult for network members to propose possible solutions to the crisis. Participants at a June 1969 Council on Foreign Relations study group on "U.S. Policy in the Middle East" suggested that it was no longer just Jewish Americans who exerted political pressure on policymakers. Following the war, one participant noted, it was "not American Jewry alone, but the whole American people who would have to be convinced of Israel's security" in any potential resolution. Popular sentiment toward Israel might have cooled by 1970, as John Campbell believed, because of the country's "uncooperative and often contemptuous attitude toward the United Nations and its reluctance to cooperate with outside powers seeking ways to move toward a political settlement," but public opinion unquestionably remained a factor in any attempt to resolve the crisis.[76]

Facing these circumstances, network specialists addressing the Arab-Israeli-Palestinian conflict diverged along two separate paths. The first, articulated most forcefully by John Campbell, recognized that a comprehensive settlement was unlikely but still urged policymakers to pursue it while at the same time trying to negotiate solutions to the individual aspects of the conflict. That prospect became much more difficult, however, as the issues now extended beyond just the refugees to include the status of Jerusalem, the occupied territories, and Israel's permanent borders. Bernard Lewis espoused a completely different alternative, premised on the belief that "the Arab-Israeli conflict, for all its importance and the attention it receives, is not the only issue in the region, nor the most decisive in the real relationship between the great powers." According to Lewis, "The Arab-Israeli crisis is not so much explosive as inflamed, not a bomb to be defused but a fever to be isolated and cooled. To this end the great powers could make some contribution by administering poultices instead of irritants." The solution, then, was to be found in deemphasizing the Middle East in U.S. policy, and minimizing the Arab-Israeli-Palestinian conflict in particular. As long as the great powers observed the situation and stepped in only to prevent another war, calmer heads might eventually prevail. As the two proposals revealed, the only real area of agreement between Campbell and Lewis, and within the wider network, was that a comprehensive solution was not likely in the immediate future.[77]

EARLY MEMBERS OF THE emerging informal network of regional specialists demonstrated only intermittent interest in the growing conflict in Palestine before World War II. Displacing those early specialists, a variety of generally pro-Zionist actors drew on enduring conceptions of the Middle East as a Judeo-Christian Holy Land and ideas of a broader sacred and secular mission to transform the region to try to convince U.S. policymakers and others to imagine a Jewish Palestine. By the mid-1940s, however, many of the old missionary hands and Orientalists inside and outside the government, supported by non-Zionist Jews, opposed the Jewish presence in Palestine because of the potential threats it posed to traditional U.S. economic, missionary, and philanthropic interests in the region. Between 1945 and 1948, pro-Zionist forces challenged and ultimately defeated these early network members in what became a vitriolic battle for Palestine.

As the Arab-Israeli-Palestinian conflict became entrenched after 1948, a new generation of specialists emerged and tried to reassert the network's authority by promoting Arab-Israeli rapprochement and an economic solution to the Palestinian refugee crisis. Along the way, they tried to adapt to a new domestic political environment in which non-network voices could exert significant pressure on specialists to protect Israeli interests. Within this context, network members remained worried about the potential dangers and apparently intractable nature of the conflict, but they were able to articulate an interpretation that reflected their acceptance of the situation and suggested that the conflict might be successfully managed.

By the mid-1960s, however, the fragile balance that network members hoped could be maintained between Arabs and Israelis—and between themselves and the pro-Israeli voices outside the network—began to break down as the conflict became more complex. An escalating arms race combined with a more politically active refugee population to force a reimagining of the Arab-Israeli-Palestinian conflict once again. Following the 1967 war, network participants struggled to develop a new interpretation and set of recommendations that offered any real hope for resolving the conflict. In effect, 1967 constituted a second defeat for many specialists. The network would not recover from this defeat, as it began to fracture and split apart under the pressures created by the war. Overall, the inability to come to terms with the Arab-Israeli-Palestinian conflict demonstrated the limits of the network's influence and abilities when confronted by an issue large and politically powerful segments of the U.S. population cared very deeply about.

EPILOGUE

From the end of World War I to the late 1960s, an evolving, informal network of specialists—somewhat transnational in scope—from academia, the business world, government, and the media was responsible for interpreting the Middle East for American audiences. In the years between World War I and World War II, that network comprised the heirs of nineteenth-century missionaries, philanthropists, educators, ancient Near East specialists, and an emerging group of policy intellectuals. Members of this nascent network combined a fundamentally Orientalist approach to interpreting the region with an evolving understanding of the United States as a great power with global interests, particularly in the natural resources of the Middle East. The absence of expertise on the contemporary Middle East became manifest during World War II and the early Cold War, and spawned efforts to create new programs and centers for training professional specialists in the modern Middle East, with the specific goal of producing knowledge for the benefit of the state. The network achieved its greatest influence from the late 1950s through the mid 1960s as policymakers implemented social science–based theories of modernization to try to transform the region.

Participants in this network imagined the Middle East of the past, the present, and the future by focusing on four key themes. Specialists turned first to Islam and what they believed was its inherent political and totalitarian nature as the most obvious marker of difference between the United States and the Middle East. They considered a potentially totalitarian Islam to be a force that dominated daily life in the region and used it to justify or explain the enduring existence of what they imagined were stagnant economic, political, and social structures there. Islam was therefore seen as the cause of an overwhelming identity crisis enveloping much of the Middle East as it entered the postwar era. As such, Islam became in the minds of network members a force with major political implications throughout the region and globally. Network members contemplated whether Muslims might determine the outcome of the Cold War. Over time, network participants came to see Islam as receding in importance and being superseded by secular nationalism as the dominant force in the Middle East. Nonetheless, they still wondered whether Islam might support the goals of nationalist leaders and movements and if the religion would therefore remain a significant factor in the Middle East and in U.S. relations with the region.

These interpretations of Islam were closely related to growing concerns over regional nationalism and its connections to mass politics, the second theme network members focused on. Initially, specialists developed two interpretations of Middle Eastern nationalism. One portrayed nationalism as a product of intellectual and anticolonial movements that took shape in the late nineteenth and early twentieth centuries and that drew inspiration from the educational initiatives of U.S. missionaries and philanthropists. The other emphasized charismatic individuals like Mustafa Kemal, Reza Khan, and ʿAbd al-ʿAziz Ibn Saʿud as the focal points of a generally benign force that offered another means of working through an overwhelming regional identity crisis and that was designed to represent the desires for political independence of the region's peoples. Mohammad Mossadegh in Iran, Gamal ʿAbd al-Nasser in Egypt, and U.S. policymakers' responses to those leaders from the late 1940s through the mid 1950s challenged this view and convinced network members that the increasingly strident nationalist movements were far less benign than originally believed. From the late 1950s through the mid-1960s, network members developed a more nuanced interpretation of Middle Eastern nationalist movements that stressed areas of common concern between movements and the United States while trying to downplay more contentious issues such as the Arab-Israeli-Palestinian conflict. Nonetheless, specialists remained ambivalent, if not openly critical, regarding the close relationship they believed continued to exist between nationalist movements and mass politics in the region.

Concerns about how to promote controlled transformation of the region, which network members believed would be inspired by spiritual crisis, rising nationalist movements, and growing pressure for more representative economic, political, and social structures, emerged as the third theme specialists focused on. The U.S. government followed a policy of liberal developmentalism during the interwar period and immediately after World War II, and the private sector—particularly U.S. oil companies like ARAMCO—played the dominant role in pursuing this agenda. By the late 1940s and early 1950s, however, a consensus emerged among specialists and U.S. policymakers that only the government was equipped to undertake such a large and coordinated effort. From the late 1950s through the mid-1960s, academic social scientists seized this opportunity to develop an overarching approach that might guide the process. They promoted modernization as the best way to get leaders such as Nasser in Egypt and the shah in Iran to focus on internal development, and modernization theory promised to increase U.S. influence over Middle Eastern countries' regional and international agendas. Modernization theory failed, however, as it presupposed the universal applicability of a single model of transformation and thus proved unable to deal with a variety of factors, including regional politics, relationships between individual leaders, and the gap between policymakers' short-term needs and network members' long-term expectations.

The Arab-Israeli conflict functioned as the fourth theme in the way network participants imagined the Middle East, though it was also the area where their credibility and expertise was subject to the greatest challenges from policymakers and a variety of influential interest groups and individuals. Between World War I and World War II, a variety of Zionist activists from outside the network worked hard to get U.S. policymakers and other interested parties to imagine a Jewish Palestine, emphasizing historical connections between Jews and the Holy Land and enduring desires to transform the region. As specialists began to devote more time to the issue during and immediately after World War II, many of the old missionary hands, Orientalists, and government specialists resisted the creation of a Jewish state in Palestine on the grounds that it would threaten U.S. economic, educational, missionary, and philanthropic interests across the region. Once a Jewish state came into existence and it became clear that high-level U.S. policymakers and powerful portions of the domestic populace supported a close U.S.-Israeli relationship, members of the informal network worked within the constraints of that relationship to develop an approach that they believed would minimize the damage to U.S. interests in the region. Maintaining the status quo while pursuing piecemeal initiatives aimed at resolving the Arab-Israeli-Palestinian conflict appeared to be the best approach in the 1950s and early 1960s. Observers struggled to come to terms with the conflict as it escalated in the mid-1960s. The Israeli occupation of the Gaza Strip, the West Bank, the Sinai Peninsula, East Jerusalem, and the Golan Heights during the June 1967 war combined with the rise of a viable Palestinian resistance movement to create a host of new issues specialists had to grapple with in the late 1960s and early 1970s.

While specialists' thinking about the Middle East tended to cluster around these themes, they were not considered in isolation. For example, network members' interpretation of Islam was influenced not only by what they did or did not know about the religion itself, but also by their understanding of Islam in relation to other forces and issues, such as nationalist movements, Cold War politics, internal pressures for social transformation, and the impact of the conflict with Israel. Looking at the themes in relation to each other, it is possible to see an overarching framework of meaning through which policymakers and other interested Americans understood the Middle East. It was premised on several fundamental assumptions, including the belief that most of the people of the Middle East, and the religion they practiced, were not only backward, but fundamentally opposed to modernity. Members of the network assumed that the region was vulnerable to those within and outside the Middle East who might mislead it and held the conviction that the United States was in the best position to bring about the region's transition to modernity. Such assumptions meant that the interpretations members of the informal network put forth reflected the biases of their time, including a clear belief in U.S. exceptionalism, an unwillingness to treat Muslims or Arabs on par with Christians or Western Europeans and Americans, and at times an overriding concern with the Cold War. Members' interpretations were also often suffused with inaccuracies and misunderstandings, as the network's early 1950s concern with the mufti of Jerusalem and its promotion in the 1960s of modernization theory indicated. While we should not view the knowledge the informal network produced in essentialist terms, we must recognize that it was very much a product of its time and place.

In arguing that an informal network of specialists developed a framework of meaning through which it saw the Middle East, I am not suggesting that all members of that network agreed on all points, that the framework as a whole was always intellectually consistent and free from contradictions, or that the framework itself led to clear policy prescriptions. Clearly none of these were the case. In the late 1950s Harold Hoskins argued against the emerging conventional wisdom that Islam was a receding threat being superseded by secular nationalism. Policy debates took place in the late 1950s and early 1960s over how accommodating the United States could have been when dealing with Nasser in Egypt, even though the multiple participants in those debates shared fairly similar interpretations of Nasser and concerns about the nature of mass politics in the region. Such interpretive debates led to diverging assessments of, and prescriptions for, the region.

Hence, it is best to think of the network and the framework it constructed as determining the contours of discussion and setting the boundaries for understanding. By identifying key themes, opening lines of debate, and laying out major interpretations, members of the informal network helped define the basic terms on which policymakers and interested citizens made sense of and interacted with the Middle East. Serious concerns and uncertainties about the nature of mass politics in the region persisted throughout this process. When discussing religion, analysts in the late 1940s and early 1950s worried about totalitarian Islam and the appeal of leaders like the mufti of Jerusalem to Muslims throughout the region. Just a few years later, analysts expressed similar concerns about Nasser and his secular, nationalist appeal to the masses not only in Egypt, but across the Arab world. Likewise, investigations of socioeconomic conditions led to speculation about whether or not the peasant classes would continue to accept their fate or rise up, especially in states ruled by conservative monarchs. And the Arab-Israeli-Palestinian conflict provided an issue, analysts argued, upon which the people of the region could focus their anger, hopes, and fears, and the issue could thus be used to mobilize virtually anyone to action.

Closely connected with this concern about mass politics in the Middle East was a tendency to highlight particular individuals as the embodiment of specialists' and policymakers' concerns about the Middle East. The network focused negative attention on the mufti of Jerusalem, Gamal 'Abd al-Nasser, Mohammad Mossadegh, and others, while holding up some Middle Eastern leaders, such as Mustafa Kemal in interwar Turkey, as models that other leaders in the region might emulate. Either way, individuals were seen to possess the ability to transform the region, either in concert with or counter to U.S. interests and desires, and therefore had to be watched closely.

Finally, and perhaps most persistently, network members clung to visions of the enduring American pursuit of a sacred and secular mission in the Middle East. The sacred and secular mission entailed an effort by a new Jerusalem to redeem an allegedly backward and defiled old Jerusalem, and had its roots in the very founding of the United States. Over time, attempts to transform the Middle East assumed an increasingly secular nature. They began with missionary and philanthropic educational efforts in the nineteenth century and moved to promoting secular nationalist movements in the 1920s and 1930s. In the 1930s and 1940s, responsibility for pursuing this sacred and secular mission fell to private oil companies following a policy of liberal developmentalism. Later, from the late 1950s through the mid-1960s, the U.S.

government itself promoted controlled transformation through modernization.

The pursuit of that sacred and secular mission relied on the production of sacred and secular knowledge about an imagined Middle East of the past, present, and future. The Orientalist approach that dominated at least through World War II emphasized the role of religion in Middle Eastern society, culture, and politics. The professionalization and institutionalization of Middle Eastern studies that began in the 1940s brought an increasing reliance on new forms of secular and allegedly scientific, objective knowledge that was used to justify U.S. involvement in the region, particularly in the late 1950s and 1960s with the implementation of modernization theory. The way specialists imagined the Middle East was the result of the integration of the production of sacred and secular knowledge with the pursuit of sacred and secular mission in the region.

Reimagining the Middle East after 1967

Events in the late 1960s led members of the informal network of specialists and other observers to reassess the Middle East, though not always in explicit or self-conscious ways. To be sure, specialists continued to draw heavily from some of the existing ways of thinking about the region, but each of the issues highlighted over the previous half-century seemed to be in a state of flux. The process of reimagining the Middle East in the late 1960s and early 1970s also led to important changes in the informal network itself and the nature of authority and expertise regarding Middle Eastern affairs. In the ten years after 1967 both the government and academia witnessed a fracturing of the informal network of Middle East specialists that had been evolving since 1918. This fracturing makes the late 1960s and early 1970s an appropriate end point for this book.

The 1967 war operated in conjunction with a host of other international events and issues to lead U.S. policymakers and regional specialists to reassess U.S. security interests in the Middle East. A U.S. economic downturn, caused in part by high spending to fund the Vietnam War and the Great Society, as well as by increasing competition from Western Europe and Asia, coincided with the rise of the Organization of Petroleum Exporting Countries (OPEC). Arab members of OPEC demonstrated the necessity of Middle Eastern oil to the maintenance of the U.S. economy and consumer culture by implementing a boycott on sales to the United States during and after the

October 1973 war between Egypt, Syria, and Israel. Meanwhile, the Soviet Union achieved relative nuclear parity with the United States, just as the United States was in the final phases of withdrawal from the quagmire in Vietnam. In combination, these events made specialists, policymakers, and the wider populace keenly aware of just how vulnerable U.S. security and ways of living were at home and abroad. Policymakers were therefore much more willing than they had been at any previous point to pursue bilateral security arrangements with regional powers in order to protect U.S. interests. President Nixon formally articulated the policy, and Presidents Ford and Carter also pursued it. In the Middle East, this new policy meant arming three regional "pillars" — Iran, Israel, and Saudi Arabia — and it remained in place at least through the Iranian Revolution in 1979.

That revolution brought back to the foreground concerns about Islam, which most specialists had largely ignored since the early 1960s, their theories about Islam's supposed opposition to modernity notwithstanding. In truth, Islam was neither as powerful a political force as observers worried it was in the 1940s and 1950s, nor as irrelevant as they believed it was at the height of the secular nationalist movements from the late 1950s through the mid-1960s. Indeed, by the mid-1960s, groups such as the Muslim Brotherhood in Egypt were beginning to split between those who wished to achieve change by operating within established political systems and those who would use religion to justify working outside political systems and pursuing their goals through violent means. The absence of extensive commentary at the time suggests that most specialists inside and outside government were either largely unaware of such events or simply found them unimportant at that moment.

While most specialists thought religion was becoming less important as a political force in the Middle East in the 1960s, they also believed the humiliating defeat that Egypt, Jordan, and Syria suffered at the hands of Israel in June 1967 had dealt a debilitating blow to the forces of secular Arab nationalism. Policymakers and specialists alike had remained intensely focused on secular nationalism since the mid-1950s, and some observers appeared to delight in watching Arab leaders deal with the consequences of the 1967 war. In a 29 February 1968 meeting with the National Security Council's Harold H. Saunders, former missionary, educator, and U.S. ambassador to Egypt John Badeau noted that nationalist movements were in decline and the United States should "show somewhat less interest in the Middle East." Badeau claimed to have "purposely rubbed in" that point when meeting with Arab leaders and elites during a December 1967 trip to the region. The next day, Saunders met for three hours with Princeton University sociologist Morroe Berger, who, according to Saunders's records, made a similar point. It was "only a matter of time" before Nasser would be gone, after which Berger believed specialists and policymakers would "wonder how he lasted so long." Finally, when the foreign ministers of the Arab League states met in Cairo in September 1968, the State Department's director of Intelligence and Research used the metaphor of a baseball game to summarize the meeting and mock Arab leaders for their apparent ineffectiveness. Thomas Hughes characterized the meeting as "Another Scoreless Inning" for Arabs, with "two hits, one walk and one man left on base."[1]

While the late 1960s suggested to specialists the demise of both Islam and secular nationalist movements as the dominant political forces in the Middle East, and the emergence of a new U.S. strategic conception of the region loomed, the post-1967 period also came to epitomize for many observers the failure of the United States to achieve its sacred and secular mission of transforming the region. The inability of the United States to find any satisfactory means of promoting controlled modernization across the Middle East by the late 1960s led to considerable frustration, as was demonstrated by the State Department's Bureau of Intelligence and Research paper "The Roots of Arab Resistance to Modernization." Most specialists struggled to suggest how the United States might ever achieve its enduring sacred and secular missions in the Middle East, though some did hope that the oil-producing states might use their enormous profits to pursue socioeconomic transformation.

Most obviously, the events of the late 1960s altered the dynamics of the Arab-Israeli-Palestinian conflict. The Israeli occupation of the Gaza Strip, the West Bank, East Jerusalem, the Golan Heights, and the Sinai Peninsula forced specialists to consider an entirely new set of questions. At the same time, the rise of a viable resistance movement among the Palestinians—fueled by the Israeli occupation—meant that Palestinian voices could no longer be ignored, as they had been for much of the preceding two decades. In combination, these new realities required specialists to imagine the Arab-Israeli-Palestinian conflict in fundamentally new ways.

While the dynamics of the late 1960s and early 1970s caused network members once again to reimagine the Middle East, perhaps the greatest reimagining took place over the basic nature of authority and expertise itself and to what ends that authority and expertise should be put. The network fractured over different conceptions of the relationship between knowledge and power that rose to the surface in the aftermath of 1967. Before 1967, specialists may have been aware of some of the tensions inherent in such a relationship and they may have disagreed on interpretations of particular issues, but they pursued the shared objective of producing knowledge that could be used for the benefit of the state. After 1967, a new generation of specialists disavowed that objective and engaged in internal battles over who could claim legitimacy as an expert on the issues and over the very reasons for the existence of the field of Middle Eastern studies. These tensions could be observed in both the academic and government realms of the network.

On the government side, fissures emerged between those who accepted that the United States had cast its lot with Israel in the Middle East and those who opposed this U.S. policy and found themselves progressively isolated from the policymaking process. According to Joseph Kraft, who publicized the dispute in the *New York Times*, these disagreements were the product of both generational and training differences. Members who generally accepted U.S. policy were usually, although not always, younger individuals who became involved in Middle Eastern affairs out of mere chance or through a pragmatic assessment of their career prospects, rather than through a basic interest in the Middle East itself. They were, according to Kraft, "bureaucratized," meaning that they felt less and less identification with the region and more with their specific jobs.

Many of the individuals who disagreed with U.S. policy had devoted long careers to Middle Eastern affairs, and found the acrimonious post-1967 environment eerily similar to that of the late 1940s when the old missionary hands, Orientalists, and government specialists lost the battle for Palestine. Some soon found themselves looking either to move out of Middle Eastern affairs or to leave government service altogether. Richard Parker, for example, requested to move to Moroccan affairs from Egyptian affairs when Richard Nixon appointed Joseph Sisco—a specialist in Soviet affairs who had never served outside of Washington—to replace Middle East expert Parker Hart as assistant secretary of state for Near Eastern affairs in 1969. Others, such as Curtis F. Jones (and Richard Parker after his retirement from government service) continued to work on U.S.–Middle East relations, but became increasingly vocal in their criticisms of U.S. policy. Jones, whom Kraft inaccurately characterized "as one of the most ardent supporters of the Arab side in the quarrel with Israel," became head of the Near East section of the State Department's Bureau of Intelligence and Research, but was soon urged to leave Middle East affairs after he openly expressed his dissatisfaction with

U.S. policy. He retired shortly thereafter and over the ensuing thirty years published numerous critiques of U.S. policy in the region. Included among Jones's published works is an insightful and introspective piece on "The Education of an Arabist," where he lamented "the gradual evolution of 'Arabist' from appellation to epithet." Jones also responded to Kraft, who he argued was "relatively kind to all Arabists but three," Richard Parker, Robert Munn, and himself.[2]

The academic component of the network also experienced this basic fracturing process brought about by the 1967 war and its aftermath. The dramatic Israeli victory and ensuing occupation led many specialists to question their profession's role in providing intellectual sustenance for some U.S. policies that generally supported Israel at the expense of Arab states and the Palestinian people. The Arab-Israeli-Palestinian conflict thus drove a wedge through the field of Middle Eastern studies after 1967, with many individuals evaluating their peers' work based on whether or not it meshed with their own political view of the conflict. The Israeli occupation became a critical issue, forcing people to take sides. A pillar of the network, Don Peretz expressed his regrets about this situation in his retrospective on his own career. Peretz noted the problem was "one of the more troublesome aspects of Middle Eastern studies . . . If an author is believed to be too 'pro-Arab' or too 'pro-Israel,' his/her work is downgraded or discounted regardless of its academic merits." The tremendous support Israel enjoyed in domestic U.S. politics contributed to the problem, leading to efforts to delegitimize scholars supportive of the Palestinian position. In addition, those academic members of the informal network who opposed U.S. policies were likely influenced by the broader opposition to U.S. foreign policy brought about by involvement in Vietnam. Lyndon Johnson explicitly linked the two conflicts as he tried to extract Israeli support for the effort in Vietnam as a quid pro quo for U.S. support of Israel. The result was increasing tension between those academic specialists who retained a policy orientation in their work and those who sought to distance themselves and their profession from U.S. involvement in the Middle East. By the mid-1970s, these tensions had reached a fever pitch, with younger academic Middle East specialists characterizing the work of their intellectual forebears as "an instrument of imperialism rather than as an objective discipline. It is an instrument of control over the peoples of the Middle East rather than a tool for those peoples' liberation through self-understanding and science."[3]

These divisions within the academic community of Middle East specialists continued, and at times even intensified, over the next four decades. Raphael Patai's *The Arab Mind* and Edward Said's *Orientalism*, both published in the 1970s, represented the two sides. Patai's work tried to describe the characteristics of "the modal Arab personality," while Said's was a sprawling work that critiqued two centuries of British, French, and American literary and policy representations of "the Orient." Both books had wide ranging impact. Despite its stereotyping and harsh characterizations of Arabs, *The Arab Mind* became virtually required reading for U.S. military and intelligence officers preparing to serve in the Middle East from the late 1970s through the early 2000s. *Orientalism*, on the other hand, laid the intellectual foundation for a generation of scholars who not only disavowed any attempts to produce knowledge for the exercise of state power, but who indeed sought to critique that very practice. In addition, *Orientalism* initiated more than two decades of debate over the production of knowledge and the nature of the knowledge itself. Said engaged in long-running intellectual and personal battles with scholars such as Bernard Lewis and Fouad Ajami, both of whom took offense at Said's critiques of the field. Lewis and Ajami also argued in numerous works that there was something inherent in either Islam or the Arab character that necessitated conflict with the United States and Western Europe. Interestingly, though perhaps not surprisingly, Ajami and Lewis both served as informal advisors to the administration of President George W. Bush after 11 September 2001, while Said was one of its harshest critics up until his death in September 2003.[4]

The events of 11 September 2001 extended the divisions among academic specialists well beyond those that existed between Ajami and Lewis on the one hand and Said on the other. Even before 9/11, Martin Kramer, a scholar who worked for the self-consciously pro-Israeli Washington Institute for Near East Policy, completed *Ivory Towers on Sand: The Failure of Middle East Studies in America*. There Kramer critiqued the entire academic system through which knowledge about the Middle East had been produced since the late 1960s for its inability to predict major regional upheavals and its overwhelming politicization. He suggested that the entire academic structure of Middle East studies should be defunded, torn down, and rebuilt from the ground up. Such views were of course quite controversial, particularly in the aftermath of 9/11, and led an array of scholars and other specialists to align against Kramer and his supporters. The most forceful of the opposing voices was Juan Cole, who began a weblog to chronicle and comment on events in the Middle East and in U.S.–Middle East relations. Kramer's and Cole's positions were also animated by their diametrically opposed views on contemporary U.S.–Middle East relations, as Kramer supported the U.S. war in Iraq, while Cole adamantly opposed it. Just as it had with respect to the conflict in government circles in the late 1960s, the *New York Times* caught wind of the intellectual battles and drew it to the attention of the broader public. In 2011, there is little indication that the fracture that emerged in the late 1960s will heal anytime soon.[5]

The intense geopolitical developments of the late 1960s and early 1970s and the tensions among academic and government specialists may have combined to usher in a new phase in the production of knowledge about the region, but one need not look very deeply to see that sacred and secular ways of imagining the Middle East have continued in the post-1967 period. Two brief examples demonstrate the point. The first concerns U.S. support for Israel, which has become much more widespread over the past four decades. Melani McAlister has shown that in the 1970s, many Americans came to view Israel "as an icon in the post-Vietnam debate about the nature of U.S. world power" based on its military successes. Closely connected to that vision of Israel was one taking hold among evangelical Christians who saw supporting Israel as a religious necessity. Christian evangelicals proved critical to the rise of the Republican Party over the following three decades and, as such, their views held tremendous sway, particularly among an emerging group of neoconservatives in the 1980s and 1990s.[6]

The second example comes from the war in Iraq that began in 2003. Ever since President George H. W. Bush decided not to topple Saddam Hussein's regime in the 1991 war, some specialists, policymakers, journalists, and policy intellectuals had been calling for "regime change" in Iraq, and it became formal U.S. policy in 1998 with the passage of the Iraq Liberation Act. Those calls escalated early this century and grew particularly loud after 9/11, when neoconservatives saw an opportunity to renew America's sacred and secular mission of transforming the Middle East. This time, however, they did so through the use of military force. Justifications for the war shifted from eliminating weapons of mass destruction to combating terrorism, to spreading democracy and using Iraq as a central point from which transformation might emanate across the region. Further illustrating the connection between the sacred and the secular as Operation Iraqi Freedom proceeded, the Defense Department under the leadership of Secretary of Defense Donald Rumsfeld included biblical references on the headings of daily intelligence briefings that were circulated at the highest levels of the government, suggesting that the U.S. military was doing God's work in Iraq.[7]

While it would require extensive research into both of these cases to carry the argument out, they do demonstrate how interpretations and imaginings of the present continue to draw on an enduring though continuously evolving framework of meaning defined by sacred and secular knowledge and mission. That framework had its roots in the earliest encounters between the United States and the Middle East, and then continued to develop into full form in the minds of the members of an informal transnational network of academics, businesspersons, government officials, and journalists as U.S. interests and involvement in the Middle East increased between 1918 and 1967. It was this foundational framework of meaning upon which all subsequent understandings and interpretations have been layered, and its reliance on sacred and secular knowledge and mission has been and continues to be a driving force in how Americans imagine the Middle East.

NOTES

Note on Sources

Materials from archival collections receive complete citations, though using the abbreviations listed below. Materials found in publications listed in the "Annual Reports, Government Publications, Newspapers, Periodicals, and Surveys" section of the bibliography are referenced in the notes with complete citations, including, when available, author, title, name of publication, volume and issue number, date, and page numbers. Articles that function effectively as primary sources receive full citations in the notes, while articles that were published more recently and that serve as secondary sources are cited fully in the bibliography and receive short citations here. All other materials that have full citations in the bibliography receive short citations here.

Abbreviations Used in Notes

CFR
Council on Foreign Relations

CIA
Central Intelligence Agency

DDEL
Dwight D. Eisenhower Presidential Library

FRUS
Foreign Relations of the United States

HSTL
Harry S. Truman Presidential Library

JFKL
John F. Kennedy Presidential Library

LBJL
Lyndon Baines Johnson Presidential Library

MEI
Middle East Institute

NSC
National Security Council

OCB
Operations Coordinating Board

PSB
Psychological Strategy Board

PUL
Princeton University Libraries

RG 59
Record Group 59: Records of the Department of State

RG 263
Record Group 263: Records of the Central Intelligence Agency

Introduction

1. President George W. Bush, "Address to a Joint Session of Congress and the American People," 20 Sept. 2001, http://archives.cnn.com/2001/US/09/20/gen.bush .transcript/.

2. Engerman, *Modernization from the Other Shore*, 1.

3. Two excellent surveys, one brief and the other more extensive, are Hahn, *Crisis and Crossfire*, and Little, *American Orientalism*. "National Intelligence Estimate: Key Problems Affecting US Efforts to Strengthen the Near East," 25 Apr. 1951, National Intelligence Estimates, 21–26, Box 213, Central Intelligence Reports, Intelligence File, President's Secretary's File, Harry S. Truman Papers, HSTL.

4. The essays in Hogan and Paterson, *Explaining the History of U.S. Foreign Relations*, provide a good sense of these tensions within the field. See, in particular, Robert McMahon, "Toward a Pluralist Vision: The Study of American Foreign Relations as International History and National History," 35–50.

5. On the rise of oil, see Yergin, *The Prize*. On the rise of consumer culture, see Cohen, *A Consumers' Republic*, de Grazia, *Irresistible Empire*, and Hoganson, *Consumers' Imperium*. Two works that place these developments in a broader interpretive framework are Hunt, *The American Ascendancy*, and Bacevich, *The Limits of Power*.

6. Harland-Jacobs, *Builders of Empire*, 23. Mann, *The Rise of the Vulcans*, x and xiv–xvii. Engerman, *Know Your Enemy*. The "China Hands" of the 1930s and 1940s constitute another group that one could consider in a similar manner.

7. Engerman, "Bernath Lecture: American Knowledge and Global Power," 600. Emphasis in original.

8. Stephenson, *Manifest Destiny*, 5. For another take on nineteenth-century notions of American exceptionalism, see Hunt, *Ideology and U.S. Foreign Policy*.

9. McAlister, *Epic Encounters*, 8–12 and 303–7. Said, *Orientalism*. For a broader discussion of how historians of U.S. foreign relations have received Said, see Rotter, "Saidism without Said."

10. Timothy Mitchell, *Colonising Egypt*, xiv.

11. I am also highly indebted to Hunt's *Ideology and U.S. Foreign Policy*, which explores three core ideas in the history of U.S. foreign relations: the belief in American exceptionalism, adherence to racial hierarchies when interpreting international affairs, and an ambivalence toward revolution. Now more than two decades old, *Ideology* remains required reading for anyone working at the intersection of culture, ideas, and policy.

12. Robert J. Allison, "Postscript: Americans and the Muslim World — First Encounters," in Lesch, *The Middle East and the United States*, 453 and 455; and Allison, *The Crescent Obscured*, xvii. Allison also makes the point, however, that the backward Muslim mirror reflected a young United States founded upon a central contradiction: the newly independent state was itself a slave society, particularly in its southern territories, and the slave system provided much of the labor on which the young nation's evolving economy rested. Even though astute observers of U.S. political and social life like Benjamin Franklin probably still adhered to popular critiques of slavery in the Arab world as an example of barbarity, they turned those criticisms against the United States. In some of their writings, Franklin and other commentators altered well-known criticisms of Muslim slavery to address the issue of slavery in their own country.

13. The elementary and secondary school figures are the aggregate totals for the five primary centers of American missionary activity in the Middle East, compiled from the individual listings published in DeNovo, *American Interests and Policies in the Middle East*, 9–10. On higher education initiatives, see DeNovo, *American Interests and Policies in the Middle East*, 13–16.

14. Sha'ban, *Islam and Arabs in Early American Thought*, and Vogel, *To See a Promised Land*, chapters 1 and 4.

15. Oren, *Power, Faith, and Fantasy*, 122–48; Smith, quoted in Sha'ban, *Islam and Arabs in Early American Thought*, 91, but see also 89–96.

16. Makdisi, "Reclaiming the Land of the Bible: Missionaries, Secularism, and Evangelical Modernity," 691, and, more generally, Makdisi, *Artillery of Heaven*.

17. On Coffing, see Edward Morris to William Seward, 16 Oct. 1862, Seward to Morris, 18 Nov. 1862, both in FRUS, 1862, 791–92. On Merriam, see Seward to Morris, 19 Sept. 1862, FRUS, 1862, 784–85; Morris to Seward, 11 Nov. 1862, 27 Nov. 1862, 11 Dec. 1862, and 30 Apr. 1863; Seward to Morris, 31 Dec. 1862, 5 Jan. 1863,

26 Jan. 1863, 2 Feb. 1863, and 13 Feb. 1863, all in FRUS, 1863, part II, 1174–76, 1181–83, and 1185–86, available at http://digital.library.wisc.edu/1711.dl/FRUS.

18. On the expansion of travel and its meaning for American national identity in the late nineteenth century, see Endy, "Travel and World Power." For travel to the Holy Land specifically, see Vogel, To See a Promised Land, chapters 2 and 3. Twain, The Innocents Abroad. See also Little, "Gideon's Band," and Suleiman, The Arabs in the Mind of America. On Melville and Dorr, specifically, as well as other travel commentary from the mid-nineteenth century, see Oren, Power, Faith, and Fantasy, chapter 7.

19. Oren, Power, Faith, and Fantasy, 133; Kuklick, Puritans in Babylon, 20–21; and Grabill, Protestant Diplomacy and the Near East, 38.

20. See Kuklick, Puritans in Babylon, for a more detailed discussion of the rise of ancient Near Eastern studies as an academic field.

21. Lockman, Contending Visions of the Middle East, especially chapter 3, and Said, Orientalism.

22. Vitalis, America's Kingdom, 28. My narrative of the Dodge family history draws heavily from Vitalis.

23. Kuklick, Puritans in Babylon; and Vogel, To See a Promised Land, chapter 7. On nineteenth-century visions of national greatness, see Stephanson, Manifest Destiny, and Hunt, Ideology and U.S. Foreign Policy, especially chapter 2; Fousek, To Lead the Free World, offers a good analysis of their applicability following World War II.

Chapter One

1. Speiser, The United States and the Near East, 229 and 232.

2. Ibid., 232–33.

3. In addition to Speiser, The United States and the Near East, xiii–xiv, see Greenberg, "In Memory of E. A. Speiser," and Hurewitz, "The Education of J. C. Hurewitz," in Naff, Paths to the Middle East, 70–72, for more biographical information on Speiser.

4. For a general overview of the late nineteenth and early twentieth centuries in the Ottoman Empire and broader Middle East, see Gelvin, The Modern Middle East. On the economy specifically, see Owen, The Middle East in the World Economy. On the rise of the United States at the end of the nineteenth century, see Hunt, The American Ascendancy, especially chapters 1 and 2.

5. On Mahan's impact on strategic thinking in the late nineteenth century, see LaFeber, The New Empire, particularly 85–101; Hunt, Ideology and U.S. Foreign Policy, 79–80; and almost any textbook on the history of U.S. foreign relations. In addition to LaFeber and Hunt, see Stephenson, Manifest Destiny, 84–87, for Mahan's views regarding civilizational conquest and uplift.

6. For Mahan's strategic thinking regarding the Middle East, see Barbir, "Alfred Thayer Mahan, Theodore Roosevelt, the Middle East, and the Twentieth Century," and

Buheiry, "Alfred T. Mahan: Reflections on Sea Power and on the Middle East as a Strategic Concept." Mahan, *The Problem of Asia*, 21, 47, 22.

7. All quotes are from the version of the 1902 *National Review* article republished as "The Persian Gulf in International Politics," in Mahan, *Retrospect and Prospect*, 217, 237, and 248–49. On his coining of the phrase "Middle East," see Roderic H. Davison, "Where is the Middle East?" *Foreign Affairs* 38, no. 4 (July 1960), 667–68; and Oren, *Power, Faith, and Fantasy*, 307–8.

8. Baram, *The Department of State in the Middle East*, 67; and DeNovo, *American Interests and Policies in the Middle East*, 18–19 and 56–57. On the broader reorganization of the State Department, see Schulzinger, *The Making of the Diplomatic Mind*.

9. Gelfand, *The Inquiry*, 38 and 44.

10. Ibid., 60–63.

11. Ibid., 227–28, 241.

12. Arthur I. Andrews, "The Koords," and J. K. Birge, "The Ottoman Turks of Asia Minor," both quoted in Gelfand, *The Inquiry*, 242–43 and 247.

13. "The King-Crane Commission Report," 28 Aug. 1919, available at http://www.gwpda.org/1918p/kncr.htm. On Armenia, see also Balakian, *The Burning Tigris*.

14. Yergin, *The Prize*, 170–77.

15. Yergin, *The Prize*, 22–55, 111–12, and 194–95. A. C. Bedford, "The World Oil Situation," *Foreign Affairs* 1, no. 1 (1922): 101, 96.

16. Halford L. Hoskins, "The Suez Canal in Time of War," *Foreign Affairs* 14, no. 1 (Oct. 1935): 93–101 and Hamilton A, R. Gibb, "Toward Arab Unity," *Foreign Affairs* 24, no. 1 (Oct. 1945): 119–29.

17. Earle, *Turkey, the Great Powers, and the Bagdad Railway*, vii, 347, 348, and 349. See also Edward Mead Earle, "The Importance of the Near East in Problems of Raw Materials and Foodstuffs," *Annals of the American Academy of Political and Social Science*, 112 (Mar. 1924): 183–86.

18. Edward Mead Earle, "American Missions in the Near East," *Foreign Affairs* 7, no. 3 (Apr. 1929), 402, 405, and 417.

19. Grose, *Israel in the Mind of America*, 141–44 and 263; and Baram, *The Department of State in the Middle East*, 74–76 and 278–79.

20. For background on Eddy, see Baram, *The Department of State in the Middle East*, 75–77; Kaplan, *The Arabists*, 77; and Vitalis, *America's Kingdom*.

21. For biographical information on Badeau, see Badeau, *The Middle East Remembered*; Killgore, "In Memoriam"; and a National Security Council biography, "John Stothoff Badeau," attached to a memorandum from R. W. Komer to the president, 11 Dec. 1962, "General 9/62–12/62," Box 168A, Country File, UAR, National Security Files, President's Office Files, JFKL.

22. On Hoskins's background, see Baram, *The Department of State in the Middle East*, 78–80; Kaplan, *The Arabists*, 133; and Manalo, "A Short History of the Middle East In-

stitute." Hoskins, *The Middle East*. Halford Hoskins was keenly aware of the confusion many people experienced when dealing with two Middle East specialists named Hoskins (Halford and Harold). At one speaking engagement, Halford Hoskins noted that he wished he would stop receiving the colonel's (Harold Hoskins) mail. Halford Hoskins, remarks at "First Annual Conference on Middle Eastern Affairs," Middle East Institute, 14 Feb. 1947, MEI.

23. For biographical information on Hurewitz, see Hurewitz, "The Education of J. C. Hurewitz," in Naff, *Paths to the Middle East*, 57–103, from which this summary is drawn.

24. John R. Starkey, "Arabists in the U.S.A.," *Saudi Aramco World* 16, no. 4 (July/Aug. 1965), http://www.saudiaramcoworld.com/issue/196504/arabists.in.the.u.s.a..htm; Farhat Ziadeh, "Winds Blow Where Ships Do Not Wish to Go," in Naff, *Paths to the Middle East*, 303–5; and John R. Starkey, "A Talk with Philip Hitti," *Saudi Aramco World* 22, no. 4 (July/Aug. 1971), http://www.saudiaramcoworld.com/issue/197104/a.talk.with.philip.hitti.htm.

25. Committee on Near Eastern Studies, *A Program for Near Eastern Studies in the United States*, 8. See also Halpern, "Middle Eastern Studies," 108–9, and Gold, "Laborers in the Vineyard," 65–67, for overviews of the ACLS report. Other works on the development and problems of Middle Eastern area studies include Bill, "The Study of Middle East Politics"; Haddad, "Middle East Area Studies"; Winder, "Four Decades of Middle Eastern Study"; Kramer, *Ivory Towers on Sand*; and Lockman, *Contending Visions of the Middle East*.

26. For broader discussions of the Cold War and the development and funding of area studies in the United States, see Chomsky et al., *The Cold War and the University*; Simpson, *Science of Coercion*; and Simpson, *Universities and Empire*.

27. Efforts to promote contemporary Asian studies and Soviet studies were well underway by the 1930s. One could even argue that African studies was ahead of Middle Eastern studies, as the African Studies Association formed in 1957, compared to 1967 for the Middle East Studies Association (and 1941 for the Association for Asian Studies). Philip K. Hitti to George C. McGhee, 19 December 1950, Decimal File 880.412/12–1950, RG 59. Committee on International and Regional Studies, "Proposal for a Program in Middle Eastern Studies," 26 March 1953, Records of President Pusey, UAI 5.169 (Middle Eastern Studies, 1953–54), Box 20, Harvard University Archives, 1, quoted in Babai, *Center for Middle Eastern Studies, Harvard University*, 2.

28. McGhee to Hitti, 3 Jan. 1951, Decimal File 880.412/12–1950, RG 59. Babai, *Center for Middle Eastern Studies, Harvard University*, 3–5. On ARAMCO's intelligence branch and its connections to the CIA, see Vitalis, *America's Kingdom*, especially 144–45.

29. My overview of the Harvard Center for Middle Eastern Studies draws heavily from Babai, *Center for Middle Eastern Studies, Harvard University*, 2–49.

30. On Gibb's views of Orientalism, see Babai, *Center for Middle Eastern Studies, Harvard University*, 9. On other universities, see Starkey, "Arabists in the U.S.A."

31. For Polk's family history, see his own engaging attempt to rediscover his lineage, *Polk's Folly*, as well as his own website, http://www.williampolk.com/html/aboutwrp.html. Polk, "What the Arabs Think," and Polk, ed., "Perspective of the Arab World: An *Atlantic* Supplement," *Atlantic Monthly* 198, no. 4 (Oct. 1956): 124–92.

32. Polk, *The United States and the Arab World*, and see Crane Brinton's foreword for an explanation of the origins and purpose of the American Foreign Policy Library. On Iraq, see Polk, *Understanding Iraq*, and McGovern and Polk, *Out of Iraq*.

33. Thomas, "From Orientalism to Professionalism."

34. See Schulzinger, *The Wise Men of Foreign Affairs*, Shoup and Minter, *Imperial Brain Trust*, and Wala, *The Council on Foreign Relations*, for good overviews of the history of the Council on Foreign Relations.

35. On Westermann's involvement in U.S.–Middle East relations going back to World War I, see Grabill, *Protestant Diplomacy and the Near East*. Westermann quoted in Schulzinger, *The Wise Men of Foreign Affairs*, 65–66. Schulzinger, *The Wise Men of Foreign Affairs*, 107.

36. For a complete list of the participants in the various study groups, consult the Records of Study Groups, CFR. John Badeau, "Islam and the Modern Middle East," *Foreign Affairs* 38 (Oct. 1959): 61–74; Campbell, *Defense of the Middle East*; Cremeans, *The Arabs and the World*; Hurewitz, *Middle East Dilemmas*; and Richard H. Nolte and William R. Polk, "Toward a Policy for the Middle East," *Foreign Affairs* 36 (July 1958): 645–58.

37. Manalo, "A Short History of the Middle East Institute," provides a good overview of the institute. A great deal of information about the institute can be gleaned from its internal newsletter, which was initiated in 1948, and from the published programs from the annual conferences the institute held, all of which are available at the MEI Library. The institute has not kept any long-term membership files, so compiling a complete list is impossible. These names were collected from the list of current members printed on the back of a program for the Fourteenth Annual Conference, May 5–7, 1960, and from Parker T. Hart, "Report of the President, Autumn 1969–Spring 1972," both located at the MEI.

38. See the published proceedings of each of these conferences for the list of participants. Franck, *Islam in the Modern World*; Franck, *Nationalism in the Middle East*; Fisher, *Evolution in the Middle East*; and Sands, *The Arab Nation*. The MEI continues to exist and to publish the *Middle East Journal*. It funds and provides office space for fellows researching topics related to the region, offers language courses, and has an extensive collection of books and periodicals dealing with the Middle East and U.S.–Middle East relations. In addition, the MEI has served as a place for retired U.S. government officials to remain involved in U.S.–Middle Eastern affairs. A number of former ambassadors—including Raymond Hare, Parker Hart, Lucius D. Battle (twice), and L. Dean Brown—have served as its president.

39. Roosevelt, *Arabs, Oil, and History*, 9. See also Speiser, *The United States and the Near*

East, 18–20; and Hurewitz, *Middle East Dilemmas*, chapter 1, all of which make this same point. Polk, "What the Arabs Think," 4–5.

40. The best discussion of the importance of the Suez Canal is Speiser, *The United States and the Near East*, 19. See also Ellen Deborah Ellis, "Tensions in the Middle East, Part I: Internal Pressures," *Current History* (May 1951): 262–65.

41. Hoskins, *Middle East Oil in United States Foreign Policy*, 1–2. Speiser, *The United States and the Near East*, 125–33.

42. CIA, NIE-14, "The Importance of Iranian and Middle Eastern Oil to Western Europe Under Peacetime Conditions," 1–2, 8 Jan. 1951, Box 1, Lot File 78 D394, Record Set of National Intelligence Estimates, Special Estimates, and Special National Intelligence Estimates, 1950–54, Records of the Bureau of Intelligence and Research, RG 59.

43. Halpern, "Middle Eastern Studies," 110 and 113.

44. Starkey, "Arabists in The U.S.A." Emphasis in original.

45. Polk, "Problems of Government Utilization of Scholarly Research in International Affairs," 237.

Chapter Two

1. For background material on Wright, especially his role as the chief historian of the War Department, see Wiley, *Historical Program of the U.S. Army*, chapters 2 and 3. Rene Millon, letter to Council on Foreign Relations members, 20 Dec. 1948, "Digest of Discussion: First Meeting of the Discussion Group on the Moslem World, 1948/49," 2 and 4, vol. 28, Records of Study Groups, CFR.

2. Rom Landau, "Peace May Be in Moslem Hands," *New York Times Magazine*, 6 Apr. 1952, 14. Office of Intelligence Research, "Problems and Attitudes in the Arab World: Their Implications for US Psychological Strategy," 19 May 1952, in Kesaris, *O.S.S./State Department Intelligence and Research Reports*, reel 1, 15.PSB, D-22, "Psychological Strategy Program for the Middle East," Annex B, "Analysis of the Middle East Mind, Basic and Current Attitudes," 6 Feb. 1953, 4, PSB Documents (Master Book of Volume III (8)), Box 16, NSC Registry Series, NSC Staff Records, 1948–61, White House Office Files, DDEL.

3. Department of the Army, "Recommendations Concerning Study of Religious Factors in International Strategy," undated [c. Apr. 1955], 1, 6, and 7. "OCB 000.3 [Religion] (File #1) (2) February 1954–January 1957," Box 2, OCB Central Files, NSC Staff Files, White House Office Files, DDEL.

4. Department of the Army, "Recommendations Concerning Study of Religious Factors in International Strategy," 5–7.

5. Department of the Army, "Recommendations Concerning Study of Religious Factors in International Strategy," 20. "Draft Project for Studies on Islam," Richard H. Sanger to Mr. Hart, 2 Feb. 1954, MEI, Box 4, Subject Files, 1953–66, Office of the Pub-

lic Affairs Advisor (NEA/P), Bureau of Near Eastern Affairs and South Asian Affairs, RG 59.

6. William L. Westermann, "Just and Practical Boundaries for the Turkish Empire," quoted in Gelfand, *The Inquiry*, 248–49.

7. Descriptions of Kemal's reforms can be found in any textbook on the twentieth-century Middle East. For examples, see Gelvin, *The Modern Middle East*, 189–92, and Yapp, *The Near East since the First World War*, 147–66.

8. Valentine Chirol, "Islam and Britain," *Foreign Affairs* 1, no. 3 (Mar. 1923), 50, 48, 50, 57–58. Earle, *Turkey, the Great Powers, and the Baghdad Railway*, 64 and 336–54.

9. Valentine Chirol, "The Downfall of the Khalifate," *Foreign Affairs* 2, no. 4 (June 1924), 571, 576, and 581.

10. Ibid., 579 and 580.

11. Ibid.

12. Gibb, *Modern Trends in Islam*, 117. See chapter 6, "Islam in the World," for the best articulation of the argument.

13. Polk, "What the Arabs Think," 9. Office of Intelligence Research, "Problems and Attitudes in the Arab World," 16. Montagne, "Modern Nations and Islam," 591–92. See also Daniel Friedenberg, "The Flaming Crescent," *New Republic*, 30 Aug. 1954, 20–21; Ishaq Husseini, "Islam Past and Present: The Basic Beliefs of the Muslim Faith," in "Perspective of the Arab World: An *Atlantic* Supplement," *Atlantic Monthly* 98 (Oct. 1956): 169–72; and the published addresses of the 1951 conference of the Middle East Institute in Franck, *Islam in the Modern World*.

14. Wilfred Cantwell Smith, "The Muslims and the West," *Foreign Policy Bulletin*, 1 Oct. 1951, 6. Smith later published *Islam in Modern History*, which was widely read in academic and policymaking circles. It was even a prominent topic of discussion in a CFR Study Group on Islam. See "Digest of Discussion: The Middle East and Modern Islam, First Meeting," George E. Gruen, Rapporteur, CFR. See also John J. Donohue, "State of the Question: The World of Islam Passes Through a Crisis," *America* 99 (27 Sept. 1958): 671–72. In neither instance was there fundamental disagreement with Smith's thesis. Rather, he was criticized because the study group found his definition of Islam too broad, while Donohue found it to be too narrow. For background on Smith, see the obituary published in the *Harvard Gazette*, 29 Nov. 2001, http://www .news.harvard.edu/gazette/2001/11.29/27-memorialminute.html.

15. See Gibb, *Modern Trends in Islam*, as well as Smith, "The Muslims and the West" on this point. PSB, "PSB D-22: Psychological Strategy Program for the Middle East," Annex B, 7.

16. This overview of the Brotherhood's rise to prominence draws heavily on Lia, *The Society of the Muslim Brothers in Egypt*, and Mitchell, *The Society of the Muslim Brothers*. Mitchell's work was originally published in 1969, and was based on extensive interviews with, and research in documents held by, members of the society who granted Mitchell access. As John O. Voll noted in his foreword to the 1993 reprint, the work

remains the best available work on the society for the first decade following World
War II.

17. Mitchell, *The Society of the Muslim Brothers*, chapter 5, but especially 133–62, provides an excellent account of the situation in Egypt and the society's role in it.

18. CIA, "ORE 54: The Current Situation in Egypt," 16 Oct. 1947, 1–2, Intelligence
Publication File HRP 92–4/001, Box 1, Estimates of the Office of Research Evalua-
tion, 1946–50, RG 263. CIA, "SR-13: The Arab States," 27 Sept. 1949, in Kesaris, *CIA
Research Reports*, 7. See also "Spearhead for Islam: The Moslem Brotherhood in Egypt,"
Christian Century 65 (25 Aug. 1948): 851–53, and "Moslem Brotherhood: Terrorists or
Just Zealots," *Reporter* 8 (17 Mar. 1953): 8–10. Montagne, "Modern Nations and Islam,"
586–87.

19. In addition to Lia, *The Society of the Muslim Brothers in Egypt*, and Mitchell, *The Society
of the Muslim Brothers*, see Salem, *Bitter Legacy*, 98–108, on the ideology of the Society of
the Muslim Brothers. Harris, *Nationalism and Revolution in Egypt*, 15 and 234.

20. Boulby, *The Muslim Brotherhood and the Kings of Jordan, 1945–1993*.

21. CIA, "SR-13: The Arab States," 65.

22. For general discussions of Kemal's reforms, see Thomas and Frye, *The United
States and Turkey and Iran*; Dankwart Rustow, "Politics and Islam in Turkey 1920–1955,"
in Frye, *Islam and the West*; and Walter Livingston Wright Jr., "Truths About Turkey,"
Foreign Affairs 26, no. 2 (Jan. 1948): 349–59. The phrase "Operation Bootstraps" is
from Thomas and Frye, who use it throughout *The United States and Turkey and Iran*.
Thomas and Frye, *The United States and Turkey and Iran*, 77. Wright, "Truths About Turkey," 352. Thomas and Frye, *The United States and Turkey and Iran*, 145–46.

23. See Frye, *Islam and the West*, particularly Niyazi Berkes, "Historical Background
of Turkish Secularism," 41–68, and Rustow, "Politics and Islam in Turkey 1920–1955,"
69–107.

24. Rustow, "Politics and Islam in Turkey," 101–6.

25. Thomas and Frye, *The United States and Turkey and Iran*, 145–46.

26. Office of Intelligence Research, "Problems and Attitudes in the Arab World:
Their Implications for US Psychological Strategy," 15. "The Moslem World," *Time*,
13 Aug. 1951, 28.

27. Millon, letter to Council on Foreign Relations members, 20 Dec. 1948, 2 and 6.
Gibb, *Modern Trends in Islam*, 85.

28. Alpers, *Dictators, Democracy, and American Public Culture*. For an earlier scholarly
assessment of American usage of "totalitarianism" in the early postwar period, see
Adler and Paterson, "Red Fascism."

29. Philip W. Ireland, "Islam, Democracy, and Communism," in Franck, *Islam in the
Modern World*, 70–72.

30. John Foster Dulles, "World Brotherhood Through the State," 8 Sept. 1946, and
"Faith of Our Fathers," 28 Aug. 1949, in Van Dusen, *The Spiritual Legacy of John Foster*

Dulles, 9 and 111–12. "Discussion at the 183rd Meeting of the National Security Council," 4 Feb. 1954, Box 5, NSC Series, Papers as President, DDEL.

31. Two good biographies of the mufti of Jerusalem are Elpeleg, *The Grand Mufti* and Mattar, *The Mufti of Jerusalem*. Three other biographies, more politically motivated, are Jbara, *Palestinian Leader Hajj Amin al-Husayni*; Schechtman, *The Mufti and the Fuehrer*; and Taggar, *The Mufti of Jerusalem and Palestine Arab Politics*.

32. Rosalind W. Graves, "The Grand Mufti of Jerusalem," *Current History* (Nov. 1946): 377, 381; "The Grand Mufti in World War II," *The Nation*, 17 May 1947, 598; and *Time*, 10 Sept. 1951, 36. See, for example, *Newsweek*, 24 June 1946, 46; *Newsweek*, 5 Aug. 1946, 39; *Time*, 24 June 1946, 31; and *New York Times Magazine*, 25 Aug. 1946, 12. *Newsweek*, 3 Sept. 1951, 28. James Bell, "Mystery Man of Islam Speaks," *Life*, 27 Oct. 1952, 145–53.

33. Speiser, *The United States and the Near East*, 96, and Hoskins, *The Middle East*, 69 and 128. Macatee, the consul general at Jerusalem, to the secretary of state, 9 Feb. 1948, FRUS, 1948, 5:611. Pinkerton, the American consul general in Jerusalem, to the secretary of state, 2 May 1946, FRUS, 1946, 7:590–91. Henderson to the secretary of state, "Certain Considerations against Advocacy by the U.S. of the Majority Plan," 22 Sept. 1947, FRUS, 1947, 5:1155.

34. Two good accounts of the decline in the mufti's influence are Mattar, *The Mufti of Jerusalem*, chapter 9, and Khadduri, *Arab Contemporaries*, 82–84.

35. Ireland, "Islam, Democracy, and Communism," 71. PSB, "D-22: Psychological Strategy Program for the Middle East," Annex B, 4–5.

36. Clifton Daniel, "The Moslem World Watches Palestine," *New York Times Magazine*, 12 June 1948, 15, and 56. Montagne, "Modern Nations and Islam," 587.

37. George F. Kennan, "Comments on the National Security Problem," 1–6 and 7. The National War College, 28 Mar. 1947, "Near and Middle East, 1947–1954," Box 20, Lot 58 D776, Subject Files of the Bureau of Intelligence and Research (INR), 1945–60, RG 59.

38. Kennan, "Comments on the National Security Problem," 7, 8–9.

39. Ibid., 9–10.

40. William Eddy to George Kennan, 28 Mar. 1947, Near and Middle East, 1947–54, Box 20, Lot 58 D776, Subject Files of the Bureau of Intelligence and Research (INR), 1945–60, RG 59.

41. Landau, "Peace May Be In Moslem Hands," 14. OCB, "Inventory of U.S. Government and Private Organization Activity Regarding Islam Organizations as an Aspect of Overseas Operations," 3 May 1957, Islamic Organizations, Box 4, OCB Secretariat Series, Records, 1948–61, NSC Staff, White House Office Files, DDEL.

42. Ireland, "Islam, Democracy, and Communism," 66–67. OCB, "Inventory of U.S. Government and Private Organization Activity Regarding Islamic Organizations as an Aspect of Overseas Operations," 1 and 4.

43. Richard N. Frye, "Islam and the Middle East," *Current History* (June 1956): 327, 328, and 331. Mein to Green; Smith to Green; and Department of State office memorandum, Marshall Green to Howard P. Jones, 22 Apr. 1957, Decimal File 611.80/4–1857, RG 59. For an even broader critique of the report, see Department of State office memorandum, Charlton Ogburn Jr. to David G. Wilson, 22 May 1957, Dedication of Islamic Center, Near Eastern Affairs, Box 4, Records Relating to Regional Matters, 1954–66, Office of the Director for Regional Affairs (NEA/RA), Bureau of Near Eastern Affairs and South Asian Affairs, RG 59.

44. Department of the Army, "Recommendations Concerning Study of Religious Factors in International Strategy," 10. Wilfred Cantwell Smith, "Islam in the Modern World," *Current History* 32, no. 190 (June 1957): 322.

45. John Badeau, "Evolution in Religion," in Fisher, *Evolution in the Middle East*, 15 and 18.

46. Philip K. Hitti, "Current Trends in Islam," in Franck, *Islam in the Modern World*, 5.

47. Franklin W. Wolf of the American embassy in Pakistan to the Department of State, "Renewed Efforts by Chaudhri Khaliquzzaman to Organize a Pan-Islamic Conference," 24 June 1950, Decimal File 880.413/6–2450, RG59. William D. Brewer of the American embassy in Saudi Arabia to the Department of State, "Saudi Press Comment on General Islamic Conference in Karachi," 21 Feb. 1951, Decimal File 880.413/2–2151, RG 59.

48. Warwick Perkins of the American embassy in Pakistan to the Department of State, "A Report on the World Muslim Conference Held at Karachi on February 9–12, 1951," 17 Feb. 1951, Decimal File 880.413/2–1751, RG 59.

49. George C. McGhee of the American embassy in Turkey to the secretary of state, 3 Apr. 1952, Decimal File 780.00/4–352, RG 59.

50. Merrell of the American embassy in Afghanistan to the secretary of state, 7 Apr. 1952, Decimal File 780.00/4–752, RG 59. Harold B. Minor of the American embassy in Lebanon to the secretary of state, 8 Apr. 1952, Decimal File 780.00/4–852, RG 59.

51. Crocker of the American embassy in Iraq to the secretary of state, 8 Apr. 1952, Decimal File 780.00/4–852, RG 59.

52. On Hare's background and status among State Department Middle East specialists, see Thomas, "From Orientalism to Professionalism," especially 79–92. Raymond Hare of the American embassy in Saudi Arabia to the secretary of state, 14 Apr. 1952, Decimal File 780.00/4–1452, RG 59.

53. Department of State telegram, Acheson to regional embassies, 10 Apr. 1952, Decimal File 780.00/4–352, RG 59.

54. S. Roger Tyler Jr., American consul general in Jerusalem, to the Department of State, 11 Dec. 1953, Decimal File 880.413/12–1153, RG 59. See Talcott Seelye of the American embassy in Saudi Arabia to the Department of State, "Proposed Arab-Islamic Congress," 18 May 1954, Decimal File 880.413/5–1854; Charles Clifford Finch of the American embassy in Turkey to the Department of State, "Moslem Conference

Sponsored by King of Jordan," 21 May 1954, Decimal File 780.00/5-2154; Jefferson Caffery, American ambassador to Egypt, to the Department of State, "Nasir Discusses Activities of Islamic Conference," 18 Aug. 1954, Decimal File 880.413/8-2754; Caffery to the Department of State, 9 Sept. 1954, "Islamic Conference Narrows Orientation," Decimal File 880.413/9-954; Caffery to the Department of State, 18 Sept. 1954, "Sadat Explains Islamic Conference," Decimal File 880.413/9-1854; Henry Byroade of the American embassy in Cairo to the Department of State, "Egypt's Pan-Islamic Relations and the Afro-Asian Conference," 2 Mar. 1955, Decimal File 880.413/3-255; and Byroade to the Department of State, "Sadat Claims Islamic Conference Successful but Nasser Expresses Opposition to Islamic Bloc Concept," 16 Apr. 1955, Decimal File 880.413/4-1655, all in RG 59.

55. OCB, "Inventory of U.S. Government and Private Organization Activity Regarding Islamic Organizations as an Aspect of Overseas Operations," 3. Mein to Green.

56. "Diary Entry by the President," 28 Mar. 1956, FRUS, 1955–1957, 15:425. See also the "Editorial Note," quoting from a memorandum from Rountree to Dulles and Hoover, 31 Mar. 1956, which describes efforts to reassure Saud that U.S. policymakers viewed "him as leader of the Arab world." FRUS, 1955–1957, 13:351. See also FRUS, 1955–1957, 15:325–26, 341–43, 352–57 for assessments of U.S.-Egyptian relations that provided the background for this initiative. Memorandum of Conversation, Eisenhower and Duncan Sandys, 1 Feb. 1957, FRUS, 1955–57, 13:444–45. See the text of Eisenhower's message to Saud in Department of State to the embassy in Saudi Arabia, 21 Aug. 1957, FRUS, 1955–57, 13.645–46.

57. Yaqub, Containing Arab Nationalism, 15, 45, and 102; and Citino, From Arab Nationalism to OPEC, 65.

58. Members of the group included John Badeau, who chaired the group, and CIA officer Charles Cremeans, ARAMCO executive James Terry Duce, Harvey Hall, Halford Hoskins, Harold Hoskins, Hal Lehrman, Harold Minor, William Polk, Kermit Roosevelt, Hamilton A. R. Gibb, and Philip Hitti, among others. Badeau ultimately wrote up the findings of the group and published them as "Islam and the Modern Middle East," Foreign Affairs 38, no. 1 (Oct. 1959): 61–74. See also John Badeau, "Islam and the Modern Middle East," and records of the study group on the Middle East and Modern Islam, especially the "Digest of Discussion: Sixth Meeting, May 18, 1959," CFR.

59. Badeau, "Islam and the Modern Middle East," 64–66. "Digest of Discussion: Sixth Meeting, May 18, 1959," 2, CFR.

60. Badeau, "Islam and the Modern Middle East," 72–73.

61. Harold B. Hoskins, "Memorandum Re Middle East Policy," 7 Aug. 1958, 1–2; Elbert G. Mathews to Mr. Rountree, "New Ideas: Proposals re Middle East Policy," 25 Aug. 1958; and William N. Rountree to Mr. Mathews, "Proposals Regarding Middle East Policy by Harold B. Hoskins," 8 Sept. 1958, 1–2, all in Decimal File 780.00/8-2558, RG 59.

62. The best available biography of Khomeini is Moin, Khomeini. For one example of

Khomeini's increasingly powerful critique, see the text of a speech he gave on 27 Oct. 1964, just a week before he would be exiled, reproduced in Moin, *Khomeini*, 122–27.

63. T. Cuyler Young, "Iran in Continuing Crisis," *Foreign Affairs* 40, no. 2 (Jan. 1962): 275–92. "Memorandum from the Assistant Secretary of State for Near Eastern and South Asian Affairs to Secretary of State Rusk," 6 June 1963, FRUS, 1961–1963, 18:571. "Telegram from the Embassy in Iran to the Department of State," 24 June 1963, FRUS, 1961–1963, 18:601–2. John W. Bowling, "The Current Internal Political Situation in Iran," 11 Feb. 1961, FRUS, 1961–1963, 18:58–59.

64. Bureau of Intelligence and Research, Department of State, "The Significance of Khomeini's Opposition to the Iranian Government," Jan. 1965, FRUS, 1964–1968, 22:122–24.

65. See Farber, *Taken Hostage*, on Iran and Mamdani; see *Good Muslim, Bad Muslim*, on Afghanistan. For a more general example of the overwhelming focus on the post-Iran period, see Gerges, *America and Political Islam*, xi, and 37–42, which claims to offer "critical historical perspective" on U.S. responses to political Islam and then covers the entire history of European and American views of Islam before 1979 in five pages.

Chapter Three

1. John C. Campbell to Russell H. Dorr, 15 Nov. 1960, "Study Group on Arab Foreign Policy, 1960–1961," Records of Groups, CFR.

2. Digest of Discussion, "Arab Foreign Policy," First Meeting, 14 Nov. 1960, 1–2, "Study Group on Arab Foreign Policy," CFR. Cremeans, *The Arabs and the World*.

3. Gelfand, *The Inquiry*, 243–50. On Egypt, see Beer, "Egyptian Problems" in *African Questions at the Paris Peace Conference*, 287–409. Beer, "The Future of Mesopotamia," in *African Questions at the Paris Peace Conference*, 420–21.

4. "The King-Crane Commission Report," 28 Aug. 1919, available at http://www .gwpda.org/1918p/kncr.htm.

5. "Confidential Appendix" to "The King-Crane Commission Report."

6. Ibid.

7. Gelvin, *The Modern Middle East*, 195. Also see Yapp, *The Near East since the First World War*, 167–180, for an overview of the rise of Reza Shah Pahlavi.

8. Bruce Hopper, "The Persian Regenesis," *Foreign Affairs* 13, no. 2 (Jan. 1935): 295, 297, 302, and 307.

9. On the breakdown of U.S.-Iranian relations in 1936 over statements in the U.S. press about Reza Shah Pahlavi, see U.S. Department of State, FRUS, 1936, 3:342–75.

10. Yapp, *The Near East since the First World War*, 188–93, and Gelvin, *The Modern Middle East*, 127–28.

11. Hans Kohn, "The Unification of Arabia," *Foreign Affairs*, 13, no. 1 (Oct. 1934): 93, 94, 95, 91, 99, and 91.

12. Joel Carmichael, "Prince of Arabs," *Foreign Affairs* 20, no. 4 (July 1942): 720, 728, and 731. In addition, see Gerald de Gaury, "The End of Arabian Isolation," *Foreign Affairs* 25, no. 1 (Oct. 1946): 82–89.

13. Kohn, "The Unification of Arabia," 96 and 99. Hans Kohn, "General Characteristics of Nationalism in the Middle East," in Franck, *Nationalism in the Middle East*, 64 and 66.

14. David G. Hogarth, "The Arab World Today," *Foreign Affairs* 4, no. 3 (Apr. 1926): 406, 407, and 408.

15. Hogarth, "The Arab World Today," 410, 412–13, 414.

16. Antonius, *The Arab Awakening*. On the State Department's familiarity with *The Arab Awakening*, see Louis, *The British Empire in the Middle East*, 401, n. 10. William L. Cleveland, "The Arab Nationalism of George Antonius Reconsidered," in Jankowski and Gershoni, *Rethinking Nationalism in the Arab Middle East*, 84. Hoskins, *The Middle East*, 295; Polk, "What the Arabs Think," 57; Campbell, *Defense of the Middle East*, 369; and Speiser, *The United States and the Near East*, 241. Speiser, 221–22, also relied heavily on Antonius for his description of U.S. missionary involvement and its contributions.

17. See Boyle, *Betrayal of Palestine*; Albert Hourani, "*The Arab Awakening* Forty Years After," in Hourani, *The Emergence of the Modern Middle East*, 193–215; and Cleveland, "The Arab Nationalism of George Antonius Reconsidered," 65–86, for overviews of Antonius's life from which this brief summary is drawn.

18. Antonius, *The Arab Awakening*, 35–37, and 43.

19. Ibid., 38 and 79–125. For the broader discussion of language, see 37–45. Cleveland, "The Arab Nationalism of George Antonius Reconsidered," 68–72.

20. Antonius, *The Arab Awakening*, chapters 7–12. Ibid., 276.

21. Ibid., 409 and 277.

22. Cleveland, "The Arab Nationalism of George Antonius Reconsidered," Hourani, "*The Arab Awakening* Forty Years Later," and Khalidi, "Arab Nationalism," are all excellent assessments of the work, its impact, and its strengths and weaknesses. Antonius, *The Arab Awakening*, 64 and 189. Cleveland, "The Arab Nationalism of George Antonius Reconsidered," 74.

23. Hourani, "*The Arab Awakening* Forty Years Later," 203–4. See ibid., 207, on the issue of Antonius's access to the various participants in interwar discussions about Palestine.

24. Report by the Coordinating Committee of the Department of State, "Aspects of the Department of State Thinking on Political and Economic Policies of the United States in the Near and Middle East for the Postwar Period," FRUS, 1945, 8:38. CIA, "ORE 25–48: The Break-Up of the Colonial Empires and Its Implications for US Security," 2 Sept. 1948, 2, Publication File HRP 92-4/001, Box 2, Estimates of the Office of Research Evaluation, 1946–50, RG 263.

25. See Kaplan, *The Arabists*, 38, 65, 72–74, and 79–81, for biographical details on

Bayard Dodge. Rene Millon, "Digest of Discussion: Fourth Meeting of the Discussion Group on the Moslem World, 1948/49," 9 May 1949, 7, 10, Records of Study Groups, Vol. XXVIII, CFR.

26. See, for example, CIA, "ORE 49: The Current Situation in Palestine," 20 Oct. 1947, Publication File HRP 92–4/001, Box 1, Estimates of the Office of Research Evaluation, 1946–50, RG 263; Hoskins, *The Middle East*, 98–141; Polk, "What the Arabs Think," 37–41; Speiser, *The United States and the Near East*, chapter 9; Hurewitz, *Middle East Dilemmas*, especially 135–55 and 250–55; and the three articles on "The Palestine Problem" by J. C. Hurewitz, Moshe Keren, and Ralph Bunche, respectively, in Frye, *The Near East and the Great Powers*, 91–118.

27. Loy Henderson to the secretary of state, 29 Aug. 1945, FRUS, 1945, 8:25, 29. Polk, "What the Arabs Think," 47–48, and Kohn, "General Characteristics of Nationalism in the Middle East," 64. Speiser, *The United States and the Near East*, 228.

28. The literature on U.S.-Iranian relations is voluminous. Some of the best works on the Mossadegh period include Bill, *The Eagle and the Lion*; Cottam, *Iran and the United States*; Mark J. Gasiorowski, "U.S. Foreign Policy toward Iran During the Mussadiq Era," in Lesch, *The Middle East and the United States*, 51–65; Heiss, *Empire and Nationhood*; and Yergin, *The Prize*, chapter 23. See Heiss, *Empire and Nationhood*, chapter 2, on U.S. efforts to achieve a more equitable oil agreement.

29. Diba, *Mohammad Mossadegh*, is a very good study of Mossadegh's life and political importance. See also Yergin, *The Prize*, 456–62, which is especially good on Mossadegh's background and personality. See, for example, memorandum of discussion at the 135th meeting of the NSC, 4 Mar. 1953, FRUS, 1952–1954, 10:692–701; Loy Henderson to John Foster Dulles, 31 Mar. 1953, 15 Apr. 1953, and 30 May 1953, all in FRUS, 1952–1954, 10:719–21, 723–25, and 730–32, respectively.

30. Yergin, *The Prize*, 456–57. Also see Hurewitz, *Middle East Dilemmas*, 38–49, for a contrasting portrayal of Mossadegh as a shrewd international politician. McGhee, *Envoy to the Middle World*, 390–91. "Developments of the Quarter: Comment and Chronology," *Middle East Journal* 7, no. 4 (Autumn 1953): 505.

31. Heiss, *Empire and Nationhood*, 229–33. Memorandum, Henderson to the Department of State, 28 July 1952, FRUS, 1952–1954, 10:416–17.

32. Telegram, Henderson to the Department of State, 22 Oct. 1951, FRUS, 1952–1954, 10:238. NSC, "Summary of NSC 136/1: Statement of Policy Proposed by the National Security Council Regarding the Present Situation in Iran," 20 Nov. 1952, FRUS, 1952–1954, 10:530. Hoskins, *The Middle East*, 184 and 186.

33. "Man of the Year: Challenge of the East," *Time*, 7 Jan. 1952, 18, 21, and 18. See Dorman and Farhang, *The U.S. Press and Iran*, 31–62, for a broader review of press coverage of Mossadegh.

34. There are several good studies of Nasser, his rise to power, and years as the leader of Egypt. See Woodward, *Nasser*; Shamir, *Egypt from Monarchy to Republic*; Kerr, *The Arab Cold War*; Gordon, *Nasser's Blessed Movement*; Waterbury, *The Egypt of Nasser and*

Sadat; Beinin, *Was the Red Flag Flying There?*; and James Jankowski, "Arab Nationalism in 'Nasserism' and Egyptian State Policy, 1952–1958," in Jankowski and Gershoni, *Rethinking Nationalism in the Arab Middle East*, 150–67. For a contemporary assessment of Nasser by an American journalist, see St. John, *The Boss*.

General Mohammad Naguib was the official leader of Egypt following the coup in July 1952. Within a few months, however, it became clear that Naguib was, at best, the one person the RCC believed could be the public face of the movement and, at worst, that he was a puppet whose strings were pulled by someone else, possibly Nasser. Through the first two years of RCC rule, Naguib and Nasser had multiple struggles for power. By 1954, Nasser made it clear that he was in control, and likely had been for much of the postrevolution period.

Nasser's work was translated and published on multiple occasions. One widely read version was Nasser, *Egypt's Liberation*.

35. Telegram from the embassy in Egypt to the Department of State, 6 Feb. 1955, FRUS, 1955–1957, 12:16. Hart, letter to the Department of State, 20 Mar. 1955, Decimal File 611.74/3–2055 RG 59. Memorandum from Parker Hart, director of the Office of Near Eastern Affairs, to George V. Allen, assistant secretary of state for Near Eastern, South Asian, and African affairs, 30 Mar. 1955, Alpha—Memos, etc., after Return from London, 11 Mar.–26 April 1955, Box 29, Miscellaneous Lot Files, Lot 59 D518, RG 59. Raymond Hare oral history interview, vol. 2, 88–89.

36. Robert C. Doty, "Closeup of Egypt's Strong Man," *New York Times Magazine*, 19 Sept. 1954, 12, 63. It is worth noting here, though, that in other areas of his analysis Doty was either not very prescient or was not clued in to how other observers might have viewed Nasser. For example, Doty also argued that "the inability of Nasser to project his personality is a serious weakness in a country which likes to adore its leaders" (ibid. 12). By 1956, most observers readily acknowledged that Nasser was supremely gifted in this very art, and argued that his ability to appeal to the Arab masses was what made him so dangerous. In a major misunderstanding of his subject, Doty also argued that Nasser's statement that neutralism "was 'possible only for the strong,'" suggested he had "renounced neutralism" (ibid. 64). More accurately, Nasser's statement reflected an honest assessment of Egypt's place in the world in the early 1950s. Richard Nolte, "Egypt in Transition," *Foreign Policy Bulletin* 33, no. 21 (15 July 1954): 1. John Badeau, "What Hope for Egypt?" *Foreign Policy Bulletin* 34, no. 8 (1 Jan. 1955): 58.

37. Spiegel, *The Other Arab-Israeli Conflict*, 65. Eisenhower, *Waging Peace*, 26 and 31. See also Immerman, *John Foster Dulles*, 149.

38. Dulles quoted in LaFeber, *America, Russia, and the Cold War*, 171. For more commentary on Dulles's tendency to equate neutralism and anticolonial nationalism with communism, see McMahon, "Eisenhower and Third World Nationalism."

39. See, for example, the discussion of neutralism in Campbell, *Defense of the Middle East*, 351 and 355–56. Nasser, quoted in Heikal, *Cutting the Lion's Tail*, 39. See also

Brands, *The Specter of Neutralism*, 241. John S. Badeau, "A Role in Search of A Hero: A Brief Study of the Egyptian Revolution," *Middle East Journal* 9, no. 4 (Autumn 1955): 380.

40. The best overview of Project ALPHA is Hahn, *The United States, Great Britain, and Egypt, 1945–1956*, 186–206. In a January 1956 diary entry, Eisenhower noted that Anderson was "one of the most capable men I know. My confidence in him is such that at the moment I feel that nothing could give me greater satisfaction than to believe that next January 20th, I could turn over this office to his hands. His capacity is unlimited and his dedication to this country is complete." "Diary Entry by the President," 11 Jan. 1956, FRUS, 1955–1957, 15:23. Eisenhower diary entry, 13 Mar. 1956, in Ferrell, *The Eisenhower Diaries*, 319. The documentary record of the Anderson Mission is available in FRUS, 1955–1957, 15:1–346. Brief overviews can be found in Brands, *The Specter of Neutralism*, 260–63; Kyle, *Suez*, 96–99; and Spiegel, *The Other Arab-Israeli Conflict*, 67.

41. Democratic Oklahoma senator Mike Monroney, quoted in Brands, *The Specter of Neutralism*, 271. For a lengthier discussion of congressional opposition to Nasser in late 1955 and early 1956, see Brands, *The Specter of Neutralism*, 268–72. Secretary of State Dulles was very well aware that there was some congressional opposition to the Aswan Dam project, and used that opposition for rhetorical effect in his discussions with the Egyptians. See "Memorandum of Conversation," 17 May 1956, FRUS, 1955–1957, 15:648.

42. Numerous scholarly works provide excellent overviews of the Suez Crisis and U.S.-Egyptian relations between 1956 and 1958. Some of the best include: Hahn, *The United States, Great Britain, and Egypt*, 211–39; Ashton, *Eisenhower, Macmillan and the Problem of Nasser*; Kyle, *Suez*; Kunz, *The Economic Diplomacy of the Suez Crisis*; Owen and Louis, *Suez 1956*; and Takeyh, *The Origins of the Eisenhower Doctrine*. Eisenhower made numerous statements to the effect that he thought Nasser had grandiose ambitions to dominate the Middle East and that he posed a serious threat to U.S. interests in the region. See, for example, two letters written to British prime minister Anthony Eden, dated 2 Sept. and 8 Sept. 1956, in Eisenhower, *Waging Peace*, 666–71.

43. "Memorandum of Discussion at the 292nd Meeting of the National Security Council," 9 Aug. 1956, FRUS, 1955–1957, 16:167–68. "Memorandum of a Conference with the President," 31 July 1956, FRUS, 1955–1957, 16:64.

44. Richard Russell, "U.S. Policies toward Nasser," 4 Aug. 1956, FRUS, 1955–1957, 16:140–42. Polk, "Our Isolation from the Arab World," *Atlantic Monthly* 200, no. 6 (December 1957): 61.

45. "Memorandum of Conversation," 12 Aug. 1956, FRUS, 1955–1957, 16:192. Allan Evans to Mr. Armstrong, 14 Aug. 1956, attached to Office of Intelligence and Research, special paper no. 2, "Hitler and Nasser: A Comparison," 14 Aug. 1956, Suez Canal Crisis, 1956, Box 11, Subject Files of the Bureau of Intelligence and Research (INR), 1945–60, Lot 58 D776, RG 59.

46. Dwight D. Eisenhower, "Special Message to the Congress on the Situation in the Middle East," 5 Jan. 1957, in *Public Papers of the President: Dwight D Eisenhower, 1957*, 13. See Takeyh, *The Origins of the Eisenhower Doctrine*, 152, on this point.

47. The best overview of U.S. policy in the wake of the Suez Crisis is Yaqub, *Containing Arab Nationalism*. On the 1957 Jordanian Crisis, see Dann, *King Hussein and the Challenge of Arab Radicalism*, especially chapters 3–5; Richard B. Parker, "The United States and King Hussein," in Lesch, *The Middle East and the United States*, 100–113; Satloff, *From Abdullah to Hussein*, especially chapters 9 and 10; and Satloff, "The Jekyll-and-Hyde Origins of the U.S.-Jordanian Strategic Relationship," in Lesch, *The Middle East and the United States*, 114–27. For lengthier analyses of the Syrian Crisis, see Ashton, *Eisenhower, Macmillan and the Problem of Nasser*, especially chapters 8 and 9; David W. Lesch, "The 1957 American-Syrian Crisis: Globalist Policy in a Regional Reality," in Lesch, *The Middle East and the United States*, 128–43; Lesch, *Syria and the United States*, especially chapters 7–11; Mufti, *Sovereign Creations*, chapter 5; and Saunders, *The United States and Arab Nationalism*, especially chapters 3 and 4.

48. The two best works on the 1958 Iraqi revolution are Batatu, *The Old Social Classes and the Revolutionary Movements of Iraq*, and a 1991 retrospective on that work, Fernea and Louis, *The Iraqi Revolution of 1958*. See documentation in FRUS, 1958, 12:307–11. Memorandum of conference with the president, 23 July 1958, staff memos, July 1958 (1), Box 35, DDE Diary Series, and Memorandum, "Discussion at the 374th Meeting of the National Security Council, 31 July 1958," Box 10, NSC Series, DDEL.

49. John Badeau, "What Suez Means to Egypt," *Foreign Policy Bulletin* 36, no. 4 (1 Nov. 1956): 25 and 33.

50. Hurewitz, "Our Mistakes in the Middle East," *Atlantic Monthly* 198, no. 6 (Dec. 1956): 50–51.

51. Polk, "Our Isolation from the Arab World," 62.

52. Ibid. See also Polk, *The United States and the Arab World*, 215–28, for a more elaborate articulation of this point.

53. The best biography of Fulbright is Woods, *Fulbright*. Other helpful works, particularly with regard to Fulbright's foreign policy thinking, include Berman, *William Fulbright and the Vietnam War*; Brown, *J. William Fulbright*; and Powell, *J. William Fulbright and America's Lost Crusade*. Berman, *William Fulbright and the Vietnam War*, 5. Brown, *J. William Fulbright*, 10.

54. Woods, *Fulbright*, 115. For the larger discussion of Fulbright's internationalism and racism, see Woods, *Fulbright*, 114–15. Fulbright, *The Price of Empire*, 159–62, and Fulbright, *The Arrogance of Power*, 69–81.

55. Fulbright, *The Price of Empire*, 154–55. Hunt, *Ideology and U.S. Foreign Policy*, chapters 4 and 5, and Packenham, *Liberal America and the Third World*, 129–50.

56. Woods, *Fulbright*, 129–36.

57. Fulbright also took his dissenter's role outside the Senate, writing several books and giving numerous speeches over the course of his career. His most popular work

was *The Arrogance of Power*, which appeared on the *New York Times* best-seller list in 1967, sold over four hundred thousand copies, and was translated into German, Italian, Japanese, Spanish, and Swedish. See Woods, *Fulbright*, 441–42. J. William Fulbright, address to the Senate, 27 Feb. 1956, in Meyer, *Fulbright of Arkansas*, 94 and 96.

58. Fulbright, *The Price of Empire*, 157–58. J. William Fulbright, address to the Senate, 14 Aug. 1957, in Meyer, *Fulbright of Arkansas*, 98.

59. Ibid., 103.

60. J. William Fulbright, Senate address, 6 Aug. 1958, in Meyer, *Fulbright of Arkansas*, 116, 122, 119, and 123.

61. On problems between Nasser and the new Iraqi leadership, see telegram from the embassy in the United Arab Republic to the Department of State, 15 Dec. 1958, and memorandum of a conference with the president, 23 Dec. 1958, both in FRUS, 1958–1960, 13:505–11. James S. Lay Jr., letter to NSC, 20 July 1958, NSC 5801/1—Policy toward the Near East (1), Box 23, Policy Papers Subseries, NSC Series, Office of the Special Assistant for National Security Affairs, White House Office Files, DDEL.

62. Yaqub, *Containing Arab Nationalism*, 238.

63. Richard H. Nolte and William R. Polk, "Toward a Policy for the Middle East," *Foreign Affairs* 36, no. 4 (July 1958): 645. Campbell, *Defense of the Middle East*, chapters 16, 18, and 19. President Johnson would later appoint Nolte U.S. ambassador to Egypt, though he was never able to serve, as Egypt broke off relations with the United States during the June 1967 war before Nolte assumed the post.

64. Second draft, untitled NSC paper, 4 Aug. 1958, Near East (5), Box 6, Special Staff Files Series, NSC Staff Papers: 1948–61, White House Office Files, DDEL.

65. Gordon Gray, "Memorandum of Conversation," meetings with the president—1958 (2), Box 3, President Subseries, Special Assistant Series, Special Assistant for National Security Affairs, Records, 1952–61, White House Office Files, DDEL. Gordon Gray oral history, 53–54.

66. William R. Polk, "The Lesson of Iraq," *The Atlantic*, Dec. 1958, http://www.theatlantic.com/issues/58dec/polk.htm.

67. Raymond Hare to secretary of state, telegram, 2 Oct. 1958, Decimal File 780.00/10–258, RG 59.

68. NSC, "NSC 5820/1: U.S. Policy toward the Near East," 4 Nov. 1958, FRUS, 1958–1960, 12:187–99.

69. "Statement on the Middle East by Senator J.W. Fulbright," 31 Aug. 1959, "Middle East," Box 791, Background Material, 1958–60, Legislation, Senate Files, Pre-Presidential Papers, JFKL. Emphasis in original.

70. See "Digests of Discussion" from the study group meetings, CFR. Also see Cremeans, *The Arabs and the World*. "Memorandum from the Assistant Secretary of State for Near Eastern and South Asian Affairs to the Acting Secretary of State," 6 July 1960, FRUS: 1958–1960, 12:259. For "NSC 6011: Statement of U.S. Policy toward the Near East," see FRUS, 1958–1960, 12:263–73.

71. Andrew Goodpaster, "Memorandum of Conversation," 23 Dec. 1958, State Department—Sept. 1958–Jan. 1959 (4), Box 3, Department of State Subseries, Subject Series, Office of the Staff Secretary, 1952–61, White House Office Files, DDEL. Robert Komer Letter to McGeorge Bundy, 30 Dec. 1963, United Arab Republic, Vol. I, Memos, 11/63–5/64, Box 158, Middle East, Country File, National Security Files, LBJL.

72. National Intelligence Estimate 36-61, "Nasser and the Future of Arab Nationalism," 27 June 1961, Folder 36: Arab World, Box 6, National Intelligence Estimates; Special National Intelligence Estimate 36.1-62, "Prospects for Nasser," 28 Mar. 1962, Folder 36.1: United Arab Republic, Box 6, National Intelligence Estimates; CIA Office of Current Intelligence, "Special Report: Nasir's Arab Policy—The Latest Phase," 28 Aug. 1964, Folder Cables, 6/64–12/64, Box 159 United Arab Republic, Vol. II, Middle East, Country File; and CIA Office of Current Intelligence, "Special Report: Nasir's Political Dilemma: How To Foster Democracy in a Totalitarian Environment," 17 Sept. 1965, Folder Memos, 6/65–6/66 (2 of 2), Box 159 United Arab Republic, Vol. IV, Middle East, Country File; all in the National Security File, LBJL. Quotes are from "Nasser and the Future of Arab Nationalism," 1, and "Nasir's Political Dilemma," 5.

Chapter Four

1. George C. Denney Jr., "The Roots of Arab Resistance to Modernization," i, 12 Sept. 1969, POL 2 ARAB, 1/1/67, Box 1/85, Central Foreign Policy Files, Subject-Numeric Files, 1967–69, Political and Defense, RG 59.

2. Denney, "The Roots of Arab Resistance to Modernization," 27, 30, and 31.

3. See Oren, Power, Faith, and Fantasy, 195–200, on Civil War veterans in Egypt.

4. George Louis Beer, "Egyptian Problems" in Gray, African Questions at the Paris Peace Conference, 289, 306–26, and 341.

5. George Louis Beer, "The Future of Mesopotamia," in Gray, African Questions at the Paris Peace Conference, 417–18, 420–21, 424, 425–26.

6. "The King-Crane Commission Report," 28 Aug. 1919, http://www.gwpda.org/1918p/kncr.htm.

7. Ibid.

8. See Rosenberg's discussion of "liberal developmentalism" in Spreading the American Dream, 7–12, and 229–34. Linda Wills Qaimmaqami modifies Rosenberg's formulation to "private sector developmentalism" in "The Catalyst of Nationalization." Rosenberg, Spreading the American Dream, 232.

9. For a fuller explanation of the Truman administration's perception of the values of and reliance on private sector investing in the non-Western world during the early postwar period, see Qaimmaqami, "The Catalyst of Nationalization," and Kaufman, Trade and Aid, 1–6.

10. Stegner, Discovery!, available in fourteen installments at www.saudiaramco

world.com. See Vitalis, *America's Kingdom*, 195–99 on Stegner's clash with ARAMCO over the publishing of *Discovery!*

11. Stegner, *Discovery!*, chapters 1 (Jan./Feb. 1968), 3 (May/June 1968, with emphasis in original), 9 (May/June 1969), and 14 (July/Aug. 1970).

12. "Aramco: a celebration"; Lyn Maby, "Footsteps in al-Hasa"; John R. Starkey, "Twitchell: '. . . Who lifted the lid on Saudi Arabia's treasure'"; and Thomas Barger, "Birth of a Dream," all in *Saudi Aramco World* 35, no. 3 (May/June 1984), www.saudi aramcoworld.com/issue/198403.

13. William Eddy letter to Mary Garvin Eddy, 17 Aug. 1948, Eddy Papers, Box 6, Folder 3, used by permission of PUL. Emphasis in original.

14. Vitalis, *America's Kingdom*, xii, and see 76–87 for a broader discussion of the construction of myths.

15. Memorandum by the under secretary of state to the secretary of state, 9 Oct. 1945, FRUS, 1945, 8:44.

16. My discussion of the Iranian case is based on Qaimmaqami, "The Catalyst of Nationalization." Qaimmaqami borrows "chosen instrument" from Rosenberg, *Spreading the American Dream*, 59–62.

17. For Qaimmaqami's overall assessment of liberal developmentalism in Iran and Thornburg's role in nationalization, see "The Catalyst of Nationalization," 29–31.

18. Gordon P. Merriam, "Draft Memorandum to President Truman," undated [Aug. 1945], FRUS, 1945, 8:46; and "Arab States Area Paper," 10 July 1950, Near East General, Pt. II, Box 1, Subject File Relating to Economic Affairs, 1947–51, Records of the Office of Near Eastern Affairs, Economic Lot Files 55 D643, RG 59. J. C. Hurewitz, "Problems of American Economic and Technical Assistance Policy in the Middle East," 8 Apr. 1952, memorandum No. 5, Group on American Policy in the Middle East, CFR. See also Hurewitz, *Middle East Dilemmas*, 211–20, for a similar evaluation.

19. Cooke, *Challenge and Response in the Middle East*. Speiser, *The United States and the Near East*, chapters 6 and 7.

20. Warriner, *Land and Poverty in the Middle East*, 1 and 39.

21. Polk, "What the Arabs Think," 22 and 57. Fisher, *Social Forces in the Middle East*, 265–66; Hurewitz, *Middle East Dilemmas*, 262; and Polk, *The United States and the Arab World*, 309.

22. Owen and Pamuk, *A History of Middle East Economies in the Twentieth Century*, 5–7 and 27. See also Beinin, "Egypt: Society and Economy," for a good discussion of the economic, social, and political problems in Egypt leading into the postwar period.

23. These points can be gleaned from almost any survey of the modern Middle East. See, for example, Cleveland, *A History of the Modern Middle East*, chapters 11–13; Milton-Edwards, *Contemporary Politics in the Middle East*, chapter 1; and Owen, *State, Power and Politics*, chapter 1.

24. Hoskins, *The Middle East*, 5; Warriner, *Land and Poverty in the Middle East*, chapter 1; and Roosevelt, *Arabs, Oil, and History*.

25. The most succinct articulation of this argument is in Polk, "What the Arabs Think," 9–11, and 22.

26. Ibid., 22.

27. Kesaris, CIA Research Reports, 65.

28. Polk, "What the Arabs Think," 7.

29. Report by the Coordinating Committee of the Department of State, "American Economic Policy in the Middle East," 2 May 1945, FRUS, 1945, 8:37.

30. Polk, "What the Arabs Think," 17.

31. The term "revolution of rising expectations" was in wide enough usage that a brief reference to it during the Annual Conference of the Middle East Institute in March 1953 did not require any further elaboration. See Arthur Z. Gardiner, "Economic Evolution," in Fisher, Evolution in the Middle East, 43. Princeton social scientist, RAND Corporation consultant, and former State Department Middle East specialist Manfred Halpern noted in 1963 that the Middle East was still influenced by the "revolution of rising expectations." See Manfred Halpern, The Politics of Social Change, vii. Polk, "What the Arabs Think," 48–49. On the contribution of education and an emerging middle class, see Habib Kurani, "Evolution in Education," in Fisher, Evolution in the Middle East, 3–12.

32. NSC, "The Position of the United States with Respect to the General Area of the Eastern Mediterranean and Middle East," 27 Dec. 1951, FRUS, 1951, 5:262. See also "National Intelligence Estimate 76: Conditions and Trends in the Middle East Affecting US Security," 15 Jan. 1953, FRUS, 1952–1954, 9:334–43.

33. "Report of the Near East Regional Conference in Cairo," 16 Mar. 1950, FRUS, 1950:, 5:4.

34. Secretary of state to the ambassador in the United Kingdom, 27 Aug. 1942, FRUS, 1942, 4:26–27. "Summary of Remarks Made by Mr. Wadsworth to President Truman on November 10 on Behalf of Himself and of Mr. Tuck, Colonel Eddy and Mr. Pinkerton," FRUS, 1945, 8:14. See also the "Summary Memorandum of Informal Conversations Relating to Social and Economic Affairs in the Middle East," prepared by American and British participants, 23–30 Oct. 1947, FRUS, 1947, 5:615, which states that if the "social, cultural and economic standards of the peoples of the area . . . are to be raised, there must be constructive foreign influences in the Middle East. It is considered that Great Britain and the United States are among the countries of the world which are in the best position to exercise such constructive influences."

35. Gordon Merriam, draft memorandum to President Truman, undated, attached as annex to Dean Acheson, memorandum by the under secretary of state to the secretary of state, 9 Oct. 1945, FRUS, 1945, 8:46.

36. Coordinating Committee of the Department of State, "American Economic Policy in the Middle East," FRUS, 1945, 8:37. "Memorandum Prepared in the Department of State," undated, FRUS, 1947, 5:545.

37. Memorandum by the under secretary of state to the secretary of state, 9 Oct.

1945, and the attached annex, in FRUS, 1945, 8:43–48, especially 44, n. 27; memorandum by the director of the Office of Near Eastern and African Affairs to the under secretary of state, 4 June 1946, FRUS, 1946, 7:7–9; and memorandum by the assistant secretary of state for Near Eastern, South Asian and African affairs to the secretary of state, 7 June 1950, FRUS, 1950, 168–73, especially 171.

38. The responses to each proposal are included with the citations listed in note 37.

39. For the text of the Truman Doctrine speech before a joint session of Congress on 12 March 1947, see *Public Papers of the Presidents: Harry S. Truman, 1947*, 178–80.

40. President Harry S. Truman, "Inaugural Address," 20 Jan. 1949, in *Public Papers of the Presidents: Harry S. Truman, 1949*, 114–15. Good overviews of Point Four can be found in Godfried, *Bridging the Gap Between Rich and Poor*, 102–9; and Packenham, *Liberal America and the Third World*, 43–49.

41. A lengthier discussion of these two initiatives can be found in Paul W. T. Kingston, "The 'Ambassador for the Arabs': The Locke Mission and the Unmaking of U.S. Development Policy in the Near East, 1952–1953," in Lesch, *The Middle East and the United States*, 30–50.

42. Warriner, *Land and Poverty in the Middle East*, 2–3 and 120. Afif I. Tannous, "Land Reform: Key to the Development and Stability of the Arab World," *Middle East Journal* 5, no. 1 (Winter 1951): 2–4. Emphasis in original. Halford L. Hoskins, "Point Four with Reference to the Middle East," in *The Annals of the American Academy of Political and Social Science* 268 (March 1950): 86–89. See also his chapter on "The Point Four Balance in the Middle East Ledger," in Halford L. Hoskins, *The Middle East*, 232–54.

43. See Kingston, "The 'Ambassador for the Arabs,'" 33, on aid for Palestinian refugees, and the entire piece on the failure of the Locke mission and U.S. foreign aid programs in the Middle East during the early 1950s.

44. I draw heavily on the works of other scholars who have written extensively on modernization theory, particularly Gilman, *Mandarins of the Future*, and Latham, *Modernization as Ideology*.

45. Lerner, *The Passing of Traditional Society*, 45.

46. Ibid., chapter 2.

47. Ibid., 88.

48. Ibid., 214 and 264–265. For a thorough response to long-standing arguments about Egyptian overpopulation, see Timothy Mitchell, "America's Egypt," especially 18–21.

49. Lerner, *The Passing of Traditional Society*, 303, 353–62, and 366–77.

50. In addition to Rostow, *The Stages of Economic Growth*, see M. F. Millikan and W. W. Rostow, "Foreign Aid: Next Phase," *Foreign Affairs* 36, no. 3 (April 1958): 418–36; and Rostow, *View From the Seventh Floor*.

51. Kunz, *Butter and Guns*, 125–26. Rostow, *The Stages of Economic Growth*, x, 4–9.

52. Rostow, *The Stages of Economic Growth*, 108–12.

53. In addition to Halpern, *The Politics of Social Change*, see Manfred Halpern, "The

Character and Scope of the Social Revolution in the Middle East," in Polk, *Developmental Revolution*, and Jessica Lautin, "Practicing Politics His Own Way: Manfred Halpern Remembered," *Daily Princetonian*, 7 Feb. 2001.

54. Halpern, *The Politics of Social Change*, vii and 25.

55. Halpern uses "Instruments of Political Modernization" as the title for the fourth of the book's five parts. See Halpern, *The Politics of Social Change*, 250, for a brief explanation of it.

56. Ibid., viii and 420.

57. Rostow, *The Stages of Economic Growth*, 164 and 26–31. See also Halpern, *The Politics of Social Change*, chapter 19.

58. Some scholars in the 1960s picked up on these and other difficulties with modernization theory almost immediately and undertook much more complex studies of social transformation. Two notable examples are Black, *The Dynamics of Modernization*, and Moore, *Social Origins of Dictatorship and Democracy*.

59. President's Committee on Information Activities Abroad, "Psychological and Informational Aspects of Foreign Economic Aid," 6 June 1960, 15, PCIAA Study No. 19, Box 13, NSC Registry Series, NSC Staff Records: 1948–61, White House Office Files, DDEL. Harold Saunders, memorandum for Mr. Komer, 20 Dec. 1961, attached to Robert Komer, memorandum to McGeorge Bundy and Carl Kaysen, 20 Dec. 1961, Iran, General, 12/11/61–12/31/61, Box 116, Country File, National Security File, Papers of the President, JFKL.

60. Kaufman, *Trade and Aid*.

61. Eisenhower, *Waging Peace*, 287. For a good overview of the Eisenhower-Jackson friendship and Jackson's career more generally, see Brands, *Cold Warriors*, chapter 6. For an overview of Jackson's and Rostow's involvement in the drafting process of Eisenhower's speech, see C.D. Jackson, "Log, July 24 to August 13, 1958—Near East Crisis," Log—1958 (2), Box 69, C.D. Jackson Papers, 1931–67, DDEL.

62. See "Editorial Note," FRUS, 1958–1960, 11:467–69. For the text of Eisenhower's speech, see *Public Papers of the Presidents of the United States: Dwight D. Eisenhower, 1958*, 606–16. The concept of a regional development bank was first mentioned in NSC 5428, which was prepared before the shift in emphasis to military assistance was complete. In NSC 5428, policymakers recommended considering the creation of "an area-wide development fund in which the West would participate, and through which states having no oil resources might benefit from those who have." The proposal resurfaced in October 1957, when the Planning Board of the NSC revisited the subject. See Robert H. Jones, letter to the planning board, 31 Oct. 1957, Near East (6), Box 6, NSC Staff Papers, 1953–61, White House Office Files, DDEL.

63. Burns, *Economic Aid and American Policy toward Egypt*, 113–18, provides an excellent overview of the development of the "Food for Peace" program, with the quoted portions on 113–14. The aid figures are from Harold Saunders, memorandum for the president, 13 Nov. 1961, attached to Saunders to Rostow, 13 Nov. 1961, General, 11/61–

12/61, Box 168, United Arab Republic, Country File, National Security Files, President's Office Files, JFKL.

64. For official statements regarding the "new look," long-term, countrywide development, and the idea of a "development decade," see W. W. Rostow, "Some Points Covered at the Foreign Aid Meeting," 14 Feb. 1961, Foreign Aid, 2/13/61–2/20/61; W. W. Rostow, "Memorandum to the President: Crucial Issues in Foreign Aid," 28 Feb. 1961, Foreign Aid, 2/24/61–2/28/61; W. W. Rostow, "A New Look at Foreign Aid," Foreign Aid, 3/1/61, all in Rostow, Staff Memos, Box 325, Meetings and Memoranda; President's Letter of Transmittal to the Congress of the United States, 21 May 1962, Foreign Aid Policy, Box 373, Carl Kaysen. Chester Bowles, "Memorandum for the President: Considerations Affecting a Possible Official Visit Here by President Nasser," 16 May 1961 and W. W. Rostow to George McGhee, 6 June 1961, both in 1/61–6/61, General, Box 168, United Arab Republic, Country File. Harold H. Saunders to W. W. Rostow, "U.S. Projects in Egypt," 21 Nov. 1961, General, 11/61–12/61, Box 168, United Arab Republic, Country File. Kennedy sent Nasser seven written or oral messages from 20 February 1961 through 1 February 1962, and received four messages from Nasser during that period. For a list of their correspondences, see William Brubeck, "Memorandum for McGeorge Bundy: Article in 25 June 1962 *New Republic* Re Nasser," 21 June 1962, 6/62, General, Box 168, United Arab Republic, Country File. All available in National Security Files, President's Office Files, JFKL. For a broad overview of U.S.-Egyptian relations in the early 1960s and the relationship between Kennedy and Nasser, see Little, "The New Frontier on the Nile."

65. Robert Komer, "Memorandum for the President: A Shift in Policy toward Nasser," 8 Dec. 1961, 11/61–12/61, General. For further documentation on the proposed action program, see Dean Rusk, "Memorandum for the President: Action Program for the United Arab Republic," 10 Jan. 1962; Komer, "Memorandum for the President: Action Program for the UAR," 15 Jan. 1962; and Komer, "Memorandum for McGeorge Bundy: Presidential Meeting on Nasser Problem," 29 Jan. 1962, all in 1/62–2/62, General. All available in Box 168, United Arab Republic, Country File, National Security File, President's Office Files, JFKL.

66. On the Mason mission, see Lucius Battle, "Memorandum to the President's Special Assistant for National Security Affairs: Objectives of Dr. Edward Mason's Mission to the United Arab Republic and United Arab Republic Expectations," 27 Feb. 1962; Komer, "Memorandum to President Kennedy: Visit of Ed Mason to the UAR," 28 Feb. 1962; and Rusk, "Memorandum to President Kennedy: Economic Action Program for the United Arab Republic," 31 Mar. 1962, all in FRUS, 1961–1963, 17:497–500, 500–501, and 566–69. On Bowles's visit with Nasser see memorandum from the deputy assistant secretary of state for Near Eastern and South Asian affairs to the president's special representative and adviser on African, Asian, and Latin American affairs, 6 Feb. 1962; telegram from the embassy in Sudan to the Department of State, 19 Feb. 1962; and airgram from the embassy in Ethiopia to the Department of State, 21 Feb.

1962, all in FRUS, 1961–1963, 17:465–67, 478–79, and 481–89. On Kaissouni's trip to Washington, see FRUS, 1961–163, 17:637–46. For an assessment of the U.S.-Egyptian relationship following the exchange visits, see Department of State, "Whither United States–United Arab Republic Relations," 24 May 1962, FRUS, 1961–1963, 17:677–82. Komer, "Memorandum to President Kennedy," 28 May 1962, FRUS, 1961–1963, 17: 686–87.

67. Two brief reviews of the conflict in Yemen are Brands, *Into the Labyrinth*, 84–87; and Cleveland, *A History of the Modern Middle East*, 306 and 438–39. On Egypt's alleged use of chemical weapons and its impact on U.S. politicians, see Robert Komer to McGeorge Bundy, 15 July 1963; and Komer to President Kennedy, 18 July 1963, both in General, 6/63–8/63, Box 169, UAR, Country File, National Security File, President's Office Files, JFKL. I have found no other primary or secondary sources that make or verify this claim, and both of the above sources place the words "poison gas" within quotation marks.

68. On Johnson and Nasser's dislike for each other, see Little, "Nasser Delenda Est." On Nasser's perceptions of the U.S. role in the 1967 war, see Fawaz Gerges, "The 1967 Arab-Israeli War: U.S. Actions and Arab Perceptions," in Lesch, *The Middle East and the United States*, 186–92.

69. Burns, *Economic Aid and American Policy toward Egypt*, 149.

70. Ibid., 215 and 126. All figures are taken from Owen and Pamuk, *A History of Middle Eastern Economies in the Twentieth Century*, 252. The annual growth rates between 1959/60 and 1964/64 in electricity, construction, and communications were 14.0, 16.6, and 11.3 percent, respectively. Komer to Bundy, 15 July 1963.

71. See William Gaud Oral History, 7–8.

72. T. Cuyler Young, "Iran in Continuing Crisis," *Foreign Affairs* 40, no. 2 (Jan. 1962): 278, 279, and 281. John W. Bowling, "The Current Internal Political Situation in Iran," 11 Feb. 1961, FRUS, 1961–1963, 17:56–65, 56–57. "Editorial Note," FRUS, 1961–1963, 17:98–99, on the formation of the Iran Task Force.

73. Robert W. Komer, "Memorandum to President Johnson," 15 Apr. 1965, FRUS, 1964–1968, 22:139–40.

74. Gerald F. Winfield, "A Proposal to Use TV to Teach Development Economics to Strengthen the New Premier of Iran," 31 May 1961, Iran, General, 23 May–31 May 1961, Box 115, Country File, National Security File, President's Office Files, JFKL.

75. K. R. Hansen, memorandum for W. W. Rostow, 13 June 1961, Iran, General, June 1961, Box 115, Country File, National Security File, President's Office Files, JFKL.

76. "Memorandum of Conversation: President Kennedy and Lieutenant General Tiemur Bakhtiar," 1 Mar. 1961; "Memorandum of Conversation: The Shah of Iran and W. Averell Harriman," 13 Apr. 1962; all in FRUS, 1961–1963, 17:38–41, 605–6. On Kennedy's discussions with the shah, see "Memorandum of Conversation," 12 Apr. 1962, and "Memorandum of Conversation," 13 Apr. 1962, both in FRUS, 1961–1963, 17:590–98 and 606–10. See also Bill, *The Eagle and the Lion*, 132–49, for a good overview

of Kennedy-era relations with the shah and the shah's attempts at reform in the early 1960s.

77. Denney, "The Roots of Arab Resistance to Modernization," 27 and 31.

78. Ibid., i–iii.

Chapter Five

1. William Eddy to General Greunther, reprinted in Cohen, "William A. Eddy, the Oil Lobby and the Palestine Problem," 175.

2. See Davidson, *America's Palestine*, 11–21, which includes the quotations from the Balfour Declaration.

3. For background on Miller and his critique of O. J. Campbell's "Report on Zionism," see Gelfand, *The Inquiry*, 51–52 and 246. Alfred L. P. Dennis, "Memorandum on the Syrian Question," quoted in Gelfand, *The Inquiry*, 251.

4. "The King-Crane Commission Report," 28 Aug. 1919, http://www.gwpda.org/1918p/kncr.htm.

5. Schoenbaum, *The United States and the State of Israel*, 18. I also draw from Davidson, *America's Palestine*, 48–52, and Christison, *Perceptions of Palestine*, 36–38, for my discussion of the 1922 resolution.

6. Dulles quoted in Davidson, *America's Palestine*, 56.

7. See Schoenbaum, *The United States and the State of Israel*, 19, for membership figures.

8. Anderson, *Biblical Interpretation and Middle East Policy*, 30–31 and 19.

9. Leonard Stein, "The Jews in Palestine," *Foreign Affairs* 4, no. 3 (April 1926): 415–32.

10. For a discussion of the broader Zionist effort to portray the late 1920s as a period of growing calm and as an indicator of the future, as well as discussion of opposition to that interpretive framework, see Davidson, *America's Palestine*, 65–75. Stein, "The Jews in Palestine," 417, 423–24, 425, 429, and 431.

11. My description of these events, including the casualty figures, is drawn largely from Davidson, *America's Palestine*, 82–92.

12. Henry W. Nevinson, "Arabs and Jews in Palestine," *Foreign Affairs* 8, no. 2 (Jan. 1930): 225, 226, and 233.

13. Felix Frankfurter, "The Palestine Situation Restated," *Foreign Affairs* 9, no. 3 (Apr. 1931): 410.

14. Ibid., 421, 423, and 434.

15. For an early acknowledgement of the potential tensions over the expansion of Jewish immigration, see Sir Andrew McFaydean, "Immigration and Labor in Palestine," *Foreign Affairs* 12, no. 4 (July 1934): 682–88. On the broader implications of the tensions of the mid-1930s, see Davidson, *America's Palestine*, 108–37. For two other contemporary discussions of the prospects for partition, see Viscount Samuel, "The Palestine Report: Alternatives to Partition," *Foreign Affairs* 16, no. 1 (Oct. 1937): 143–55;

and H. St. John B. Philby, "The Palestine Report: The Arabs and the Future of Palestine," *Foreign Affairs* 16, no. 1 (Oct. 1937): 156–66.

16. For documents relating to the State Department's response to the events of the mid-1930s, see FRUS, 1936, 3:433–59 and FRUS 1937, 2:881–922.

17. On anti-Zionist Jews and Arab-American opposition, see Davidson, *America's Palestine*, 34–38, 102–4, and 119–22.

18. Wallace Murray to Edward R. Stettinius, 27 Oct. 1944, FRUS, 1944, 5:625. For other examples, see memorandum by the director of the Office of Near Eastern and African Affairs to the secretary of state, 24 Aug. 1945, FRUS, 1945, 8:728; "Memorandum: Views of the Department of State Concerning American Promises Regarding Palestine," 2 Oct. 1945, FRUS, 1945, 8:755; the discussion of a memorandum from Loy Henderson to Robert Lovett, 24 Sept. 1947, contained in FRUS, 1947, 5:666, n. 1; and Richard Sanger, "Memorandum of Conversation," 26 Dec. 1947, FRUS, 1947, 5:668. "Memorandum by the Joint Chiefs of Staff to the State-War-Navy Coordinating Committee," 21 June 1946, FRUS, 1946, 7:632–33, though not originating from within the network, also fits into this vein. Duce, via Loy Henderson to Secretary of State George C. Marshall, 26 May 1948, quoted in Yergin, *The Prize*, 426.

19. On the impact that Henderson's years dealing with Soviet affairs had on him and his approach to the Middle East and other issues, see Brands, *Inside the Cold War*. Memorandum, Henderson to Acheson, 21 Oct. 1946, FRUS, 1946, 7:712. Memorandum, Henderson to the secretary of state, 22 Sept. 1947, FRUS, 1947, 5:1153–54. For a reiteration of these points, see memorandum, Henderson to Lovett, 24 Nov. 1947, FRUS, 1947, 5:1281–82.

20. Memorandum, Henderson to Acheson, 1 Oct. 1945, FRUS, 1945, 8:752. Memorandum by the chief of the Division of Near Eastern Affairs to the under secretary of state, 8 May 1946, FRUS, 1946, 7:598.

21. Memorandum, Henderson to Acheson, 21 Oct. 1946, FRUS, 1946, 7:712; and memorandum, Henderson to the secretary of state, 22 Sept. 1947, FRUS, 1947, 5:1155. Merriam to Loy Henderson, 27 Dec. 1946, FRUS, 1946, 7:732. CIA, "ORE 49: The Current Situation in Palestine," 20 Oct. 1947, 1, Intelligence Publication File HRP 92–4/001, Box 1, Estimates of the Office of Research Evaluation, 1946–50, RG 263. CIA, "ORE 7–48: Possible Developments in Palestine," 28 Feb. 1948, 6, Intelligence Publication File HRP 92–4/001, Box 1, Estimates of the Office of Research Evaluation, 1946–50, RG 263.

22. Memorandum, Henderson to the secretary of state, 22 Sept. 1947, FRUS, 1947, 5:1154–56.

23. See Roosevelt, *Arabs, Oil, and History*, 173–95, for his views on Palestine.

24. Tivnan, *The Lobby*, 23. "President Truman to the British Prime Minister," 8 May 1946, FRUS, 1946, 7:596–97.

25. Kolsky, *Jews against Zionism*, ix. Grose, *Israel in the Mind of America*, 226, claims Sulzberger was essentially one of the founding members of the group. Elmer Berger

recalls, however, that Sulzberger believed "it would not be wise to be so closely associated with a partisan view in such a controversial issue. But the paper, we were as-
sured, would give fair and even sympathetic coverage to our views." Berger, *Memoirs of
an Anti-Zionist Jew*, 14.

The distinction between Reform Judaism and traditional Judaism is critical, as most
anti-Zionist Jews initially came from the Reform group. Reform Judaism emerged in
Europe after the French Revolution, and embraced its ideas of liberty, equality, and
fraternity. There are many distinguishing features, but the most important for this
discussion are: Reform Judaism affirmed the traditional idea of divine revelation but
argued that it did not mean every word in the Bible should be interpreted literally,
as God's direct words; Reform Judaism rejected the notion that Jews were a separate
people and submitted instead that they were "chosen" only as being messengers of
God; Reform Jews believed that human reasoning and the development of democratic
processes would allow Jews to live in equality with others in any country and, thus,
Jews did not need a separate nation of their own. This last point also indicated that
Jews should be loyal to the nations in which they lived, rather than reserve their loyalty for a Jewish state. Reform Judaism, under the leadership of I. M. Wise, gained a
large following within the United States in the latter half of the nineteenth century.
The movement began to be challenged between 1880 and 1920, however, when large
numbers of Jewish immigrants from Eastern Europe—where Jews had traditionally
been treated as a people apart—arrived in the United States. Those immigrants that
joined Reform Judaism pushed it toward a stance that acknowledged Jewish unique-
ness and separateness. But it was not until the narrow passage of the Columbus Plat-
form in 1937 that Reform Judaism in the U.S. made an official statement in support
of a Jewish homeland in Palestine. Between 1937 and 1943, a spirited debate over the
issue continued, but as news of the Holocaust emerged, and as a Jewish state came
nearer to a reality in the 1940s, Reform Jews increasingly supported the creation of
a Jewish state. The ACJ was created by a group of Reform rabbis who continued to
adhere to the well-established antinationalist Reform point of view. See Norton Mezvinsky, "Reform Judaism and Zionism: Early History and Change," in Tekiner, Abed-
Rabbo, and Mezvinsky, *Anti-Zionism*, 313–39, and Kolsky, *Jews against Zionism*. Berger,
Memoirs of an Anti-Zionist Jew, 12.

26. On Levison and his government contacts, see Kolsky, *Jews against Zionism*,
138–39. Kolsky, *Jews against Zionism*, 136–37. Telegram, the acting secretary of state
(Acheson) to the charge in the United Kingdom (Gallman), 30 Aug. 1946, FRUS, 1946,
7:690–91.

27. Good discussions of the activities of the American Zionist Emergency Council,
and of postwar Jewish lobbying efforts more generally, can be found in Grose, *Israel in
the Mind of America*, 172–76, and Tivnan, *The Lobby*, 24–28.

28. Davidson, *America's Palestine*, 147.

29. Chaim Weizmann, "Palestine's Role in the Solution of the Jewish Problem," *For-*

eign Affairs 20, no. 2 (Jan. 1942): 324–38. *The Gallup Poll: Public Opinion, 1935–1971*, vol. 1 (New York: Random House, 1972), 554 and 584.

30. Davidson, *America's Palestine*, 130–31. Grose, *Israel in the Mind of America*, 113–16 and 145–48. For one version of the statement, see letter from the minister in Iraq to the secretary of state, 11 Mar. 1944, FRUS, 1944, 5:588. Grose, *Israel in the Mind of America*, 145, also contains portions of the statement. On the protests by Middle Eastern leaders and U.S. diplomats to the statement and the congressional resolutions, see FRUS, 1944, 5:580–91. The secretary of state to the minister resident in Saudi Arabia, 13 Mar. 1944, FRUS, 1944, 5:589–90. Memorandum of conversation between the king of Saudi Arabia and President Roosevelt, 14 Feb. 1945, FRUS, 1945, 8:2.

31. Five excellent accounts of the evolution of Truman's thinking on Palestine that reach different conclusions about his motivations are Cohen, *Truman and Israel*; McCullough, *Truman*, 595–620; Schoenbaum, *The United States and the State of Israel*, 34–62; Spiegel, *The Other Arab-Israeli Conflict*, 16–49; and Davidson, *America's Palestine*, chapter 8. See, for example, memorandum by the president's special counsel to President Truman, 8 Mar. 1948, FRUS, 1948, 5:690; and memorandum of conversation, 12 May 1948, FRUS, 1948, 5:975. For a more general discussion of this issue, see Snetsinger, *Truman, the Jewish Vote and the Creation of Israel*. Spiegel, *The Other Arab-Israeli Conflict*, 19–20, and Brands, *Into the Labyrinth*, 25. Rusk, *As I Saw It*, 147.

32. Good overviews of the State Department and White House policies during this period are Brands, *Into the Labyrinth*, 19–30; Schoenbaum, *The United States and the State of Israel*, chapter 2; and Spiegel, *The Other Arab-Israeli Conflict*, 20–38. Truman, quoted in Davidson, *America's Palestine*, 173. Memorandum by the director of the Office of Near Eastern and African affairs to the secretary of state, and memorandum by the chief of the Division of Near Eastern Affairs, both dated 31 Aug. 1945, FRUS, 1945, 8:734–36.

33. The most explicit statement of government Middle East specialists' resistance to the partition plan is a paper that Loy Henderson presented to Secretary of State George Marshall, a paper with which, according to Henderson, all members of Near Eastern Affairs concurred. Henderson to Marshall, 22 Sept. 1947, and the attached paper, "Certain Considerations against Advocacy by the U.S. of the Majority Plan," FRUS, 1947, 5:1153–58. Clifford was a political operative whose main focus was to ensure Truman's election in 1948, and Niles was a Jewish immigrant from Poland who, according to historian Lawrence Davidson, was Truman's "advisor on minority affairs" and his liaison with the Jewish community. The level of Truman's involvement in the attempt to sway votes is unclear. Christison, *Perceptions of Palestine*, 69–72; Davidson, *America's Palestine*, 175 and 187; and Grose, *Israel in the Mind of America*, 248–54.

34. Zionists had even contacted Truman's mother and sister in hopes they would convince him to support partition. Ferrell, *Off the Record*, 65–66 and 127. Both Schoenbaum, *The United States and the State of Israel*, 59, and Spiegel, *The Other Arab-Israeli Conflict*, 34, confirm that Truman made this secret pledge to Weizmann.

35. On the issue of anti-Semitism in the State Department, see Richard D. Breitman

and Alan M. Kraut, "Anti-Semitism in the State Department, 1933–1944: Four Case Studies," in Gerber, *Anti-Semitism in American History*, 167–97. They conclude that while some State Department employees likely were anti-Semitic, such sentiments were rarely the determining factor in the formation of U.S. policy. See also Christison, *Perceptions of Palestine*, especially 34–35, where she addresses the issue going back to the Wilson presidency; and Kaplan, *The Arabists*, 7, 19, and 86–90. Harry S. Truman, *Years of Trial and Hope*, 165. Hart quoted in Joseph Kraft, "Those Arabists in the State Department," *New York Times Magazine*, 7 Nov. 1971, 82.

36. On the blocking of Henderson's appointment as U.S. ambassador to Turkey, see Davidson, *America's Palestine*, 219.

37. Hahn, *Caught in the Middle East*.

38. Eisenhower and Dulles stressed the administration's desire to pursue an impartial policy in the Arab-Israeli conflict on numerous occasions. See, for example, the memorandum of conversation from Dulles's meeting with Lebanese officials, 16 May 1953, FRUS, 1952–1954, 9:75; memorandum of discussion at the 147th Meeting of the NSC, 1 June 1953, FRUS, 1952–1954, 9:385–86; and the memorandum of conversation between the secretary of state and the president, 21 Apr. 1954, FRUS, 1952–1954, 9:1528–29. See also Spiegel, *The Other Arab-Israeli Conflict*, 50–54, and Schoenbaum, *The United States and the State of Israel*, 92. For specific examples of opposition to Israeli policies, see documentation in FRUS, 1952–1954, 9:1319–20; 1403–09; 1432–34; 1442–44; and 1590–91. See also Deborah J. Gerner, "Missed Opportunities and Roads Not Taken: The Eisenhower Administration and the Palestinians," in Suleiman, *U.S. Policy on Palestine*, 97–99 and 101–4.

39. Michelle Mart, "Tough Guys and American Cold War Policy," 357, 359, and 360. For a lengthier treatment of the cultural construction of Israel as a U.S. ally, see Mart, *Eye On Israel*. On the image of the "weak" Jew, see Breines, *Tough Jews*.

40. Hunt, *Ideology and U.S. Foreign Policy*. Department of State, "The Potential Military Manpower in the Arab States and Israel," 27 Dec. 1950, FRUS, 1951, 5:12–13.

41. For contemporary comparisons between Arabs and Israelis on these issues, Vera Micheles Dean, "Israel and Egypt: Two Enemies—Same Goals," *Foreign Policy Bulletin*, 1 Oct. 1955, 9–11 and 16; Foreign Policy Forum, "Three Views on Israel," *Foreign Policy Bulletin*, 15 Mar. 1957, 101–3; and Don Peretz, "Israel's First Decade: 1948–1958," *Foreign Policy Bulletin*, 1 Apr. 1958, 109–12.

42. Berger, *Memoirs of an Anti-Zionist Jew*, 27–49. See also Elmer Berger, "Zionist Ideology: Obstacle to Peace," in Tekiner, Abed-Rabbo, and Mezvinsky, *Anti-Zionism*, 1–32.

43. Kolsky, *Jews against Zionism*, 191–92, and Berger, *Memoirs of an Anti-Zionist Jew*, 40–44.

44. L. D. Battle to McGeorge Bundy, 19 June 1961, Memoranda to the White House, Box 4, Office of Near Eastern Affairs, Records of the Director, 1958–63, Bureau of Near Eastern Affairs and South Asian Affairs, RG 59.

45. On Dorothy Thompson's relationship with AFME, and for her views on the

Middle East more broadly, see Kurth, *American Cassandra*, 422–30, and Sanders, *Dorothy Thompson*, 334–41. Department of State memorandum, Shepard Jones to Mr. Henry Byroade, 15 Aug. 1952, American Friends of the Middle East, Box 4, Office of the Director for Regional Matters, 1954–66, Bureau of Near Eastern Affairs and South Asian Affairs, RG 59. The description of the founding of AFME is taken from this document, from Kurth, *American Cassandra*, 422–28, and Sanders, *Dorothy Thompson*, 335–38. American Friends of the Middle East, Inc., "First Annual Report of the Executive Vice President to the Board of Directors and the National Council of the American Friends of the Middle East, Inc., May 15, 1951 to June 30, 1952," (New York: AFME, Inc., 1952), 18; American Friends of the Middle East, Inc., "Third Annual Report of the Executive Vice President to the Board of Directors and the National Council of the American Friends of the Middle East, Inc., July 1, 1953 to June 30, 1954," (New York: AFME, Inc., 1954), 41; and each of the subsequent years.

46. For an example of a letter from Garland Evans Hopkins (executive vice president of AFME) to the secretary of state, written in a language that demonstrates a certain level of familiarity between the two, see Hopkins to John Foster Dulles, 19 June 1953, Decimal file 611.80/6-1953, RG 59. For an example of a meeting between representatives of AFME and upper-level State Department employees (including the secretary of state) concerned with Middle Eastern affairs, see memorandum of conversation, "Views of Three American Editors regarding Middle East Problems," 8 Jan. 1954, Decimal File 611.80/1 854, RG 59. Kurth, *American Cassandra*, 422, mentions that the CIA funded the AFME.

47. Damon to Sanger, 2 Apr. 1953, and Sanger to Damon, 3 Apr. 1953, and memorandum from Richard Sanger to Mr. Allen, 21 Jan. 1955, all in "American Friends of the Middle East," Box 4, Records Relating to Regional Matters, 1954–66, Office of the Director for Regional Affairs (NEA/RA), Bureau of Near Eastern Affairs and South Asian Affairs, RG 59. Kurth, *American Cassandra*, 446, and Sanders, *Dorothy Thompson*, 340–41. A current description of AMIDEAST, including its mission statement, can be found at www.amideast.org.

48. Hoskins, *The Middle East*, 107. See also Campbell, *Defense of the Middle East*, 81–84.

49. Campbell, *Defense of the Middle East*, 321. Vera Micheles Dean, "Egypt: Nation in Search of Personality," *Foreign Policy Bulletin* 15 Oct. 1955, 24.

50. Henry Byroade, "The Middle East in New Perspective," speech before the Dayton, Ohio, World Affairs Council, 9 Apr. 1954, *Department of State Bulletin* XXX, no. 774 (26 Apr. 1954): 632, and also excerpted in *Time*, 19 Apr. 1954, 35. See Campbell, *Defense of the Middle East*, 301–4, on these points and for an overall assessment of the Arab-Israeli conflict that is quite similar to Byroade's.

51. Byroade, "The Middle East in New Perspective," 632.

52. The best overview of the rise of the Israel lobby in the United States in the 1950s is Tivnan, *The Lobby*, 29–51. For a more controversial take, see Mearsheimer and Walt, *The Israeli Lobby and U.S. Foreign Policy*.

53. For information on Goldmann, see Tivnan, *The Lobby*, 23, 26–7, and 40–1. Edwin Wright, who was a vocal anti-Zionist and adamantly opposed to the Jewish lobby, claims to have helped Byroade draft the 1954 speech. For Wright's account, see the Wright oral history available at http://www.trumanlibrary.org/oralhist/wright.htm.

54. There has been much debate, in both scholarly and policy circles, about the causes of the refugee problem, specifically over whether the refugees voluntarily vacated their homes and land or whether the Israelis forced them to flee. The best work on the subject is Benny Morris, *The Birth of the Palestinian Refugee Problem*, though Morris later reconsidered some of his assertions in *The Birth of the Palestinian Refugee Problem Revisited*. Morris concludes that a combination of factors—voluntary departure, fleeing to avoid military battles, Arab evacuation orders, and forced evacuations by the Israeli Defense Force—created this very real human tragedy. The United States consistently footed the majority of the bill for U.N. relief efforts for Palestinians. Even after relief efforts were scaled back in the late 1950s and early 1960s, the United States still paid about $23 million annually, or about 70 percent of United Nations Relief and Works Agency funds for Palestine. See "Circular Telegram from the Department of State to Certain Near Eastern and North African Posts," 15 Apr. 1961, FRUS, 1961, 17:85.

55. Georgiana G. Stevens, "Arab Refugees: 1948–1952," *Middle East Journal* 6, no. 3 (Summer 1952): 288. Stevens estimated that as much as 65 percent of the refugees lived outside the camps. See Stevens, "Arab Refugees," 290. Don Peretz, "The Arab Refugee Dilemma," *Foreign Affairs* 33, no. 1 (Oct. 1954): 134.

56. Stevens, "Arab Refugees," 290–91.

57. Peretz contended that by 1954, the final year of the U.N. plan, only 10 percent of the allocation had been used for its intended purpose and "not even 3,000 Palestinians" had "been made self-sufficient." Peretz, "The Arab Refugee Dilemma," 140. For a broader discussion of the problems of repatriation and the need for an economic solution, see Peretz, "The Arab Refugee Dilemma," 137–48, and Stevens, "Arab Refugees," 291–93.

58. For the basic outline of the "Johnson Plan," named after Joseph Johnson, see memorandum from Acting Secretary of State Bowles to President Kennedy, 28 Apr. 1961; and "Editorial Note," both in FRUS, 1961–1963, 17:91–92, and 221–22, respectively. See Zaha Bustami, "The Kennedy-Johnson Administrations and the Palestinian People," in Suleiman, *U.S. Policy on Palestine*, 114, for the text of the relevant paragraph of the 1948 U.N. resolution. Bustami also presents a good overview of the Kennedy and Johnson administrations' approaches to the refugee issue.

59. Komer to McGeorge Bundy, 14 Sept. 1962, Komer, 9/62–10/62, Staff Memoranda, Meetings and Memoranda; Komer to Carl Kaysen, 22 Sept. 1962, Palestine Refugees, General, 8/62–9/62, Box 148, Palestine, Country File; Komer to President Kennedy, 5 Dec. 1962, Palestine Refugees, General, 12/62–11/63, Box 148, Palestine, Country File, all in National Security File, President's Office Files, JFKL.

60. See Khalidi, *Palestinian Identity* for a good overview of the rise of Palestinian nationalism.

61. Campbell, *Defense of the Middle East*, 297. Cremeans, *The Arabs and the World*, 180. See "Study Group Reports: Arab Foreign Policy," fourth meeting, 28 Feb. 1961, CFR.

62. Regarding French weapons sales to Israel, consider that in early 1956 President Eisenhower decided that the United States had "no objection" to France's sale of twelve jet fighters to Israel. Eisenhower later complained, however, that those twelve jets "would display a rabbitlike capacity for multiplication." See Eisenhower, *Waging Peace*, 29.

63. See Little, "The Making of a Special Relationship," 567–73. Memorandum of conversation, 27 June 1960; and memorandum from the under secretary of state for political affairs to the secretary of state, 15 July 1960, both in FRUS, 1958–1960, 13:341–44 and 349–50, respectively. Memorandum of conversation, 8 May 1961; and memorandum of conversation between President Kennedy and Prime Minister Ben Gurion, 30 May 1961; both in FRUS, 1961–1963, 17:102–3 and 135–37, respectively.

64. On opposition to selling HAWKs to Israel, see memorandum from the assistant secretary of state for Near Eastern and South Asian affairs to the under secretary of state for political affairs, 7 July 1960, FRUS, 1958–1960, 13:344–49. Memorandum from the assistant secretary of state for Near Eastern and South Asian affairs to Secretary of State Rusk, 7 June 1962, and the attached paper entitled "Israel and United States Policy"; telegram from the embassy in Greece to the Department of State, 15 June 1962, which summarized the views of the annual Conference of Chiefs of Mission to Near Eastern and North African Countries; memorandum from the acting assistant secretary of state for Near Eastern and South Asian affairs to Secretary of State Rusk, 17 June 1962; and memorandum from Robert W. Komer of the NSC Staff to the president's special assistant for national security affairs, 22 June 1962, all available in FRUS, 1961–1963, 17:710–18, 728–30, 734–36, and 747–48, respectively. See also memorandum from Secretary of State Rusk to President Kennedy, 7 Aug. 1962, and the attached paper, "United States Policy toward Israel," FRUS, 1961–1963, 18:27–32. "Circular Telegram from the Department of State to Certain Posts," 14 Sept. 1962, and memorandum from Robert W. Komer to the president's special assistant for national security affairs, 14 Sept. 1962, both in FRUS, 1961–1963, 18:94–95, and 96–97, respectively.

65. On State Department Middle East specialists' position on arms sales to Jordan and Israel, see memorandum of conversation, 25 Jan. 1965, and memorandum from Secretary of State Rusk to President Johnson, 1 Feb. 1965, along with the attached papers on the problem, which were drafted by specialists, all in FRUS, 1964–1968, 18:277–81, and 283–87, respectively.

66. For the American perspective on the first mission, see memorandum for Robert W. Komer of the NSC staff, 10 Feb. 1965; telegram from the embassy in Israel

to the Department of State, 13 Feb. 1965; telegram from the Department of State to the embassy in Israel, 13 Feb. 1965; telegram from the embassy in Israel to the Department of State, 15 Feb. 1965; and memorandum from Robert W. Komer of the NSC Staff to President Johnson, 16 Feb. 1965. All in FRUS, 1964–1968, 18:323–28, 330–32, and 334–36. On the choice of Harriman and the problem of his notoriety, see memorandum of telephone conversation, George Ball and the President, 5:15 p.m., 7 Feb., 1965, "Jordan [4/14/64–3/12/65]," Box 4, George Ball Papers, LBJL.

67. Robert Komer oral history, 50 and 49. Memorandum of telephone conversation, George Ball and John D. Jernegan, 7 Feb. 1965, Jordan [4/14/64–3/1265], Box 4, George Ball Papers, LBJL. Komer oral history, 52–54. See also Robert Komer, memorandum for the record, conversation with Israeli Minister Gazit, 14 May 1963, FRUS, 1961–1963, 18:535–38.

68. For Komer's support of the initiative to aid Nasser, see Komer to Walt Rostow, 2 June 1961, General, 1/61–6/61, United Arab Republic, Box 168, Country File, and Komer to McGeorge Bundy, and attached memorandum for the president, 8 Dec. 1961, General, 11/61–12/61, United Arab Republic, Box 168, Country File, both in National Security File, President's Office Files, JFKL. Memorandum of telephone conversation, George Ball and the president, 5:25 p.m., 7 Feb. 1965, Jordan [4/14/64–3/12/65], Box 4, George Ball Papers, LBJL.

69. Memorandum of conversation, 14 Jan. 1965, FRUS, 1964–1968, 18:269–71. Telegram from the embassy in Lebanon to the Department of State, 5 Feb. 1965, FRUS, 1964–1968, 18:298–302.

70. Ibid.

71. For Peretz's own take on his early career, see Don Peretz, "Vignettes — Bits and Pieces," in Naff, *Paths to the Middle East*, 231–61. Don Peretz, "The Arab Refugees: A Changing Problem," *Foreign Affairs* 41, no. 3 (Apr. 1963): 558–70.

72. Peretz, "The Arab Refugees," 558, 559, and 560–65.

73. CIA, "Israel, the Arab States, and Palestine 'Liberation' Activities," 3 Dec. 1965, 1, Israel, vol. V, Memos and Miscellaneous, 12/65–9/66, Box 139, Middle East, Country File. Telegram from the American embassy in Israel to the secretary of state, 8 Sept. 1965, Israel, vol. IV, 2/65–11/65 (2 of 2), Box 139, Middle East, Country File. Memorandum from Walt Rostow for Henry Wilson, 19 Sept. 1966, based on an overview of the Palestine Liberation Army provided by White House Middle East specialist Harold Saunders, 16 Sept. 1966. Both documents are attached to a covering memorandum from Saunders to Rostow, 19 Sept. 1966, Israel, vol. VI, Memos, 12/66–7/67, Box 140–141, Middle East, Country File. All available in the National Security File, LBJL.

74. See Charles W. Yost, "The Arab-Israeli War: How It Began," *Foreign Affairs* 46, no. 2 (Jan. 1968): 304 and 318; and Badeau, *The American Approach to the Arab World*, 169–70. Don Peretz, "Arab Palestine: Phoenix or Phantom," *Foreign Affairs* 48, no. 2 (Jan. 1970), 325–27. On this same point, see Donald Bergus of the U.S. embassy in Cairo to the Department of State, Aug. 1968, Visitors — 1968 (WWR), I, Box 17–18,

Rostow Files, National Security File, LBJL. Bergus argued that Israel's "basic fallacy" was "its failure to recognize emergence of Palestinianism as a political and military force which is self-financing, capable of intimidating Arab rulers (including once-mighty Nasser), with far-flung capabilities, and increasing imagination" (ibid. 2). Peretz made an explicit call to include Palestinians in the negotiating process in "Arab Palestine," 333. See discussion at a Council on Foreign Relations study group on the Middle East in the aftermath of the third round, sixth meeting, 16 Apr. 1968, CFR.

75. Bernard Lewis, "The Arab-Israeli War: The Consequences of Defeat," *Foreign Affairs* 46, no. 2 (Jan. 1968): 334–35. John C. Campbell, "The Arab-Israeli Conflict: An American Policy," *Foreign Affairs* 49, no. 1 (Oct. 1970): 52. See also Lewis, "The Arab-Israeli War: The Consequences of Defeat," 331.

76. Council on Foreign Relations study group on "U.S. Policy in the Middle East," third meeting, 16 June 1969, 20, CFR. Campbell, "The Arab-Israeli Conflict," 53–54.

77. Campbell floated the idea in several different places. See, for example, Campbell, "The Arab-Israeli Conflict," his working paper for a CFR study group on U.S. policy in the Middle East, called "The Arab-Israeli Conflict: Long-Term Considerations," and on which the *Foreign Affairs* article is based; see also "The Middle East: U.S. Policy in the Absence of a Settlement," prepared for the State Department's Policy Planning Council, Dec. 1968, "Transition: Policy Planning Council Paper—Middle East," Box 50, Subject File, National Security File, LBJL. Lewis suggested this policy in two separate articles, "The Consequences of Defeat," and "The Great Powers, the Arabs, and the Israelis," *Foreign Affairs* 47, no 4 (July 1969): 652.

Epilogue

1. Harold H. Saunders, "Memorandum for the Record: Conversation with John Badeau," 5 Mar. 1969, and Harold H. Saunders, "Memorandum for the Record: Talk with Professor Morroe Berger," 5 Mar. 1968, both in Saunders Memos, Box 7, Name File, National Security File, LBJL. Thomas L. Hughes to the secretary of state, 24 Sept. 1968, POL 3 Arab League, 1/1/67, Box 1844, Political Defense, Subject-Numeric Files, Central Foreign Policy Files, RG 59.

2. Kraft, "Those Arabists in the State Department," *New York Times Magazine*, 7 Nov. 1971, 82, 88, 89, and 92. The term "Arabist" originally referred to anyone who was trained in the Arabic language and made the study of the Middle East his or her life's work. Over the last four decades, however, it has been used in a more specific and derogatory manner to refer to those government Middle East specialists, most with Arabic-language training, who have spent extensive time in the Middle East and are seen to identify with the Arab cause or generally to be "pro-Arab." In addition to Kraft on this point, see Kaplan, *The Arabists*, and Parker, "The Arabists." Curtis F. Jones, "The Education of an Arabist," *Foreign Service Journal* 59, no. 11 (Dec. 1982): 19 and 31. For his critiques of U.S. policy, see Curtis F. Jones, "The Questionable Alliance," *Foreign Service*

Journal 62, no. 2 (Feb. 1985): 17–21, as well as his various contributions to the online journal *American Diplomacy*, http://www.unc.edu/depts/diplomat.

3. Peretz, "Vignettes—Bits and Pieces," 254. Johnson and Tucker, "Middle East Studies Network in the United States," 20. See also Hajjar and Niva, "(Re)Made in the USA," which was a follow-up report on the state of the field.

4. Patai, *The Arab Mind*, and Said, *Orientalism*. For a broader discussion of the impact of Said and *Orientalism*, see Lockman, *Contending Visions of the Middle East*, especially 182–214. On Ajami, his role as an advisor to both Bush administrations and his feud with Said, see Adam Shatz, "The Native Informant," *The Nation* (28 Apr. 2003): 15–28.

5. Kramer, *Ivory Towers on Sand*. Juan Cole, "Informed Comment," available at www.juancole.com. See also Juan Cole, *Engaging the Muslim World*, which addresses the current state of knowledge production about the region and provides his thoughts on contemporary U.S.–Middle East relations. Richard Bernstein, "Experts on Islam Pointing Fingers at One Another," *New York Times*, 3 Nov. 2001.

6. McAlister, *Epic Encounters*, 157.

7. For a revealing assessment of Rumsfeld and the biblical headers on intelligence reports, see Robert Draper, "And He Shall Be Judged," *GQ*, June 2009, http://men.style.com/gq/features/landing?id=content_9217.

BIBLIOGRAPHY

Primary Sources

MANUSCRIPT COLLECTIONS

Abilene, Kans.
  Dwight D. Eisenhower Library
    John Foster Dulles Papers
    Dwight D. Eisenhower Papers as President (Ann Whitman File)
    Dwight D. Eisenhower Records as President, White House Central Files
    C. D. Jackson Papers
    C. D. Jackson Records
    White House Office Files
      National Security Council Staff, Papers
      Office of the Special Assistant for National Security Affairs, Records
      Office of the Staff Secretary, Records
Austin, Tex.
  Lyndon Baines Johnson Library
    George Ball Papers
    McGeorge Bundy Papers
    Lyndon Baines Johnson Archives
      Pre-Presidential Papers
      Presidential Papers
    Tom Johnson Notes of Meetings
    Henry Cabot Lodge Correspondence
    National Security Files
    David G. Nes Correspondence
    Walt W. Rostow Papers
    White House Central Files
Boston, Mass.
  John F. Kennedy Library
    McGeorge Bundy Papers
    John Fitzgerald Kennedy Papers

National Security Files
 Country Files
 Robert W. Komer Files
Pre-Presidential Papers
President's Office Files
White House Central Files
White House Staff Files
Dean Rusk Papers
James C. Thomson Papers
College Park, Md.
 National Archives,
  Record Group 59: General Records of the U.S. Department of State
  Decimal File
  Middle East Lot Files
  Miscellaneous Lot Files
  Records of the Bureau of Intelligence and Research
  Records of the Foreign Service Posts of the Department of State
  Records of Offices Responsible for Near Eastern, South Asian, and African
   Affairs
  Records of Secretaries of State and Principal Officers of the Department of
   State
  Subject Numeric Files
 Record Group 273: Records of the National Security Council
 Record Group 283: Records of the Central Intelligence Agency
 Record Group 286: Records of the Agency for International Development
 Record Group 306: Records of the United States Information Agency
  Records of the Office of Research
 Record Group 353: Records of Interdepartmental and Intra-departmental
  Committees (Department of State)
 Record Group 469: United States Foreign Assistance Agencies, 1948–1961
Independence, Mo.
 Harry S. Truman Library
 Dean Acheson Papers
 Harry Howard Papers
 George C. McGhee Papers
 Harry S. Truman Papers
  President's Secretary's File
  Staff Member and Office Files
   Psychological Strategy Board Files
  White House Central Files

Confidential Files
Official Files
Student Research File
New York, N.Y.
Council on Foreign Relations
Records of Study Groups
Princeton, N. J.
Seeley G. Mudd Library, Princeton University
Hamilton Fish Armstrong Papers
Allen W. Dulles Papers
William A. Eddy Papers
Council on Foreign Relations Records
Washington, D.C.
Middle East Institute
General Records

ORAL HISTORIES

Author's Possession
Findley Burns
William Dale
Curtis Jones
Walt Whitman Rostow
Abilene, Kans.
Dwight D. Eisenhower Library
Gordon Gray
Raymond Hare
Austin, Tex.
Lyndon Baines Johnson Library
Lucius D. Battle
Robert W. Komer
Dean Rusk
Boston, Mass.
John F. Kennedy Library
William F. Gaud
Independence, Mo.
Harry S. Truman Library
George Allen
Henry Byroade
Loy Henderson
Harry Howard

Edwin Locke Jr.

George C. McGhee

David G. Nes

Edwin M. Wright

EDITED PAPERS AND MEMOIRS

Acheson, Dean. *Present at the Creation: My Years in the State Department*. New York: W. W. Norton, 1969.

Badeau, John S. *The Middle East Remembered*. Washington, D.C.: Middle East Institute, 1983.

Ball, George W. *The Past Has Another Pattern: Memoirs*. New York: W. W. Norton, 1982.

Berger, Elmer. *Memoirs of an Anti-Zionist Jew*. Beirut: The Institute for Palestine Studies, 1978.

Copeland, Miles. *The Game of Nations: The Amorality of Power Politics*. New York: Simon and Schuster, 1969.

Eisenhower, Dwight D. *The White House Years: Mandate for Change, 1953–1956*. Garden City, N.Y.: Doubleday, 1963.

———. *The White House Years: Waging Peace, 1956–1961*. Garden City, N.Y.: Doubleday, 1965.

Eveland, Wilbur Crane. *Ropes of Sand: America's Failure in the Middle East*. New York: W. W. Norton, 1980.

Ferrell, Robert, ed. *The Eisenhower Diaries*. New York: W. W. Norton, 1981.

———. *Off the Record: The Private Papers of Harry S. Truman*. New York: Harper & Row, 1980.

Gray, Louis Herbert, ed. *African Questions at the Paris Peace Conference, with Papers on Egypt, Mesopotamia, and the Colonial Settlement*. New York: Negro University Press, 1969. First published in 1923 by Macmillan.

Johnson, Lyndon Baines. *The Vantage Point: Perspectives of the Presidency, 1963–1969*. New York: Holt, Rinehart and Winston, 1971.

Kesaris, Paul, ed. *CIA Research Reports: The Middle East, 1946–1976*. Frederick, Md.: University Publications of America, 1979.

———. *O.S.S./State Department Intelligence and Research Reports, XII: The Middle East, 1950–1961, Supplement*. Frederick, Md.: University Publications of America, 1979.

McGhee, George C. *Envoy to the Middle World: Adventures in Diplomacy*. New York: Harper and Row, 1983.

Meyer, Karl E., ed. *Fulbright of Arkansas: The Public Positions of a Private Thinker*. Washington, D.C.: Robert B. Luce, 1963.

Murphy, Robert. *Diplomat Among Warriors*. Garden City, N.Y.: Doubleday, 1964.

Roosevelt, Archie. *For Lust of Knowing: Memoirs of an Intelligence Officer*. Boston: Little, Brown, 1988.

Rusk, Dean. *As I Saw It*. Edited by Daniel S. Papp. New York: W. W. Norton, 1990.

Truman, Harry S. *Memoirs, Volume 2: Years of Trial and Hope*. Garden City, N.Y.: Doubleday, 1956.

Van Dusen, Henry P., ed. *The Spiritual Legacy of John Foster Dulles: Selections From His Articles and Addresses*. Philadelphia: Westminster Press, 1959.

ANNUAL REPORTS, GOVERNMENT PUBLICATIONS,
NEWSPAPERS, PERIODICALS, AND SURVEYS

America

American Friends of the Middle East Annual
  Reports

Annals of the American Academy of Political
  and Social Science

Atlantic Monthly

Christian Century

Congressional Digest

Current History

Department of State Bulletin

Foreign Affairs

Foreign Policy Bulletin

Foreign Relations of the United States

Foreign Service Journal

The Gallup Poll

Life

Middle East Journal

Nation

National Review

New Republic

Newsweek

New York Times

New York Times Magazine

Public Papers of the Presidents

Reporter

Saudi Aramco World

Time

Secondary Sources

Adler, Les K., and Thomas G. Paterson. "Red Fascism: The Merger of Nazi Germany and Soviet Russia in the American Image of Totalitarianism, 1930's–1950's." *American Historical Review* 75, no. 4 (April 1970): 1046–64.

Allison, Robert J. *The Crescent Obscured: The United States and the Muslim World, 1776–1815.* New York: Oxford University Press, 1995.

Alpers, Benjamin L. *Dictators, Democracy, and American Public Culture: Envisioning the Totalitarian Enemy, 1920s–1950s.* Chapel Hill: University of North Carolina Press, 2003.

Alterman, Jon B. "American Aid to Egypt in the 1950s: From Hope to Hostility." *Middle East Journal* 52, no. 1 (Winter 1998): 51–69.

Anderson, Irvine. *Biblical Interpretation and Middle East Policy: The Promised Land, America, and Israel, 1917–2002.* Gainesville: University Press of Florida, 2005.

Antonius, George. *The Arab Awakening: The Story of the Arab National Movement.* New York: G.P. Putnam's Sons, 1946.

Appy, Christian G., ed. *Cold War Constructions: The Political Culture of United States Imperialism, 1945–1966.* Amherst: University of Massachusetts Press, 2000.

Ashton, John Nigel. *Eisenhower, Macmillan and the Problem of Nasser: Anglo-American Relations and Arab Nationalism, 1955–59.* New York: St. Martin's, 1996.

Babai, Don, ed. *Center for Middle Eastern Studies, Harvard University: Reflections on the Past,*

Visions for the Future, Fiftieth Anniversary Volume. Cambridge, Mass.: Harvard University Center for Middle Eastern Studies, 2004.

Bacevich, Andrew. *The Limits of Power: The End of American Exceptionalism.* New York: Metropolitan Books, 2008.

Badeau, John. *The American Approach to the Arab World.* New York: Harper & Row, 1968.

———. "A Role in Search of A Hero: A Brief Study of the Egyptian Revolution." *Middle East Journal* 9, no. 4 (Autumn 1955): 373–84.

———. "What Suez Means to Egypt." *Foreign Policy Bulletin* 36, no. 4 (1 November 1956).

Balakian, Peter. *The Burning Tigris: The Armenian Genocide and America's Response.* New York: Harper Collins, 2003.

Bar-Siman-Tov, Yaacov. "The United States and Israel since 1948: A 'Special Relationship'?" *Diplomatic History* 22, no. 2 (Spring 1998): 231–62.

Baram, Phillip J. *The Department of State in the Middle East, 1919–1945.* Philadelphia: University of Pennsylvania Press, 1978.

Barber, Benjamin. *Jihad vs. McWorld.* New York: Times Books, 1995.

Barbir, Karl K. "Alfred Thayer Mahan, Theodore Roosevelt, the Middle East, and the Twentieth Century." *Journal of Middle Eastern and North African Intellectual and Cultural Studies* 2, no. 1 (Spring 2004), http://mena.binghamton.edu/karlkbarbir.htm.

Batatu, Hanna. *The Old Social Classes and the Revolutionary Movements of Iraq.* Princeton, N.J.: Princeton University Press, 1978.

Beinin, Joel. "Egypt: Society and Economy, 1923–1952." In *The Cambridge History of Egypt: Volume 2, Modern Egypt, from 1517 to the End of the Twentieth Century*, edited by M. W. Daly, 309–33. New York: Cambridge University Press, 1998.

———. *Was the Red Flag Flying There?: Marxist Politics and the Arab-Israeli Conflict in Egypt and Israel, 1948–1965.* Berkeley: University of California Press, 1990.

Ben-Zvi, Abraham. *Decade of Transition: Eisenhower, Kennedy, and the Origins of the American-Israeli Alliance.* New York: Columbia University Press, 1998.

Berman, William C. *William Fulbright and the Vietnam War: The Dissent of a Political Realist.* Kent, Ohio: Kent State University Press, 1988.

Bill, James A. *The Eagle and the Lion: The Tragedy of American-Iranian Relations.* New Haven, Conn.: Yale University Press, 1988.

———. "The Study of Middle East Politics, 1946–1996: A Stocktaking." *Middle East Journal* 50, no. 4 (Autumn 1996): 501–12.

Binder, Leonard. *The Ideological Revolution in the Middle East.* New York: Wiley & Sons, 1964.

Black, C.E. *The Dynamics of Modernization: A Study in Comparative History.* New York: Harper & Row, 1966.

Boulby, Marion. *The Muslim Brotherhood and the Kings of Jordan, 1945–1993.* Atlanta: Scholars Press, 1999.

Bowie, Robert, and Richard H. Immerman. *Waging Peace: How Eisenhower Shaped an Enduring Cold War Strategy.* New York: Oxford University Press, 1998.

Boyle, Susan Silsby. *Betrayal of Palestine: The Story of George Antonius*. Boulder, Colo.: Westview, 2001.

Brands, H. W. *Cold Warriors: Eisenhower's Generation and American Foreign Policy*. New York: Columbia University Press, 1988.

————. *The Devil We Knew: Americans and the Cold War*. New York: Oxford University Press, 1993.

————. *Inside the Cold War: Loy Henderson and the Rise of the American Empire, 1918–1961*. New York: Oxford University Press, 1991.

————. *Into the Labyrinth: The United States and the Middle East, 1945–1993*. New York: McGraw-Hill, 1994.

————. *The Specter of Neutralism: The United States and the Emergence of the Third World, 1947–1960*. New York: Columbia University Press, 1989.

Breines, Paul. *Tough Jews: Political Fantasies and the Moral Dilemma of American Jewry*. New York: Basic Books, 1990.

Brown, Eugene. J. *William Fulbright: Advice and Dissent*. Iowa City: University of Iowa Press, 1985.

Brown, L. Carl. "The Middle East: Patterns of Change, 1947–1987." *Middle East Journal* 41, no. 1 (Winter 1987): 26–39.

Brown, Michael. *The Israeli-American Connection: Its Roots in the Yishuv, 1914–1945*. Detroit: Wayne State University Press, 1996.

Buheiry, Marwan R. "Alfred T. Mahan: Reflections on Sea Power and on the Middle East as a Strategic Concept." In *The Formation and Perception of the Modern Arab World: Studies by Marwan R. Buheiry*, edited by Marwan R. Buheiry and Lawrence I. Conrad, 157–69. Princeton, N.J.: Darwin, 1989.

Burns, William J. *Economic Aid and American Policy toward Egypt, 1955–1981*. Albany: State University of New York Press, 1985.

Buzzanco, Robert. "Where's the Beef? Culture without Power in the Study of U.S. Foreign Relations." *Diplomatic History* 24, no. 4 (Fall 2000): 623–32.

Campbell, John C. *Defense of the Middle East: Problems of American Policy*. New York: Harper & Brothers, 1958.

Childers, Erskine B. *Common Sense about the Arab World*. New York: Macmillan, 1960.

Chomsky, Noam, et al. *The Cold War and the University: toward an Intellectual History of the Postwar Years*. New York: New Press, 1997.

Christison, Kathleen. *Perceptions of Palestine: Their Influence on U.S. Middle East Policy*. Berkeley: University of California Press, 1999.

Christopher, John B. "Middle East: National Growing Pains." *Headline Series*, no. 148 (July–Aug. 1961). New York: Foreign Policy Association–World Affairs Center, 1961.

Citino, Nathan. *From Arab Nationalism to OPEC: Eisenhower, King Saʿūd and the Making of U.S.-Saudi Relations*. Bloomington: Indiana University Press, 2002.

Cleveland, William L. *A History of the Modern Middle East*. Boulder, Colo.: Westview, 2000.

Cohen, Lizabeth. *A Consumers' Republic: The Politics of Mass Consumption in Postwar America.* New York: Vintage, 2003.

Cohen, Michael J. *Truman and Israel.* Berkeley: University of California Press, 1990.

———. "William A. Eddy, the Oil Lobby and the Palestine Problem," *Middle Eastern Studies* 30, no. 1 (Jan. 1994): 166–80.

Cole, Juan. *Engaging the Muslim World.* New York: Palgrave MacMillan, 2009.

Committee on Near Eastern Studies. *A Program for Near Eastern Studies in the United States.* Washington, D.C.: American Council of Learned Societies, 1949.

Connelly, Matthew. *A Diplomatic Revolution: Algeria's Fight for Independence and the Origins of the Post–Cold War Era.* New York: Oxford University Press, 2003.

———. "Taking Off the Cold War Lens: Visions of North-South Conflict during the Algerian War for Independence." *American Historical Review* 105, no. 3 (June 2000): 739–69.

Cooke, Hedley V. *Challenge and Response in the Middle East: The Quest for Prosperity, 1919–1951.* New York: Harper & Bros., 1952.

Cottam, Richard W. *Iran and the United States: A Cold War Case Study.* Pittsburgh: University of Pittsburgh Press, 1988.

Cremeans, Charles. *The Arabs and the World: Nasser's Arab Nationalist Policy.* New York: Praeger, 1963.

Cullather, Nick. "Research Note: Development? It's History." *Diplomatic History* 22, no. 4 (Fall 2000): 641–53.

Daniel, Norman. *Islam and the West: The Making of an Image.* New York: Oneworld, 1993.

Dann, Uriel. *King Hussein and the Challenge of Arab Radicalism: Jordan, 1955–1967.* New York: Oxford University Press, 1989.

Davidson, Lawrence. *America's Palestine: Popular and Official Perceptions from Balfour to Israeli Statehood.* Gainesville: University Press of Florida, 2001.

Dawisha, Adeed. *The Arab Radicals.* New York: Council on Foreign Relations, 1986.

De Grazia, Victoria. *Irresistible Empire: America's Advance through Twentieth Century Europe.* Cambridge, Mass.: Belknap Press, 2005.

DeNovo, John A. *American Interests and Policies in the Middle East, 1900–1939.* Minneapolis: University of Minnesota Press, 1963.

Diba, Farhad. *Mohammad Mossadegh: A Political Biography.* London: Croom Helm, 1986.

Donohue, John J. "State of the Question: The World of Islam Passes Through a Crisis," *America,* 99 (27 September 1958): 671–72.

Doran, Michael. *Pan-Arabism before Nasser: Egyptian Power Politics and the Palestine Question.* New York: Oxford University Press, 1999.

Dorman, William A., and Mansour Farhang. *The U.S. Press and Iran: Foreign Policy and the Journalism of Deference.* Berkeley: University of California Press, 1987.

Earle, Edward Mead. *Turkey, the Great Powers, and the Bagdad Railway: A Study in Imperialism.* New York: Macmillan, 1923.

Edwards, Holly. *Noble Dreams, Wicked Pleasures: Orientalism in America, 1870–1930.* With

Brian T. Allen, Steven C. Caton, Zeynep Celik, and Oleg Grabar. Princeton, N.J.: Princeton University Press, 2000.

Elpeleg, Zvi. *The Grand Mufti: Haj Amin al-Hussaini, Founder of the Palestinian National Movement.* Translated by David Harvey. London: Frank Cass, 1993.

Endy, Christopher. "Travel and World Power: Americans in Europe, 1890–1917." *Diplomatic History* 22, no. 4 (Fall 1998): 565–94.

Engerman, David C. "Bernath Lecture: American Knowledge and Global Power," *Diplomatic History* 31, no. 4 (September 2007): 599–622.

———. *Know Your Enemy: The Rise and Fall of America's Soviet Experts.* New York: Oxford University Press, 2009.

———. *Modernization from the Other Shore: American Intellectuals and the Romance of Russian Development.* Cambridge, Mass.: Harvard University Press, 2003.

Esposito, John. *The Islamic Threat: Myth or Reality?* New York: Oxford University Press, 1992.

Farber, David. *Taken Hostage: The Iran Hostage Crisis and America's First Encounter with Radical Islam.* Princeton, N.J.: Princeton University Press, 2005.

Fernea, Robert A., and William Roger Louis, eds. *The Iraqi Revolution of 1958: The Old Social Classes Revisited.* London: I. B. Tauris, 1991.

Fisher, Sydney Nettleton, ed. *Social Forces in the Middle East.* Ithaca, N.Y.: Cornell University Press, 1955.

———, ed. *Evolution in the Middle East: Reform, Revolt, and Change.* Washington, D.C.: Middle East Institute, 1953.

Fousek, John. *To Lead the Free World: American Nationalism and the Cultural Roots of the Cold War.* Chapel Hill: University of North Carolina Press, 2000.

Franck, Dorothea Seelye, ed. *Nationalism in the Middle East.* Washington, D.C.: Middle East Institute, 1952.

———, ed. *Islam in the Modern World.* Washington, D.C.: Middle East Institute, 1951.

Fraser, T. G. *The USA and the Middle East since World War 2.* New York: St. Martin's, 1989.

Friedenberg, Daniel. "The Flaming Crescent." *New Republic*, 30 August 1954, 20–21.

Frye, Richard N. *The Near East and the Great Powers.* Cambridge, Mass.: Harvard University Press, 1951.

———, ed. *Islam and the West: Proceedings of the Harvard Summer School Conference on the Middle East, July 25–27, 1955.* The Hague: Mouton, 1957.

Fulbright, J. William. *The Arrogance of Power.* New York: Random House, 1966.

———. *The Crippled Giant: American Foreign Policy and Its Domestic Consequences.* New York: Random House, 1972.

———. *The Price of Empire.* With Seth P. Tillman. New York: Pantheon, 1989.

———. *Prospects for the West.* Cambridge, Mass.: Harvard University Press, 1963.

Gallagher, Nancy Elizabeth, ed. *Approaches to the History of the Middle East: Interviews with Leading Middle East Historians.* London: Ithaca Press, 1994.

Gasiorowski, Mark J. *U.S. Foreign Policy and the Shah: Building a Client State in Iran.* Ithaca, N.Y.: Cornell University Press, 1991.

Gelfand, Lawrence E. *The Inquiry: American Preparations for Peace, 1917–1919*. New Haven, Conn.: Yale University Press, 1963.

Gelvin, James. *The Modern Middle East: A History*. 2nd ed. New York: Oxford University Press, 2008.

Gendzier, Irene L. *Managing Political Change: Social Scientists and the Third World*. Boulder, Colo.: Westview, 1985.

———. *Notes From the Minefield: United States Intervention in Lebanon, 1945–1958*. New York: Columbia University Press, 2006.

Gerber, David A., ed. *Anti-Semitism in American History*. Urbana: University of Illinois Press, 1986.

Gerges, Fawaz A. *America and Political Islam: Clash of Cultures or Clash of Interests?* New York: Cambridge University Press, 1999.

———. "The Kennedy Administration and the Egyptian-Saudi Conflict in Yemen: Co-opting Arab Nationalism." *Middle East Journal* 49, no. 2 (Spring 1995): 292–311.

———. *The Superpowers and the Middle East: Regional and International Politics, 1955–1967*. Boulder Colo.: Westview, 1994.

Gibb, Hamilton A. R. *Modern Trends in Islam*. Chicago: University of Chicago Press, 1947.

Gilman, Nils. *Mandarins of the Future: Modernization Theory in Cold War America*. Baltimore: Johns Hopkins University Press, 2003.

Godfried, Nathan. *Bridging the Gap Between Rich and Poor: American Economic Development Policy toward the Arab East, 1942–1949*. New York: Greenwood, 1987.

Gold, Andrew. "Laborers in the Vineyard: Foreign Service Arabists and American Middle East Policy, 1948–1960." Ph.D. diss., University of Southern California, 1997.

Goode, James F. *The United States and Iran: In the Shadow of Mussadiq*. New York: St. Martin's, 1997.

Gordon, Joel. *Nasser's Blessed Movement: Egypt's Free Officers and the July Revolution*. New York: Oxford University Press, 1992.

Grabill, Joseph L. *Protestant Diplomacy and the Near East: Missionary Influence On American Policy, 1810–1927*. Minneapolis: University of Minnesota Press, 1971.

Greenberg, Moshe. "In Memory of E. A. Speiser." *Journal of the American Oriental Society* 88, no. 1 (Jan.–Mar. 1968): 1–2.

Griffith, Robert. "The Cultural Turn in Cold War Studies." *Reviews in American History* 29 (2001): 150–57.

Grose, Peter. *Israel in the Mind of America*. New York: Knopf, 1983.

Haddad, Yvonne Y. "Middle East Area Studies: Current Concerns and Future Directions." *MESA Bulletin* 25, no. 1 (July 1991): 1–13.

Hahn, Peter L. *Caught in the Middle East: U.S. Policy toward the Arab-Israeli Conflict, 1945–1961*. Chapel Hill: University of North Carolina Press, 2004.

————. *Crisis and Crossfire: The United States and the Middle East since 1945*. Washington, D.C.: Potomac Books, 2005.

————. "Special Relationships." *Diplomatic History* 22, no. 2 (Spring 1998): 263–72.

————. *The United States, Great Britain, and Egypt, 1945–1956: Strategy and Diplomacy in the Early Cold War*. Chapel Hill: University of North Carolina Press, 1991.

————. "The View from Jerusalem: Revelations about U.S. Diplomacy from the Archives of Israel." *Diplomatic History* 22, no. 4 (Fall 1998): 509–32.

Hajjar, Lisa, and Steve Niva. "(Re)Made in the USA: Middle East Studies in the Global Era." *MERIP Reports* 27, no. 4 (Oct.–Dec. 1997): 2–9.

Halliday, Fred. *Islam and the Myth of Confrontation: Religion and Politics in the Middle East*. New York: I. B. Tauris, 1996.

Halpern, Manfred. "Middle Eastern Studies: A Review of the State of the Field with A Few Examples." *World Politics* 15, no. 1 (Oct. 1962): 108–22.

————. *The Politics of Social Change in the Middle East and North Africa*. Princeton, N.J.: Princeton University Press, 1963.

Hare, Paul J. *Diplomatic Chronicles of the Middle East: A Biography of Ambassador Raymond A. Hare*. Lanham, Md.: University Press of America, 1993.

Harland-Jacobs, Jessica L. *Builders of Empire: Freemasonry and British Imperialism, 1717–1927*. Chapel Hill: University of North Carolina Press, 2007.

Harris, Christina Phelps. *Nationalism and Revolution in Egypt: The Role of the Muslim Brotherhood*. The Hague: Mouton, 1964.

Heikal, Mohamed H. *Cutting the Lion's Tail: Suez Through Egyptian Eyes*. New York: Arbor House, 1987.

Heiss, Mary Ann. *Empire and Nationhood: The United States, Great Britain, and Iranian Oil, 1950–1954*. New York: Columbia University Press, 1997.

Hertzberg, Arthur. *The Jews in America: Four Centuries of an Uneasy Encounter, a History*. New York: Simon and Schuster, 1989.

Hodson, Joel C. *Lawrence of Arabia and American Culture: The Making of a Transatlantic Legend*. Westport, Conn.: Greenwood, 1995.

Hogan, Michael J., ed. *America in the World: The Historiography of American Foreign Relations since 1941*. New York: Cambridge University Press, 1995.

Hogan, Michael, and Thomas Paterson, eds. *Explaining the History of U.S. Foreign Relations*, 2nd ed. New York: Cambridge University Press, 2004.

Hoganson, Kristin. *Consumers' Imperium: The Global Production of American Domesticity, 1865–1920*. Chapel Hill: University of North Carolina Press, 2007.

Holland, Matthew F. *America and Egypt: From Roosevelt to Eisenhower*. Westport, Conn.: Praeger, 1996.

Hoskins, Halford L. *Middle East Oil in United States Foreign Policy*. Westport, Conn.: Hyperion, 1976. First published in 1950 by the Library of Congress.

————. *The Middle East: Problem Area in World Politics*. New York: Macmillan, 1954.

Hourani, Albert. *The Emergence of the Modern Middle East*. Berkeley: University of California Press, 1981.

Hudson, Michael. "To Play the Hegemon: Fifty Years of US Policy toward the Middle East." *Middle East Journal* 50, no. 3 (Summer 1996): 329–43.

Hunt, Michael H. *The American Ascendancy: How the United States Gained and Wielded Global Dominance*. Chapel Hill: University of North Carolina Press, 2007.

———. *Ideology and U.S. Foreign Policy*. New Haven, Conn.: Yale University Press, 1987.

Huntington, Samuel P. *The Clash of Civilizations and the Remaking of World Order*. New York: Simon & Schuster, 1996.

Hurewitz, J. C. *Middle East Dilemmas: The Background of United States Policy*. New York: Council on Foreign Relations, 1953.

———. *The Struggle for Palestine*. New York: Norton, 1950.

Immerman, Richard H. *John Foster Dulles: Piety, Pragmatism, and Power in U.S. Foreign Policy*. Washington, D.C.: Scholarly Resources, 1999.

Jankowski, James, and Israel Gershoni, eds. *Rethinking Nationalism in the Arab Middle East*. New York: Columbia University Press, 1997.

Jbara, Taysir. *Palestinian Leader Hajj Amin al-Husayni: Mufti of Jerusalem*. Princeton, N.J.: Kingston, 1985.

Johnson, Peter, and Judith Tucker. "Middle East Studies Network in the United States." *MERIP Reports* 38 (June 1975): 3–20, 26.

Kamalipour, Yahya R, ed. *The U.S. Media and the Middle East: Image and Perception*. Westport, Conn.: Greenwood, 1995.

Kaplan, Robert D. *The Arabists: The Romance of an American Elite*. New York: Free Press, 1995.

Karabell, Zachary. "The Wrong Threat: The United States and Islamic Fundamentalism." *World Policy Journal* 12, no. 2 (Summer 1995): 37–48.

Kaufman, Burton I. *The Arab Middle East and the United States: Inter-Arab Rivalry and Superpower Diplomacy*. New York: Twayne, 1996.

———. *Trade and Aid: Eisenhower's Foreign Economic Policy, 1953–1961*. Baltimore: Johns Hopkins University Press, 1982.

Kennedy, Dane. "Imperial History and Post-Colonial Theory." *Journal of Imperial and Commonwealth History* 24, no. 3 (1996): 345–63.

Kerr, Malcolm. *The Arab Cold War: Gamal ʿAbd al-Nasir and His Rivals, 1958–1970*. London: Oxford University Press, 1971.

Khadduri, Majid. *Arab Contemporaries: The Role of Personalities in Politics*. Baltimore: Johns Hopkins University Press, 1973.

Khalidi, Rashid. "Arab Nationalism: Historical Problems in the Literature." *American Historical Review* 96, no. 5 (Dec. 1991): 1363–73.

———. *Palestinian Identity: The Construction of Modern National Consciousness*. New York: Columbia University of Press, 1997.

———. *Sowing Crisis: The Cold War and American Dominance in the Middle East*. Boston: Beacon, 2009.

Killgore, Andrew I. "In Memoriam: Dr. John Stothoff Badeau, 1903–1995." *Washington Report on Middle East Affairs* 14, no. 6 (Jan. 1996): 17.

Klein, Christina. *Cold War Orientalism: Asia in the Middlebrow Imagination, 1945–1961.* Berkeley: University of California Press, 2003.

Kolsky, Thomas A. *Jews against Zionism: The American Council for Judaism, 1942–1948.* Philadelphia: Temple University Press, 1990.

Kramer, Martin S. *Ivory Towers on Sand: The Failure of Middle Eastern Studies in America.* Washington D.C.: Washington Institute for Near East Policy, 2001.

Kuklick, Bruce. *Puritans in Babylon: The Ancient Near East and American Intellectual Life, 1880–1930.* Princeton, N.J.: Princeton University Press, 1996.

Kuniholm, Bruce R. *The Origins of the Cold War in the Near East: Great Power Conflict and Diplomacy in Iran, Turkey, and Greece.* Princeton, N.J.: Princeton University Press, 1980.

———. "Retrospect and Prospect: Forty Years of US Middle East Policy." *Middle East Journal* 41, no. 1 (Winter 1987): 7–25.

Kunz, Diane B. *Butter and Guns: America's Cold War Economic Diplomacy.* New York: Free Press, 1997.

———. *The Economic Diplomacy of the Suez Crisis.* Chapel Hill: University of North Carolina Press, 1992.

Kurth, Peter. *American Cassandra: The Life of Dorothy Thompson.* Boston: Little, Brown, 1990.

Kyle, Keith. *Suez.* New York: St. Martin's, 1991.

LaFeber, Walter. *America, Russia and the Cold War 1945–1992.* 7th ed. New York: McGraw-Hill, 1993.

———. *The New Empire: An Interpretation of American Expansion, 1860–1898,* Thirty-Fifth Anniversary Edition with a New Preface. Ithaca, N.Y.: Cornell University Press, 1998.

Latham, Michael. *Modernization as Ideology: American Social Science and "Nation Building" in the Kennedy Era.* Chapel Hill: University of North Carolina Press, 2000.

Lautin, Jessica. "Practicing Politics His Own Way: Manfred Halpern Remembered." *Daily Princetonian,* 7 February 2001.

Lerner, Daniel. *The Passing of Traditional Society: Modernizing the Middle East.* Glencoe, Ill.: Free Press, 1958.

Lesch, David W. *Syria and the United States: Eisenhower's Cold War in the Middle East.* Boulder, Colo.: Westview, 1992.

———, ed. *The Middle East and the United States: A Historical and Political Reassessment.* 2nd ed. Boulder, Colo.: Westview, 1999.

Levey, Zach. *Israel and the Western Powers, 1952–1960.* Chapel Hill: University of North Carolina Press, 1997.

Lewis, Bernard. *Islam and the West.* New York: Oxford University Press, 1993.

Lewis, Martin, and Karen Wigen. *The Myth of Continents: A Critique of Metageography.* Berkeley: University of California Press, 1997.

Lia, Brynjar. *The Society of the Muslim Brothers in Egypt: The Rise of an Islamic Mass Movement, 1928–1942.* Reading, Pa.: Ithaca Press, 1998.

Little, Douglas. *American Orientalism: The United States and the Middle East since 1945.* 3rd ed. Chapel Hill: University of North Carolina Press, 2008.

———. "Cold War and Covert Action: the United States and Syria, 1945–1958." *Middle East Journal* 44, no. 1 (Winter 1990): 51–75.

———. "A Fool's Errand: America and the Middle East, 1961–1969." In *The Diplomacy of the Crucial Decade: American Foreign Relations During the 1960s,* edited by Diane B. Kunz, 283–319. New York: Columbia University Press, 1994.

———. "From Even-Handed to Empty-Handed: Seeking Order in the Middle East." In *Kennedy's Quest for Victory: American Foreign Policy, 1961–1963,* edited by Thomas G. Paterson, 156–77. New York: Oxford University Press, 1989.

———. "Gideon's Band: America and the Middle East since 1945." *Diplomatic History* 18, no. 4 (Fall 1994): 513–40.

———. "The Making of a Special Relationship: The United States and Israel, 1957–1968." *International Journal of Middle East Studies* 25 (1993): 563–85.

———. "Nasser Delenda Est: Lyndon Johnson, the Arabs, and the 1967 Six Day War." In *The Foreign Policies of Lyndon Johnson: Beyond Vietnam,* edited by H. W. Brands, 145–67. College Station: Texas A&M University Press, 1999.

———. "The New Frontier on the Nile: JFK, Nasser, and Arab Nationalism." *Journal of America History* 75, no. 2 (Sept. 1988): 501–27.

Lockman, Zachary. *Contending Visions of the Middle East: The History and Politics of Orientalism.* New York: Cambridge University Press, 2004.

Louis, William Roger. *The British Empire in the Middle East, 1945–1951: Arab Nationalism, The United States, and Postwar Imperialism.* Oxford: Clarendon Press, 1984.

Mahan, Alfred Thayer. *The Problem of Asia and Its Effect Upon International Policies.* Boston: Little, Brown, 1900.

———. *Retrospect and Prospect: Studies in International Relations, Naval and Political.* Boston: Little, Brown, 1902.

Makdisi, Ussama. *Artillery of Heaven: American Missionaries and the Failed Conversion of the Middle East.* Ithaca, N.Y.: Cornell University Press, 2008.

———. "Reclaiming the Land of the Bible: Missionaries, Secularism, and Evangelical Modernity." *American Historical Review* 102, no. 3 (June 1997): 680–713.

Mamdani, Mahmood. *Good Muslim, Bad Muslim: America, the Cold War, and the Roots of Terror.* New York: Pantheon, 2004.

Manalo, Kathleen. "A Short History of the Middle East Institute." *Middle East Journal* 41, no. 1 (Winter 1987): 64–73.

Mann, James. *The Rise of the Vulcans: The History of Bush's War Cabinet.* New York: Viking, 2004.

Mart, Michelle. *Eye On Israel: How America Came to View the Jewish State as an Ally.* Albany: State University of New York Press, 2006.

———. "Tough Guys and American Cold War Policy: Images of Israel, 1948–1960." *Diplomatic History* 20, no. 3 (Summer 1996): 357–80.

Mattar, Philip. *The Mufti of Jerusalem: Al-Hajj Amin al-Husayni and the Palestinian National Movement.* New York: Columbia University Press, 1988.

McAlister, Melani. *Epic Encounters: Culture, Media, and U.S. Interests in the Middle East, 1945–2000.* 2nd ed. Berkeley: University of California Press, 2005.

McCloud, Aminah Beverly. *African American Islam.* New York: Routledge, 1995.

McCormick, Thomas J. *America's Half-Century: United States Foreign Policy in the Cold War.* Baltimore: Johns Hopkins University Press, 1989.

McCullough, David. *Truman.* New York: Simon and Schuster, 1992.

McGovern, George, and William R. Polk. *Out of Iraq: A Practical Plan for Withdrawal Now.* New York: Simon and Schuster, 2006.

McMahon, Robert J. *The Cold War on the Periphery: The United States, India, and Pakistan, 1947–1965.* New York: Columbia University Press, 1994.

———. "Eisenhower and Third World Nationalism: A Critique of the Revisionists." *Political Science Quarterly* 101, no. 3 (1986): 453–73.

Mearsheimer, John, and Stephen Walt. *The Israeli Lobby and U.S. Foreign Policy.* New York: Farrar, Straus, and Giroux, 2007.

Milton-Edwards, Beverley. *Contemporary Politics in the Middle East.* Malden, Mass.: Blackwell, 2000.

Mitchell, Richard P. *The Society of the Muslim Brothers.* New York: Oxford University Press, 1993.

Mitchell, Timothy. "America's Egypt: Discourse of the Development Industry." *Middle East Report* 21, no. 2 (Mar.–Apr. 1991): 18–34, 36.

———. *Colonising Egypt.* Berkeley: University of California Press, 1988.

Moin, Baqer. *Khomeini: Life of the Ayatollah.* New York: St. Martin's, 1999.

Moore, Barrington, Jr. *Social Origins of Dictatorship and Democracy: Lord and Peasant in the Making of the Modern World.* Boston: Beacon, 1966.

Morris, Benny. *The Birth of the Palestinian Refugee Problem, 1947–1949.* New York: Cambridge University Press, 1987.

———. *The Birth of the Palestinian Refugee Problem Revisited.* New York: Cambridge University Press, 2004.

Morris, James. *Islam Inflamed: A Middle East Picture.* New York: Pantheon, 1957.

Mousa, Issam Suleiman. *The Arab Image in the U.S. Press.* New York: Peter Lang, 1984.

Mufti, Malik. *Sovereign Creations: Pan-Arabism and Political Order in Syria and Iraq.* Ithaca, N.Y.: Cornell University Press, 1996.

Naff, Thomas, ed. *Paths to the Middle East: Ten Scholars Look Back.* Albany: State University of New York Press, 1993.

Nasser, Gamal Abdul. *Egypt's Liberation: The Philosophy of the Revolution.* Washington, D.C.: Public Affairs, 1955.

Oren, Michael B. *Power, Faith, and Fantasy: America in the Middle East, 1776 to the Present.* New York: W. W. Norton, 2007.

Ovendale, Ritchie. *Britain, the United States, and the Transfer of Power in the Middle East, 1945–1962.* London: Leicester University Press, 1996.

Owen, Roger. *The Middle East in the World Economy, 1800–1914.* New York: I. B. Taurus, 1993.

———. *State, Power and Politics in the Making of the Modern Middle East.* New York: Routledge, 2000.

Owen, Roger, and Sevket Pamuk. *A History of Middle East Economies in the Twentieth Century.* Cambridge, Mass.: Harvard University Press, 1999.

Owen, Roger, and William Roger Louis, eds. *Suez 1956: The Crisis and Its Consequences.* New York: Clarendon, 1989.

Packenham, Robert. *Liberal America and the Third World: Political Development Ideas in Foreign Aid and Political Science.* Princeton, N.J.: Princeton University Press, 1973.

Parker, Richard. "The Arabists: A Review Essay." *Journal of Palestine Studies* 24, no. 1 (Autumn 1994): 67–77.

Patai, Raphael. *The Arab Mind, Revised Edition, With a New Forward by Norvell B. De Atkine.* New York: Hatherleigh, 2002.

Paterson, Thomas G. *Meeting the Communist Threat: Truman to Reagan.* New York: Oxford University Press, 1988.

Plummer, Brenda Gayle. *Rising Wind: Black Americans and U.S. Foreign Affairs, 1935–1960.* Chapel Hill: University of North Carolina Press, 1996.

Polk, William. *Polk's Folly: An American Family History.* New York: Doubleday, 2000.

———. "Problems of Government Utilization of Scholarly Research in International Affairs." *Background* 9, no. 3 (Nov. 1965): 237–59.

———. *Understanding Iraq: The Whole Sweep of Iraqi History, from Genghis Khan's Mongols to the Ottoman Turks to the British Mandate to the American Occupation.* New York: Harper Collins, 2005.

———. *The United States and the Arab World.* Cambridge, Mass.: Harvard University Press, 1965.

———. "What the Arabs Think." *Headline Series,* no. 96 (Nov.–Dec. 1952). New York: Foreign Policy Association, 1952.

Polk, William, ed. *Developmental Revolution: North Africa, Middle East, South Asia.* Washington, D.C.: Middle East Institute, 1963.

Powell, Lee Riley. *J. William Fulbright and America's Lost Crusade: Fulbright's Opposition to the Vietnam War.* Little Rock, Ark.: Rose, 1984.

Prados, John. *Keepers of the Keys: A History of the National Security Council from Truman to Bush.* New York: William Morrow, 1991.

Pratt, Mary Louise. *Imperial Eyes: Travel Writing and Transculturation.* New York: Routledge, 1992.

Qaimmaqami, Linda Wills. "The Catalyst of Nationalization: Max Thornburg and The Failure of Private Sector Developmentalism in Iran, 1947–1951." *Diplomatic History* 19, no. 1 (Winter 1995): 1–31.

Rist, Gilbert. *The History of Development: From Western Origins to Global Faith*. London: Zed Books, 1997.

Roosevelt, Kermit. *Arabs, Oil, and History: The Story of the Middle East*. New York: Harper & Brothers, 1949.

Rosenberg, Emily. *Spreading the American Dream: American Economic and Cultural Expansion, 1890–1945*. New York: Hill and Wang, 1982.

Rostow, W. W. *The Stages of Economic Growth: A Non-Communist Manifesto*. New York: Cambridge University Press, 1960.

———. *View from the Seventh Floor*. New York: Harper & Row, 1964.

Rotter, Andrew J. "Christians, Muslims, and Hindus: Religion in U.S.–South Asian Relations, 1947–1964." *Diplomatic History* 24, no. 4 (Sept. 2000): 593–613.

———. *Comrades at Odds: The United States and India, 1947–1964*. Ithaca, N.Y.: Cornell University Press, 2000.

———. "Gender Relations, Foreign Relations: The United States and South Asia, 1947–1964." *Journal of American History* 81, no. 2 (1994): 518–42.

———. "Saidism without Said: Orientalism and U.S. Diplomatic History." *American Historical Review* 105, no. 4 (Oct. 2000): 1205–17.

Said, Edward W. *Covering Islam: How the Media and the Experts Determine How We See the Rest of the World*. New York: Pantheon, 1981.

———. *Culture and Imperialism*. New York: Vintage, 1994.

———. *Orientalism*. New York: Vintage, 1979.

Salem, Paul. *Bitter Legacy: Ideology and Politics in the Arab World*. Syracuse, N.Y.: Syracuse University Press, 1994.

Sanders, Marion K. *Dorothy Thompson: A Legend in Her Time*. Boston: Houghton Mifflin, 1973.

Sands, William, ed. *The Arab Nation: Paths and Obstacles to Fulfillment*. Washington, D.C.: Middle East Institute, 1960.

Satloff, Robert B. *From Abdullah to Hussein: Jordan in Transition*. New York: Oxford University Press, 1994.

Saunders, Bonnie F. *The United States and Arab Nationalism: The Syrian Case, 1953–1960*. Westport, Conn.: Praeger, 1996.

Schechtman, Joseph B. *The Mufti and the Fuehrer: The Rise and Fall of Haj Amin el-Husseini*. New York: Thomas Yoseloff, 1965.

Schoenbaum, David. "More Special Than Others." *Diplomatic History* 22, no. 2 (Spring 1998): 273–83.

———. *The United States and the State of Israel*. New York: Oxford University Press, 1993.

Schulzinger, Robert D. *The Making of the Diplomatic Mind: The Training, Outlook, and Style of United States Foreign Service Officers, 1908–1931*. Middletown, Conn.: Wesleyan University Press, 1975.

———. *The Wise Men of Foreign Affairs: The History of the Council on Foreign Relations*. New York: Columbia University Press, 1984.

Sha'ban, Fuad. *Islam and Arabs in Early American Thought: The Roots of Orientalism in America.* Durham, N.C.: Acorn Press, 1991.

Shamir, Shimon, ed. *Egypt from Monarchy to Republic: A Reassessment of Revolution and Change.* Boulder, Colo.: Westview, 1995.

Shoup, Laurence H., and William Minter. *Imperial Brain Trust: The Council on Foreign Relations and United States Foreign Policy.* New York: Monthly Review, 1977.

Simpson, Christopher. *Science of Coercion: Communications Research and Psychological Warfare, 1945–1960.* New York: Oxford University Press, 1994.

———, ed. *Universities and Empire: Money and Politics in the Social Sciences During the Cold War.* New York: New Press, 1998.

Smith, John Allen. *The Idea Brokers: Think Tanks and the Rise of the New Policy Elite.* New York: Free Press, 1991.

Smith, Wilfred Cantwell. *Islam in Modern History.* Princeton, N.J.: Princeton University Press, 1957.

Snetsinger, John. *Truman, the Jewish Vote, and the Creation of Israel.* Stanford, Calif.: Hoover Institution Press, 1974.

Solecki, John. "Arabists and the Myth." *Middle East Journal* 44, no. 3 (Summer 1990): 446–57.

Speiser, E. A. *The United States and the Near East.* Cambridge, Mass.: Harvard University Press, 1947.

Spiegel, Steven L. *The Other Arab-Israeli Conflict: Making America's Middle East Policy from Truman to Reagan.* Chicago: University of Chicago Press, 1985.

Spurr, David. *The Rhetoric of Empire: Colonial Discourse in Journalism, Travel Writing, and Imperial Administration.* Durham, N.C.: Duke University Press, 1993.

Stegner, Wallace. *Discovery! The Story of Aramco Then.* Available in fourteen installments at www.saudiaramacoworld.com.

Stephenson, Anders. *Manifest Destiny: American Expansion and the Empire of Right.* New York: Hill and Wang, 1995.

Stivers, William. *America's Confrontation with Revolutionary Change in the Middle East, 1948–83.* New York: St. Martin's, 1986.

———. *Supremacy and Oil: Iraq, Turkey, and the Anglo–American World Order, 1918–1930.* Ithaca, N.Y.: Cornell University Press, 1982.

St. John, Robert. *The Boss: The Story of Gamal Abdel Nasser.* New York: McGraw Hill, 1960.

Suleiman, Michael. *The Arabs in the Mind of America.* Brattleboro, Vt.: Amana Books, 1988.

Suleiman, Michael, ed. *U.S. Policy on Palestine: From Wilson to Clinton.* Normal, Ill.: Association of Arab-American University Graduates, 1994.

Taggar, Yehuda. *The Mufti of Jerusalem and Palestine Arab Politics, 1930–1937.* New York: Garland, 1986.

Takeyh, Ray. *The Origins of the Eisenhower Doctrine: The US, Britain and Nasser's Egypt, 1953–57.* New York: St. Martin's, 2000.

Tekiner, Roselle, Samir Abed-Rabbo, and Norton Mezvinsky, eds. *Anti-Zionism: Analytical Reflections*. Brattleboro Vt.: Amana Books, 1989.

Thomas, Lewis V., and Richard N. Frye. *The United States and Turkey and Iran*. Cambridge, Mass.: Harvard University Press, 1951.

Thomas, Teresa Ann. "From Orientalism to Professionalism: United States Foreign Service Officers in the Middle East since 1946–the Training and Foreign Policy Role of State Department Arabists." Ph.D. diss., Clark University, 1996.

Thornburg, Max Weston. *People and Policy in the Middle East: A Study of Social and Political Change as a Basis for United States Policy*. New York: W. W. Norton, 1964.

Tillman, Seth P. *The United States in the Middle East: Interests and Obstacles*. Bloomington: Indiana University Press, 1982.

Tivnan, Edward. *The Lobby: Jewish Political Power and American Foreign Policy*. New York: Simon and Schuster, 1987.

Turner, Richard Brent. *Islam in the African-American Experience*. Bloomington: Indiana University Press, 1997.

Twain, Mark. *The Innocents Abroad, or The New Pilgrim's Progress, Being Some Account of the Steamship Quaker City's Pleasure Excursion to Europe and the Holy Land*. New York: Book League of America, 1929.

Vitalis, Robert. *America's Kingdom: Mythmaking on the Saudi Oil Frontier*. Stanford, Calif.: Stanford University Press, 2007.

Vogel, Lester I. *To See a Promised Land: Americans and the Holy Land in the Nineteenth Century*. University Park: Pennsylvania State University Press, 1993.

Von Eschen, Penny M. *Race against Empire: Black Americans and Anticolonialism, 1937–1957*. Ithaca, N.Y.: Cornell University Press, 1997.

Wala, Michael. *The Council on Foreign Relations and American Foreign Policy in the Early Cold War*. Providence: Berghahn Books, 1994.

Warriner, Doreen. *Land and Poverty in the Middle East*. London: Royal Institute of International Affairs, 1948.

Waterbury, John. *The Egypt of Nasser and Sadat: The Political Economy of Two Regimes*. Princeton, N.J.: Princeton University Press, 1983.

Weinbaum, Marvin G. *Egypt and the Politics of U.S. Economic Aid*. Boulder, Colo.: Westview, 1986.

Wiley, Bill I. "Historical Program of the U.S. Army: 1939 to Present [1945]." Office of the Chief of Military History, Department of the Army, www.army.mil/cmh-pg/reference/History/wiley-fm.htm.

Williams, Patrick, and Laura Chrisman, eds. *Colonial Discourse and Post-Colonial Theory: A Reader*. New York: Columbia University Press, 1994.

Winder, R. Bayly. "Four Decades of Middle Eastern Study." *Middle East Journal* 41, no. 1 (Winter 1987): 40–63.

Woods, Randall Bennett. *Fulbright: A Biography*. New York: Cambridge University Press, 1995.

Woodward, Peter. *Nasser*. London: Longman, 1992.

Yapp, M.E. *The Near East since the First World War: A History to 1995*. 2nd ed. Harlow, U.K.: Longman, 1996.

Yaqub, Salim. *Containing Arab Nationalism: The Eisenhower Doctrine and the Middle East*. Chapel Hill: University of North Carolina Press, 2004.

Yergin, Daniel. *The Prize: The Epic Quest for Oil, Money and Power*. New York: Simon & Schuster, 1992.

Zegart, Amy B. *Flawed by Design: The Evolution of the CIA, JCS, and NSC*. Stanford, Calif.: Stanford University Press, 1999.

INDEX

Morris, Edward Joy, 16

Mosque of Omar, 195

Mossadegh, Mohammad, 10, 92, 96, 112–18, 123, 126, 130, 137–38, 184, 211, 236, 239

Mufti of Jerusalem. *See* Husseini, Hajj Amin al-

Mujahedeen, 94

Munn, Robert, 244

Murray, Wallace, 201–2

Muslim Brotherhood, 63, 65–68, 118, 241

Mussolini, Benito, 74

Mutual Security Program, 162–63

Nasser, Gamal ʿAbd al-, 37, 66, 93, 95–96, 113, 218, 220, 223, 225–26, 228, 236–39, 242; U.S. efforts to use Islam to counter appeal of, 87–89; rise and early U.S. views of, 117–19; tensions in relations with U.S., 119–26; U.S. comparisons to Hitler, 122, 124; and Suez crisis, 122–23; critiques of U.S. responses to, 126–28, 130–31; U.S. efforts to work with, 131–37; continuing U.S. discomfort with as symbol of Arab nationalism, 137–39; U.S. uses of modernization theory toward, 141, 174–80, 184

National Geographic, 12

Nationalism, 2, 14, 33–34, 39, 47–48, 96, 138–39, 142, 169, 236, 238–39, 241; and Islam, 58, 61, 64, 78, 82–93, 103–4; interwar interpretations of, 97–112; and Iran in the 1950s, 112–17; and U.S. concerns about Egypt in the 1950s, 117–26; U.S. reassessments of in the late 1950s and 1960s, 126–38; and Palestinians, 223

National Security Council (NSC), 56, 73, 116, 132–33, 135–36, 158, 172, 181, 227

Network of specialists, 4–6, 10–12, 19–20, 24–25, 44–54, 70, 77, 93, 95, 112, 117, 132–34, 138, 141, 158, 186, 235–40; and transnational nature of, 18–19, 33, 44–45, 60, 152–53, 163, 235; and challenges presented by Arab-Israeli-Palestinian conflict, 188–89, 200–201, 212–13, 221, 224–25, 231–34; and post-1967 period, 240–47

Neutralism, 87, 120–21, 133, 135

Nevinson, Henry, 195–96

New York Times, 77, 80, 117, 119, 205, 217, 243, 246

Niles, David, 210

Nixon, Richard M., 131, 184, 241, 243

Nolte, Richard, 119, 132–33, 135, 185

North Africa, 13–14, 29, 37, 40, 64, 73, 80, 99, 151, 169–70, 187

October 1973 War, 241

Office of Strategic Services (OSS), 24, 35, 37, 39–40, 50, 204

Oil, 3–4, 8–9, 11–12, 25–27, 29, 32–33, 35, 38–39, 41, 43, 46, 50–53, 78–79, 88, 127, 133–34, 158, 180, 240; and Iran, 51, 113–15; and promoting private sector development, 141, 144–51, 236, 239; using revenue for modernization, 182, 184, 242, 273 (n. 62); and tension over Palestine/Israel, 200–202, 212

Operation Iraqi Freedom, 246

Operation Straggle, 125

Operation TPAJAX, 114–15

Operation Wappen. *See* Operation Straggle

Operations Coordinating Board (OCB), 81–82, 87

Oren, Michael, 15

Organization of Petroleum Exporting Countries (OPEC), 240–41

Russia, 1, 12–13, 25, 27–28, 39, 50, 79–80, 100, 130, 196
Rustow, Dankwart, 69–70

Said, Edward, 9–10, 16, 245
Said, Nuri al-, 125, 127
Salisbury, Edward, 18
Sandys, Duncan, 88
Sa'ud, 'Abd al-'Aziz Ibn (King Ibn Saud of Saudi Arabia), 36–37, 96–97, 100, 102–5, 145, 201, 208, 236
Sa'ud, Sa'ud bin 'Abd al-Aziz al- (King Saud of Saudi Arabia), 88–89
Saudi Arabia, 9, 28, 36–37, 62, 84–85, 88–89, 102–4, 118, 125, 154, 177, 187, 201, 208, 211, 241; and liberal developmentalism in, 145–49, 151
Saunders, Harold H., 241–42
Schoenbaum, David, 192
Self-determination, 97, 104–5, 111, 128, 133, 157, 190, 199–200, 209
September 11, 2001, attacks, 1, 245
Sha'ban, Fuad, 15
Shari'a law, 72, 74, 100, 102
Silver, Abba Hillel, 207–8
Sinai Peninsula, 237, 242
Sisco, Joseph, 243
Six Day War (June 1967), 178, 184, 186, 189, 224, 231–32, 234, 237, 240–46
Smith, Eli, 15
Smith, Wilfred Cantwell, 45, 49, 64–65, 82
Soviet Union, 3–4, 6, 42, 50–51, 88, 103, 125, 128, 132, 159–60, 171, 173, 180, 241; and Islam, 79–81; and Egypt/Nasser, 119–21; and Arab-Israeli-Palestinian conflict, 202, 204, 209, 212, 215, 221, 224–26, 229
Speiser, Ephraim Avigdor, 23–25, 38, 40, 42, 46, 51, 111–12, 152

Spiegel, Steven, 120
Sputnik, 131
Standard Oil of California, 145
Starkey, John, 53, 148
Stegner, Wallace, 146–49
Stein, Leonard, 194–96
Stephanson, Anders, 7, 13
Stettinius, Edward, 201
Stevens, Georgiana, 221
Straits of Tiran, 89
Suez Canal, 27, 33, 38, 50, 66, 87, 117; and crisis, 89, 121–31, 220
Sulzberger, Arthur Hays, 205
Sykes-Picot Agreement, 108
Syria, 25, 28, 34, 59, 80, 88, 97, 99, 104–5, 107, 109, 125, 144, 151, 153, 166, 220–21, 224, 241
Syrian Protestant College. See American University of Beirut

Talbot, Phillips, 92, 229
Tannous, Afif, 163–64
Thomas, Lewis, 69–70
Thomas, Teresa, 46, 85
Thompson, Dorothy, 216–17
Thornburg, Max, 150–51
Time, 71, 116–17, 123
Tivnan, Edward, 205
Totalitarianism: U.S. comparisons with Islam, 3–8, 58, 71–77, 81, 83–84, 91, 93, 96, 108, 124, 156, 170, 235, 239; U.S. comparisons with Nasser and Arab nationalism, 124, 137–39
Trans-Arabian Pipeline (TAPLINE), 20
Transjordan, 25, 28, 153, 194
Travel literature, 4, 12–13, 17, 20, 26, 35, 41, 151
Tripartite Declaration, 224
Truman, Harry S., 55, 65, 78, 81, 114–15; and Palestine/Israel, 37, 189, 208–10,